VISHVAPANI BLOMFIELD became a Buddhist at the age of 14. He took a First in English at Cambridge University, edited *Dharma Life* magazine for nine years, and is a prominent member of the Triratana Buddhist Order. He lives in Cardiff with his wife and son and contributes regularly to BBC Radio 4's 'Thought for the Day'.

Gautama Buddha

Vishvapani Blomfield

Quercus

First published in Great Britain in 2011 by Quercus

This paperback edition published in 2012 by
Quercus
55 Baker Street
Seventh Floor, South Block
London
W1U 8EW

A CIP catalogue record for this book is available
from the British Library

ISBN 978 0 85738 830 8

10 9 8 7 6 5 4 3 2 1

Text and plates designed and typeset by Ellipsis Digital Ltd
Map and family tree by David Hoxley
Printed and bound in Great Britain by Clays Ltd. St Ives plc

For Leo

GAUTAMA'S FAMILY TREE

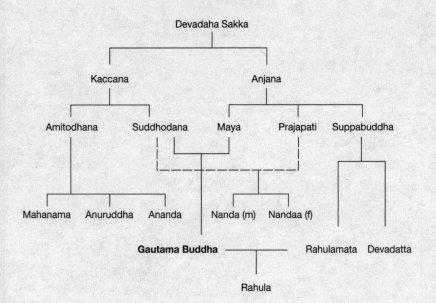

The sources for this family tree are the c.1st century CE Mahavastu and the Buddhist Commentaries

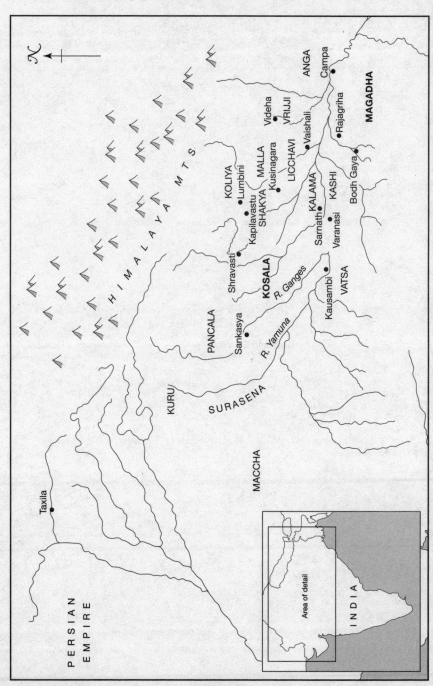

Gautama's India

Contents

Acknowledgements

Despite the limitations brought by his health, Sangharakshita offered advice and encouragement throughout the period of writing whenever I asked, and kindly read two completed chapters and offered his comments. For all my efforts to find fresh insights, my approach to the Buddha is essentially learned from him. Ven Analayo also read several chapters, and offered penetrating critiques in three languages, informed by his considerable knowledge of both the Nikayas and the Agamas. Dharmachari Subhuti read through the whole manuscript and, with characteristic incisiveness, illuminated many points of dharma and pointed out numerous shortcomings in my text. This book would have been very different without his generous help. Alan Sponberg (Saramati) read the final chapter and appendix and offered helpful comments from his perspective as a Buddhist historian.

I am also grateful to Dhivan and Nagabodhi, who read chapters relatively early in the writing process, and to Jayarava for his perceptive comments via email. Many other friends helped by listening to me talking about the Buddha and responding helpfully, when they could get a word in edgeways. I learned much from speaking with Stephen Batchelor, who was writing his own account of Gautama's life as I wrote this one, and highlighted for me two key issues the material throws up: how to treat the chronology of the

Buddha's post-Enlightenment career, and how to present the teachings in a way that is integrated with the life. My understanding of a third issue – the need to do justice to both the human and the more-than-human aspects of the Buddha – comes from Sangharakshita. I should add that my overall understanding of Buddhism itself has developed over many years thanks to my other teachers, colleagues, friends and students in the Triratna Buddhist Order. I am also grateful to Tony Morris, who commissioned the book, and my editors at Quercus.

The house style for notes permits only direct citations, rather than acknowledgments of the scholars who have influenced my presentation. At times the debt is so considerable that this limitation is an embarrassment. The Select Bibliography cites the works from which I have learned most, but I wish to acknowledge, among recent scholars, my particular debts to Richard Gombrich, Johannes Bronkhorst, Rupert Gethin, Sue Hamilton, Geoffrey Samuel and Bhikkhu Analayo.

Over the last two decades new translations have revolutionised the relationship of English speakers to the Pali texts. I am deeply indebted to Bhikkhu Bodhi for his immense labours in translation and for the commentary and scholarship that accompanies his texts. I have also benefited from the admirable efforts of Thanissaro Bhikkhu and the staff of Access to Insight and the other internet sites that are making Buddhist texts far more easily available. Translations of Rupert Gethin, Andrew Olendzki and others are bringing a new literary subtlety to English translations of key Pali texts and I have used these wherever possible.

Finally, my heartfelt love and thanks go to Kamalagita for her support while I was writing, even when she was pregnant and caring for a new baby, and to Leo, who joined us near the end.

INTRODUCTION

Gautama and the Buddha

It is morning; the sun is hot but not yet overwhelming and a man named Bahiya scours the streets of Shravasti. His gaunt frame is covered by a rough tunic that is stitched together from pieces of tree bark and he is weary after walking night and day from India's west coast. But he draws little attention from the townspeople, who recognise him as a holy man: a part of the tide of spiritual seekers that washes constantly through the city.

Shravasti is the capital of the kingdom of Kosala and a major metropolis of the culture that thrives in the central Ganges Valley. We have no detailed descriptions of its streets to fill out the scene, but the city's ruins have been partially unearthed and reveal that it was a large town, guarded by huge ramparts, at the junction of three important trade routes. A slightly later text evokes the profusion of such a city:

> furnished with solid foundations and with many gateways and walls
> ... behold the drinking shops and taverns, the slaughterhouses and
> cooks' shops, the harlots and wantons ... the garland-weavers, the
> washermen, the astrologers, the cloth merchants, the gold workers
> and the jewellers.[1]

With such clues we may imagine the scene that confronted Bahiya: the wattle-and-daub houses with domed roofs of tiles or thatch, the sturdier brick-built civic buildings and homes of the wealthy; the main streets clogged with mules, oxen, chariots and pedestrians; the elephants lumbering impassively along the roadway laden with produce; the alleys spidering out from the main thoroughfare, thick with smells and resounding with the cries of food-sellers.

As Bahiya jostles through the press, he catches sight of a singular figure and knows instantly that it is the man he seeks. He is in the middle years of his life and the Bahiya Sutta – the account of this meeting in the ancient Buddhist scriptures – describes him as 'pleasing, lovely to see, with calmed senses and tranquil mind, possessing perfect poise and calm'.[2] He stands silently at a doorway, his eyes cast downwards, as the woman of the house places a little food in his bowl. Like other townspeople, he wears lengths of cloth draped around his midriff and across his shoulder to make a robe. But their mud-yellow fabric is much coarser than the embroidered muslin used by the rich, or even the plain cotton of the poor. It is a patchwork sewn together from scraps gathered on rubbish heaps or from the charred remnants of the shrouds that covered corpses in the cremation grounds. These robes, along with the bowl made from dried palm leaves that he holds before him, a needle and thread, a girdle, a razor and a water-strainer, are the sum of his possessions. Most people call him 'Gautama', the name of the clan into which he was born in Shakya, Kosala's north-eastern province; but his disciples address him by a host of titles, especially 'Bhagavat', meaning Blessed Lord; 'Tathagata' – 'the one who is like that'[3] – and 'Buddha' – the Awakened.

The encounter is intense and dramatic. Bahiya throws himself at Gautama's feet and cries: 'Please teach me! Teach me the Truth that will be for my lasting benefit.' Gautama spoke to no one when he was collecting food, so he tells Bahiya, 'Come to me later and I will answer your questions.' But Bahiya insists he cannot wait. 'It is hard to know how long you or I will live!' At the third time of asking, Gautama turns to face Bahiya and speaks a few spare words:

> Bahiya, you should train yourself thus: In the seen will be merely what is seen. In the heard will be merely what is heard. In the sensed will be merely what is sensed. In the cognised will be merely what is cognised. In this way should you should train yourself . . . Then, Bahiya, you are not 'in that'. When you are not 'in that', then you will be neither here nor beyond nor between the two. Just this, is the end of suffering.[4]

A sudden moment of communion cocoons the men beyond time or place, and something happens to Bahiya. Exactly what is hard to say, but its effect is shattering. It is bound up with the meaning of Gautama's words, but that meaning is mixed with the sense that Gautama, himself, embodies them completely and has inwardly expanded into the open spaces they disclose. A shift occurs deep in Bahiya's consciousness – a silent opening. And then the moment is over. The street noises return, Bahiya walks away and Gautama returns quietly to his alms round.

The term rendered as 'the Truth' in Bahiya's request is 'dhamma' in Pali, or 'dharma' in Sanskrit. It was a crucial word in Gautama's India that had many meanings, but here it means the underlying nature of things and also the way a person should act to be in accord with it. Bahiya was asking Gautama to show him the true nature of existence, and Gautama's reply, which compresses his realisation into a concentrated essence, instructs Bahiya to train himself to experience the world in new way: 'In the seen there will be merely the seen; in the heard there will be merely the heard.'

That was his message . . . but what did it mean? What does it mean for there to be no 'you' in experience? And if Gautama truly embodied his teaching, who or what was he – this man who was 'neither here nor beyond nor between the two'?

Gautama said the Dharma he had discovered was 'profound, hard to see and hard to understand; peaceful, sublime, beyond the sphere of mere reasoning, subtle and to be experienced only by the wise'.[5] He offered many explanations of it, and Buddhist tradition has added many more, but his words often point to something that language cannot contain and the same is true of Gautama, the man. Asked if Gautama was wise, one of his disciples replied that he didn't know, but he could deduce Gautama's accomplishments by examining external signs, in the way that an elephant tracker knows the dimensions of the beast he is following from the size of the footprint it leaves behind. This book will approach Gautama like that elephant hunter, examining his words and his impact in the hope of deducing the dimensions of their elusive author.

We find such clues in the many stories about Gautama that have come down to us in the Buddhist scriptures. By their account, for forty-five years after his Awakening Gautama travelled continually across the Ganges Valley. The dust of its roadways caked his feet, he gathered food amid the grime and bustle of its cities and he gave talks in the parks just outside them where religious wanderers stayed. Wherever he went he met people – full-time religious seekers like Bahiya or householders from each and every walk of life: merchants and musicians, kings and lepers, priests and prostitutes. He spoke with the curious, the sceptical and the intensely devout, and he tried, again and again, to communicate his explosive understanding of existence. He stretched the meanings of the words and concepts that people already knew; and he invoked venerable, established ideas but turned them on their heads.

For all the glimpses in the scriptures of this vividly real Gautama of the plains, cities and wilderness tracks, we encounter unavoidable difficulties when we try to thread them together into a coherent and credible narrative. The first is the nature of our evidence. Gautama wrote nothing himself; in fact, we have no reason to think he was literate and writing may not even have existed in his society. The Bahiya Sutta is one of the many 'discourses' of the Buddhist canon (Buddhist tradition counts 17,505 of them) on which we must rely for our information about Gautama. According to the traditional account, they are accurate records of actual events that were preserved thanks to the phenomenal memory of Ananda – Gautama's confidant, assistant and companion for the last twenty-five years of his life, while a monk named Upali recalled the incidents surrounding the establishment of the monastic rules that are recorded in a body of texts called the Vinaya – the monastic code. Historians, however, regard this account as a pious fiction, and, whatever truth the Discourses contain, they were clearly reshaped, as they were remembered (by monks who weren't trained from childhood in memorising skills), then repeated and finally rendered into the ancient Indian languages of Pali and Sanskrit. They are full of repetitions and stock formulas, and Gautama's teachings often come in a great list. It is hard to think that Gautama, or anyone else, ever spoke in their convoluted way. These conventions only make sense as ways of helping the monks memorise the words.

The process of committing the Pali versions of the Discourses to writing began in Sri Lanka in the first century BCE, when the material was already at least 300 years old. Sanskrit versions of the early texts have a different history, but almost all of them were lost when Indian Buddhism disappeared in the twelfth century. The original palm-leaf manuscripts of both the Pali and the Sanskrit scriptures sweltered and crumbled in the tropical humidity. They were recopied repeatedly and very few Buddhist manuscripts, barring some fragments, are more than 500 years old (though we do have much older rock-cuttings and inscriptions). Finally, the scholar-monks, for whom memorising, editing and interpreting the texts became a full-time activity, reshaped them in the light of their own concerns.

The earliest evidence about Gautama that we can date reliably comes from inscriptions left by the Buddhist Emperor Ashoka, around 150 years after Gautama's death. Consequently, some authorities think that any attempt to locate the historical Buddha – the figure behind the legends and the texts – is inherently 'quixotic'[6] and some even doubt that we can say for certain that an historical individual called Gautama Buddha existed at all. This book follows a different approach. Someone must have founded the Buddhist tradition and the early Buddhists themselves were convinced that it was Gautama. They strove mightily to preserve the oldest teachings as accurately as possible, even before they were written down, and they zealously excluded other material from their canon. Most Indian religious scriptures that preceded Gautama and most that followed him (including Buddhist ones) are plainly mythological, or else concern highly abstruse metaphysics and analysis. By contrast, the Discourses present a vivid and credible portrait of an historical society that matches the political situation prevailing in Gautama's time and is largely backed by archaeology. What's more, their portrait of Gautama is vibrant and individual, as if they are depicting an actual person, and while the teaching contains some inconsistencies, in broad terms it expresses a coherent and strikingly original account of life. My approach, therefore, is to trust the texts unless there are good reasons to doubt them, and where things are uncertain we can draw on the battery of methods that scholars have developed to assess them.* Other sources fill out what we can glean from the Discourses, especially the remarkable poems of the *Theragatha* ('Songs of the Monks') and *Therigatha* ('Songs of the Nuns') in which Gautama's immediate disciples recount their experiences, including their meetings with the master himself.

Sometimes the Discourses themselves give us the evidence we need to sort out fact from legend. For instance, the popular account tells us that the young Gautama was a prince who never left his palace or saw the outside world. Aged twenty-eight or twenty-nine he stepped out and saw an old man, a sick man and a corpse, and was shocked to discover that life included suffering. Finally, he saw a wandering spiritual seeker (a *shramana*) and became one himself. It's a powerful myth, but the Discourses never mention the episode, though they do relate that Gautama left home out of disillusionment. The story was lifted by later storytellers from a text called the Mahapadana Sutta in which Gautama recounts the life of a pre-historical Buddha named Vipassi. Thus, we can confidently say that the story of the Four Sights is a legend, not a fact.

This book will make many such deductions, like an elephant-tracker, but we shall never know for certain what the historical Gautama 'really' did or said. The best we can hope for is a plausible

---

* Among the many methods of 'higher criticism' of the Buddhist texts that have been used over the last century are various approaches to assessing the age of the language and verse forms they use, comparing Pali texts with Chinese translations of the Sanskrit versions of the Discourses and identifying details that serve no polemical purpose and seem to contain the memory of actual events. After all these efforts, there is some agreement but no consensus about Gautama's original teachings. It is worth adding that while some historians would reject the approach to the Buddhist scriptures in this book, leading figures like Richard Gombrich and Johannes Bronkhorst follow a similar method.

account. As the Discourses were intended as records of Gautama's teaching, not repositories of data about his life or his environment, this means scavenging information from scattered comments and weighting our portrait towards passages with the best claim to being the oldest and therefore closest to Gautama's actual words. A particular problem is that, while the early Buddhist scriptures contain a narrative of Gautama's life up to the start of his ministry and his final year, we can only guess at the sequence of the many incidents in the intervening period. There is much we can say about what happened in that period, but we cannot say when it happened or in what order. So this book will explore the major themes of that time: Gautama's teaching career, how he developed a monastic community and his engagement with society.

There are many things about the historical Gautama that we cannot say. For example, we don't know his full name. Buddhist tradition called him Siddhartha (or Siddhattha in Pali), meaning 'he whose aim is accomplished', but the name never appears in the earliest sources. In the Discourses, people who weren't his followers usually call him Gautama, or Master Gautama, which was his clan name – the equivalent of a surname – and it will suffice for this book. We also cannot be certain when he lived. Buddhist traditions agree that Gautama gained Enlightenment aged thirty-five and lived to eighty, and South Asian Buddhists place his death in 484 BCE. But this date was worked out centuries after the event, and other traditions placed it in 486, 428 or 384 – a difference of up to a century. Most historians prefer the later dates, and this book places his birth around 484 BCE, his Enlightenment in 449 BCE and his death in 404 BCE.[7]

Two further issues bear on any biography of Gautama. Firstly, the Discourses present the world as ancient Indians experienced it, not as modern westerners do. Nature is a vivid presence, and the gods and demons that embody natural forces pack the texts, along with displays of supernormal powers and miraculous events. As the modern Buddhist teacher Sangharakshita argues, excluding these on the grounds that they are 'unrealistic' would change the meaning of the sources: 'The gods and goddesses are not there simply as ornamentation. Their presence is part of the teaching. They provide glimpses of an ancient mode of human consciousness fully integrated into a universe of value, worth and purpose. To miss them is to miss the poetry, and the heart, of the Buddha's message.'[8] This poetry is present, for example, in Mara, the figure who is said to have appeared when Gautama was on the cusp of Enlightenment. He is presented both as a demon who accosts Gautama and as a personification of his doubts and limitations. Both meanings are presented as 'literally' true and the story's resonance is lost unless we keep both in mind.

The second issue is what we individually bring to the attempt to reconstruct Gautama's life. Harold Bloom goes to the heart of the matter in commenting on the many attempts to write a biography of the 'historical Jesus', the historical figure who is hidden behind the 'theological' Jesus of the New Testament in his book *Jesus and Yahweh: The Names Divine*. Any account of Jesus, he says, must choose how to interpret the Gospels, but as these texts were intended to convert us, not to pass on historical data, how an author interprets them depends on their faith or scepticism. Bloom concludes that biographers merely *'find themselves* and not the elusive and evasive Yeshua'.[9] I hope for a little more than that in my search for Gautama, but Buddhist texts have similar designs upon us. As we are all subject to the frailty of the human condition, none of us can be objective or indifferent in the face of Gautama's words on 'suffering, the origination of suffering and the cessation of suffering' and his startling claim to have found 'a way leading to the cessation of suffering'.

One's faith or scepticism about this claim will shape one's interpretations, and my view of Gautama is shaped by the fact that I
am Buddhist and committed to trying to practise his teachings.
His qualities move me because I want to develop them myself and
because I believe that they are important for others, and I have
tracked Gautama because I want to see those qualities more clearly.
For me, that means seeing him as a recognisably human being who
struggled with actual events and engaged with the religious, cultural and political forces of his world, and as a result the Gautama
who emerges from these pages is not quite the figure who has been
revered by the Buddhist tradition. But engaging with the Gautama
of whom we read in the texts means grappling with the nature of
the state he claimed to have attained: the way of seeing, acting and
experiencing he discovered when he attained the state of Awakening or Enlightenment or Realisation which he called 'Nirvana'.
The figure this book presents is the Enlightened Buddha and assumes
that Gautama really did attain a new kind of existence through
realising and becoming one with the Dharma: reality itself, the true
nature of existence that holds at all times and in all places, whether
or not a Buddha has explained it. And I approach Gautama's teaching
on the assumption that he was trying to explain the reality that he
directly apprehended.

The biographer's task, therefore, is to place Gautama in a credible historical setting without assuming that he was really just an
ordinary person, albeit an exceptionally wise and kindly one. For
one thing, that would distort our sources, which agree that Gautama was something other than an ordinary human being. The
Discourses recall a meeting with a Brahmin priest called Dona who
saw something remarkable in Gautama and attempted to locate
him within the categories of Indian cosmology. Was he a god, Dona
asked, or one of the various kinds of spirit? Gautama replied that

he was not. Was he then a human being? 'No, Brahmin,' Gautama said, 'I am not a human being.' Gautama told Dona he had 'abandoned the conditions by which I would be a god or a man' and explained himself with an image: 'Just as a red, blue, or white lotus – though born in the water and grown in the water, rises up and stands unsoiled by the water, so, Brahmin, though born and grown in the world, I have overcome the world and dwell unsoiled by the world. Consider me a Buddha: "one who has Awakened".'[10]

Even the apparently naturalistic elements in Gautama's story are imbued with archetypal significance. For the early Buddhists Gautama's biography started not with his birth, but with the countless lifetimes that preceded it, and even the events of his final life, which this book describes, are said to conform to the pattern or 'rule'[11] that shaped the lives of all previous Buddhas, right back to Buddha Vipassi ninety-one aeons ago. As Reginald Ray comments: 'Gautama, in his own time and in subsequent times, was able to be the Buddha precisely because he was understood to embody, in a complex way, the cosmic and transcendent. Far from being incidental to who he was, the myth and cult defined his essential person, for his earliest followers as for later Buddhists.'[12]

We can find many clues in the Discourses to the character of Gautama's realisation. For example, they often describe the shattering effect that meeting Gautama had on people like Bahiya. The Bahiya Sutta tells us that, in an instant of unbiased perception, the craving that normally warps human experience fell away and he saw reality as Gautama saw it. The seen *was* just the seen, the heard *was* just the heard and he was 'freed from the taints because he ceased grasping'.[13]

And in the midst of such dramas we sometimes encounter a commanding poetry that seems to speak from a distant and uncanny dimension of consciousness. The account of Gautama's meeting

with Bahiya, for instance, is accompanied by an inspired, spontaneous 'verse of uplift' (*udana*):

> Where water, earth, fire, and wind have no footing:
> There the stars do not shine, the sun sheds no light,
> The moon does not appear and darkness is not found.
> And when a sage, a brahman through wisdom,
> Has known this for himself, then he is freed
> from form and the formless, from bliss and from pain.[14]

Gautama seems to be describing a realm that can only be evoked
by negating everything we have experienced, and yet he instructed
Bahiya to focus on direct perception. That combination of the
timeless and the concrete is at the heart of the figure we encounter
in the early sources. He is intelligent but also wise; he demonstrates ordinary human kindness but also exemplifies compassion;
he is gracious and courteous but can be devastatingly direct. The
issues that were current in his culture shaped his teachings, but
he rethought and re-imagined them with startling originality. His
spiritual search took place within a subculture of fellow seekers –
the *shramanas*, or 'strivers', who lived on the edges of mainstream
society; but he sharply criticised many of them and founded a
new shramana community in an effort to reform their world. His
ideas developed in dialogue with other religious practitioners as
he responded to their questions and the deep, unspoken assumptions they revealed, but they defied those beliefs and challenged
the established religions. He relied on wealthy supporters, but he
also questioned the drives for money and power that fired the
booming economy of the Ganges Valley, and was even more crit-
ical of the culture of Brahminism with its magical thinking and
rigid social stratification. The alternatives Gautama proposed prob-

ably had only a marginal effect in his lifetime, but they eventually inspired a vast, international Buddhist civilisation and a spiritual tradition whose influence touched much of the human race, and producing countless realised masters.

Gautama once said that the whole world, how it arises and how it ceases, is to be discovered in the actuality of 'this fathom-long body'.[15] That is an encouraging assertion for those who go in search of the historical Gautama and hope to keep sight of the Enlightened Buddha. Let us turn, then, to the concrete and historical beginnings of Gautama's story: his birth in approximately 484 BCE in a provincial town of the Ganges Valley called Kapilavastu.

1

A World in Ferment

Kapilavastu

Kapilavastu was much smaller than Shravasti, but to Gautama's cousin Mahanama it was a 'rich and prosperous, populous, crowded' metropolis. His remarks are part of a dialogue in which Mahanama complains to Gautama about the town's busy evening traffic and the risk of colliding with 'a stray elephant, a horse, a chariot, a cart or a pedestrian'.[1] Mahanama's words are evocative, but they are the only concrete depiction of Kapilavastu in the Discourses, and one of their few descriptions of place or environment. The ruins of two towns from roughly this period – one on each side of the Nepalese–Indian border – are claimed by their supporters as the 'true' Kapilavastu, but while both places contain ancient remains, their claims to be Gautama's birthplace have as much to do with national sentiment as with evidence. The only reliable testimony for Kapilavastu's location comes from two Chinese Buddhist pilgrims who travelled to India a thousand years after Gautama and wrote eloquent accounts of what they saw. They seem to place the town in a spot where some ruins lie, some distance to the south of either site. When Fa-hsien visited in the fifth century CE the region was largely abandoned, and two centuries later Hsuan Tsang (c.602–664 CE) reported, 'There are some ten deserted cities in this country, wholly desolate and ruined. The capital is overthrown and in ruins. The royal precincts within the city were all built of brick. The foundation walls are still strong and high. It has long been deserted.'² He adds that the 'royal precincts within the city' – that is, the fortified area that included the palace and its surroundings – 'measure some 14 or 15 li around'. This is about 7 km, which suggests a population of 8,000 or so.* From this eyewitness account of Kapilavastu's ruins, and from fragments in early texts, we can sketch a rough portrait of the town where Gautama grew up.

Kapilavastu was the capital of Shakya – the land of the Shakyans – and home to the Gautamas, the leading clan of the ruling nobility. Beyond the town, in a cultivated area known as its 'field', Shakyan villagers lived with their animals in fragile shelters of bamboo plastered with mud, as many Indians still do today. Kapilavastu means 'Kapila's farm', and the lives of most townspeople were tied to the farmlands and the crops they produced. Much of this land had been reclaimed from the wilderness by felling trees or draining marshes, and the work it required varied according to the seasons of the tropical year. In the hot months when the River Rohini, which skirted Kapilavastu, dried to a sluggish trickle, labourers in muddy cotton clothes stooped over the cracked earth, tending their limp crops and digging inundation ditches. Then came the monsoon, which swelled in cumulus clouds blowing in from the Arabian Sea and burst on the land in a buffeting deluge. Then the fields filled with shoots, withered shrubs burst into leaf, the earth erupted with barley, wheat and rice, and soon it was time for the harvest.

---

* These estimates are made by H. W. Schumann in his book *The Historical Buddha*, p.18. He estimates that Shakya's population was 180,000.

Most people knew only their village or locality and never ventured to the great cities. They continued the work of their fathers, maintained the customs of the clan and were bound to the cycles of agriculture and the seasons. Many townspeople also owned farmland or traded in its produce, and perhaps the most telling description of Shakyan life is a passage in the Vinaya in which Mahanama persuades his brother Anurudha that, notwithstanding his frail constitution, he should renounce his householder existence and become a wandering monk. Mahanama convinces him with a detailed account of the routines that regulated the lives of even the Shakyan elite:

> First, you have to get your fields ploughed; then you have to get them sown; then you have to get the water led down over them; then you have to get the water led off again; then you have to get the weeds pulled up; then you have to get the crop reaped; then you have to get it carried away; then you have to get it arranged into bundles; then you have to get it trodden out; then you have to get the straw picked out; then you have to get all the chaff removed; then you have to get it winnowed; then you have to get the harvest garnered; then you have to do just the same the next year and the same all over again the year after that. The work is never over.[3]

Life was tied to the never-ending cycle of the seasons and the demands of the harvest.

Provincial though it was, Shakya was at the northern edge of a great civilisation and linked to it by the very thoroughfare that Mahanama describes. This was the trade road that ran east from Shravasti and passed through the centre of Kapilavastu, bringing travellers from across the region. The territory between towns was

mostly covered by dense woodland, and even a thousand years later
Fa-hsien noted that 'you seldom meet any people on the roads for
fear of the white elephants and the lions'.[4] Bandits and tribesmen
were still more dangerous, and merchants often travelled in prover-
bially noisy convoys that were protected by Kosalan soldiers and
could include several hundred ox-drawn wagons.

Beyond Shravasti the road forked and a southern limb ran down
the western coast of India to what is now Maharashtra and Kerala.
The northern branch crossed the Rajputana desert to Taxila and
north-west India and continued to Persia, where a powerful and
ancient civilisation flourished. When Gautama was born, c.484 BCE,
modern-day Pakistan and Kashmir were Persian territories, and on
the empire's distant north-eastern border a fierce war was raging
with the Greeks who, in turn, were developing a new kind of culture which Pericles, Sophocles and Socrates – all born in the decades
around Gautama's birth – would soon raise to unprecedented
heights. An ancient civilisation also flourished in distant China,
where Confucius was developing his social philosophy; and in Judea,
an eastern province of Persia, the tribal cult of the Jewish nation
had evolved dramatically into a coherent religion with a powerful
and original world view.

To the north of Kapilavastu the land rose in a haze of brown to
foothills covered with a dense jungle that bounded the region as a
whole. Thick undergrowth of jujuba and elephant grass made the
terrain virtually impassable and it was home to dangerous wild
animals like rhinoceros and tigers. On the horizon loomed the
jagged rock wall of the Mahabharata Mountains, the first in a series
of ranges that culminate in the mighty Himavat – the Himalayas
– about which little was known. Dark-skinned tribesmen lived in
the lands leading to its slopes, and it was said that the cities of the
gods were hidden amid their peaks. A track probably skirted the

marshes and led from Kapilavastu across high passes to the lands
that would one day be called Nepal and Tibet.

South of Kapilavastu was the western Ganges Valley, an expanse
of flat terrain 1,000 km wide and 300 km deep, where Gautama
spent virtually his whole life.* The trade road ran east from Kapilavastu, skirting the Himalayan foothills, and then turned south
towards the Ganges. The river was a mile wide when it was in flood
and travellers crossed by ferry to the southern shore and the kingdom
of Magadha. Downstream of the crossing point, boats sailed from
the great port of Campa to southern India, and perhaps beyond,
returning with jewels and spices. Upstream was Varanasi where
people travelled to die free of sin, having purified themselves in
the Ganges. The river flooded during the rains, and land near it
was so fertile when it was drained and irrigated that it yielded two,
or even three, harvests a year. This abundance fed a growing
population, and the largest cities, containing up to 100,000 inhabitants, were among the greatest in the world.

Shakya was perhaps 200 km across and contained eight towns
besides Kapilavastu, though most of its inhabitants probably lived
in villages and worked on the land. It was less fertile than lands
nearer the Ganges, but productive enough to generate a healthy
food surplus. Wealthy citizens bought gems and spices from the
south and decorated their houses with the lustrous black pottery
that was popular across the Ganges Valley. Shakya followed an
ancient form of self-government called *gana* community, or 'com-

---

* There is no convenient term for this region, so I will refer to it as 'the Ganges
Valley', although, strictly speaking, the valley extends further east and west than
the region the Buddha inhabited. According to the Discourses, his travels also took
him to Kuru, beyond the Ganges Valley, where he is said to have taught the famous
Satipatthana Sutta.

munity of equals', which it shared with a band of territories running eastwards from Shakya. The smaller city states were named
after the ruling clans: the Moriyas, the Mallas, the Koliyas and so
on; but the strongest *gana* community was the Vrijian Federation,
based in the thriving city of Vaishali, which united eight or nine
independent clans.

So far as we can tell, Gautama's father, Suddhodana, was a Shakyan
aristocrat, and some sources call him a 'raja'. But despite the version of Gautama's life made familiar in legendary accounts, this
didn't mean that he was a king (they were called 'maharajas'). It is
possible that he was simply one aristocrat among many, but
according to some sources, Suddhodana was the Shakyans' chief
raja. We know from descriptions of other *gana* communities that
chieftains were elected in a meeting of representatives of aristocratic families at the assembly hall: usually an open space with a
thatched roof supported by sturdy pillars, in the middle of the town
at the junction of the main thoroughfares. They made decisions
by mutual agreement or else by a vote, so historians sometimes
call the *gana* communities 'republics', and Gautama always thought
that their collective aspect – 'meeting in harmony, breaking up in
harmony and carrying on their business in harmony'[5] – brought
them strength. But those who weren't part of the nobility couldn't
participate in decision-making and *gana* communities certainly
weren't democracies in the modern sense.

The sources that give Suddhodana this role tell us that he held
the position when Gautama was born and died still in post thirty-
six years later. The chief raja had many responsibilities and would
have had only a rudimentary administration to help him collect
taxes, decide court cases according to Shakyan customs and enact
public works such as building roads, reservoirs and dams. He also
had to manage the unruly noblemen's assemblies. A Brahmin called

Ambatha told Gautama that at one meeting he had attended the Shakyans sat on their high seats 'poking each other with their fingers, laughing and playing about'.[6] There were also tensions between Shakyans and the Koliyas, who lived on the eastern bank of the Rohini, and on at least one occasion the two groups quarrelled over the right to use the river's water for irrigation.

Young Gautama

To allay political tensions and maintain the purity of their bloodline, the custom among Shakyan nobles was to intermarry with the Koliyas, who were their close relatives. Suddhodana married two Koliyan sisters, who were also his cousins, and eventually the elder sister, Maya (also known as Mayadevi and Mahamaya), became pregnant with Gautama. In keeping with the custom that women should return home to give birth, Maya set out from Kapilavastu to Devadaha when the birth approached. After several kilometres she paused to rest in 'a pleasure grove'[7] at Lumbini, and feeling her child coming she reached out to grasp the branch of a plaksa tree. The legends recount that the child emerged from her right side amid many miraculous signs and was lowered to the ground by the gods. Having rested, Maya triumphantly bore her baby son back to Kapilavastu.

One event stands out oddly from the joyful recitation of events in the Discourses that describe Gautama's birth: 'Seven days after the birth of the Bodhisatta [i.e. Gautama], his mother died and was reborn in the Tushita heaven.'[8] The speaker, Ananda, adds: 'This, too, I remember as a wonderful and marvellous quality of the Blessed One.' That strikes a dissonant note, as if an uncomfortable but important fact has somehow survived within the litany of marvels. Women commonly died in childbirth, but Gautama must have been affected by the knowledge that his mother had perished so that he might live, and that his very existence was bound up with her suffering.

Following Maya's death, Gautama's aunt, Prajapati (or Pajjapati), became his stepmother and, as Ananda later mentioned, she 'suckled [Gautama] at her own breast'[9] and tended to his upbringing. At seven, boys of the Kshatriya, or warrior, class were entrusted to men who educated them in the skills of a warrior; but when Gautama described his upbringing he called it 'delicate, exceedingly delicate',[10] and there is no reason to dispute the traditional image of Gautama growing up in luxury. Indian palaces of this era had cool, spacious apartments built around courtyards, and gardens filled with lotus ponds. 'In one of them blue lotuses bloomed', Gautama recalled; 'in another white lotuses, and in a third red lotuses, just for my enjoyment.' Such pools were often surrounded by gardens brightly decorated with flowers and ornamental birds such as peacocks and red-crested brahmany ducks, and we know that Indian nobles of somewhat later times loved flowering trees like the tall, pale-flowered shirisa, the fragrant kadamba and the beautiful ashoka tree, which blossoms in a mass of crimson and orange. Classical Indian literature contains many accounts of aristocratic life, and, allowing for some anachronism, descriptions such as the following passage from the second century CE erotic text, the *Kama Sutra*, are helpfully evocative:

The outer room, balmy with rich perfumes, should contain a bed, soft, agreeable to the sight, covered with a clean white cloth, low in the middle part, having garlands and bunches of flowers upon it and a canopy above it and two pillows, one at the top, another at the bottom. There should be also a sort of couch besides, and at the head

of this a sort of stool, on which should be placed the fragrant oint-
ments for the night, as well as flowers, pots containing collyrium and
other fragrant substances.[11]

Gautama tells us that he dressed only in fine robes made of
muslin brought from Varanasi's markets, and used only the best
sandalwood paste to cool his skin in the hot season. He also said
he had three palaces, 'one for the summer, one for the winter, and
one for the rainy season', which may mean that he had separate
quarters for each season, or that he relocated to the hills when the
heat grew unbearable. A telling detail is his comment that even the
servants were well fed: 'While in other people's homes servants and
slaves receive a meal of broken rice together with sour gruel, in my
father's house they were given choice rice and meat.'[12]

Later versions of Gautama's biography expanded a final detail
in his account into a key part of the legend of his childhood. He
says, 'I did not come down from the palace during these months.'
This probably means that he stayed there during the rains, but the
echo of Buddha Vipassi's seclusion prompted the legend that Suddhodana had confined Gautama to the palace and concocted an
idyllic existence from which all signs of sickness and suffering were
removed. That is an evocative fable, but it is more plausible that
Gautama simply experienced a luxurious childhood and that his
father tried to inculcate the outlook of a nobleman.

A credible tradition, which survives in the later accounts of Gautama's childhood, relates that he grew up in a tight-knit group of
aristocratic Koliya and Gautama children who were related through
a web of marriages. These childhood connections, and perhaps
rivalries, remained important in his later life when several of his
companions became prominent members of his order. Gautama's
wife-to-be is said to have been another cousin – the daughter of

Maya and Prajapati's brother, Suppabuddha – and *her* brother was Devadatta, with whom Gautama had the most serious falling-out of his career. Buddhist legends suggest that the pair were at odds even in their boyhood, and that the rivalry had grown over many lifetimes. Gautama had a half-brother, Nanda, and a half-sister, Sundari Nanda, who were the children of Suddhodana and Prajapati, while other members of the family included three cousins on his father's side – Mahanama, Anuruddha and Ananda. Also important in palace life were Gautama's servants, including Chandaka, his loyal retainer.

Little is recorded of Gautama's childhood in the Discourses, but one of them lists games which he may have played with his companions:

> games on boards with eight or ten rows, visualised board games, hopscotch, spillikin dice, hitting sticks, ball games, painting shapes with the hand, blowing through toy pipes, playing with toy ploughs, turning somersaults, playing with toy windmills made of leaves, playing with toy measures, toy carts or toy bows; guessing at letters or thoughts, mimicking deformities.[13]

Then there were popular entertainments, including 'dances, singing, music, fairs, recitations, hand-clapping, the chanting of bards, fairy scenes [and] acrobatics', which travelling troupes would have performed when they passed through Kapilavastu, as well as fights between 'elephants, buffaloes, bulls, goats, rams and cocks'.[14] Poetry, dance and music are more probable diversions for the cultivated atmosphere of the palace, and Gautama tells us that in the rainy season, during which he 'did not come down from the palace', he spent his time 'enjoying myself with female musicians only'.[15] In later life Gautama associated such pursuits with distracting sensual pleasures and told actors that they were destined for an unhappy rebirth. But he also congratulated a singer that 'the sound of your strings blends so well with your song'[16] and spoke knowledgeably about the 'imaginative, traditional, didactic and extempore'[17] genres of poetry.

Gautama's warrior training doubtless included wrestling, sword fighting and archery, but, alas, there is no basis in the Discourses for later tales that made him a master archer who alone could bend the mighty bow of his grandfather. The truth was that Shakyan nobles grew up to be farmers or administrators. The tales of Vedic India's heroic age in the great epic the *Mahabharata* (then being collated in the Brahmin lands to the west) evoke an era when warrior clans ruled themselves and rode to war, but they culminate in a cataclysmic battle. If Gautama were told such stories he may have heard in them a lament for the end of the warrior's ancient nomadic life. A similar pathos haunts his own descriptions of battle: 'Men take swords and shields and buckle on bows and quivers, and they charge into battle massed in double array with arrows and spears flying and swords flashing; and there they are wounded by arrows and spears and splashed with boiling liquids and crushed under heavy weights and their heads are cut off by swords.'[18]

Gautama often transposed martial imagery to the inner battle of spiritual development: 'Though one should conquer thousands upon thousands of men,' he said, 'he who conquers himself is truly the greatest in battle.'[19] Another thread in the Discourses that may echo Gautama's childhood years is his appreciation of the craftsman's mastery of his materials, which he used as an image for the command and attention required to develop the mind. He usually mentioned the relatively narrow range of professions he would have seen in the streets of Kapilavastu and the fields of Shakya: 'Irrigators draw off water; fletchers shape arrows; carpenters carve wood; the spiritually mature discipline themselves.'[20]

A succinct account survives in the Discourses of a childhood incident that became crucially important for Gautama when he recalled it at a pivotal moment in his later life. He remembered 'sitting in the cool shade of a rose-apple tree while my Shakyan father was engaged in work'[21] and entering spontaneously into a state of deep tranquillity. According to late sources, the occasion was a festival to mark the start of the annual ploughing season that came after the monsoon rains, when the land was moist and firm. The chieftain initiated the ploughing and verses were recited; similar, perhaps, to those of the *Atharva Veda*: 'Successfully let the good ploughshares thrust apart the earth; successfully let the ploughmen follow the beasts of draught; Shunashira, do ye two dripping with oblation make the herbs rich in berries for this man!'[22]

Seated cross-legged in the shade, Gautama entered a peaceful and concentrated state, which he later recalled as a deeply satis-fying state of inner flourishing: 'I spent time having attained the joy and happiness of the first absorption, which is accompanied by thinking and examination and is born of seclusion.'[23] 'The first absorption, or *dhyana*, is a state of meditative concentration and later, when he had grown familiar with meditation, Gautama described it in greater detail:

> Gladness arises, and when one is glad, joy arises. When the mind is joyful, the body becomes tranquil, and when the body is tranquil one experiences happiness; the mind of someone who is happy becomes concentrated ... He suffuses, fills, soaks and drenches his very body with the happiness and joy that come from seclusion so that there is no part of his body that is untouched.[24]

In this experience Gautama tasted a new kind of awareness, which didn't depend on the physical senses, in which his mind opened effortlessly into an unsuspected, expansive dimension of being.

Everyone married, and Gautama did so when he was sixteen or seventeen, according to Buddhist tradition. Some versions of the legend imagine a passionate romance between Gautama and his bride, but in Gautama's world marriage meant fulfilling the duty to provide sons, rather than a path to emotional fulfilment. His later comments on marriage in general suggest that while Gautama understood its appeal he found it constricting. We know nothing for certain about his wife, not even her name, and in the early texts she is referred to only as Rahulamata ('the mother of Rahula' – Gautama's son). In later tradition she is best known as Yashodhara, but she is also called Baddhacacca, Bimba, Gopa, Subhaddaka and Migaja. Whatever we say about her is speculation. It is even possible that Gautama had more than one wife and that the various names refer to each. Buddhist tradition also mentions a harem (perhaps the 'female singers' who waited on him in the rains), and identifies several nuns, whose memory survives through verses they composed, as former members.

Crowded Waters

If we discount the legend that Gautama had no contact with the outside world before he left the palace, we can surmise that when he had completed his education he took his place among the nobles in the Shakyan assembly and helped his father with his work. His later confidence in dealing with kings, and canny political sense, suggests that he learned from the experience, but Shakya's position was complex and vulnerable, and its difficulties must have affected him. Although Suddhodana and the assembly decided the nation's day-to-day affairs, Shakya was in fact a province of Kosala, the kingdom ruled from Shravasti that controlled the western part of the Ganges Valley to the north of the river. Gautama was happy to say of his race: 'In the foothills of the Himalayas live a people who are indigenous to Kosala. They come from the race of the sun and they are Shakyans by birth. That was the people from which I went forth.'[25] But the Shakyan nobility was notorious for a racial pride that Gautama himself sometimes echoed. By 'the race of the sun', he meant the descent the Shakyans claimed from the 'solar lineage' of primordial monarchs and 'Universal Rulers' that culminated in the legendary King Okkaka. Gautama himself told the story of Okkaka's banished sons whom the Shakyans called their ancestors:

[They] made their home on the flank of the Himalayas beside a lotus pond where there was a big grove of teak trees. And for fear of contaminating the stock they cohabited with their own sisters. The King Okkaka asked his ministers, 'Where are the princes living now?' and they told him. At this King Okkaka exclaimed, 'They are strong as teak trees, these princes, they are real Shakyans.'[26]

This lineage made the Shakyans superior, in their own eyes, to Brahmins like Ambattha, for whose benefit he told the story, and also to their Kosalan rulers. But one discourse tells us that 'the Shakyans are vassals of King Prasenajit of Kosala. They bow down before him, salute him respectfully, bow with cupped hands and are at his service.'[27] In practice this probably meant that Shakya paid the Kosalan Maharaja a share of its income as a tax and could not wage war independently. It may be that Kosala had conquered Shakya, or that Kosala's sphere of influence expanded until it encompassed the Shakyans, who accepted the king's suzerainty in return for his protection.*

While Kosala overshadowed Shakya, other forces challenged Kosala itself. At the start of Gautama's life it was probably the strongest of the Ganges nations, buoyed by the unprecedented wealth that washed through the entire region thanks to international trade and agricultural surpluses. But Kosala's administration was weak and swathes of the country were lawless. Magadha, bolstered by iron and copper mines, was the growing power, and throughout Gautama's life the kingdoms of Kosala, Magadha and Kasi jockeyed with each other and with the Vrijian Federation for control of the fertile Ganges farmlands and the lucrative river trade. But if some kingdoms were expanding more quickly than others, the kingdoms as a whole were growing stronger and more centralised, and swallowing up *gana* communities like Shakya. To start with, the king had probably been a distant figure who left his subjects to rule themselves according to their customs. But the power of central governments was growing. Kings encouraged industry and supported trade, and as their power grew they extracted more money from the peasants and larger tributes from dependent territories. They issued laws, took a sixth of income in tax and claimed ownership of uncultivated land, which they drained and irrigated using forced labour to establish vast royal estates that enriched them further. Spy networks underpinned their rule and, in time, standing armies backed it.

A new culture was growing in the cities that disrupted long-standing, settled ways of life. When Ajatashatru (Magadha's king

---

* According to the Burmese *Glass Palace Chronicles*, both Shakya and neighbouring Koliya were conquered at a time when the kingdoms of Kosala and Pancala were united, the cause being an insult by the Shakyans to the Pancalan king.

in the latter part of Gautama's life) described his society to Gautama he listed the occupations of his subjects: 'Elephant riders,
cavalrymen, charioteers, archers, spies, standard-bearers, high-
ranking royal officers, household slaves, cooks, barbers, bath attendants, sweet-makers, garland-makers, washermen, weavers,
basket-makers, potters, those skilled in accounts and calculation,
and various other professions of a similar sort.'[28]

These cities were booming, turning themselves into power
centres protected by massive, newly constructed ramparts. Bankers
extended credit and merchants made fortunes, while ruin could
come to even the most venerable families. Members of the same
clan had previously shared land, but landowners now amassed
huge estates tended by hired workers and slaves. For most people,
life was hard. Gautama observed: 'On account of the craft by which
a clansman has to make a living . . . he has to face cold, he has to
face heat, he is injured by gadflies, mosquitoes, wind, sun and
creeping things.'[29]

For a while, Gautama may well have shared Suddhodana's pre-
occupations and perhaps tasted the same pressures. Bhaddiya,
another Shakyan raja, recalled that he had lived within 'lofty, encir-
cling walls, firm battlements and sturdy gates',[30] surrounded by
armed guards who accompanied him wherever he went, but, even
so, he was constantly 'anxious, fearful and on alert'.[31] We hear a
similar anxiety in the Attadanda Sutta in which Gautama describes
Shakyan life as a fight for survival in a confined space with people
'flopping around, like fish in water too shallow'.[32]

Spiritual Crisis

In a discourse called 'The Noble Quest', in which Gautama gave his fullest account of the events leading to his Enlightenment, he says that when he left home he was 'still a young man with a head of black hair and the advantages of being in the first flush of youth'.[33] In another discourse he adds, 'I was twenty-nine years of age when I went forth in search of what is good.'[34] Buddhist tradition accepted twenty-nine as the age of Gautama's 'going forth', but it seems rather too old, leaving too much time in the palace and too little between his departure and his Enlightenment to encompass the events that are described. A younger age, perhaps the late teens or early twenties, also fits better the intense emotions that stirred him.

The classical biographies use the story of Gautama's Four Sights to account for his crisis. While we cannot treat this as fact, it is a helpful reminder that he was prompted not by psychological mal-adjustment but by a visceral realisation of inescapable aspects of the human condition. He marvelled that people ordinarily remain oblivious to the presence of old age, sickness and death despite seeing around them those who are 'tottering, frail, youth gone, teeth broken', the 'afflicted, suffering and gravely ill, lying fouled in [their] own excrement', and the 'bloated and oozing'[35] bodies of the dead. Seeing these harsh realities, Gautama threw off the 'intoxication with youth, health and life'[36] that had clouded his awareness, and suddenly understood that old age, sickness and death are inescapable facts. He called them 'divine messengers' who tell human beings something vitally important about their state.

In later life, when he had formulated his teachings, Gautama used a term current in the religious discourse of his time to explain his motivation for leaving home. All ordinary human life, he said, is *dukkha*. The word is often translated as 'suffering', and it includes physical pain and distress, but the root meaning is 'not fitting well', or perhaps 'standing badly', and it also means 'difficulty' and 'uneasiness'.[37] *Dukkha* encompasses all the unsatisfactoriness that is inherent in life, and the sense that something is awry even when things go well. For Gautama, this was more than a mild unease: it was a shattering awareness of aspects of reality he had previously ignored. He had a remarkable talent for identifying the universal truths in particular experiences, but he may have been helped by spiritual teachings he heard in Kapilavastu. He later quoted powerful verses, attributed to an ancient teacher called Araka, which say that that human life vanishes as quickly as

> a dewdrop on the tip of a blade of grass . . .
> a bubble on the surface of the water . . .
> a line drawn on water . . .
> a river that has arisen far away in the mountains . . .
> a ball of spit . . .
> a piece of meat thrown into an iron pan . . .
> a cow led to the slaughterhouse and each step takes her closer
> to death.[38]

'The life of humans is brief and fleeting and full of pain and despair', the verses continue. 'You should heed advice, do what is wholesome, practise the spiritual life; there is no escape from death for one who is born.'

In 'The Noble Quest', Gautama describes the deep disillusionment that followed his observation of how people lived. Everyone seemed to be on a quest to find happiness and security. Most sought it in external things, like the must-have items of Gautama's society: 'men and women slaves, goats and sheep, fowl and pigs, elephants, cattle, horses and mares'.[39] But these 'objects of attachment' bring suffering because people become 'tied to these things, infatuated by them and utterly committed to them'. In another discourse, Gautama comments that, typically, when a man encounters old age, disease and death, he feels 'horrified, humiliated and disgusted'.[40] But that response seemed self-indulgent to the young Gautama and he relates that the visceral shock of his realisation was such that 'all my pride in my life vanished'.[41]

Gautama sensed that *dukkha* couldn't be allayed by solving his worldly problems, or even by changing the world itself. Its source lay much deeper. The Attadanda Sutta is the most vivid description we have of the shattering emotions Gautama felt (and it is significant that it belongs to what scholars consider the very earliest of the Discourses).

> Fear is born from arming oneself.
> Just see how many people fight!
> I'll tell you about the dreadful fear
> that caused me to shake all over:
> Seeing creatures flopping around,
> Like fish in water too shallow,
> So hostile to one another!
> – Seeing this, I became afraid.

Then came an insight that determined what came next in Gautama's life and shaped its future course.

> This world completely lacks essence;
> It trembles in all directions.
> I longed to find myself a place
> Unscathed – but I could not see it.

Seeing people locked in conflict,
I became completely distraught.
But then I discerned here a thorn
– Hard to see – lodged deep in the heart.
It's only when pierced by this thorn
That one runs in all directions.
So if that thorn is taken out –
one does not run, and settles down.[42]

He understood that people create the world's troubles through their efforts to alleviate their insecurity and confusion; and he saw that he was afflicted, just as they were, by the thorn in his heart. He understood that he needed to change himself in some radical, fundamental way. But how?

The Endless Round

Gautama's testimony in 'The Noble Quest' and the Attadanda Sutta vividly evokes the emotions and experiences that prompted his crisis, but understanding what he did next means expanding our focus from Kapilavastu and the Shakyan court to the wider culture in which he lived. Gautama's quest was a response to issues that face people in every society and at every time, but it was shaped by the specific time and place in which he grew up. Every culture has a distinctive world view – a way of understanding life that answers fundamental questions about its meaning and yet also raises certain problems. Gautama's Greek contemporaries considered that human beings live in the shadow of the gods, vulnerable to mortality and fate; and the afterlife was a ghostly echo. Gautama's contemporary Socrates wrestled with this philosophy and revolutionised his countrymen's outlook by urging them to trust their reason and develop inner qualities. The Hebrew universe, meanwhile, was framed by man's relationship to God, who dictated the moral law and presided over death. But what had begun as a tribal covenant between Yahweh and the Jews became a religion of personal moral effort when Isaiah and Jeremiah proclaimed that God had renewed the covenant by writing 'the law in their minds and on their hearts'.[43]

An important difference in the view of life prevailing in the Ganges Valley was that its inhabitants considered the world both incredibly old and inconceivably vast. A discourse that describes Gautama's birth offers a Miltonic evocation of the enormity of the boundless universe he envisaged: 'A great immeasurable light surpassing the splendour of the gods appeared in the world ... even in those abysmal world interspaces of vacancy, gloom and utter darkness, where the sun and moon, mighty and powerful as they are, cannot make their light prevail.'[44]

What's more, the cosmos is 'without discoverable beginning',[45] as Gautama later said, and has existed for innumerable aeons, expanding and collapsing in a giant cosmic cycle.* A single aeon, or *kalpa*, is so long that it cannot be reckoned in years or centuries, only evoked. Years after his departure from Kapilavastu, sitting beneath the night sky with its infinite stars, Gautama himself told his disciples to imagine a great mountain of rock, five miles long, high and broad. If, at the end of every hundred years, a man were to brush the mountain just once with a fine cloth woven in Kasi, the mountain would be at length be worn away, he said, but, 'the aeon would still not have come to an end'.[46]

---

* This seems to have been the prevalent view of the Ganges Valley religions. Brahminical texts offer different ideas, including the belief that the world was created, and Gautama knew that such views existed.

This unbounded cosmos staggers the imagination, and as it is without a beginning, there is no creator god to rule and make sense of it. Such a cosmos would dwarf the individual were it not for another aspect of Ganges Valley cosmology: the belief that each individual, or at least his or her soul, is as ancient as the universe and has been reborn repeatedly throughout the ages. But if belief in rebirth gave the individual a place in the cosmos, it raised fresh concerns for thinking Indians like Gautama. The early sources speak not of rebirth but of 're-death', and the prospect of dying thousands of times was overwhelming. Gautama told his followers that in their previous lifetimes they had left behind 'a pile of bones higher than a mountain',[47] and shed 'more tears than the waters of the four great oceans' as they 'experienced again and again the death of a mother, father, son or daughter'.[48]

Our lot, Gautama's contemporaries believed, is to wander through death and rebirth in the sphere Indians called *samsara*. The world of human experience, they believed, is part of the realm of form and sensation, which also includes the realms of the lower gods, gruesome hell-realms, and four great continents that lie at the points of the compass. Above it is a divine realm of 'form only' whose inhabitants are self-luminous and feed on delight, and beyond that is the highest sphere, which is without either form or sensation.* Rebirth in any of the divine realms brings a life of prolonged bliss, but birth in the hells or the macabre ghostly domains means unimaginable pain. Whatever one's destination, the endlessly repeating

---

* There are thirty-one spheres in all, according to Theravada Buddhism: four form-less spheres (*arupa-lokas*), and sixteen spheres of the realm of form (*rupa-lokas*), all with their heavenly inhabitants; while the world of form and sense (*kama-loka*) includes six god realms and the realms of humans, animals, hungry ghosts and the inhabitants of hell.

cycles of birth, death and rebirth offer no resting place and give no sense of purpose.

But how is one's post-mortem destination determined? The answer depended on a certain idea of *how things happen*, and this would also be a central issue in Gautama's thinking. Anyone could see that actions have consequences in this life, and certain forms of religion held that prayers and sacrifices affect events in unseen ways. By the same token, people believed that a person's actions – or *karma* – determined where they were reborn. Good actions meant a happy rebirth while bad ones bound one to a darker fate. For Gautama, as for his Ganges Valley contemporaries, rejecting belief in karma was unthinkable – it would have meant rejecting the whole basis of ethics, while rejecting rebirth would leave only a chilling nihilism. But a further, crucial, question remained: *which* actions bring beneficial merit, and which bring harmful consequences? Here the consensus broke down, and the region's competing religious traditions had sharply different answers.

Culture Wars

The popular religion of *gana* communities like Shakya focused on the shrines of local gods and spirits.* Some were benevolent, but most were capricious and dangerous, and had to be propitiated by offerings at the deity's shrines – a sacred tree in a grove outside a village or town. Each place had its local deity, usually a fierce *yaksha*, and some sources say that Gautama was presented as a child to Shakyavardana, the *yaksha* spirit who presided over the Shakya

---

* Buddhism designated these spirits 'earth gods', and distinguished them from the spirits that reside in the higher heavenly realms.

clan. Some scholars have also identified goddess cults, including benign spirits that presided over fertility, and destructive figures that brought disease and killed children. This folk religion satisfied most people. Its rituals were interwoven with clan traditions and the cycles of the year, and Gautama noted that 'many people, out of fear, flee for refuge to sacred hills, woods, groves, trees and shrines'.[49] But though Gautama felt deep affection for spirit shrines throughout his life, he commented that, in reality, they were not 'a safe refuge'. For him, real security from the sufferings of old age, disease and death meant going beyond samsara altogether.

In Gautama's story of Vipassi's encounter with the old man, sick man and corpse, he added that Vipassi then saw a shaven-headed figure dressed in yellow robes and learned that this man had *gone forth*. He had renounced possessions, status and caste and become 'one who truly follows dharma, who truly lives in serenity, does good actions, is harmless and truly has compassion for living beings'.[50] Such a man was a *shramana*, a wandering religious seeker, rather like the sadhus who are still a common sight in India. According to one classical source, their lives included 'complete control of the organs of sense, abstaining from all kinds of work, disowning money, keeping from society, begging in many places, dwelling in forests, and purity both internal and external'.[51]

The shramanas' origins lie far back in Indian history. Gautama clearly believed that his culture was already very old, and told stories of ancient cities lost in the jungle. Some trace the shramanas' origins to the Harrappan civilisation that thrived around the Indus Valley in the north-east of the subcontinent between 3000 and 1500 BCE, and a seal found in the buried city of Mohenjo Daro depicts a cross-legged figure with his hands resting on his knees and his eyes narrowed, perhaps in meditation. Harrappan civilisation declined when the River Saraswati dried up and it is impossible to say what its religious legacy may have been. But we do know that in the centuries preceding Gautama's birth holy men in the Ganges Valley were exploring methods of spiritual development called 'yoga', which may have included some sort of meditation. The Jains, one of the best-established shramana communities, traced their traditions back through a series of teachers to the distant past, and at least the last of these teachers, Parsva, was an historical figure who was said to have lived about 300 years before Gautama.

Religious wanderers passed through Kapilavastu on their travels between the major cities, and it was common for aristocrats like Gautama to engage them in conversation. The Discourses record a visit by Gautama in later life to the yogic hermitage of 'Bharandu the Kalama'[52] near Kapilavastu, whose residents followed the teachings of a great meditation master called Arada Kalama. The Pali commentary adds that the hermitage had existed in Gautama's youth, which suggests the possibility that he had visited it as a young man and met the yogis who lived there. One way or another, it would have been natural for Gautama to meet shramanas and perhaps discuss with them his questions about life. Some householders mocked these wandering mendicants, most did not understand them, but many still respected them deeply and set aside a little of the food they cooked each day to place in their bowls when they came on their alms rounds. That gained them karmic merit that could bring a better rebirth in the next life or good fortune in this. Many towns had a park outside the walls where wanderers stayed, and some towns – though, apparently, not Kapilavastu – had a special shramana rest house. There is some evidence that wanderers also provided medicine, which would have brought householders into contact with them when they went for treatment.

The shramana tradition seems to have been indigenous to the Ganges Valley, and a natural response to its philosophy of karma and rebirth. A second culture, which coexisted uneasily with it, had spread from the west – the culture of the Aryas. Because, in the long run, the Aryas' descendants dominated the subcontinent, Aryan texts survived and until recently historians assumed that the inhabitants of the Ganges Valley (barring peripheral groups, tribes and perhaps the lower social orders) were among their descendants. Even Buddhist works from a few centuries after Gautama's time depict him as an Arya who grew up in a society that followed the Aryan religion of Brahminism. But in recent years a more complex picture has emerged in the work of historians such as Romila Thapar, Johannes Bronkhorst and Geoffrey Samuel.

The Aryas came to India from Persia in a series of migrations starting in about 1500 BCE, just as Harrappan civilisation was declining. These weren't full-scale invasions, but the ancient Aryan texts called Vedas recall battles for territory. The oldest of them, the *Rig Veda*, divides people between those who are *arya*, or noble, and those who are *dasa*, or servants, suggesting a distinction between victorious tribes and those they conquered. Ancient texts also speak of *aryavarta* – the sacred 'Aryan land' where 'the door to the world of the Fathers'[53] stood open and their culture prevailed. The historic centre of aryavarta was the Punjab, and in Gautama's day distant Taxila remained an important Aryan centre, despite its incorporation into the Persian Empire. Aryavarta territory expanded as Aryan influence spread east and south over the centuries until, as one ancient text rhapsodically declared, aryavarta lay 'to the east of the sunset and to the west of the sunrise, and (ran) as far as the high mountains reach and the sacred rivers flow'.[54] But there were definite limits. As late as 150 BCE Patanjali, in his work on Sanskrit grammar, wrote that the eastern boundary of aryavarta was the dense 'Kalaka forest'[55] at the confluence of the Ganges and the Yamuna rivers. This was the western boundary of the central Ganges

Valley, placing Kosala, Shakya and the lands to the south and east of them firmly outside aryavarta.

One Brahminical text recounts a legendary battle between the Aryas and the 'demonic people of the east' (the 'Asuras') in which 'the gods drove out the Asuras, their rivals and enemies, from the region, and being regionless they were overcome'.[56] This legend may recall an ancient rift between Aryan tribes, or perhaps battles between Aryas and indigenous people, as well as the migration of the defeated peoples to the inhospitable marshes and forests around the Ganges. Once there, the migrants drained the land, cleared some of the forests and made the Ganges Valley so suitable for cultivation that, when agriculture was properly established, the economy boomed and the region's population swelled far beyond that of aryavarta itself.

On the eastern side of the Yamuna were Kuru and Pancala. In the centuries before Gautama, some historians believe, they developed into the first truly Brahminical states, where a rigorous new religion evolved out of the ancient rites. At its heart stood the Brahmin priests who preserved the Aryan lore and rituals recorded in the Vedas which, they believed, the gods had recited to ancient sages when they entered a hallucinogenic 'intoxication of ecstasy'.[57] The priests memorised the hymns along with prescribed ritual gestures and chanted them in the sacrifices that constituted Brahminism's central rites. Three sacrificial fires burned constantly in a Brahminical home – one to prepare food, one to receive the offerings and the third to ward off evil spirits; and the devout, who believed that gods dwelled within the fires, would rather extinguish their own lives than let them go out. One can still see Brahminical rituals – with their mass of flames and smoke, the sweet smell of burning butter and the droning throb of the ancient hymns – performed in the Hindu temples that inherited these traditions.

The sacrifice was powerful magic. It promised success in crucial events like childbearing, warfare and the harvest, and the Vedas include charms against being killed by anything from fever to a missile flung by the gods. Later Vedic hymns declared that the true importance of the sacrifice was that it repeated the primordial creative act, and that the universe itself only continued when its essential power (called *rta*, or *dharma*, and later, *Brahman*) was touched. That only happened if a sacrifice was perfectly enacted, so priests became highly trained specialists who studied for twelve years before they could officiate. For those with faith, Brahmins were a link to the mysterious forces that governed the universe: a 'refuge' from life's storms, and a protection against the primordial terrors that threatened to plunge humanity back into chaos.

Across northern India, more and more peoples spoke 'Indo-Aryan' languages and adopted aspects of Aryan culture. Vedic gods like Indra and Brahma became widely accepted and some Aryan rituals may have been familiar parts of the whole region's religious culture. The magical powers claimed by the Brahmins were an attractive addition to the old spirit cults, and some priests were probably invited to move east because of their expertise in ritual and magic. We hear of Brahmins conducting rituals across the Ganges Valley and of long-established sacred sites like Varanasi and Gaya that were becoming important Brahminical centres. Kings were drawn to the Brahmins by the promise of powerful sacrifices to sanctify their rule and they compensated the priests for leaving aryavarta with money or the lordship of a village 'full of grass, timber, water and corn'.[58] Other Brahmins who travelled east may simply have been settlers looking for land to farm. By Gautama's time, the native culture of local cults and shramanas existed side by side in the Ganges Valley with the imported culture of the Brahmins, and people heard their differing views of life and competing visions of society.

The caste system, which still governs much of Indian life, lay some centuries in the future. But the Brahminical societies of Kuru and Pancala had built on distinctions inherited from Vedic times in dividing people into four orders or *varnas*, with the Brahmins at the top. The priestly claim to supremacy challenged the *Kshatriyas*, the warriors and nobles who had previously dominated Aryan life, and for centuries the two groups vied for primacy. Legends survive of Brahmins who condemned Kshatriyas and kings who declared war on the priests. *Vaishyas*, the merchants and farmers, came a poor third, but were still among the three 'twice-born orders' whose male members underwent Brahminical initiation at puberty. In the fourth category were *Shudras*, who were expected to serve members of the other orders; and at some point a fifth group was identified, beyond the serfs and outside society proper: the caste-less *Chandalas* for whom, as Gautama observed, 'there is little food or drink and it is hard to survive, food and clothing is obtained with difficulty'.[59] The Vedas declared that this way of organising society was divinely ordained, and a well-known passage describes how the varnas were created when the gods carved up the primordial man:

> The Brahmin was his mouth, of his arms were made the warrior
> His thighs became the Vaishya, of his feet the Shudra was born.[60]

The reassuringly static Brahminical ideal of a society in which everyone knew their place had made substantial inroads into the Ganges Valley by Gautama's time. Rulers were flattered to receive a respected place in the Aryan social order, and across northern India aristocratic clans identified themselves as Kshatriyas. Many people, Gautama included, identified strongly with the clan into which they were born, and the varna system reinforced that identity.

But as the economy of the Ganges Valley boomed, money spoke loudest and Brahminical social distinctions seemed misplaced. Gautama observed that 'if a Kshatriya, a Brahmin, a Vaishya or a Shudra prospers in wealth, corn, gold or silver, there are Kshatriyas, Brahmins, Vaishyas and Shudras who are eager to do what he tells them, please him and speak sweetly to him'.[61] We hear in the Discourses of Brahmins who worked as accountants, craftsmen and especially farmers. The most important figure in the countryside was the *gahapati*, the head of an extended household whose power came from his wealth, regardless of whether he had been born as a priest, merchant or nobleman. Merchants discovered that if they were successful in business they could change their standing. They saw with their own eyes the contrasting lives of villagers and townspeople and the differing customs and beliefs of the countries they visited. Tales even reached Gautama of a distant land called Ionia (Yona) where there were no Brahminical varnas and 'masters [could] become slaves and slaves masters'.[62]

There is no sign that Brahminism, with its emphasis on magical powers and external rituals, ever appealed to Gautama, and we cannot even say if he encountered it before he left Kapilavastu. Shakya was not only outside aryavarta, it was far from the major Ganges cities in which Brahmin influence was strongest. The only official distinction within Shakyan territory was between Kshatriyas and their subjects, and while there are mentions in the Discourses of Brahmins from Kosala, Magadha and elsewhere, we find no Shakyan Brahmins. Shakyan nobles were fiercely proud of their status, and one Vedic source calls the clans of the gana communities 'degenerate Kshatriyas'[63] because they disrespected the priests. That echoes Ambattha's complaint that the Shakyan Kshatriyas 'do not know how to pay homage to Brahmins', and were 'fierce, rough-speaking, touchy, violent and of menial origin'.[64] However, the

Shakyans' claim that they were descended from Okkaka suggests that, like many others, they accepted aspects of Aryan culture that bolstered their prestige.

Full-time religious practitioners in the Ganges Valley were often lumped together as 'brahmanas and shramanas' – but the two traditions were at odds. Patanjali cites *brahmana–shramana* as a phrase that compounds two things that are actually hostile, like 'cat and mouse' or 'snake and mongoose', between whom 'there is eternal conflict'.[65] Priests like Ambattha looked down on shramanas and considered them ritually impure. That is probably the explanation for the incident in Gautama's later life when he approached a village and the local Brahmins, seeing 'bald-pated' shramanas approaching, threw chaff down the well to stop them drinking the water and thereby polluting it.[66] The competition between the two groups would continue for another 1,500 years and its echoes can be heard in the religious life of modern India.

But Brahminism was changing even as its influence on Ganges Valley life increased. The Vedas instructed Brahmins to live frugally and avoid towns, but their wealthy lives in the Ganges cities were anything but simple. Gautama pointedly asked Ambattha:

Those first sages . . . did they enjoy themselves, well bathed, perfumed, their hair and beards neatly trimmed, adorned with garlands and wreaths, indulging in the pleasures of the five senses? Did they eat special fine rice, or amuse themselves with women, or ride around in chariots drawn by mares with braided tails, or have themselves guarded in fortified towns with palisades and barricades?[67]

Even though renunciation and celibacy had no place in the Vedas, Gautama's criticisms touched a nerve because the shramanas seemed closer to the Vedic sages' frugality and virtue than their priestly heirs. Perhaps in response to the shramanas, an ascetic tradition was developing among the Brahmins themselves, and a century after Gautama, a Greek ambassador to the Indian court called Megasthenes described these Brahmin ascetics: 'They live in simple style, and lie within a moderate-sized enclosure on rushes or deer-skins. They abstain from animal food and sexual pleasure and spend their time in listening to serious discourse and in imparting their knowledge to such as will listen to them.'[68]

The mystical teachings of these men are found in scriptures called the Upanishads, which were passed in secret from teacher to disciple and included ideas such as the philosophy of karma and rebirth, which they may also have learned from the shramanas. Gautama had more respect for Brahminical ascetics than for their priestly peers, but they still remained for him a pale reflection of the real spiritual heroes of his culture – the shramanas. It was to them that he turned in his crisis.

Going Forth

When he became a shramana himself, Gautama had to make sense of the contradictory answers shramana teachers proposed to the problems of the human condition. But those differences didn't concern him as he contemplated joining them. What he could see, as he explained in 'The Noble Quest', was that household life bound one to a meaningless existence whose repetitions echoed the cycles of lives. However, just leaving home would not be enough. He needed to escape samsara altogether: 'Suppose that, being myself subject to birth, having understood the danger in what is subject to birth, I seek the unborn supreme security from bondage: Nirvana. Suppose that being myself subject to sickness, death, sorrow and defilement I seek the unageing, unailing, deathless, sorrowless, supreme security from bondage: Nirvana?'[69]

According to the traditional account, the climax of Gautama's crisis came a week after the birth of his first son. Rather than bringing pride, the event exacerbated Gautama's feeling that his existence was constricted and meaningless, and he named his son 'Rahula', which means 'fetter'. Later depictions of Gautama's departure in Buddhist art and literature describe a pathos-filled drama in which he creeps at night through the darkened palace and, unable to resist a last look at his family, steals into the room where his wife is sleeping, her hand shielding the head of their newborn son. He feels an urge to hold the child one last time, but turns away, promising himself that he will return when he has true wisdom to offer. Then he wakes Chandaka, who saddles Kanthaka, his favourite horse, and together they ride into the night. 'The Noble Quest' offers a rather less romantic account, according to which Gautama left only after a period of painful argument with his father and stepmother who 'wept, their faces covered by tears'.[70] It may be that Gautama had made an agreement with Suddhodana not to leave until he had provided a grandchild. It has recently been suggested that the entire tradition of Gautama having a son is a later addition to his biography.*

Whatever the truth, the story of Gautama's decision to abandon his wife and child, disappoint his father's hopes and renounce his clan retains the power to shock. But becoming a shramana was a respected option in Gautama's society, though it was not without an emotional cost. Gautama believed a higher duty called him, and a discourse which is in the voice of a very early biographer suggests how the choice between the palace and the open road appeared:

* Rahula appears in the Pali Discourses, but Gautama's abandonment of him does not.

I shall tell you about the renunciation, the manner in which the one with insight renounced the world and the manner of the inquiry which led him to choose the life of renunciation: 'In a home,' thought that man, 'a life is stifled – impurity is everywhere, like dust. For the wanderer,' thought that man, 'there is space – he lives out in the open in the air.' He saw this was so and set off.[71]

From Gautama's perspective, household existence was the real escapism because those undertaking it ignored the harsh truths of old age, sickness and death. The mention of Nirvana is anachronistic, as the term seems to have been coined later in his life by Gautama himself; but it does evoke the faith he must surely have felt that he would find a truly fulfilling alternative to the ills of samsara.

Legend relates that at dawn Gautama and Chandaka crossed the Anoma River, which marked the edge of the Shakyan lands. Then Gautama shaved his flowing hair and beard, sadly bade farewell to Kanthaka and exchanged his princely robes for the rags of a beggar. The change from householder to wanderer was both a literal and a metaphorical transition. Gautama was giving up his old identity, renouncing the warrior's duty to rule over society and abandoning security, status and comfort. He was leaving everything he knew and the people he loved to join an alternative world in which religious wanderers lived outdoors and survived on scraps donated by respectful householders. For Gautama, it was not his race, his Kshatriya birth, nor the ideas of the Brahmins that made him *arya* – noble. Nobility lay in the quest on which he now embarked. He set out, literally, on the path that led from Kapilavastu to the world beyond it, and he also started to walk the figurative 'path' of spiritual practice that led away from the cyclic repetitions of the world and towards a shimmering alternative:

Over and over, the seeds all get planted;

Over and over, the rain-god sprinkles rain.

Over and over, the farmer farms the field;

Over and over, the food grows in the realm ...

Over and over, he tires and he struggles;

Over and over, the fool goes to the womb.

Over and over, he's born and he dies;

Over and over, they bear him to his grave.

But one whose wisdom is wide as the earth

Is not born over and over,

For he's gained the path

Of not becoming over again.[72]

2

The Search for Wisdom

The Spiritual Marketplace

Later in Gautama's career, having spent many years as a wandering shramana, life in the wilderness became second nature. He sometimes appeared as untamed as the land itself:

> In places where frightening serpents abide,
> Lightning clashes and the rain-god thunders,
> In the blinding darkness of the deepest night,
> There he sits – the monk who's vanquished his dread.[1]

But this wasn't how Gautama felt as he set out from Shakya in his wanderer's rags. The journey took him south, down the trade road that passed through the lands of the Koliyas and Mallas, and gave Gautama his first taste of the rough conditions that would be his lot from now on. Householders gave him his food, probably placing it in his cupped hands rather than in a bowl (which seems to have been a Buddhist innovation). Sometimes that meant scraps left over from a meal, sometimes nothing at all. At night he lay down wherever he could, under the stars or beneath a banyan tree, whose

branches coiled down to the earth like garbled pipework. All around
the jungle hummed – no wonder most people saw it as a place of
'fear and dread'.[2]

The Ganges Valley is now open fields and farmland, but in Gautama's time a settlement was an island in a sea of trees. Ancient
sources speak of four great forests in northern India, but wilderness of one sort or another was pervasive. The trees, including
banyan, palmyra, coconut, acacia and palm, teemed with life and
resounded with birdsong. But the wilderness was generally considered inhospitable and dangerous. 'Delightful parks, groves, beautiful landscapes and lotus ponds are few', Gautama later said, 'while
rough hills and slopes, impassable rivers and rugged mountains
covered with stumps and thorns are many.'[3] The jungle's perils
included dangerous snakes and wild animals, including tigers and
boar, and bandits who preyed on travellers. There was the constant
irritation of mosquitoes, the gadflies that bit deep into the flesh,
and the 'cold and heat, hunger and thirst, wind and the heat of the
sun'.[4] Merchants were always 'happy and relieved'[5] when they made
it through a forest without being attacked by bandits, and other
reports speak of indigenous tribes – 'rough, untamed people who
belong to the wilds on the borderlands and follow a different way
of life',[6] as the Emperor Ashoka described them some time later.
Plundering war-bands would sometimes 'surround the countryside', as Gautama related. 'A mother cannot reach her son, nor the
son his mother.'[7]

The wilderness also had a symbolic role. It represented everything that was unpredictable and foreign to settled existence, and
possessed an extremely dangerous, untamed power. Those who
stayed in the jungle reported chilling encounters with ghosts, spirits
and demons, and Brahmin priests performed sacrifices to free the
wild tracts between villages of the 'ogres, man-tigers, thieves,

murderers, and robbers'[8] that haunted them. The young Gautama agreed with the consensus that 'remote jungle-thicket resting places are hard to endure, seclusion is hard to practise and it is hard to enjoy solitude. The jungle must rob a monk of his mind if he has no concentration.'[9]

Only a few of Gautama's fellow wanderers chose to live away from civilisation entirely. Megasthenes reported to his compatriots that a hard core of forest renunciates lived frugal lives in the woods 'where they subsist on leaves of trees and wild fruits and wear garments made from bark of trees'.[10] It was common knowledge that they were also magicians who could shrink themselves to the size of an atom, make themselves as light as wool or as heavy as a stone, touch any object at any distance, and either bend others to their will or grant their wishes. Later accounts tell us that householders offered alms and gifts to these sages when they were living and honoured their funeral mounds (or *stupas*) after their deaths. Such was their prestige, Megasthenes says, that kings consulted them 'regarding the causes of things' and 'through them, worship and supplicate the deity'.[11]

Although Gautama declared that his teaching was unique, Buddhist tradition holds that solitary seers, or *pratyekabuddhas*, had lived before him and found realisation in the remote wilderness: 'Their hair and beards shaved ... dressed in yellow robes ... not attached to family or tribe ... like clouds torn by wind.'[12] The legendary figures of whom Gautama spoke may recall real holy men who once lived deep in the jungle and were glimpsed from afar by awestruck villagers, burning with fiery realisation. According to both Buddhists and Jains, such men remained silent in public rather than sharing their insights, and they sometimes disappeared into mountain caves and 'were never seen again'.[13] Gautama also spoke of six prehistoric figures whose Buddhahood had been as complete as his own and this, too, may recall a lineage of ancient saints.*

Most shramanas' lives were less extreme than those of the hermits. They had renounced mainstream society with its stress on family and social duty; they were celibate; they had no personal property; and they wandered from place to place and often slept rough. But they spent most of their time on the outskirts of villages, towns and cities, not in the depths of the forest, and Megasthenes noted that they received food, usually consisting of barley meal, 'for the mere asking'.[14] These wanderers formed a parallel society around the new urban centres and banded together in groups, each of which was led by a teacher, or *guru*. For Gautama, the shramanas' existence in its ideal form expressed 'the spiritual life in all its fullness and purity, like a polished shell'.[15] But scandals were frequent, and Gautama also observed that some male wanderers 'divert themselves with women wanderers who wear their hair bound in a topknot', and thought that happiness lay in touching their 'soft and downy arms'.[16]

When shramanas met each other on the road they asked, 'Who is your teacher and what teaching [dharma] do you follow?' To start with, we must assume, Gautama had no answer – only the dissatisfaction that had set him on the path. But other wanderers constantly discussed their beliefs, the practices they undertook and the relative merits of their teachers. In this way Gautama would have heard the names of the most famous gurus and been told that he needed one to guide him. So he made his way 640 km south from Kapilavastu, across the Ganges to Rajagriha, the cap-

---

* Buddhist tradition expanded the list to twenty-seven, with Gautama as the twenty-eighth Buddha. According to most Buddhist traditions, Maitreya will be the next Buddha.

ital of Magadha, where many of the most famous teachers were based.

Rajagriha was the greatest city in India and the oldest in the Ganges Valley. It was a natural fortress guarded by a ring of five hills along whose ridges ran a 40 km protecting wall while an inner ring of fortifications encircled the city itself. When the gates were closed, Rajagriha was impregnable. The city had grown wealthy on iron and copper from mines in the mountains to the south, revenues from the thriving river trade, and the surplus from the intensely fertile farmland in the plains stretching down to the Ganges. The population was growing so fast that a new city was built around Gautama's time beyond the old walls, and later in his life Rajagriha was said to contain the houses of 36,000 merchants. Many trees were felled for timber, and wild elephants, which had long roamed the hills, were trapped for use by the army. A dense monsoon jungle covered the mountains and stretched far beyond them, and Hsuan Tsang reported that 'a great bamboo forest'[17] still covered the hillsides to the south-west of the city in the seventh century. Eventually, the mountains became a barrier to communication and at the end of his life Gautama witnessed the fortification of Pataligama (now Patna) on the Ganges, which became Magadha's new capital and a base from which the King could control the river.

Gautama always enjoyed Rajagriha's 'lovely parks, groves, meadows and ponds',[18] and the forests and caves were ideal dwellings for wanderers, who walked to the city each morning to beg for food. Vultures' Peak – one of the Rajagriha mountains – commands a spectacular view across the valley, and Gautama returned there throughout his life, perhaps finding the powerful, eerie atmosphere created by its jagged rocks and boulders conducive to meditation. At the foot of the mountains were holy springs. Hsuan Tsang saw ten, but he reported that 'there were formerly 500 warm springs [which] have their origin to the south of the Snowy Mountains from the Anavatapa Lake and, flowing underground, burst forth here'.[19] Even in his day, Hsuan Tsang continued, 'These spots being surrounded by mountains and supplied with water, men of conspicuous virtue and wisdom take up their abode here, and many hermits live here in peace and solitude.'

Each morning, shramanas entered the city to beg for food. Some had regular patrons, but the more austere preferred (like Gautama's disciple Mahakasyapa in later years) to go to those streets that were home to 'the poor and needy, the streets of the weavers'.[20] Then they gathered in parks just outside the town to debate their ideas about 'the nature of man'.[21] A shramana called Kunaliya described his lifestyle to Gautama: 'I stay around monastic parks and attend gatherings. After the meal, when I have finished my breakfast, it is my custom to wander from park to park and from garden to garden. There I see ascetics and Brahmins engaged in discussion for the sake of defending their ideas and condemning those held by other people.'[22]

The shramanas themselves, with their 'hairy bodies and long nails',[23] presented a bizarre spectacle. Some shaved their hair, as Gautama had, or pulled it out at the roots, while others wore matted dreadlocks. Many were naked, and some allowed their fingernails to grow immensely long. Regarding the body as a source of impurity or distraction, many practised forms of self-mortification, and as a result they appeared 'lean, wretched, unsightly, jaundiced, with veins standing out on their limbs'.[24] But perhaps the oddest were the shramanas who devoted themselves to acting and thinking like an animal, and would 'curl up like a dog'[25] when they sat down.

In this campus-like atmosphere of discussion and debate Gautama may have felt that he was finding *too many* answers to his questions. Arguments were fierce, and a dizzying proliferation of opinions and ideas swirled amid the uproar, the supporters of each vehemently propounding their own views while denouncing their opponents. Judging by his later comments, Gautama seems to have found the atmosphere distasteful. He disliked the constant chatter about 'kings, robbers, ministers, armies, dangers, battles, food, drink, clothing, beds . . . relatives, vehicles . . . women, heroes . . . the dead, trifles, the origin of the world . . . and whether things are so or not so',[26] and felt that some debaters were simply addicted to argument. He later mimicked their discussions:

'You don't understand this teaching and discipline – I do!' 'How could you understand it?' 'Your practice is quite wrong – mine is right!' 'What I say can be backed up, what you say can't.' 'You are stating last what ought to come first and first what ought to be said last.' 'What you have thought out has been overturned.' 'Your point has been bettered – You're refuted!'[27]

Gautama offered a brilliant analysis of the philosophies on offer, identifying sixty-two separate 'views' among them. But he was less struck by the content of the shramanas' ideas than by the emotions that fuelled their debates:

Seeking controversy, they plunge into assemblies, but regard one another as fools. Relying on others' authority, he speaks in debate and claims to be a expert. Anxious and desiring praise, he grows nervous and becomes dejected if his argument is refuted. He gets angry and seeks the weak points in his opponents' arguments. There is the elation of victory and the dejection of defeat.[28]

Around fifty shramana communities jostled for support and prominence in the Ganges Valley, but a few major teachers stood out (the Buddhist texts usually list six), all with 'communities and followings', and all 'well known and of some repute . . . and thought holy by many'.[29] Most of these sects died out long ago, so our information comes from references in Buddhist and Jain scriptures that are likely to be biased against them. One such Buddhist discourse presents a conversation between Gautama and Ajatashatru, the King of Maghada, who says he has met the teachers, heard their teachings from their own lips, and questioned them – with the impatience of a man with no time for metaphysical speculation – about the practical benefits, 'evident here and now',[30] of their beliefs.

For most shramanas, rebirth, karma and the need to free oneself from the effects of karma were the heart of the existential problem, and their aim was to escape the cycle of lives. Doing this required some kind of inner realisation, but the nature of the 'self' that would achieve it perplexed them. 'Did I exist in the past, or did I not?' they asked. 'What was I and what shall I be in the future? . . . Am I now? Am I not now? *What* am I? *How* am I? Where has this being come from? Where will it go?'[31] The answer for most shramanas was that everyone has an eternal Self or soul – the *atman* or *purusha* – that existed before birth and continued after death. This Self was the immaterial, permanent and blissful core of one's being that survived death, and, in its pure state, possessed infinite knowledge. Because it was different from either the body or the mind, it was untouched by actions or thoughts, and hence free of karma. The task of the religious practitioner was to gain a direct knowledge of this *atman* and thereby find liberation from karmic retribution.

A few shramanas rejected these ideas. For example, Ajatashatru reported that Ajita of the Blanket of Hair had told him:

Good and bad deeds have no fruit or result, there is no this world and the next . . . A person is formed of the four elements and when one dies the earth part returns to and merges with the general mass of earth, the water with water, the fire part with fire, the air part with air; the sense faculties pass into the ether.[32]

Ajita and similar teachers have often been seen as rationalist free-thinkers, but they may simply have been Brahmins who rejected karma, which played no part in Vedic thinking, and had only rudimentary ideas about rebirth if they believed in it at all. The Buddhists who compiled the discourse deemed such views 'nihilism' and a denial of the moral order, and Ajatashatru reports that a teacher called Purana Mahakasyapa spelled out the horrifying implications: 'If someone were to take a razor-edged discus and make of all the creatures of the earth a single heap of flesh, there would be nothing bad in that, nothing bad would come of it.'[33]

Such thinkers were in the minority and Gautama had little interest in their ideas. The Jain community, however, was probably the largest of the shramana groups and it influenced him greatly. Its leader was Vardhamana, usually known as Mahavira ('the Great Hero'), who was said to have found liberation by following the teachings of a shramana community that already had a long history in the Ganges Valley, (though he seems not to have joined the community itself). According to the Jain scriptures, Mahavira defined the Self as 'being without form',[34] and said that to free it the practitioner must stop accruing fresh karma. That meant practising non-violence (ahimsa), and scrupulously avoiding killing living beings, even insects. But the implications of this teaching went much further. As all actions had a karmic result, Jain ascetics – who included women as well as men – should eventually cease to act altogether:

A monk should examine a spot and when he has found it free of living beings he should spread out his layer of grass there. He should lie there without food; if temptations should affect him in this regard, then he should bear them ... If [animals or birds] feed on his flesh and blood, he should not kill them or wipe them away.[35]

Jain ascetics presented a grim spectacle. They refused to wash and their followers praised them for being 'filthy'.[36] Gautama once observed a group dwelling on one of the Rajagriha mountains who practised 'continuous standing, rejecting seats, and experienced painful, racking, piercing feelings due to exertion'.[37] In this way, they burned up their past karma and prepared for the culmination of their practice, which came when they stopped eating altogether and died. That brought liberation because 'by doing no actions there will be no consequences ... [and] all suffering will be exhausted'.[38] The Jains' fervour won them many supporters who admired their efforts to escape the world.

A similar group, the Ajivakas, survived for 2,000 years after Gautama's time; but their teachings have only recently been convincingly reconstructed. According to the Jain Bhagavati Sutra, the Ajivaka teacher, Makkhali Gosala, was a student of Mahavira's who fell out with him. He agreed that inactivity was the way to avoid creating karma, but he thought it was impossible to eradicate old karma. According to Buddhist accounts, the Ajivakas held that 'No human action, no force, no effort, no striving, no human endeavour has any effect.'[39] The consequences of past actions were like a ball of thread that had been thrown and would run on till it was completely unravelled, which would take millions of lifetimes. In the meantime they practised austerities. Jambuka, an Ajivaka monk who became a follower of Gautama, recalled that 'for fifty-five years I wore dust and dirt, eating a meal once a month. I tore out my hair and beard. I stood on one leg, I avoided a seat, I ate dry dung, and I did not accept any special food.'[40] Such practices brought an unblinking focus on an unconditioned level of being at which 'there is no deed performed either by [one's own] self or by [the self] of others'.[41] But in Gautama's view, Ajivaka teachings also undermined the basis for making an effort, and he once called Makkhali an 'infatuated man' who had caused more 'loss, discomfort and sorrow'[42] than anyone living.

To decide which shramana sect to follow, Gautama needed to assess their competing claims. Years later, when he was a teacher himself, Gautama visited the land of the Kalamas in the Vrijian Federation where a group of citizens who found themselves in a comparable situation asked for his aid. Many teachers had passed through their city, they said, all claiming that their ideas were the complete truth, and they had listened in the hope of finding guidance. 'They come to Kesaputta and set out and explain only their theories while attacking, insulting, disparaging and rejecting the theories of others.' Some time later, other teachers would arrive in the town and do exactly the same thing. 'Sir, we are doubtful and uncertain about who are telling the truth and who lies.'[43] Gautama's reply has become famous as advice on finding a path through spiritual confusion, and its incisiveness and practicality suggests that it was informed by his own struggles. He started by sympathising with the Kalamas' situation and encouraged them to have an open, enquiring attitude because, he said, 'your uncertainty concerns something that is indeed a matter of doubt'. Then he went through the grounds on which people usually adopt a belief and rejected them all: 'You should not go along with something just because of what you have been told, because of tradition [or] because of accordance with scripture.' That encapsulated the ways in which people unthinkingly fall into step with a religious faith, or defer to the authority of ancient scriptures, such as those of Brahminism. But Gautama also told the Kalamas that impressive arguments didn't necessarily mean that something was true or right: 'You should not go along with something ... on the grounds of reason, on the grounds of logic, because of analytical thought, because of abstract theoretical pondering, because of the appearance of the speaker, or because some ascetic is your teacher.'

The thoroughness with which this list demolished the pretensions of both religion and philosophy evokes the mind of the young Gautama as we might imagine him in Rajagriha's shramana parks: self-contained, deeply sincere, highly intelligent, determined to see through pretension, and passionately intent on finding something that addressed his yearning to pull out the thorn in his heart that produced his spiritual unease. He advised the Kalamas to consider the effect of the teachings they heard. Did those who followed them become more or less greedy? Were they more loving or more filled with hatred? Did they grow wiser or become more confused? How did they act? He said they should both listen to people they considered wise and use their own judgement. Above all, they should try out the teachings for themselves and see their effect. 'When you know for yourselves that particular qualities are wholesome, blameless, praised by the wise, and lead to good and happiness when taken on and pursued, then you should engage in them and live by them, Kalamas.'[44]

Gautama's quest was existential, not philosophical, and before he became a shramana he may have known nothing of the competing beliefs of his day. His search had started with his distress at common and observable features of human experience, and, so far as we can tell, he had no prior assumptions about what would solve his problem. That left him free to consider ideas without prejudice and to understand things, as he later counselled others, by 'seeing them with wisdom'.[45]

Initiation

According to 'The Noble Quest', Gautama now studied under two great meditation masters: first Arada Kalama (whose reputation he may have heard in Kapilavastu) and then Udraka Ramaputra, one of the most prominent yogis in the Ganges Valley.* He threw himself into their practices, but he later commented that he had, all the while, maintained his independence and 'looked among' the teachings of these gurus, 'without grasping them'.[46]

Arada assured Gautama at their first meeting that a capable pupil could quickly 'experience and attain for himself through direct knowledge what the teacher has understood',[47] and Gautama joined the other students in reciting and memorising the teachings. Soon, Gautama tells us, he knew Arada's teachings, 'as far as mere mouthing the words, mere repeating of what had been repeated to me' was concerned. This theoretical knowledge was enough for some, and to start with it satisfied Gautama, but he sensed that Arada, who was a renowned meditator, had more to offer. 'How far have you experienced and attained [your teaching] for yourself through direct knowledge?'[48] Gautama asked him. Then Arada revealed the inner meaning of the sacred formulas Gautama had been reciting by disclosing a way to reach the goal of spiritual life. In a special initiation, Arada told Gautama of an incredibly refined state called 'the sphere of Nothingness' that lay far beyond ordinary experience and

---

* There is good evidence, put forward in Alexander Wynne's book, *The Origins of Buddhist Meditation*, that Arada and Udraka are actual historical figures, but we know only a little about their lives. Arada may have lived in Shakya (in which case, Gautama may not have travelled south at all), or in mountains in the Vajjian Confederation. Some later accounts say that he studied with other teachers as well.

could only be reached through mastery of demanding meditation practices. Undaunted, Gautama reflected, 'Arada Kalama has faith, energy, mindfulness, concentration, and wisdom. That is how he has mastered these teachings. But I have these qualities too. If I make the same effort, perhaps I can realise this teaching for myself.'[49] Filled with confidence, Gautama applied himself, and before long he reached the state of which Arada had spoken.

According to Buddhist tradition the sphere of Nothingness is one of the highest levels of meditative absorption, reached only once the meditator has passed through the stage of experiencing the mind as infinite space and then experiencing it as infinite consciousness. One discourse tells us of yogis who believed that such an experience was 'Nirvana here and now',[50] which seems to have been Arada's view. It explains that some yogis believed that in this state they left behind the deluded self of ordinary experience and by contemplating 'There is Nothing' they realised 'another self'.[51] Brahminical texts such as the Upanishads, which may record the beliefs that Arada himself followed, say much more about these states.* According to them, the yogi's meditation reverses the process by which the universe came into existence, stripping away the layers that cover the *atman* until the meditator reaches the undifferentiated, primordial Nothingness that existed before creation itself. Then, 'like a shining flame without smoke, like the bright sun, like a fork of lightning in the sky, [the meditator] sees the self with the self'.[52] He becomes *atman* and realises its unity with *brahman*.

---

* Buddhist tradition says that Arada and Udraka were shramanas, but the parallels between the states they describe and those described in the Upanishads and elsewhere suggest that they may in fact have been Brahminical sages, like those the texts described. Another possibility is that Brahmins learned meditation from yogis like Arada and Udraka.

'The Noble Quest' tells us that when Gautama emerged from this meditation he reported his experience to Arada, who was delighted. At last, he said, he had discovered 'a companion in the spiritual life' who shared his deepest realisation. 'The teaching which I declare . . . is the one you live, having experienced and attained for yourself through direct knowledge!'[53] As Gautama had no more to learn, Arada proposed that they share the leadership of the community. Arada died not long after and he may already have been searching for a successor when he saw his heir in the young Gautama.

Despite the honour, something felt wrong. The sphere of Nothingness had disappointed Gautama. Arada had probably instructed him to merge with the Absolute by losing himself in the experience of Nothingness and becoming one with it. From his perspective, there could be nothing beyond that. But when Gautama later discussed this state, he emphasised that it was possible to inhabit it while 'possessing mindfulness'.[54] If that had happened when he meditated under Arada he would have seen that what he had attained was not a sublime, mystic union with God, but simply a state of mind that had developed through his efforts. Having emerged from meditation he left that state behind and saw he was fundamentally unchanged. He told himself that Arada's teaching 'did not conduce to dispassion, cessation, peace, direct knowledge, Awakening or Nirvana, but only to rebirth in the sphere of Nothingness'. He still hadn't answered the questions about birth, death and suffering that had spurred him on his quest, and he hadn't removed the thorn, 'hard to see – lodged deep in the heart',[55] that was the essence of the human problem. He used a potent phrase to describe his response to Arada's teaching: 'Finding *no satisfaction* in that teaching, I lost my enthusiasm for it and left.'[56] He was dissatisfied with the meditative state he had reached; dissatisfied, perhaps, with the philosophy that explained it; and dissatisfied to find he was still so far from the wisdom he yearned for.

Hoping that another teacher might show him how to go beyond the sphere of Nothingness, Gautama travelled back to Rajagriha where he heard of a famous guru, now dead, called Rama, who had attained a state that went beyond Nothingness called 'the Sphere of Neither-Perception-nor-Non-Perception'. Rama's community was now led by Udraka Ramaputra ('Rama's son'), a famous and revered teacher who lived with 700 disciples and was venerated by nobles and kings, who showed him 'great obeisance, saluting him, placing [their] hands together, and paying homage'.[57] Words fail entirely in describing the state of 'Neither-Perception-nor-Non-Perception' and Udraka just said enigmatically, 'He sees, but does not see.'[58] However, this state, or something very like it, is described in the Mandukya Upanishad, where it is the ultimate aspect of the self or *atman*:

> perceiving neither what is inside nor what is outside, nor even both together; not as a mass of perception, neither as perceiving nor as not perceiving; as unseen; as beyond ordinary transaction; as ungraspable; as without distinguishing marks; as one whose essence is the perception of itself alone; as the cessation of the visible world . . . That is the self, and it is that which ought to be perceived.[59]

Gautama's account of his study under Udraka is similar to that of his time with Arada. Udraka taught him and, once again, Gautama quickly mastered his method. The only difference was that when he told Udraka about this experience Udraka offered him sole leadership of the community. After all, Gautama had reached the state that Udraka only knew of from Rama. Once again, Gautama felt disappointment with the limits of what he attained and left to continue his quest.

Gautama never forgot his early gurus and when, after his Awakening, he wondered who might be able to share his realisation he thought first of Arada and Udraka. But he also believed that they had been seduced by the exalted spiritual experiences they had attained. Gautama remarked that Udraka wrongly claimed that he had pulled up 'the tumour's root'[60] of craving, when in fact he had succumbed to a more subtle kind of attachment. When Gautama taught his followers about the states Arada and Udraka had shown him, he urged them to recognise that they were products of the meditator's experience and that, even in the sphere of Nothingness, 'change takes place'.[61] So when a monk entered such a state, he should tell himself to 'abandon it!' and 'surmount it!'[62]

The Way of Pain

If the great meditation teachers couldn't help Gautama, he would have to find the path by himself. In the ancient accounts of his endeavours he seems driven forward by an overwhelming desire to find something that is real and true and ultimate. Gautama reflected that trying to overcome his spiritual ignorance by using his mind was like trying to light a fire with 'a wet, uncured piece of wood that had been left in water'.[63] The cause lay deeper. Jains would have said that he was still producing the karma that bound human beings to samsara and he should stop acting and punish the flesh. In Gautama's religious world these were powerful arguments and, while he did not become a Jain himself, he did take up the practice of self-mortification.

A discourse describing the ascetic practices of Gautama's day tells us that a self-mortifier 'plucks out his hair and beard, sleeps on thorns or in a garment of mud, lives on filth or drinks no

water',[64] and to this day the Indian sadhus who inherit these traditions induce pain by fasting, lying on a bed of nails, hanging
from a tree or holding an extreme posture such as standing on one
leg. The young Gautama, filled with single-minded determination,
was undaunted by the prospect of such hardships and he decided
to place no limits whatsoever upon the effort he applied.

Five companions joined Gautama in his endeavours: Ashvajit,
Bhaddiya, Mahanama, Vapshya and Kaundaniya. The 'Group of
Five' are usually said to have been Shakyans, like Gautama, though
many aspects of this story are unconvincing. Another tradition
relates that they were fellow students of Udraka who had been so
impressed by Gautama that they decided to follow him. In fact, we
know nothing for sure about the men who shared this stage of
Gautama's career and appear again in his story after his Enlightenment. But a local legend relates that, at least for a while, Gautama and his companions stayed in a cave in the Mahakala hills
called Pragbodhi ('Before Awakening'), across the river from the
Bodh Gaya pilgrimage site, where a lip of rock conceals the cave,
and the dark, rough-walled space has just enough room for six
men to sit or stand.

The Discourses describe Gautama's period of self-mortification
in great detail, though their accounts read more like a compendium
of practices than a description of what a single individual actually
did. At the end of Gautama's life, one discourse relates, he was rem-
iniscing with his disciple Shariputra about the intensity of his efforts
as a young man. He says he went naked, rejecting conventions,
ignoring other people and even hiding if need be. Rather than begging, he lived on food he could scavenge: 'greens or millet or wild
rice or hide-parings or moss, grass or cow dung ... forest roots
and fallen fruits'.[65] He stopped washing and became so dirty that
the dirt flaked off his skin; he slept outside in the winter and stayed

in the sun in the blazing heat of the hot season. Sometimes he stood or squatted continuously, or slept on a mattress of spikes. On one occasion he was sleeping in a cremation ground with the bones of the dead for his pillow when some boys came across him. They spat at him, urinated on him and poked sticks in his ears, but, he says, 'I do not recall that I felt any hatred, such was my equanimity.'[66]

Another account occurs in a dialogue with a Jain called Saccaka. Gautama tells Saccaka that he started by engaging in intense yogic practices whose purpose was to reshape his mind as if it were his enemy. He clenched his teeth, pressed his tongue against the roof of his mouth and sweat poured from him as he tried to 'mentally hold down my mind with my mind, crush it and overwhelm it'.[67] We read of this practice in one of the Upanishads, while *praniyama*, another yogic practice that Gautama mastered, is described in the Brahminical Yoga Sutra. This is the art of controlling the breathing and making it slower and slower until it stops altogether. When this happened, Gautama reports:

> I had terrible winds pushing up in my head as if a strong man were twisting a sharp knife in my head [or] fastening a turban around my head with a leather strap. I had terrible winds cutting through the abdomen as if a skilled butcher were cutting through [it] with a sharp butcher's knife. I had a terrible burning sensation in my body as if two strong men were to grab a weaker man by his two arms and roast him through in a pit of hot coals.[68]

Gautama passed out, and, as he lay unconscious, the forest spirits gathered around. 'He's dead,' said one. 'No, he isn't dead,' said another, 'but he's dying.' A third said, 'Oh, he's just a holy man [*arahant*]. This is how they live.'[69]

Gautama stopped eating, aiming perhaps to 'renounce his body',[70] like a Jain monk or to 'live on air',[71] like a Brahminical yogi. The spirits begged him not to die, the discourse tells us, and Gautama sent them away, determined to continue his ordeal by eating nothing at all. But the gods continued to feed Gautama through the pores of his skin with 'divine nourishment', and he opted to eat the smallest amount possible:

> It occurred to me that I might take very little food, just a morsel at a time, of mung-bean soup, lentil soup, chickpea soup or pea soup. My body became extremely emaciated: my limbs became like the jointed stems of creepers or bamboo; my backbone, bent or straight, became like corded beads; my ribs jutted and stuck out like the broken rafters of an old house; the pupils of my eyes sunk deep in their sockets were like the glint of water seen down at the bottom of a deep well; my scalp became like a fresh bitter gourd that has been withered and shrivelled by the wind and sun. When I wanted to touch the skin of my belly I felt my backbone. When I wanted to urinate or defecate I fell over right there on my face. I stroked my limbs with my hand to soothe my body, but the hair, whose roots had grown rotten, dropped from my body.[72]

Images of Gautama in this period are among the most striking figures in Buddhist art. The statue in the Pragbodhi cave, for instance, shows a body shrunk down to the skeleton, but nonetheless sitting erect in meditation posture. There is something compelling in this image, but also something that, to modern eyes, verges on the insane; and in the end that was how Gautama saw it. His struggle to crush his mind and free his spirit from his body had pushed him to the limits of endurance and brought him to the verge of death, but he asked himself if he was any nearer to the realisation for which he yearned. Gautama's efforts to destroy his attachment to the senses had merely involved him in them even more deeply, and he later compared the self-mortifier to a dog who tries to run away from a post to which he is tied and 'just keeps circling it'.[73]

A memory rose from the depths of Gautama's mind. He was a child again and sat beneath the rose-apple tree in the beautiful countryside as his father ploughed his field, with joy and wonder arising in him as naturally as leaves sprouting on a tree. The memory of that moment of spontaneous blossoming was a message from a time of innocence which contained all that was missing from his grim struggles with the flesh. The happiness he had felt was utterly different from attachment or craving and the web of emotions connected with them. He recalled: 'I asked myself why I feared this happiness, which had nothing to do with sense pleasures [or] unwholesome qualities. Then I decided I would not fear it.' Then he asked, 'Might this in fact be the path to Awakening?'[74] and he knew with utter certainty that it was. It is usually said that Gautama gained his insights into the nature of existence when he attained Enlightenment, but this passage suggests that some at least came before it. He was learning to see life in terms of what he came to call the Dharma, the underlying structure of reality which he later articulated in his teachings. More insights were to follow.

At last, Gautama decided to eat.* In some later versions of this story a girl from a local village, usually named Sujata, discovers him near the Naranjara River, not far from the Pragbodhi cave, and gives him food. Imagine the sight that would have confronted her: slack skin hanging from a skeleton, its golden hue starved to an uncanny char; a lank beard clinging to gaunt cheeks, and eyes

* As with so many elements of Gautama's story, we cannot say how long the period of his austerities lasted, but the sources give the impression that it was some years.

like mineshafts – their primeval glimmer akin to the ancient light of a distant star. Sujata thought he was one of the many ghosts that haunted Gaya, and she offered him milk-rice, as she would when she made an offering to propitiate a spirit. Gautama was living, even if he had gazed into the land of the dead, and slowly, painfully, he ate. Then he walked to the broad and sandy banks of the Naranjara and bathed himself in its cool water. In this way, the story goes, after his years of striving Gautama was restored, at last, by accepting help; and it came not from the gods but from an ordinary person and a simple act of kindness.

Gautama's five fellow self-mortifiers were disgusted by the change. There was a confrontation and angry words were spoken. They had followed him and he had let them down. They would not hear his explanations and they told one another: 'He has given up the struggle and reverted to a life of excess.'[75] The five bade Gautama a cold farewell and said they would continue without him on the path of pain.

The Forest Path

Gautama was thirty-five years old, and Buddhist tradition states that it was six years since he had left the palace – though that seems too short a time for the many turns in his journey. Once again he was alone, and his solitude was more complete than ever. He had left behind conventional society – the world of family, responsibility, pleasure and power. The shramanas' world of ideas and training had also failed to answer his questions, for all its ancient roots and spiritual masters. Now he was abandoning his companions, the practice of self-mortification and the beliefs that underlay it. No one could accompany him where he now wished to travel.

In Gautama's most vivid account of this period – a discourse called 'Fear and Dread' – he says that he lived deep in the jungle, like the hermits Megasthenes described. Gautama had heard the warnings that life in the wilderness could drive people mad; but the jungle was the ideal place for the naked confrontation with the truth he desired. He was ready to enter the jungle as 'one of the noble ones',[76] whatever demons it contained; and he sensed that the self-awareness, ethical purity and inner peace he had developed meant he could face anything at all without being overwhelmed. Directly confronting his experience was a different kind of challenge from that of attaining mystical states or the self-mortifier's battle with life, and more genuinely demanding than either. Gautama's intuition guided him, and he felt like 'a man wandering through a forest' who comes on a forgotten 'ancient path travelled upon by people in the past'.[77]

Buddhist tradition relates that Gautama was living in the region around Gaya, and if this is true, it is also significant. In legend and popular belief, Gaya has always been associated with ghosts, spirits and the dead. The *Mahabharata* names it as the best place to perform funeral rites, and even today thousands of Hindu pilgrims travel there to visit spirit shrines and perform *puja* for their ancestors. In Gautama's day, some of these shrines were in the hills overlooking the plains: Ghost Hill, Pragbodhi – where Hsuan Tsang heard that Gautama had found himself sharing a cave with 'a dragon'[78] – and a peak formerly known as Ghost Mountain, which was surrounded by temples with fearsome fire-shrines that housed powerful serpent-gods. Gautama later returned to these shrines and continued his engagement with their deities.

Gautama relates that certain spots in the midst of dark woodland or around sacred trees undeniably possessed an unnerving atmosphere. Beneath the trees were shrines scattered with the bones of sacrificed animals that were dedicated to the ferocious spirits that were said to live in them. People visited the shrines to perform ceremonies that propitiated the spirits, but otherwise they were shunned. Despite hearing of the overwhelming 'fear and dread' these places prompted, Gautama visited them at the very times they were most to be avoided: the nights that marked the phases of the moon when the earth's energy was roused and the spirits walked abroad. 'There in the darkness or the moon-cast shadows I would hear an animal approaching, or a peacock would break off a twig, or the wind would rustle the fallen leaves, and I thought, "Is this it coming now, the fear and dread?"'[79]

Worshippers had long believed that in propitiating a spirit they were also appeasing the wild and destructive forces of nature, so in facing the demons, Gautama was also engaging with these threatening powers. And he was confronting the secret places of his own mind that led him to fear them. As he sat, he asked himself: 'What am I doing here, wanting this to happen? And if it does happen, why should I not drive it out?' Then it came – again and again: fear and terror pulsing through him. But each time the feeling rose up, he refused to be deflected from what he was doing. If he was sitting, he continued to sit; if he was walking, he continued to walk. In that way, he says, 'I faced that fear and dread, just as it found me, and I drove it out.'

Gautama's confrontation with the Gaya shrines was a particularly dramatic instance of his practice in this period. Whatever happened, he simply observed his experience without interpreting it or getting caught in habitual reactions – a practice Gautama came to call 'mindfulness'. Past experiences that had 'left their impression on the heart'[80] sometimes resurfaced; and sometimes he found himself thinking about the future or getting distracted by things around him. But he learned to notice these thoughts when they arose and became sensitive to the emotions that underlay them and how they affected him. He saw his experience as a flow of 'mental states', one developing out of another. Some states, especially those associated with craving, hatred and cruelty, carried a compulsive power that grew stronger if he dwelt on it. These emotions were constricting, and in that sense they brought him suffering; if he acted on them they would bring suffering to others as well. Then there were states like renunciation, friendliness and compassion that blossomed, if he paid them attention, into deep calm and positivity. Gautama started to assess his thoughts in these terms: 'The thought occurred to me: "Why don't I keep dividing my thinking into two sorts?" So I made thinking imbued with sensual desire, ill will and cruelty one sort, and thinking imbued with renunciation, non-ill-will and harmlessness another.'[81]

Gautama learned to guide his thoughts. 'Sensual desire' arose again and again, he recalled, and he applied a sensitive but nonetheless 'diligent, ardent and resolute' effort to address it: a middle way between lazily indulging himself and attempting to storm Enlightenment through sheer willpower. When ill will or another destructive emotion arose he became aware of it, reflected that it would 'obstruct wisdom, and lead away from Nirvana', and it naturally subsided. Conversely, he encouraged positive emotions when they arose. His mind became concentrated, and the mention of 'non-ill-will' suggests that powerful impulses of renunciation and compassion also welled up. It may be that Gautama undertook practices which seem to have been current among shramanas, that amplified loving kindness and similar emotions until they suffused the meditator's experience:

With his heart filled with unbounded, abundant loving kindness, compassion, sympathetic joy or equanimity he dwells suffusing the whole world, upwards, downwards, across, everywhere. Like a mighty trumpeter making a proclamation to the four quarters of the universe, by this meditation, by this liberation of the heart he leaves nothing untouched.[82]

Gautama had discovered a crucial principle about how consciousness works: 'Whatever a monk dwells on and keeps thinking about becomes the inclination of his awareness.'[83] He learned that the mind continually creates and recreates itself through the way it responds to experience, and that with greater awareness these responses could be a matter of conscious choice rather than automatic reaction. *That* was the path: a process of mental cultivation that had moral as well as psychological significance. Around the world, other great figures of the 'Axial Age' were also looking inwards and examining their minds, but Gautama's precise observation of his thoughts and his sense of their ethical weighting is unique.

Gautama recalled that he often focused his attention on the breath and let go of distracting thoughts, using the reflection: 'Contemplating relinquishment, I breathe in ... Contemplating relinquishment, I breathe out.'[84] In that way, he inhabited a state of deep calm and absorption, 'completely secluded from sense desires and unwholesome qualities of mind',[85] and dwelled in these states for days at a time. He reflected deeply, and then relaxed his thinking and settled back into meditation, 'so that my mind should not be strained'.[86] But so much energy was released, he says, that 'neither my body, nor my eyes became fatigued'.[87]

This way of deepening his awareness matched the harmonious tranquillity that had filled Gautama beneath the rose-apple tree. But the significance of that experience went further: his mind had opened into a new dimension of consciousness. Our understanding of what other contemplatives did in Gautama's time is too fragmentary to say for certain whether others practised in the same way. But it is possible that Gautama discovered this dimension, which he called *dhyana*, for himself and introduced it to Indian spirituality.* Dhyana can be translated as 'absorption', and Gautama identified a series of four successively deeper stages of concentration. First came the steady awareness and open, sensitive enjoyment of the first absorption – the first dhyana. This was the same state of ease and bliss that Gautama had experienced under the rose-apple tree. Thoughts continued, but the mind was suffused by the peaceful pleasure of meditative awareness, and Gautama compared it to the saturation of soap powder by liquid. Then Gautama stilled his thoughts and entered the second absorption – a state of inner clarity and mental unification that is 'without thinking and examining, and born of concentration'.[88] Inner calm and oneness of heart took over and he felt joy and inspiration come 'welling up from below',[89] like springwater in a lake. Letting go of joy, or even interest in it, he entered the third level of absorption, and became entirely 'equanimous, mindful and fully aware',[90] like a lotus flower resting on the surface of a lake that was cooled 'from root to tip'[91] by the surrounding water. Letting go of happiness and unhappiness, he entered the fourth absorption, a state of perfect equanimity and 'pure bright awareness'. Images can hardly encompass this level of experience, and Gautama compared it, rather mysteriously, to emerging from a bath and cloaking oneself in a white robe.

* The suggestion that Gautama 'discovered' the dhyanas/jhanas has been made by in recent years by Bronkhorst, Vetter and others. Strictly speaking we can only say that, as Gethin puts it, the dhyanas 'first surface in Buddhist writings . . . and are a central feature of Buddhist texts' (Gethin 1992, pp.347, 348). The implication is that the meditative states taught by Arada Kalama and Udraka Ramaputra (*arupa-samapattis*), were rather different, even though they are integrated with the rupa-dhyanas in developed Buddhist thought.

In what seem to be the oldest accounts of Gautama's Awakening he says that his breakthrough came through the practice of these four absorptions. In contrast to the descriptions of meditation in the Upanishads, which mix accounts of actual experiences with religious or mystical beliefs about the nature of the universe, Gautama's account of the absorptions is a detailed and precise description of what was taking place in his consciousness. What he describes also differs from the practices undertaken by Jains and other shramanas, which involved forcing the mind on the principle that 'happiness ... can only be reached by pain'.[92] The dhyanas showed Gautama a new and unsuspected dimension of consciousness that was relaxed, peaceful and joyful and which, he sensed, was preparing the mind for a transforming insight.

In these profoundly concentrated states Gautama's mind was free from the distractions and hindrances that cloud ordinary experience, and powerful, positive forces became available to it. Gautama said that his awareness was 'open and unenveloped', his experience was 'imbued with luminosity',[93] and he realised that, as he became more concentrated, the scope of his awareness expanded. He reflected: 'When my concentration is immeasurable, my vision is immeasurable and with immeasurable vision I perceive immeasurable light and see immeasurable form.'[94] This could last 'for a whole day and night'. The more he practised, the more successful his efforts became, and the more fully present he felt: 'Tireless energy was aroused in me and unremitting mindfulness was established, my body was tranquil and untroubled, my mind concentrated and unified.'[95]

On the full-moon day of May/June, in the blazing summer's heat, Gautama crossed the Naranjara at a shallow ford and came to a clearing in the forest near a village called Uruvilva. The place is now called Bodh Gaya. He recalled, 'I saw an agreeable piece of ground, a beautiful grove with a clear-flowing river with pleasant, smooth banks, and nearby a village for alms.'[96] A grass-cutter offered him a seat of fragrant *kusa* grass, some versions tell us, and he sat down by the silver trunk of a spreading fig tree, shrouded by the cooling bowl of its heart-shaped leaves. He faced west into the setting sun and the realm of night, darkness and 'the deep and mighty ocean',[97] and he sat motionless in the violet air.

Legends relate that the trees bent forward to protect Gautama, and the animals and birds remained quiet to avoid disturbing his efforts. In 'The Noble Quest' Gautama recalls that he had said to himself: 'This will serve for striving.'[98] That is pleasingly straightforward, but later accounts placed into his mouth the more stirring injunctions he urged on his disciples: 'My flesh may wither away and my blood may dry up until only skin, sinews and bones remain, but I will not give up till I have found what firmness, persistence, and effort can bring!'[99] 'Until I have found liberation, I will sit here unflinching and utterly still.'[100]

3

Nirvana

Mara's Assault

Gautama sat down beneath the Bodhi Tree and did not get up again. The next day, so Buddhists say, a new person sat there – a realised sage who would be known henceforth by his title, *Buddha*: the Awakened.

This night was the pivot on which Gautama's life turned, but an observer of his vigil would simply have seen a man absorbed, stock-still, in concentration. He insisted that the full truth of that night could not be reached by mere thinking, but that didn't make it an incomprehensible mystery to be revered in silence. He believed others could repeat his breakthrough, and the Discourses contain numerous descriptions of what happened. These accounts use several different kinds of language to evoke Gautama's experience, perhaps because Gautama himself tried out various approaches in communicating it, or perhaps because different groups among the monks who compiled the texts understood his Enlightenment in different ways.

Sometimes Gautama personified the forces involved and hinted at a drama that unfolded in some grand, visionary dimension on the borderland between myth and experience. Some accounts focus on the meditative experiences he passed through and describe the nuances of attitude and attention that enabled him to ascend the levels of absorption until he found something beyond them. Others describe how Gautama saw more and more deeply into his mind until he gained an insight into the nature of reality that he later expressed in his teachings. Finally, he described a vision of existence that somehow encompassed all the other approaches.

Let us start with the myth.

In a discourse called 'Striving' Gautama says that, having sat down beside the Naranjara, 'I engaged in deep struggle, practising meditation with all my strength in the effort to find freedom from bondage.'[1] Then his efforts were interrupted. A figure appeared and Gautama heard a voice. The speaker, Mara, was a powerful god and a kind of a demon, but he spoke calmly and used words that seemed full of sympathy to insinuate himself into Gautama's thoughts:

> You are so thin and pale. Why – you're near to death. My dear sir, do live. It is far better to live! You could accumulate merit if you stayed alive. You could lead the religious life, perform the offerings to the fire – it's a sure way to get lots of merit. What's the point of all this exertion?[2]

Other discourses give slightly different versions of the words with which Mara tried to sap Gautama's resolve. Mara said he was unworthy of Enlightenment because he had given up ascetic practice; or else Mara was a voice of shame and loneliness, rebuking Gautama for skulking in the forest.

Did Gautama intend us to see Mara literally, as a real demon accosting him from the outside, or did he represent forces within Gautama's mind? Mara is both, dwelling on the uncertain border between literal truth, allegory and myth, and in time Buddhists distinguished three or four aspects. First, Mara is a real demon who 'exists' independently of Gautama; and even after Gautama's Awakening he reappears again and again in the Discourses disguised as a farmer, a lion, a giant elephant or simply, 'a cloud of smoke, [a] swirl of darkness'.[3]

Secondly, Mara is the 'Lord of Death', who presides over the realm of death and rebirth that is samsara. In coming to Gaya, Gautama had journeyed to a sacred centre dedicated to death rituals, and Mara's throne – the Vajrasana, or 'diamond throne' – is said to have been located in Bodh Gaya itself. Where better than Bodh Gaya for one seeking 'the deathless' to confront the forces that shackled him? By extension, Mara is 'the Lord of the Realm of Desires' – the desires that produce the karma that binds people to the cycle of rebirth Gautama wished to escape.

But Mara is also the embodiment of destructive emotions and personifies all the hidden evasions, doubts and desires that still held Gautama back. In that sense, defeating Mara meant overcoming himself. Gautama's encounter with Mara echoes his description in 'Fear and Dread' of facing his terror by sitting unflinchingly in haunted forest shrines. But in 'Striving' Mara is the voice of doubt rather than fear: a silver-tongued Mephistopheles who says he has followed Gautama for seven years, ever since he first considered leaving his palace. Gautama replies: 'I see your armies surrounding me', and identifies these armies as the forces of sensual desire, discontent, hunger and thirst, craving, sloth, terror, doubt and ambition.

For Gautama, the mind and the world weren't separate spheres. Because our experience of the world is filtered through the mind and shaped according to its biases it was quite possible for Mara to be *both* an aspect of Gautama's psychology *and* a force at work in the world – a metaphor and a demon. For Gautama's contemporaries, gods and demons were real presences, and Gautama himself correlated the realms they inhabited with various states of mind. In one discourse Mara describes himself as 'a snare moving in the sky, something mental which moves about'.[4] This way of thinking intertwines psychology and cosmology, and mythic language is better at expressing it than concepts. Thus 'Mara' is called the 'lord of limitation', and in 'Striving', Gautama calls him 'Namuci', the name of a drought demon of Vedic mythology that means 'one who withholds the waters',[5] because Mara prompts the gnawing desires through which we block the fresh water of life.

Mara's role in the story of Gautama's Awakening makes it a drama – a contest between two figures rather than one man's inner experience; and this may be why he became a central figure in the myths that grew around the Enlightenment. The key was Gautama's metaphor of the army, which was vastly elaborated into a host of blood-curdling demons. A text included in the Discourses initiated this in its description of an attack by Mara's army on an assembly of gods, urged on by Mara himself:

> Come on, seize and bind them all! With lust
> We'll catch them all! Surround them all about,
> Let none escape, whoever he may be!'
> Thus the war-lord urged on his murky troops.
> With his palm he struck the ground, and made
> A horrid din, as when a storm-cloud bursts
> With thunder, lightning, and with heavy rain.[6]

When Mara suggested to Gautama that he should content himself with fire sacrifices, he spoke as if he were addressing a Brahmin; but 'Striving' relates that Gautama replied as a warrior: 'I can see the troops all around me, with Mara mounted on an elephant, and I go forward into the struggle.'[7] In a rousing battle cry Gautama declared his willingness to fight and even die rather than be defeated: 'When the wind blows, even rivers and streams are dried up. So why shouldn't it dry up my blood while I am in the struggle . . . Even though the whole world and its gods cannot defeat that army of yours, I will destroy it with the power of wisdom!'[8]

The assault of Mara's hordes was a favourite scene for Buddhist poets of later centuries, one which they described in bloodthirsty detail. The *Lalitavistara* described his soldiers as grotesque, deformed figures with twisted faces and eyes shining with rage – a writhing mass of hatred and desolation, their bodies covered in blood and their mouths spewing vomit. They breathe fire, wear necklaces of human bones around their necks and wield axes, chains and bolts of lightning. In the developed myth Mara attacks Gautama many times, using the power of the elements – whirlwind, torrential rain, clouds of fiery ash, showers of rock and boundless darkness – while Gautama sits motionless. Buddhist art depicts him protected by an invulnerable aura, which turns the fearsome missiles into a rain of petals and incense that falls harmlessly at his feet.

A further episode, which does not appear in the Discourses, came to epitomise the battle between Gautama and Mara in Buddhist myth, and suggested the universal significance of their battle. The spot where Gautama sat was considered the diamond throne (Vajrasana), which represented the pinnacle of existence. In the *Nidana Katha*, at the height of the battle Mara declares that he, not Gautama, deserves to sit on this throne. Gautama asks who can testify to Mara's worthiness and a cry goes up from the attackers: '*I am his witness, I am his witness.*'[9] Mara asks who will testify for Gautama, and in reply Gautama tells Mara that he has practised kindness, generosity, patience and meditation for incalculable life-times. He extends his right hand to touch the earth – which is how Buddhist images often show him – and declares, 'Let this great and solid earth, non-sentient as it is, be my witness.' In reply, the earth thunders with 'a hundred thousand echoes'. In the *Lalitavistara* the earth is personified as the goddess Sthatavara. The upper part of her body emerges from the ground, surrounded by a host of other goddesses, and she replies to Gautama, 'It is as you have declared. We appear to attest to it. Moreover, you have become the supreme witness to the realms of the humans and the gods!'[10]

According to both the Discourses and later biographies, Mara had one further means of attack. The army vanished, the glade grew quiet and three beautiful young women faced Gautama. 'Is it because you are unhappy that you have hidden yourself away in the woods, all alone?'[11] one said, her voice filled with soft consola-tion. 'Perhaps you are ashamed of something you have done, or you are pining for what you have lost. Why don't you make any intimate ties?' The woman was Mara's daughter, Craving, and her sisters, Lust and Discontent, accompanied her. But despite their efforts Gautama's attention did not waver. The three sisters told their father that any ordinary man would have shrivelled up, or gone mad with lust, but Mara replied, 'You might as well have tried to find a foothold in an abyss.'[12]

Finally, Mara accepted defeat, and, according to 'Striving', he aban-doned the fight with a regretful comparison. 'I remember once seeing a crow hovering above a lump of fat on the ground below. "Ah, food!" it thought. But the lump turned out to be a rock, hard and inedible, and the crow flew away disgusted.'[13] Mara's lute slipped from his hands, we read elsewhere, and he shrank, suddenly, into a wretched figure who 'sat down cross-legged, with his shoulders drooping, downcast, dismayed, brooding, unable to speak and scratching the ground with a stick.'[14] He said he felt like a crab whose claws had been broken off by children and who was unable to return to the pond. 'All my distortions, manoeuvres and contortions have been cut off',[15] he lamented.

With Mara defeated, the visionary forms vanished like mist and Gautama was alone at last. A light wind rippled through the glade. The moon was full and the morning star was rising in the east.

The Depths of the Mind

Many of Gautama's accounts of Awakening leave aside myth entirely and present, instead, a description of the experiences he passed through (which were also instructions for others wishing to do the same). While these accounts are detailed and precise, their descriptions are far beyond the range of normal experience. They point to an unimaginably concentrated state of mind outside the familiar categories of language. Nonetheless, Gautama described his progress through these increasingly refined states in great detail.

He said that he felt focused and confident and discovered that he was free from anger and his conscience was clear. Later Buddhists tell us that Gautama practised the mindfulness of breathing meditation to focus his mind, but the Discourses simply relate that he deepened his concentration and passed through the four absorptions until his mind was 'purified and cleansed – stainless, without defilements, having become sensitive, workable and steady, reaching a state that is unshakeable'.[16] When he taught others how to attain this state he told them it was as powerful, stable and supple as molten gold and in it he could mould his consciousness like a goldsmith: '[He] prepares a furnace, heats up a crucible and places gold in it with a pair of tongs. He blows on it, sprinkles water and examines it again and again, so that the gold becomes flawless, free from dross, and is pliant, malleable and luminous, and he can form it into whatever shape he wishes.'[17]

At the fourth level of absorption Gautama's mind was completely calm, as still as a lake, and he discovered a new way of relating to his experience. 'By letting go of happiness and unhappiness, as a result of the earlier disappearance of pleasure and pain, I lived having attained equanimity and mindfulness.'[18] He was able simply to rest in awareness and explore his mind with what he sometimes called 'controlled perception'.[19] Relaxing his conscious awareness into a state of complete receptivity, Gautama opened himself to all the fears, lusts and hatreds that lurked in the fathomless psychic darkness of his mind – the primal insecurities that drove people to bind themselves to samsara. Perhaps this is the meaning of his battle with Mara. The thousand soldiers who attacked Gautama would then symbolise the exploded fragments of his unconscious, and the transformation of their weapons into a rain of flowers would represent their reintegration and sublimation within his conscious awareness.

Some accounts of Gautama's Awakening say that as his concentration deepened, Gautama left behind mental activity and entered a stage of 'cessation' (*nirodha*). This is sometimes described as new level of absorption at the very 'limit of perception'[20] in which he let go of the most basic ways in which his experience formed itself: the desire to exist and its alternative, the desire for annihilation. Gautama saw the impermanent and conditioned nature of even the subtlest substratum of the mind, and his stillness was undisturbed by even the slightest ripple of craving or attachment, even to the experience of equanimity.

As the forces that produced craving dissolved away, Gautama emerged into a fundamentally different relationship with experience, which he called 'Nirvana in this life'. 'Nirvana' means 'blown out', because the 'fire' of craving has been extinguished. It suggests a way of being rather than a fixed state, and certainly not a place to which one might travel. Without even the urge to exist or not to exist, Gautama was free not to cling to anything. He had discovered an entirely new way of being.

Seeing the Truth

Gautama often spoke of what happened to him beneath the Bodhi Tree as a way of seeing the world. It was an entirely new perspective on life, not just an exalted state of mind, and he found it, he says, by seeing through his former illusions. Many of the descriptions of Enlightenment in the Discourses present it as the realisation of one or other of the concepts that comprised his later teachings. Buddhists have debated for many years whether Gautama gained these insights while he dwelt in deep meditation or if he had to withdraw from them in order to reflect. In the Discourses, however, absorption and insight are impossible to separate.

Gautama's intense concentration gave him the poise and detachment needed to make a deep 'inward investigation'[21] of the mind, which was also an investigation of existence as it presented itself to him. His quest had started with an anguished awareness that suffering was a universal fact of life. Now he reflected again: 'This world has fallen deep into trouble. It is born, ages and dies, yet it does not understand an escape from this suffering.'[22] Beyond the horizon of death lay rebirth and a repeat of the cycle – and no one had found a way out. Gautama pressed his mind with 'careful attention' against the implacable problem of the human condition, and sensed that the sufferings of samsara had a cause. 'When what exists do ageing and death come to be?' he asked of himself.[23] The cause shaped his experience, but it lay, invisible to him, somewhere beyond his conscious awareness, like an ocean surge affecting tidal rivers far upstream: 'That causes the rivers to surge, the rivers surging cause the lakes to surge and the lakes surging cause the pools to surge.'[24] But what was the unseen cause, the distant tidal swell, that made him as he was? Unlike teachers who answered this question with metaphysical concepts about man's relation to the divine, Gautama was spurred by a wish to grapple with an experience – the experience of *dukkha* – so he directed his investigations towards the nature of experience itself. Finding the source of the *dukkha*, and whatever it was that tied people to samsara, meant investigating the mind.

Gautama once said, in a famous verse, 'Experiences are preceded by mind, led by mind and produced by mind.'[25] He came to understand that consciousness filtered and shaped everything he thought he knew about the world, how he made sense of it and how he responded; and yet his consciousness was always changing and guided by tendencies and biases of which he was unaware. Meditating in the forest, Gautama had been learning to see the patterns of his thoughts. He had understood that what happens in one moment produces the next instant of awareness and so on in a stream of experiences. But there is also something compulsive, driven and fettered in the way the mind works. Thoughts and feelings constantly combine with deep-seated habits to draw attention towards pleasures, possessions and ideas, and then cling to them. Gautama called this force *craving*. Accompanying it are *aversion* – the urge to push painful experience away – and *ignorance* – the desire to avoid what is happening. These are 'three fires' that set the mind ablaze.

The Discourses suggest that Gautama examined the nature of

his experience through reflective meditation while his mind was in an intensely concentrated state and saw it in a new way. Some discourses say he dwelt on the five 'heaps' or categories of subjective experience (the *khandhas* or *skhandas*). Others say that he investigated the elements that were believed to constitute the cosmos and saw he could not identify himself with any of them, or that he noted the shifting and conditioned 'feelings' that determined how he related to the world.[26] We shall return to these ideas in exploring Gautama's teaching, especially the accounts that say he understood and then unravelled the sequence through which experience comes into being and binds us to samsara. For now it will suffice to say that each formulation shows that neither he nor anyone else existed in a fixed or independent way. 'Through careful attention', Gautama said, 'there took place in me a breakthrough by wisdom',[27] and he grasped that everything in his experience was impermanent and insubstantial. There was no question of a fixed self apart from the flow of 'mental events', still less an eternal *atman* and, by extension, there could be no *Brahman*, no God at the heart of existence.

This was a revelation, not a cool acquisition of knowledge. Gautama noted the 'gratification' afforded by identifying one aspect of experience as 'self', and the 'danger' of becoming attached to it. Then he saw the way to 'escape' that attachment: 'Whatever pleasure and joy there is in the world, this is its gratification; that the world is impermanent, bound up with suffering and subject to change, that is the danger in the world; the removal and abandoning of desire and lust for the world, this is the escape from the world.'[28]

Gautama said that he penetrated the ignorance that coloured his experience, saw the human condition for what it was and understood how to stop sowing seeds of future suffering. He gained 'knowledge and vision that is in accordance with reality'[29] and, as one discourse puts it, he *became* the insight he attained: 'knowing, he knows; seeing, he sees; he is vision'.[30] If ignorance meant he had been asleep, then understanding meant waking up to reality, and the wisdom this brought was unshakeable because it was founded on the truth.

Vision

A final way in which Gautama described what happened that full-moon night took the language of seeing a stage further. 'Ignorance was banished, knowledge arose, darkness was banished, light arose',[31] he said. 'Insight into things not previously heard came to me – knowledge, understanding, wisdom, light.'[32] At the culmination of his enquiry, it seems, he had an enveloping and transforming vision of existence that shaped his insights in terms of the world view that had framed his quest.

Gautama looked back through his life with its tangle of fears and desires, which he was only now unravelling. Back through the times that had moulded him, back through his childhood, and past his birth to the darkness beyond it. In a flash, he glimpsed the infinity of past lives through which he had wandered as the universe itself waxed and waned. The intimate details of each existence flew back – his name, his family, his appearance, where he found pleasure and what had brought pain, and the hundred thousand deaths he had suffered. Above all, he saw the pattern of those lives: how the effects of actions rippled across lifetimes and impelled him to repeat them. Gripped by ignorance, craving and hatred, Gautama had forged his own suffering over and over, and seeing that was so, he knew he could stop.

Gautama called this awareness of his own previous existences the first 'true knowledge', or, perhaps, 'visionary insight' (*vijja*).

Then came a second. He turned his mind to the pattern of other people's lives and saw the multitude of beings vanishing and reappearing over endless aeons, and moulding themselves through their actions. He saw how minds condition the reality they experience, and the universe of change he apprehended was deeply moral. While selfish and cruel actions lead to suffering, kind and generous ones bring happiness. That is the true meaning of karma.

Gautama's understanding of the course of karma and rebirth stayed with him throughout his life, and for his Ganges Valley contemporaries this was a crucial aspect of his attainment. Expressing these insights in other terms, one could say that Gautama understood the forces that had made him who he was, that shaped others' lives and that operated in the world. One Discourse says that he gained the power to understand 'the results of actions with possibilities and causes ... the ways leading to different destinations [after death] ... the world with its many and different elements ... [and] how beings have different inclinations'.[33]

At the first flicker of dawn, Gautama's visions culminated in a final breakthrough: a shaft of wisdom that fused his insights into the pattern of lives with his grasp of the nature of the mind. It rippled through Gautama, transforming him utterly, and he knew that the deep, instinctive 'taints' (*asavas*) at the very core of his being had been destroyed. He would continue to act, but he would no longer generate karma. At last, he was free.

> In the course of knowing and seeing this, my mind was freed from the taint of sense desire, my mind was freed from the taint of being, my mind was freed from the taint of ignorance. And when it was freed, there was knowledge that it was freed: I understood, Birth is destroyed. The spiritual life has been lived. Done is what should be done. There is nothing further required to this end.[34]

Gautama's breakthrough – whether we approach it through his battle with Mara, his experience in deep meditation, his insights into reality or his vision of the pattern of lives – changed him completely. Perhaps fearing that people would make his Enlightenment into a fixed entity, like the *Brahman* of which the Brahmins spoke, he often chose to say simply what he was not. He even did that in speaking of 'Nirvana', which is the act of 'blowing out' the fire of craving. But Gautama's negations added up to something. He sometimes suggested that he had discovered a sphere beyond this world, and beyond even the immaterial realms, in which 'there is no coming, no going, no staying, no deceasing, no uprising'.[35] However, he warned against thinking of Nirvana as a place, and said he had left behind notions of place altogether. Often he preferred metaphors to definitions in describing his attainment. He called it 'the harbour of refuge', 'the cool cave', 'the island amidst the floods', 'the place of bliss', 'emancipation', 'liberation', 'safety', 'the transcendental', 'the uncreated', 'the tranquil', 'the home of ease', 'the calm', 'the end of suffering', 'the medicine for all evil', 'the unshaken', 'ambrosia', 'the immaterial', 'the imperishable', 'the abiding', 'the further shore', 'the unending', 'the bliss of effort', 'the supreme joy', 'the ineffable', 'detachment'.[36] But even metaphors have limitations and Gautama's disciple Shariputra remarked, 'Even the great sea, the earth, a mountain and the wind are not applicable in simile to the Teacher's excellent release.'[37]

Perhaps the best way to encapsulate the meaning of Gautama's Enlightenment is to say that he realised the Dharma, the true nature of reality that holds 'whether or not there is the arising of a Tathagata'[38] to understand it; and realising it, he became one with it. So a way of considering what Gautama became in his Enlightenment is to explore what he had understood and what he taught when he came to 'declare, teach, describe, set forth, reveal and explain'[39] the Dharma.

The River of Life

For seven days after his Awakening, we are told, Gautama 'sat without stirring, cross-legged at the foot of the Bodhi Tree, enjoying the bliss of liberation'.[40] At first he was immersed in an absorption of incredible depth and intensity, beyond thoughts or words; but slowly a reflective quality eddied into his mind, and at some point he declared to himself the fact of his Enlightenment. The words vary from text to text. In some versions he declares his understanding of a particular doctrine; elsewhere he utters a victory cry: 'When things become clear to the ardent meditating sage, he stands, scattering the troops of Mara, like the sun that lights up the sky!'[41]

A legend of this period offers a powerful image for the depth of Gautama's absorption. He sat in the glade beneath a muchalinda tree when the sky darkened, the temperature fell and a pre-monsoon storm blew up. To protect him, a serpent, or *naga*, rose from the lake and wound its coils seven times around his meditating figure, sheltering it with his hooded head. In Indian mythology the nagas live in the depths of the ocean and in symbolic traditions of later Buddhism and Hinduism (the Tantra) the serpent represents the fiery energy of the unconscious mind and the universal water element. The image of a serpent protecting Gautama symbolises the sublimation of these energies in his Awakening. It also suggests the kinship between Gautama's experience and the natural world. Gautama declared:

> Blissful is detachment for one who is content,
> For one who has learned Dharma and who sees;
> Blissful is non-affliction in the world,
> [and] restraint towards living creatures.[42]

Gautama once said that 'one suffers if one lives without reverence',[43] and following his Enlightenment he felt a powerful need to look up to someone or something. For a week he simply gazed, unblinking, at the Bodhi Tree that had sheltered him, but he could think of no one in the realm of men or gods who was truly worthy of his reverence. However, he was deeply absorbed in the reality he had discovered – the Dharma – and that was something he could respect. From now on the Dharma was the object of his veneration.

Buddhist tradition devised an elaborate scheme that specified exactly what Gautama did in each of the weeks after his Awakening. The Discourses are less precise, but they agree that, early on, he reflected on what it told him about the world, and his new understanding started to distil into thoughts. In one sense, what Gautama had realised could not be expressed in language, but even Nirvana is something 'one can talk about',[44] he said, provided one did not become attached to the words.

As Gautama sat in the Uruvilva grove he must have gazed often at the Naranjara River. The channel was 100 metres wide, and in the heat of midsummer it was shallow enough to cross by foot; but Gautama had also seen it after the rains when it was a surging torrent. The river matched what he had to say. It was an apt image for the *dukkha* that had set him on his quest, and he sometimes compared the human condition to that of 'a man who has fallen into an overflowing river with deep water and a rapid current [and is] carried away by its swift-flowing current'.[45] One way or another, you have to find dry land by crossing the stream and getting to the farther shore. But the river also became an image for the insights at the heart of Gautama's Realisation.

Naming a flowing channel of water 'Ganges' or 'Naranjara' made it seem solid and knowable; but, in truth, the water swirled in an endless process of change. In distant Greece, Gautama's contemporary Heraclitus declared that 'you cannot step twice into the waters of the same river'. Gautama went a step further and declared, with his characteristic capacity to deduce general principles from particular observations, that impermanence was a universal characteristic of existence. The processes that form a river suggested another: 'Just as when the god brings rain in huge drops upon a mountaintop, and the water runs down the slope filling up the mountain crevices, clefts and gullies . . . they fill up the pools . . . they fill up the lakes . . . they fill up the rivers . . . [and] they fill up the oceans and seas.'[46]

A river isn't a *thing*, Gautama understood: it is a *process*. The same is true of a person. As Gautama pondered what he had learned about the human condition he saw that a human being is also not a fixed entity – and the yogis' belief that the *atman* is their essential self was a great diversion from this truth. People shape their experience and bind themselves to the cycle of birth, death and rebirth according to the same principle that shapes a river. A river has no single cause. Millions of drops of water come together to create it, and the form they take depends on the climate, the underlying geology of the land and so on. Similarly, a person's state of mind in any given moment is the result of countless experiences; it is shaped both by their culture and the underlying habits and tendencies that have developed throughout their life (and perhaps over previous lifetimes, as well). So the best way to express how either a river or a mind comes into existence is to say that it arises because of, or in dependence upon, an array of prior conditions. By extension, what exists now will create, or 'condition', the future. If it rains heavily, the river will rise, and it might dry up altogether if a dam is built or if the water is diverted into irrigation channels.

This pattern reveals a universal principle of how things work that is evident in plants, animals, stars, planets and galaxies: it is a law, like the laws of mathematics. Gautama called it the principle of *dependent arising*. His classic expression, which became a defining credo for the early Buddhist movement, was more precise still: 'When this exists, that comes to be. With the arising of this, that arises. When this does not exist, that does not come to be. With the cessation of this, that ceases.'[47]

Abstract as this formulation sounds, it expresses a revolutionary insight. It shares with a modern scientific or empirical perspective a concern with the process of cause and effect, and in that respect it distanced Gautama from the magical thinking of Brahminism and folk religion. But Gautama was not interested in scientific principles per se; he had gained an insight into the nature of reality, which he called the Dharma, and been so completely transformed that henceforth he lived 'within' it and experienced life from its perspective. This Dharma was the truth of existence at every level. It described the inner world of experience in either deep meditation or ordinary life, and the outer world of nature and society. But when he came to communicate his teaching, Gautama only mentioned external phenomena (such as the patterns that form a river) as metaphors for the patterns of consciousness. His concern was how the mind works, how it produces what we call 'experience', how it creates suffering and how one can find liberation.

According to one discourse, a week after his Awakening 'the Lord emerged from that concentration and gave well-reasoned attention to dependent arising: This being, that is; from the arising of this, that arises.'[48] This is perhaps the earliest example of the classic formula, but, even at this early stage of Gautama's reflections on the Dharma, he is said to have formulated further applications. In particular, the discourse tells us that he teased out various links, or *nidanas*, through which human beings create their experience and, typically, bring suffering on themselves.* Gautama may also have reflected on other subjects that became important in his developed teachings: how consciousness is constituted; how dependent arising connects with the traditional idea of karma; and its relevance not just to the creation of suffering, but also to the developmental process that leads away from it.

It must have taken many years for Gautama (or, perhaps, later Buddhist tradition) to develop the complex and sophisticated ideas we find in the Discourses' doctrines, and some scholars think that the various versions of them in the Discourses mark stages in this process. Subsequent chapters will suggest how this may have happened to Gautama. What never changed was the vision, which came to Gautama with his Awakening, of life as a moral drama in which people act for good or ill and bring themselves either suffering or liberation in both this life and lives to come.

Deciding to Teach

As Gautama reflected, a doubt arose: 'It occurred to me that the Truth I had found was profound, hard to see, hard to understand, peaceful, sublime, beyond the sphere of mere reasoning, subtle, [and only] to be experienced by the wise.'[49] How could experience be put into words when it transcended language? Moreover, his

* This is the first instance of the famous chain of twelve *nidanas*, which is mentioned many more times in the Discourses and depicted, for example, on the outer rim of the Tibetan wheel of life. But there are signs that this detailed exposition of how dependent arising shapes experience and brings rebirth developed more slowly. For an interpretation of how this happened see Richard Gombrich, *What the Buddha Thought*, pp.129ff.

message was also extremely challenging – it went 'against the stream' of normal instincts and aspirations. To understand him, people would have to look unflinchingly at their motivations, and he knew very well that most of them were so attached to external things like belongings and possessions, and so 'impassioned by greed, enveloped in a thick darkness', that it would be hard for them to see 'the possibility of things having specific causes and arising in dependence upon things'. Trying to teach, he thought, would be 'distressing and hurtful for me', and he 'inclined to the least discomfort, not to teaching the Truth', preferring the prospect of resting in deep meditation.

From the earliest times Buddhists have found this episode problematic. It seems unthinkable that the supreme embodiment of compassion would have considered keeping his wisdom to himself. Perhaps, they suggested, it was a kind of game, a way of dramatising the altruistic impulse that is inseparable from Enlightenment. But in 'The Noble Quest', Gautama's uncertainty seems real enough, and the Indian tradition of forest hermits, recalled by Buddhist tradition as 'solitary Buddhas', suggests that remaining in the forest was, indeed, an option for someone in his position. The Discourses record several occasions in Gautama's later life when he showed distaste for the 'bother' that went with his involvement in the world. Once, feeling unable to live 'at ease'[50] in a busy environment, he just walked off into the forest; another time, he told a group of rowdy monks, 'I dismiss you! You cannot live with me!'[51] These incidents suggest Gautama's abiding love of a peaceful forest life and perhaps a determination to live in his own way, without compromise.

'The Noble Quest' tells us that, as Gautama paused, a celestial figure intervened. This was Brahma Sahampati, a member of the highest class of gods, who were 'of stunning beauty'[52] and luminous radiance. Some Brahmins considered Brahma the creator God himself, although Gautama held that the various Brahmas merely thought they were supreme beings, and that, in time, they would experience 'change and reverse'.[53] This story shows Brahma acknowledging Gautama's superiority to him because Gautama has gone beyond creation altogether. He implores Gautama to teach, and insists that his efforts shall not be in vain: 'There are beings with little dust in their eyes who will be lost if they do not hear the Truth . . . Rise up, a hero, the victor in battle, leader of the caravan, owing nothing, wanderer in the world. Let the Blessed One teach the Truth, there will be those who understand.'[54] Brahma is sometimes interpreted as the voice of Gautama's conscience, or perhaps his compassion, impelling him to act altruistically, however much 'trouble' it might be, but his appearance also dramatises the subordination of the Brahminical way of thinking to Gautama's.

Whatever the significance of Brahma's request, Gautama's response bears the authentic stamp of his visionary imagination.

Aware of Brahma's request, and out of compassion for beings, I surveyed the world with the vision of one Awakened. As where there is a clump of blue lotuses, red lotuses or white lotuses, some of [them] do not rise out of the water but thrive while still immersed in it; some remain level with the surface of the water; and some rise out of the water and remain untouched by [it]. In exactly the same way, I saw beings with little dust in their eyes and with much dust in their eyes, with keen faculties and with dull faculties, of good habits and of bad habits, easy to teach and difficult to teach.[55]

Lotus pools are still common in India, appearing in parched landscapes as miracles of colour. The tiny hairs on a lotus leaf wick away dirt and water, leaving it entirely clean, and that made the lotus a symbol for the purity of the sage who was undefiled by passion. The original element in Gautama's vision is the image of humanity in different stages of life and growth. It suggests that the capacity to grow towards Enlightenment is a natural potential within life, rather than an imposition upon it, and that to practise Gautama's dharma would be to blossom into fullness, if the conditions were right.

Buddhist tradition connected Gautama's decision to teach with a powerful new feeling – a 'great compassion' that some saw as a further unfolding of his Awakening experience. But who would understand his message? He thought of Arada Kalama: 'He is wise, clever, learned, someone who had long had little dust in his eyes . . . He would quickly understand this Truth.'[56] But the gods told Gautama that Arada had died a week earlier. Then he thought of Udraka Ramaputra, but learned that he had died the previous night. Finally he thought of his five former companions: 'They had been very helpful to me while I applied myself to the struggle. Suppose I were to teach the Group of Five monks the Truth first.'

Gautama learned through his 'divine eye' that the five were staying in Isipatana, a shramanas' meeting place in a deer park in Sarnath, near the holy city of Varanasi. Seven weeks after his Awakening he left Uruvilva, the Bodhi Tree and the forest grove, and started to walk.

4

The Awakening Movement

Stepping into the World

Hsuan Tsang arrived in Bodh Gaya in the year 637 CE, eight years after leaving China. His journey had taken him through cloudless deserts and freezing mountains; he had escaped robbers and charmed Mongol warlords; he had seen regions where Gautama's dharma thrived and others where the monasteries lay crumbling and abandoned. But when Hsuan Tsang at last reached Bodh Gaya, his biographer tells us, his response was far from joy:

> The Dharma Master . . . prostrated himself on the ground and cried in sorrow and anguish, bitter tears streaming down his face: 'I have no idea where I was or what type of rebirth I had when the Buddha gained Enlightenment. Now in the age of the Counterfeit Law I have finally arrived here at this place. Why is my evil karma so profound?' That very day was the final day of the summer rainy season and several thousand monks had gathered there, but everyone wept as they saw the great Dharma master weeping.[1]

Hsuan Tsang was desolate at the heart of the vast international Buddhist civilisation because Gautama was absent. Even twelve centuries after Gautama's death, the memory endured of his living presence, and a sense that he had communicated not just his ideas but his Dharma – the understanding of life that he apprehended and embodied – so that others might grasp it, too.

That direct communication was Gautama's aim as he walked from Uruvilva to Sarnath – about 210 km as the crow flies, and considerably further by the winding track Gautama followed, which still runs beside the new highway. It was the end of the hot season, so he probably set off very early in the morning and waited in the shade for much of each day until the heat subsided. Then he had to cross the River Ganges, using the ferry on which shramanas travelled free of charge. He walked at a steady pace, but he wasn't hurrying and the journey must have taken around two weeks.

At the very start of his journey, before he had even reached Gaya, Gautama met a naked Ajivaka wanderer called Upaka who asked Gautama the usual questions about his guru and the dharma he followed. Gautama replied, 'I have no teacher, no one exists like me anywhere in all existence and I have no peers. I am the supreme teacher and I alone am fully Enlightened. I am now travelling to set turning the wheel of Dharma in a world that has grown blind.'[2] No doubt, many seekers claimed to have found realisation, some of them sincere and some quite mad. Gautama was claiming not just a degree of spiritual attainment, but to have reached the supreme goal of spiritual life. 'By your claims, friend, you are an Absolute Victor,' Upaka said. Gautama replied: 'The Victors are those like me who have destroyed their taints. I have done just that, so, yes, I am a Victor.' Upaka waggled his head in the Indian way that suggests equivocal acknowledgement. Such an attainment was impossible according to the Ajivaka belief that 'happiness and unhappiness come in fixed measures, and the round of rebirth has a definite limit'.[3] For them, liberation came only after millions of aeons when a person's karma had exhausted itself. 'May it be so, friend,' Upaka said, and he took care as he walked away to follow a different road from Gautama.

Upaka's indifference to Gautama's pronouncement showed that some people simply would not be open to Gautama's teaching and he would need to do more than simply declare his realisation if he wanted to convince others. Another discourse relates that just a week after his Awakening a 'certain haughty Brahmin'[4] called Nigrodha had approached him and also failed to recognise his attainment. And something similar happened when Gautama reached Sarnath. As the July moon was becoming full and the monsoon breaking, Gautama arrived at the Isipatana deer park where Ashvajit, Bhaddiya, Mahanama, Vapshya and Kaundaniya were sitting together deciding what they should do. 'He has given up the struggle and reverted to a life of excess,' said one. 'We will not get up for him, [but] if he wants to he can sit down.'[5] As Gautama came near, the companions could not contain themselves. They greeted him warmly; but he told them he was not the person he had been:

Listen! The deathless has been achieved. I will give instruction, I will teach the Truth. If you practise as instructed then soon you will come to live, having experienced and attained here and now for yourselves through direct knowledge the ultimate goal of the spiritual life.[6]

One of the five expressed the doubts they all felt. Gautama had achieved no special breakthrough while practising self-mortification, so how could he have done so when he was living in a way that, to their eyes, was indulgent and sensual? Gautama insisted he hadn't reverted to luxury, and eventually the five admitted that they had never before heard him speak as he did now. They settled down to hear what he had to say.

'The Noble Quest', whose account of Gautama's actions has been so detailed up to this point, now merely says, 'I was able to convince the five monks',[7] but it gives no hint of what Gautama said. When later Buddhist monks compiled their monastic code in the Vinaya, they introduced it with an account of Gautama's life in the year that followed his Awakening – the *Mahavagga*, which was the first biography of Gautama. As 'The Noble Quest' didn't mention what he said to the monks, the compilers inserted a discourse called 'Setting in Motion the Wheel of the Teaching' (Dhammacakkapavattana Sutta), which seemed to be an account of that teaching. It relates that Gautama expounded two lists – the Four Truths and the Eightfold Path – and this became a classic formulation of Buddhist teachings that is still repeated in most textbooks. But in the discourses that scholars consider the earliest, Gautama usually speaks directly and informally rather than in lists, stressing principles rather than detailed doctrines. Richard Gombrich comments:

> Of course we do not really know what the Buddha said in his first sermon – no one was there with shorthand or a tape recorder – and it has even been convincingly demonstrated that the language of the text as we have it is in the main a set of formulas, expressions which are by no means self-explanatory but *refer* to already established doctrines.[8]

We shall get a better sense of Gautama's meeting with the five ascetics if we broaden the focus and consider how, in the years following his Enlightenment, he communicated what he had understood to many others.

Meeting the Buddha

Throughout Gautama's life, and perhaps especially at the start of his career, his sheer presence made a powerful impact. Although no single account gives us a credible physical description of Gautama, it is possible to assemble a portrait by scavenging among the Discourses. It seems he was shaven-headed, well built, of normal height and strikingly 'handsome, good-looking and of the most beautiful complexion'.[9] We hear that he had 'golden-coloured skin'[10] and sometimes seemed, literally, to shine and glow like the sun. 'It's marvellous how serene [is your] air, Master Gautama,' one person exclaimed: 'how clear and translucent [your] complexion!'[11] Another says: 'You have a perfect body, you are shining, well proportioned, beautiful to look at ... you have very white teeth ... clear eyes, a round face, you are large, straight, splendid.'[12] There is more than a hint of saintly iconography in such comments, and it is more likely that Gautama's skin was tanned dark by his outdoor life and hardened by the wind and heat. Near the end of Gautama's life, Ananda remarked: 'his complexion is no longer clear and radiant, his limbs are all flaccid and wrinkled and his body is stooped'.[13]

The most detailed description of Gautama in the Discourses is much closer to hagiography. It is placed in the mouth of a young Brahmin called Uttara whose guru sent him to observe Gautama and see if he conformed to the image of the superman of Brahminical lore. Uttara reported that not only had he seen all thirty-two of the distinctive physical characteristics such a person was expected to display, he had also observed Gautama's grace, elegance and decorum. Gautama's 'table manners', for example, were impeccable:

When he receives rice, he does not raise or lower the bowl, or tip it forwards or backwards. He receives neither too little rice, nor too much. He adds sauces in the right proportion; he does not exceed the right amount of sauce in the mouthful. He turns the mouthful over two or three times in his mouth and then swallows it, and no rice kernel enters his body unchewed; then he takes another mouthful.[14]

This chimes with reports of the purposeful, considered, self-aware character of Gautama's actions that displayed the 'mindfulness' for which he was renowned. As Uttara said, 'He tastes his food experiencing the taste, though not experiencing greed for the taste.'

For their part, Brahmins made sense of Gautama's attainment in terms of the Vedic precedents. The iconography with which he is depicted in Buddhist art is based on the thirty-two marks, which include long ears, webbed fingers and a bump at the crown of the head. But in many discourses there is no hint that Gautama possessed such unusual features, and the people who met him usually noticed nothing special about his appearance beyond his air of calm. One wanderer, with whom he happened to share a shelter for the night, remarked that he was searching for 'Gautama, who went forth from the Shakyan clan',[15] and noticed nothing special in his companion that suggested he had found him already.

The uncertain line between observation and hagiography may reflect the gradual overlay of religious piety upon historical reality; but even in the earliest texts, Gautama's followers believe that they encounter more than an ordinary human being. The notion that Gautama's life recapitulated the pattern followed by the previous Buddhas, who dominated the history of the universe, encouraged his disciples to regard him as the embodiment of a timeless archetype whose Awakening was significant for the entire cosmos, from the lowest hell to the highest heaven. Every step of his career is watched over by hosts of divine beings, and the earth itself shakes in response to the principal events of his life.

Gautama once said, 'I often abide in voidness.'[16] That could mean that he existed on a transcendental plane distinct from the worldly one – an important belief for many later Buddhists. But Gautama also said that what made him distinctive was that he lived according to the insight that experience is a shifting stream of phenomena that arises in dependence upon conditions and is therefore 'void' of a fixed essence. He still got ill and experienced pain, but there was no alteration in his 'lucidity'.[17] When a stone splinter cut his foot he simply observed the pain, 'mindful and clearly comprehending, without becoming distressed'.[18] The true 'wonder and marvel', Gautama declared, was not his supernormal powers, or the truth or otherwise of the legends that surrounded his life, but his capacity to observe his 'feelings . . . perceptions . . . and thoughts . . . as they arise, as they are present and as they disappear'.[19] In a similar vein, he once redefined the mythic superman of the Brahmins as 'a master of the mind in the ways of thought'[20] because he could think any thought he wanted to think and not think about something if he didn't want to.

However we read these descriptions of Gautama, it is clear that he was an extraordinary individual. Strangers sensed the majesty beneath Gautama's quiet demeanour, and disciples sometimes compared the impression he made to the massive grandeur of an elephant or the prowling watchfulness of a tiger. Perhaps the most successful literary attempt to evoke this elusive power is Gautama's brief appearance in Herman Hesse's novel *Siddhartha*:

> His peaceful countenance was neither happy nor sad. He seemed to be smiling gently inwardly. With a secret smile, not unlike that of a child, he walked along, peacefully, quietly. He wore his gown and

walked along like all the other monks, but his face and his step, his downward glance, his peaceful, downward-hanging hand, and every finger of his hand spoke of peace, spoke of completeness, sought nothing, imitated nothing, reflected a continuous quiet, an unfading light, and invulnerable peace.[21]

Sometimes, if he thought a person was ready, Gautama directed the full force of his consciousness towards them. That's what happened in his meeting with Bahiya, with which this book started. Those on the receiving end reported feeling overwhelmed, transported and sometimes transformed. It was a kind of spiritual energy, but also an engulfing sense of Gautama's compassion. He was said to 'abide in loving-kindness',[22] and the Vinaya suggests that Gautama could direct his goodwill towards others like a force field. Once, it tells us, he subdued a rampaging elephant in this way, and when a resident of Malla called Roja remarked that he was 'not much impressed' by him, Gautama 'suffused Roja with a mind of love',[23] and Roja became a disciple.

Gautama enjoyed 'living in the remote jungle, where there is little noise . . . places that are undisturbed and utterly secluded',[24] but he probably spent relatively little time there after his Enlightenment. He usually passed the annual rains retreat in a monastic centre on the outskirts of a major city (most often in Shravasti). For the rest of the year he wandered, but, as his overriding project was spreading his teachings, he tended to travel back and forth along the trade roads that linked these cities, often accompanied by a substantial entourage. Unless he was meditating or collecting his food, he was happy to strike up a conversation with people he met on the road, whether they were farmers, Brahmins or merchants. At other times shramanas and householders, including leading members of society, visited Gautama in his lodgings; he also spent

time instructing his own monks. He didn't care whether the person
to whom he spoke was of high or low caste or if they were con-
ventionally respectable, and he was happy to share his teachings
with prostitutes, robbers and at least one murderer. He is traditionally said to have taught people on the level they could understand, reserving advanced teachings for the most receptive listeners.
The Discourses don't quite bear this out, and there are many examples of people failing to grasp his meaning; but he could sometimes pick out those with the capacity to understand him more
fully. An example is the story of the leper named Suppabuddha
who approached a group of people thinking, 'Surely some food
must be being distributed.'[25] Notwithstanding his disappointment
at discovering that they were, in fact, listening to Gautama's teaching,
he sat down to listen. Gautama wondered, 'Who here is capable of
understanding the Dharma?' and his eyes alighted on Suppabuddha.
He recognised something in the leper and directed his talk to him,
finding just the right words to communicate his insight and understanding, and Suppabuddha made an instant spiritual breakthrough.

Whatever the circumstances, the Discourses represent Gautama
as an immensely skilled communicator with an uncanny ability to
establish rapport. Whoever he was with, he recalled at the end of
his life: 'I matched my appearance to their appearance, I matched
the sound of my voice to the sound of theirs, and I instructed them
with talk about the teaching, encouraging, enthusing and inspiring
them.'[26] However strongly people expressed their views, Gautama
avoided getting into arguments and developed a way of accepting,
at least to start with, the value of the qualities they praised. If they
were interested in exciting mystical experiences, he asked them to
imagine the most valuable fruit of meditation. They usually agreed
that this was realisation, not ecstasy. If they thought that virtuous
action meant performing a sacrifice, he asked them what the highest

sacrifice would be. He used images of cultivation when speaking to farmers and spoke of discipline in speaking with an animal trainer. This brought Gautama a reputation for charm and courtesy, even among Brahmins. Sonadanda, for example, had heard that Gautama was 'kindly of speech, courteous, genial, clear'.[27] Sonadanda wanted to meet the remarkable shramana but was worried he would be shown up if Gautama asked philosophical questions from the perspective of the Ganges Valley religion, about which he knew nothing. He needn't have worried. The impeccably considerate Gautama put Sonadanda at ease by asking him to describe the qualities of the true Brahmin. Then Gautama led him, step by step, towards his own way of thinking until Sonadanda agreed (to the dismay of his companions) that being a true Brahmin ultimately had nothing at all to do with birth, appearance or knowledge of the sacred mantras.

Uttara noted Gautama's combination of charm and directness when he spoke in public. His words were 'distinct, intelligible, melodious, audible, ringing, euphonious, deep and sonorous', and he refused to flatter or disparage his listeners, choosing instead to 'instruct, urge, rouse and encourage' them.[28] This contrasted with the Brahminical way of chanting scriptures, which was a ritual rather than an attempt to convey ideas. Gautama's preference for speaking in the 'local language',[29] rather than priestly Sanskrit, may reflect his identification with the spiritual traditions of the Ganges Valley, but it also helped put people at their ease, allowing them to make their own connections with his message.

Richard Gombrich comments that Gautama 'had a clear and compelling vision of the truth and was trying to convey it to a wide range of people with different inclinations and varying presuppositions, so he had to express his message in many different ways'.[30] To this end, Gautama used metaphors, parables and stories,

as well as ideas, to convey his meaning. From the start, Gautama
had a remarkable talent for articulating insights that defied the
usual categories of thought in clear and powerful concepts. But
even these were a means to an end. He compared his teachings to
a raft that could help a person cross a stretch of water and then
be left behind. 'The raft's purpose is for crossing over, not for holding
on to.'[31] Gautama explained.

The results could be dramatic. An ageing Brahmin called Pingiya
recalled his first meeting with Gautama. 'I am old,' he told him.
'My body is weak and my skin is pale. I can hardly see and I hear
only with difficulty. Don't let me die while I am still in confusion,
but teach me about the way things are.'[32] Gautama replied: 'Pingiya,
you must let go of the body and of forms.' This mysterious message
somehow touched the man with a startling immediacy. He said,
'Up till now, before I heard Gotama's teaching, people had always
told me: "This is how it has always been, and this is how it will
always be"; only the constant refrain of tradition.' Gautama's teaching
differed profoundly from the 'bleary half-light' of the ancient mystical beliefs Pingiya had previously followed, and Pingiya declared:
'There is nothing else quite like it anywhere in the world.'[33]

Hearing the Truth

The River Ganges is the heart of the region in which Gautama
lived. For orthodox Hindus it is a goddess – Ganga – whose course
mirrors the flow of life towards death. It runs south from the
Himalayas, and then winds eastwards towards the Bay of Bengal;
but at one point it makes a sharp turn north-east, seeming to reverse
its natural course, and Hindus see this as a symbol for the transition from death to rebirth in a new body. In Gautama's time a city

named Varanasi had already grown up around the port and the bathing places on the western bank, facing the rising sun and the huge floodplain on the east. For those wanting to find a favourable rebirth, the crook in the river is an ideal place to be purified and die. The corpses lie in rows and are dipped in the water before being placed on one of the funeral pyres that litter the bank. Acrid smoke rises as the flesh melts and the bones char to ashes that are thrown back into the river. Bodies of the unclean, like lepers and pregnant women, and of the wholly pure, like cows and children, are tied to a rock and dropped from boats into the stream. Many rise again, and the grisly detritus is washed onto the farther shore. Meanwhile, crowds of pilgrims stand up to their waists in the river and murmur sacred verses before immersing themselves in its holy yet utterly filthy water.

Varanasi was at the eastern edge of the Ganges Valley, just out-side the Aryan lands, and had recently been absorbed into Kosala along with the kingdom of Kasi, of which it was the capital. Hindus claim that the city is 3,000 years old, but archaeologists report that the town's fortifications and oldest stone buildings were constructed in Gautama's time: 460–440 BCE.[34] The Discourses don't portray the city as the centre of Brahmin worship and training it became, and trainee priests still travelled to the colleges of Taxila far to the north-west. But many people, both Brahmins and non-Brahmins, believed that 'whoever, young or old, does an evil action is released from [it] by ablution in water',[35] and it is reasonable to suppose that, even then, people bathed in the Ganges in the hope of win-ning a better rebirth.

The belief that an act like ablution had spiritual merit in and of itself opposed everything Gautama had learned in his Awakening. 'Purity and impurity are matters of personal experience',[36] he said, and when he saw a group of renunciants performing ritual ablutions he commented that only 'truth and Dharma'[37] would make them pure. Gautama wanted to direct people's attention away from external observances and towards their states of mind, as well as the patterns of cause and effect. That's what he did, according to 'Setting in Motion the Wheel of the Teaching', when he addressed the Group of Five. The ascetics put their faith in practices that cultivated pain and suffering, and Gautama addressed this preoccupation in his teaching of the Four Noble Truths; but he introduced a new perspective by drastically expanding the meaning of suffering. The first Truth suggests that there is no need deliberately to accentuate suffering through self-mortification. *Dukkha* is everywhere in the inherent unsatisfactoriness and inescapable difficulty of human life. Its cause, he explained in the second Truth, lies in the mind's tendency to respond to experience with craving; and, conversely (the third Truth), if craving ceases, *dukkha* will cease as well. Therefore, the fourth Truth is that one must transform one's experience until one is without craving, and that means following the Eightfold Path.

We cannot say if Gautama's message took precisely this form, and in a sense it doesn't matter. We know that he communicated his insight into dependent arising and can assume that he did so in terms that addressed his listeners' concerns. According to 'Setting in Motion the Wheel of the Teaching', Kaundaniya was the first to understand Gautama's meaning, and when he did so the universe reverberated:

There arose in the venerable Kaundaniya a vision of truth, without blemish, untarnished: 'The nature of everything whose nature it is to arise is to cease ... The Gods of the Earth proclaimed: 'This wheel of Truth that the Blessed One has turned in Varanasi, at Isipatana in the animal park, no ascetic or Brahmin, nor god, nor Mara, nor Brahma, nor anyone in the world can stop.'

This was a key event in the history of the universe, according to Buddhist mythology, and the gods in the ascending heaven-realms took up the cry, up to the apex of existence: 'This ten-thousandfold world system shook, trembled and quaked. A boundless splendid radiance appeared in the world surpassing the majesty of the gods. Then the Blessed One breathed a sigh: "Kaundaniya has understood! Kaundaniya has understood!"'[38]

Gautama spoke further with the remaining four members of the group. They took turns to beg food, and, one by one, they made the same breakthrough as Kaundaniya. When Gautama gave a talk explaining that nothing possessed any essential selfhood, they made another and then, the Mahavagga tells us, 'there were six perfected ones (*arahants*) in the world.'[39]

Varanasi was a trading city and an important centre for the manufacture of fabrics, perfumes and sculpture, so it was home to wealthy merchants. The Mahavagga relates that Yasha, the son of such a family, watched his beautiful attendants as they slept, and was plunged into turmoil: 'One with a lute in the hollow of her arm, one with a tabor at her neck, one with a drum in the hollow of her arm, one with dishevelled hair, one with saliva dripping from her mouth, muttering in their sleep, like a cemetery before his very eyes.'[40]

Gautama's biographers inserted this scene into their accounts of his decision to leave the palace. In the original version, Yasha declares, 'Alas! what distress; alas! what danger!' He wanders into the Deer Park, Gautama calls the young man over, and when they speak, Yasha immediately understands his teaching.

Yasha's father came looking for his son, and when he met Gautama the same thing happened. Then Gautama spoke to Yasha's mother and his wife, and they were convinced as well. Word spread among Yasha's friends that something extraordinary was taking place, and more and more of them visited Isipatana. Each in turn was convinced by Gautama and took ordination. They shaved their heads, donned the shramanas' robes and slept rough among the trees. Each day they walked to Varanasi to get food, and they spent the rest of their time meditating or discussing the Dharma. Soon, the Mahavagga tells us, there were sixty-one arahants.

Buddhist tradition holds that, as arahants, the disciples had reached final liberation and had no more to learn, and later Buddhists were puzzled by the apparent ease with which they attained this state. The Discourses also relate that listeners, starting with Kaundaniya, often made a dramatic breakthrough on hearing a single teaching, or perhaps after a week or two of putting Gautama's instructions into practice. In later years progress seemed much slower, and some suggested that times had become less propitious for Dharma practice. Others said that the difference in Gautama's time was the impact of meeting 'the giver of the Deathless',[41] Gautama himself.

The tradition that such an encounter could have this revelatory impact is strong in the Discourses: 'When the Buddhas arise in the world, the radiance-makers, they make visible this Dharma that leads to the calming of dukkha and [men] hearing them acquire wisdom [and] regain their hearts.'[42] This makes sense if we read the encounters described in the Discourses as recapitulations of an archetype, but they are puzzling if we regard them as realistic descriptions of what happened. The notion that simply hearing Gautama's words might catapult a listener into Awakening runs counter to his emphasis on self-reliance and his message that 'one man cannot purify another'.[43] Gautama told one interlocutor, 'I am not able to release anyone who has doubts, but if you understand the most excellent Dharma you will cross the flood for yourself.'[44] He said that, while people *could* sometimes make a sudden breakthrough, the usual pattern was 'gradual training, gradual practice, gradual progress in the Dharma',[45] and he compared Awakening to the slow ripening of crops or 'the slope of the Ganges to the east'.[46]

Another explanation is that after Gautama's death a later generation, looking back at the heroic days of their community's pioneers, inflated the original meaning of their attainments. The Discourses identify arahants as those who have 'lived the spiritual life, done what has to be done, laid down the burden, utterly destroyed the fetters of existence and [are] completely liberated through final knowledge'.[47] They are said to have 'done their work' so completely that they 'are no longer capable of being negligent'.[48] But in the texts we find that Ashvajit declares he is 'still a beginner, newly gone forth in this Dharma', even after becoming an arahant, and Mahakasyapa repeatedly loses his temper.

What had happened to these men? The process that led people to practise Gautama's teaching, the Discourses often relate, started with the appearance of a Tathagata – a fully Enlightened person:

> He teaches the Truth that is beautiful in the beginning, beautiful in the middle and beautiful in the end, both in its spirit and in its letter. He makes clear the spiritual life in all its perfection. A householder gains faith in the Tathagata [and] reflects: 'Living in a house is restricted and cluttered, going forth is a life wide open.' After some time he might abandon his possessions and leave behind his circle of relatives. Then he might shave off his hair and beard, put on ochre robes, and go forth from home into homelessness.[49]

At some point a shift took place, usually under Gautama's influence, and listeners 'made the breakthrough'[50] to a new way of seeing the world. Sometimes Gautama spoke of this breakthrough as *renunciation* – a change from looking for happiness in sense pleasures to finding it in a simple, uncluttered existence and a deepening of experience. For some, that meant giving up household life and becoming a full-time renunciant, but this wasn't a penance: 'If by renouncing a lesser happiness one would see an abundant happiness, let the spiritually mature person . . . sacrifice the limited happiness,'[51] as Gautama said. Sometimes he spoke of the change as the arising of *faith*, an emotion that includes trust, confidence and inspiration and is grounded in experience. At other times he spoke of it as *right view* or *seeing truly*. Technically, right view is defined as fully grasping the Four Truths, which express, in précis, the insights that constituted Gautama Enlightenment.

When this breakthrough is truly decisive it is as if a 'Dharma-Eye' opens to supplement the usual senses. An account of an encounter between Gautama and a lay follower called Upali includes a detailed description of this experience:

> When Gautama knew that Upali's mind was ready, receptive, free from hindrances, elated and confident, he explained the teaching that is unique to the Buddhas: dukkha, its origin and cessation and the path leading from it. Just as a clean cloth would take dye evenly, so while Upali sat there the spotless, immaculate Dharma Eye arose in him: 'Whatever is subject to origination is subject to cessation.' He fathomed the Dharma, and passed beyond doubt.[52]

Such a person is fundamentally different from an ignorant, ordinary person (a *prattagjana*), and has joined the ranks of the 'noble ones' – the true Aryans who are not to be confused with those who merely belong to the Aryan race. He or she becomes a *shravaka* – 'one who has heard'.

> What others speak of as happiness, that the Aryans say is dukkha;
> what the others say is dukkha the Aryans know as happiness. For
> those enveloped there is darkness, blindness for those who cannot
> see; whilst for the wise there is an opening, like light to those with
> sight. Fools unconversant with the Dharma, though in its presence,
> do not discern it.[53]

Someone who is Aryan in this sense, Gautama said, has 'entered
the course of rightness, entered the plane of superior persons and
transcended the plane of the worldlings'.[54] He or she acquires 'unwavering confidence'[55] in the Buddha, Dharma and Sangha, and
possesses the moral virtues that are 'dear to the noble ones'.[56] Most
Shravaka were renunciants, but the difference between a *shravaka*
and a *prattagyana* was their spiritual attainment, not how they
lived. Numerous householders made the same breakthrough without
renouncing their possessions, while some monks remained members of the 'un-Aryan company'.[57] Occasionally someone like Suppabuddha 'crossed over doubt, attained to complete confidence and
became independent of others in the Teacher's teaching',[58] without
making any formal commitment at all. Usually, though, if a listener was convinced by Gautama's teaching they made an act of
commitment by 'going for refuge'. The only reliable refuge, Gautama said, is something that isn't caught up in the tangles of samsara, and that means the Buddha – Gautama himself and the ideal
he embodies; and the Dharma – his teachings and the truth they
describe. The third refuge is the Sangha, which can mean the community of those who have who realised the Dharma, the community of all Buddhists, or the monastic community – which is how
many later Buddhists understood it.

In time, this initial inspiration deepens. Faith can become a
growing commitment and openness to the truth; seeing truly can

become a deepening understanding that culminates in transformative wisdom; renunciation can become the practice of letting go of craving and the end of attachment in Nirvana. Going for refuge fully to the ideals represented by the Buddha, Dharma and Sangha means embodying them. The whole of life can be a path and then, shifting the metaphor, it can become a stream. Living in this way, one is no longer swept along in the unconscious, habitual patterns of the world, but borne by a new, inner current. Just as water flows from a mountain-top to the ocean, Gautama said, with faith, the practitioner's experience transmutes into multiple 'streams of merit'[59] that feed happiness and 'flow on' to joy, tranquillity, concentration, insight, liberation and 'the destruction of the taints'.[60]

Starting a Movement

Having gathered a number of disciples around him, Gautama had, in effect, started a new shramana community, and at some stage he gave it a name: 'You are people of different birth, with different names, from different lineages and families, who have gone forth from home into homelessness. If you are asked who you are you should affirm: "We are ascetics, sons of the Shakyan – *Shakyaputra shramanas*."'[61]

The early Shakyaputras did not live like the Buddhist *bhikkhus* and *bhikkhunis* of later times, whose activities are regulated by hundreds of rules; and even the Christian terms 'monks' and 'nuns' are somewhat misleading (though there are no adequate alternatives). The Shakyaputras didn't dwell in monasteries, at least to start with, and the difference between renunciates and householders in the Shakyaputra movement was a matter of how they lived, not the sacramental distinction that separates ordained Roman Catholic clergy from the laity. But those who had formally 'gone forth' from the household life were different because their time was wholly devoted to practising Gautama's teachings. Their main responsibility was to find Awakening, but, even before the rains' retreat had finished, Gautama introduced another element. He told them to share their understanding with others:

> Wander, monks, for the blessing of the many, for the happiness of the many, out of compassion for the world, for the benefit and welfare, blessing and happiness of gods and men. No two of you should go the same way. Communicate the Dharma, which is lovely in the beginning, middle and end, and share both the letter and the spirit of the spiritual life in all its fullness and purity. There are those with little dust in their eyes, who are suffering from not hearing the Dharma.[62]

These stirring words show the character of the movement Gautama was starting. He believed that his dharma applied to everyone, and telling the monks to wander for 'the benefit of the many' suggested that it wouldn't be a movement of shramanas alone. His teachings wouldn't be passed only to chosen disciples, in the Upanishadic manner, or restricted to certain castes, like the Vedic traditions. The Jains and the Ajivakas (so far as we can tell) also considered their teachings to be universally true; but we encounter nothing in their scriptures comparable to the sense of mission these words express. It helps explain Buddhism's capacity to spread across Asia while the other Ganges Valley sects never left the subcontinent, and Hinduism remained an essentially Indian religion.

However, one Discourse relates an incident that seems to have occurred during Gautama's stay in Sarnath. A man called Dhammadinna (not to be confused with a famous nun of the same name) travelled from Varanasi to see Gautama with other householders, and requested a teaching. Gautama told his listeners to 'enter and dwell upon those discourses ... that are deep, deep in meaning, supramundane, dealing with emptiness.'[63] This would be hard, exclaimed Dhammadinna, for people 'living in a home crowded with children, enjoying Kasian sandalwood, wearing garlands, scents and unguents, and receiving gold and silver'. He and his companions were familiar with Gautama's ethical precepts, he said, and they just wanted to know the next step on the path. Gautama replied that they should develop faith in the Buddha, Dharma and Sangha and the 'virtues dear to the noble ones'. The incident is ambiguous, but it suggests that Gautama had overestimated how much these householders could understand and was exploring how to communicate with them.

According to the Mahavagga, Gautama's instruction to spread his teachings inspired the new monks. They spread out quickly and new recruits started to arrive at Isipatana even before the rains had finished. Gautama could have stayed in Sarnath and made it his headquarters, but instead he decided that the Shakyaputras would have a decentralised structure. Gautama told the monks:

> I permit you to grant the going forth and conduct ordinations yourselves. First the candidate must have his hair and beard shaved off, then he must put on a robe and cover the left shoulder with it. He must salute the feet of the ordaining monk and then squat down and salute the ordaining monk with joined palms and recite 'I go for Refuge to the Buddha; I go for Refuge to the Dharma; I go for Refuge to the Sangha.'

Taming the Spirits

Once the monsoon was finished Gautama walked through a rejuvenated land, down the trade road that had brought him to Sarnath. 'The climate is soft, the crops abundant, the fruit trees flourishing and the underwood thick in every place',[64] wrote Hsuan Tsang. Gautama was heading towards the great metropolis of Rajagriha, but he stopped in Uruvilva and spent several months there. He said he wanted to repay the householders who had supported him during his stay in the forest grove and perhaps in the preceding years, but he also had unfinished business with the Gaya spirits and the religious cults that propitiated them. Along the Naranjara were 'hermitages' led by three brothers, all called Kasyapa, who were Jatila ascetics. Another discourse relates that Gautama saw Jatilas in the middle of winter performing fire sacrifices and 'plunging in and out of the water'[65] to purify themselves. These rituals resemble those of the Brahmins, but the Jatilas may also have been practitioners of an indigenous Magadhan fire-worshipping spirit cult.

The Mahavagga relates that Gautama asked the priest of the Uruvilva shrine – Uruvilva Kasyapa – if he could spend a night in the fire chamber. Kasyapa agreed, but warned Gautama, 'The shrine is home to a dreadful, venomous naga king who possesses great magical power.' That night the priests watched in horror as flames spewed from the chamber, but the next morning Gautama stepped out unscathed and showed them the snake – its inner 'fire' extinguished. When the full moon came he did the same in a second hermitage, and this time when he left the fire chamber his body was still flickering with 'multi-coloured flames, dark green, then red, crimson, yellow and crystal-coloured'.[66] On other nights a mysterious glow lit the grove where Gautama was staying, and he reported the next day that gods had visited him. Further 'miraculous' displays followed, including splitting logs for the sacrifice with the power of his mind, and at length Kasyapa and his disciples were won over.

This story presents Gautama as a master of the gods, a wizard or thaumaturge with supernormal abilities, and a shaman with power over the spirit world. Gautama told the Uruvilva priests that his connection with the gods had developed with his Awakening. At first, he said, he had only been able to see the light from their bodies, but later he could 'distinguish their forms, talk with them, discover how they came to be born in their different spheres and understand their experiences'.[67] As for 'miracles', the Discourses in general consider it an unremarkable fact that the absorptions enabled a meditator to create a 'mind-made body' and develop an array of psychic powers:

Being one he becomes many; being many he becomes one; he appears then vanishes; he passes unhindered through house walls, through city walls and through mountains as if through air; he rises up out of the earth and sinks down into it as if it were water; he walks on water as if it were solid earth; he travels through the sky cross-legged as if he were a bird and strokes with his hand things of such power and mastery as the sun and moon.[68]

Other powers included the ability to read others' thoughts (which Gautama often does in the Discourses), to hear sounds at a distance, to cause earthquakes and to prolong life. If this seems unrealistic we should recall that 'miracle'-performing saints and prophets are found in every culture, as are shamans who claim to enter the spirit world. Commentators who want to make Gautama the proponent of their own rational world view suggest that accounts of his miraculous feats are later constructions, but displays of Gautama's psychic powers are everywhere in the Discourses. By their testimony, he was both the teacher of a down-to-earth, psychologically convincing message *and* a wonder-working saint, and the difficulty in reconciling these aspects reflects the difference between the modern world view and that of a pre-modern society. In some aspects Gautama *was* a remarkably modern figure who relied on his direct experience, evaluated it pragmatically and asks others to do the same. But everyday reality in his culture included gods, miracles, karma, rebirth and higher states of consciousness.

Gautama's victory over the Gaya nagas continues the confrontation with the region's spirits that had preceded his Awakening, and the battle with Mara that symbolised it. But something had changed. Now he stood apart from the universe 'with its gods, Maras, Brahmas . . . princes and people',[69] and no spirit, however fearsome, had any hold over him because he was free from the fear and clinging that made ordinary people susceptible. The Uruvilva priests were so impressed that they decided to join Gautama's order. Kasyapa later recalled:

> Seeing the marvels of the famous Gautama, I did not at once fall down before him, being deceived by envy and pride. Knowing my intention, the charioteer of men urged me on. Then there arose in me hair-raising agitation. Despising what little supernormal power I had had previously, when I was an ascetic with matted hair, I went forth in the conqueror's teaching.[70]

Mainstream Buddhist tradition, and perhaps Gautama himself, later became deeply ambivalent about displays of miracles, but it seems that, at least in this early period, he was willing to use them. Miracles impressed priests, who saw ritual as a way of channelling power, because it showed whose power was superior. But Gautama's true message was more subtle. The Uruvilva priests shaved their matted hair and threw it into the river, and when the priests of the other hermitages saw the locks floating past they came to investigate. Gautama gathered them all on Gayasisa hill, a few miles from the river, and in this awe-inspiring landscape – 'with its sombre valley, streams and steep and dangerous crags',[71] as Hsuan Tsang says – Gautama gave one of his most brilliant and compressed talks. Moving from magic to metaphor, he inverted the meaning of the fire they had worshipped:

> All is burning, monks. And what is the all that is burning, monks? The eye is burning . . . The ear is burning . . . The nose is burning The tongue is burning . . . The body is burning. The mind is burning, ideas are burning, stimulation of the mind is burning; and whatever . . . feeling that comes about conditioned by stimulation of the mind, that, too, is burning. Burning with what? I say it is burning with the fire of greed, the fire of hatred, the fire of delusion; burning with birth, with old age, with death, with grief, with lamentation, with pain, with sorrow, with despair.[72]

Whether the Jatilas were Brahmins or Magadhan fire worshippers, the descriptions of fire chambers and sacrifices show that fire had been at the heart of their religion. Gautama's talk shifted their attention from the elemental force that promised power over the world to the emotions and instincts that had led them to desire power in the first place.

Rajagriha

From Uruvilva, Gautama travelled to Rajagriha, and the Mahavagga tells us that he arrived with a retinue of 1,000 newly ordained monks. The Shakyaputras created a sensation in the city's religion-fuelled life. King Bimbisara met Gautama in a formal reception at a holy grove outside the walls, and many citizens (the text says 120,000) came to watch. We must imagine a grand but wary reception as Bimbisara (seated beneath the white royal banner), the court, and the other Rajagriha citizens weighed up this new claimant to spiritual mastery. Gautama's shramana community was already larger than the one Udraka Ramaputra had gathered over many years, and its young teacher, who claimed to have gained full realisation, had rejected the other gurus. The astonished citizens spotted Kashyapa, the guardian of Gaya's holy fire-shrines, among the monks and wondered who was really the teacher. Gautama put the question to Kashyapa: 'Why have you deserted your shrine?' Kashyapa replied: 'The sacrifices praise tangible things and offer worldly rewards. But I have seen a state that is free from attachment to sensual existence. Therefore I take no more delight in sacrifices and offerings.' Kashyapa rose from his seat, prostrated himself before Gautama and said: 'The Lord is my teacher, I am a disciple.'[73]

According to the Mahavagga, Kasyapa's display of faith in Gautama convinced Bimbisara that he was a genuinely Enlightened master, and Bimbisara asked to become a lay follower, declaring that he had fulfilled his life's ambition to meet a realised teacher and understand his message. Many other Rajagriha citizens followed the king's example. It is hard to take this at face value as relatively few discourses relate further discussions between Bimbisara and Gautama, who spent much more time in Shravasti, and the

Jains also claim that Bimbisara converted to their faith (along with thirteen of his wives and twenty-three of his sons). Most likely, Bimbisara recognised Gautama as a guru (perhaps even one who had gained full Enlightenment) who should be respected within the Magadhan religion, and he may even have become a patron of the Shakyaputra community, as the tradition asserts. But there is no indication that he gave Gautama his exclusive loyalty.

Bimbisara's recognition, whatever it meant exactly, was a coup for Gautama and an important step for his community. In the weeks after his arrival in Rajagriha, interest in the Shakyaputras swept the city and they attracted important recruits. Two wanderers called Upatissa and Kolita, who had been friends since childhood, had made a pact to tell the other if either of them discovered 'the way to the Deathless'. They became followers of the sceptical shramana teacher, Sanjaya Belatthaputta, and travelled India in search of deeper teachings. Shortly after their return to Rajagriha, Upatissa saw Ashvajit on his alms round and was drawn by his air of calm. He asked Ashvajit what dharma he followed, and Ashvajit replied in verses that were later repeated throughout the Buddhist world:

> Those things that arise from a cause, of these the Truth-finder
>   has told the cause,
> And that which is their stopping – the great recluse has such a
>   doctrine.[74]

Ashvajit didn't even explain what these causes were or how they worked, but the mere suggestion that the world could be looked at as a process of cause and effect transformed Upatissa. He realised: 'Whatever is of the nature to arise all that is of the nature to stop.' The Dharma Eye opened, and when he told Kolita what he had learned, the same happened to his friend.

The two men sought out Gautama, and he ordained them with the simple words, 'Come, monks! Dharma is well proclaimed. Adopt the pure life and make an end of suffering.'[75] They took the names Shariputra and Maudgalyayana, and both quickly became arahants. For a fortnight, Gautama says, Shariputra probed his mind more and more deeply and saw into the nature of his mental states 'one by one, as they occurred'.[76] He passed through the absorptions and at each stage he 'ferreted out' the elements of his experience; whatever occurred, 'he did not cling to it, welcome it or hold to it', and in this way, Shariputra freed himself from the limitations those states brought. 'Known to him those states arose, known to him they were present, known to him they disappeared. He understood thus: "So indeed, these states, not having been, come into being; having been, they vanish" . . . Regarding those states, abided unattracted, unrepelled, independent, detached, free, dissociated, with a mind free of barriers.'[77]

Eventually, the discourse tells us, he reached the stage of neither-perception-nor-non-perception, and then the further stage of 'the cessation of perception and feeling'. Bringing mindful awareness to even this incredibly refined state, 'his taints were destroyed by his seeing with wisdom' and Sariputra realised, 'There is no escape beyond.'[78]

Gautama declared that every Buddha had two chief disciples and Shariputra and Maudgalyayana were his. He had known them in many previous lifetimes and their meeting in this life was the fulfilment of aeons of development. In Buddhist art they are often depicted standing beside Gautama or reverentially gazing up at him. Gautama saw that Shariputra (with his exceptional intellect) and Maudgalyayana (with his extraordinary psychic powers) could be important allies in developing his movement. What's more, the Mahavagga relates, their defection persuaded many of Sanjaya's followers to do the same, and a group of intellectually minded sceptics joined Gautama's order alongside the former priests, yogis and laymen. Sanjaya was so distraught that he died of a haemorrhage.

Then came the popular backlash. Anger spread among Rajagriha's citizens that the 'home-breaker' Gautama was taking away their sons and husbands: 'Who will he poach next?' The monks depended on the townspeople for their food, and they ran the gauntlet of abuse when they made their alms rounds each day. Gautama said the unrest would last a week and advised the monks to stay calm. He gave them a verse of their own to repeat to people who chanted anti-Shakyaputra slogans:

> Great heroes, Truth finders, led by what is true Dharma.
> Who could be jealous of the wise, leading according to Truth?[79]

The criticism died down, as Gautama had anticipated, but the episode showed that the Shakyaputra movement, with its message of renunciation, was vulnerable to the popular mood. He needed to take care not to alienate those who were left behind.

Even if Gautama's focus, at least in the early years, was sharing his wisdom with full-time religious practitioners, his insights illuminated the reality that everyone experienced. Everyone's experience arose in dependence upon conditions, and the Dharma could help them understand the patterns of their lives. The fundamental cause of the world's problems lay in the minds of human beings, Gautama taught. 'In dependence upon feeling there is craving; in dependence upon craving there is pursuit,' he once said. The chain continued with 'gain', then 'decision-making', 'desire', 'lust', 'attachment ... possessiveness ... niggardliness [and] defensiveness'. As a result, 'various evil, unwholesome things originate – the taking up of clubs and weapons, conflicts, quarrels and disputes, insults, slander and falsehood.'[80]

Gautama linked his insights into the mind with the traditional notion of karma and the belief that it determined future rebirth. While Gautama had little time for the Brahminical identification of karma with the 'purifying action' of rituals such as the sacrifice, he strongly believed that actions had consequences in both 'this world and the next'.[81] That brought him close to the Jain belief, which seems to have been especially influential in Magadha, that all actions produce karma. For the Jains this meant that all action is bad, which Gautama found absurd, but their teachings also made karma into a universal principle, connecting it to a compassionate desire to avoid harming others. Gautama agreed with the Jains that regulating behaviour to avoid destructive actions was vital, at least as a starting point, and he formulated five ethical precepts that may well have been based upon the precepts for Jain householders. These are abstaining from 'the destruction of life'; from 'taking what has not been given'; from sexual misconduct and from lying. The fifth Jain precept was giving up possessions, but Gautama probably thought this unrealistic for householders and, instead, he asked householder disciples to 'abstain from wines, liquors and intoxicants which are the basis for negligence'.[82]

The fifth precept connected Gautama's ethical teachings to the mind, hinting that, for him, being ethical and acquiring beneficial karma really depended on the state of mind with which a person acted. In time, as we shall see, Gautama reinterpreted the meaning of karma by saying that 'by karma I mean intention'.[83] That was perhaps too subtle for some people, but they could understand his insistence that they should develop loving-kindness, generosity, contentment, honesty and mindfulness.

The Shakyaputras would always be dependent on their householder supporters, but they already had an asset of their own. The Mahavagga tells us that Bimbisara had donated a plot of land called the Venuvana, or 'Bamboo Park', just outside the city, and to start with the monks slept rough in the squirrels' feeding ground. As individual monks weren't allowed to own property, Gautama accepted the land on behalf of the Shakyaputras as a whole. It gave the order some economic security, and the Venuvana's location helped define the monks' relationship to townspeople. It was 'neither too far from a village nor too near, suitable for coming and going, accessible for people whenever they want, not crowded by day, having little noise at night . . . conducive to privacy and suitable for meditation'.[84] But accepting the property was also a step towards making the order an institution in its own right.

Rajagriha was always an important centre for the new movement, but the Jains and other non-Buddhist wanderers were well established and some groups may have been active for centuries. The city was never Gautama's main base, but he returned to Rajagriha often, and at the end of his life he recalled with deep affection the sacred mountains and caves where he had stayed: 'Vulture's Peak, Gotama's Banyan Park, Robbers' Cliff, the Sattapanni Cave on the slope of Vebhara, Black Rock on the slope of Isigili, the Sita grove in the Sappasondika ravine . . . the bamboo grove at the squirrels' feeding ground, Jivaka's Mango Grove, the Maddakucchi deer park'.[85] In each place he had exclaimed to Ananda: 'How delightful!'

Kapilavastu

It was about seven years since Gautama had left Shakya, and tradition says that Suddhodana sent Kaludayin, one of Gautama's childhood friends, to persuade him to return. Kaludayin composed a beautiful set of verses that evoked Shakya just as the land was exploding into flower after the rains.

Crimson now, Sir, are the trees of the forest,

Having shed their foliage, they're eager to fruit,

Their flowers are blazing forth like brilliant flames ...

The blossoming trees, so pleasing to the mind,

Spread their fragrance in every direction,

Surrendering their leaves and longing for fruit ...

My Lord, let the Shakyas and Koliyas see you

Facing westward and crossing the Rohini.[86]

Gautama was ready to return. The quest for meaning that had impelled him to leave Shakya was over, and the King of Magadha (the most powerful man in the Ganges Valley) had recognised his achievement. He had a message he believed could benefit his kinsmen, and had started a movement that could be established in Shakya. Besides, Kapilavastu was on the main trade road between Rajagriha and Shravasti, and if he were to travel freely across the region he could hardly avoid it.

Many legends cluster around Gautama's return home, but there is a particular ring of authenticity to several incidents that suggest his reception was mixed. When Gautama arrived he was taken to the Nigrodha Grove, just outside the city. The next day he made his alms round and when Suddhodana saw him in the street his anger flared: 'How can a Shakyan beg in the streets barefoot and wearing rags?' Gautama's reply reiterated his rejection of his father's values and claimed a new independence: 'I am not of the Shakyan lineage but of the Buddha lineage, and I beg because that is what Buddhas do.'[87]

According to the *Nidana Katha*, Gautama met a similar response from the 'proud' older Shakyans who visited him at Nigrodha Grove. They refused to bow to the young Gautama and told their children, 'You bow; we'll sit behind you.'[88] Gautama performed another miracle – a spectacular display he repeated several times – in which he rose into the air and streams of water and flames shot from his body. The Shakyans were captivated.

Whatever the impact of Gautama's first visit on Shakya as a whole, it had a huge effect on his immediate family. The young men he had grown up with still looked up to him, and he understood their hopes and frustrations. Now he presented them with a compelling vision of an alternative way of living. Chandaka, his servant and charioteer, was eager to become one of Gautama's monks and became an ardent partisan of 'our order, our teaching'.[89] The tide of enthusiasm even caught up Gautama's half-brother Nanda, who admitted that he was 'conceited, vain and addicted to sensual pleasures'.[90] Gautama arrived at the festivities celebrating Nanda's wedding to the beautiful Janapadakalyani, took his brother aside and suggested he become a monk. Nanda accepted reluctantly. At some point, Gautama's paternal cousins Ananda and Anuruddha joined the order along with his maternal cousin Devadatta, plus their friends Bhagu and Kimbila. The principal tradition states that this happened on Gautama's first visit to Kapilavastu, but other evidence places it some years later. These men quickly became leading Shakyaputras and part of Gautama's inner circle, and both Ananda and Devadatta were to play important, though very different, roles in its history.

But what of the people they left behind? When Anuruddha told his mother that he and his brother wanted to become Shakyaputras, she replied: 'You two boys are dear to me. One day, death will separate you from me against my will. So how can I allow you to enter the homeless state while I am still alive?'[91] Eventually, she relented. But another story relates that Prajapati, Gautama's stepmother, had lost the power to cry in his absence, and recovered it while bathing her eyes in water that had flowed from his body. A final legend, usually placed somewhat later in Gautama's biography, relates that he visited his mother in the heaven to which she had departed, and milk spurted from her breasts when she heard his teaching.

These stories suggest healing of the injuries Gautama's departure had inflicted, but others give a different impression. Gautama's wife told the seven-year-old Rahula to find Gautama and make a request that carried the weight of her frustration. As his mother had directed, Rahula demanded: 'Give me my inheritance!' Gautama responded by asking Shariputra to give Rahula novice ordination. The family crisis deepened and Suddhodana stepped in. He told Gautama: 'When you went forth, it was very painful for me and I felt the same when Nanda did so. But when it came to Rahula my pain was overwhelming. A father's love for his son cuts into the skin; it cuts into the hide, the flesh, the ligaments, the bones. It reaches the marrow and it lives there.'[92]

Gautama agreed that, in future, novice ordination would require the parents' permission, but in Rahula's case he was adamant. The boy would become a monk and Shariputra and Maudgalyayana would be his tutors.

Gautama left Shakya after some months, but the commentaries relate that he returned four years later. Suddhodana was dying and Gautama hurried to his father's bedside. Then another crisis broke out. A drought had dried the Rohini, which flowed between the lands controlled by Shakya's two leading clans, the Koliyas and the Gautamas. The river had been dammed and the clans shared the water, but when the reservoir dwindled the Koliyan labourers told their Shakyan counterparts: 'If this water is diverted to both sides of the river, there won't be enough for you and us too. But our crops will ripen with just a single watering. Let us have the water.'[93] The Shakyans protested that they would be forced to beg their food from the Koliyas and insisted that they should have the water instead. Fights broke out, insults were exchanged and soon the Koliya and

Gautama warriors faced each other across the Rohini. The two sides of Gautama's family prepared for battle.

According to the commentaries, this was the occasion on which Gautama gave the powerful speech evoking his youth in Shakya when he described people as 'flopping around, like fish in water too shallow',[94] and then turning on each other. In this setting, his image of the thorn 'lodged deep in the heart' becomes an arrow that echoes the real arrows that might soon kill the soldiers if the battle proceeded. His proposed solution also gains poignancy: 'Once it is pulled out, the running is finished.'[95] According to one version of the story, Gautama then turned to the generals and asked, 'How much is water worth?' 'Very little, Reverend Sir,' they replied. 'And how much are warriors worth?' 'Warriors are beyond price.' 'It is wrong to destroy these priceless warriors for the sake of a little water,'[96] said Gautama, and the commanders were silent.

The image of fish struggling with each other in a drying river was a traditional Indian metaphor for anarchy, and texts on statecraft agreed that averting anarchy was a leader's principal responsibility. The commentary informs us that Gautama told the commanders, 'If I hadn't been here you would have unleashed a river of blood. Ask yourselves, why do you act in this way? It is because you are blindly driven by your passions and therefore live in continual conflict.'[97] Finally, he offered a kind of prayer – an aspiration for a better world that is found in the Dhammapada:

> Happy indeed we live, friendly amid the haters.
> Among men who hate we dwell free from hate.
> Happy indeed we live, healthy amid the sick.
> Among men who are sick we dwell free from sickness.
> Happy indeed we live, content amid the greedy.
> Among men who are greedy we dwell free from greed.[98]

The battle was averted.

Before his father died, we are told that Gautama gave him a final teaching and Suddhodana became an arahant. The stories of Gautama's intervention at the Rohini and on Suddhodana's deathbed suggest a further healing. He had averted a familial and national calamity and mediated between the clans, just as his father would have done; but he also contributed the perspective of Awakening and spoke with a voice of sanity at a moment of communal madness. According to the Vinaya, following Gautama's teaching at the Rohini several hundred Shakyans became monks, and Mahanama later noted that 'many distinguished young Shakyan men have gone forth in imitation of the Lord'.[99] For some, it was a matter of pride that at least one member of the family should follow suit.

Gautama often passed through Shakya in his wanderings. Its problems and the troubles of its unruly nobles, with their aristocratic pride and unstable allegiances, affected him throughout his life. In the years that followed, his field of activity included the entire Ganges Valley and beyond. It is impossible to give a chronological account of Gautama's life after his visit to Kapilavastu, as the narrative of his life recorded in the ancient sources peters out and the story is picked up again only in his final years. In place of a narrative, we must examine the main themes of Gautama's life as the Shakyaputras expanded and his activity developed in several dimensions. In the next chapter we shall explore how Gautama's encounters with other religious practitioners, especially his fellow shramanas, shaped the way his teachings developed. Then we shall consider the development of the monastic community. And then we come to Gautama's relationship with the wider society in which he lived.

5

Dialogue

The Great Wanderer

Picture a winding road in Magadha: dirt and stones beaten smooth by horses' hooves and cartwheels. Beside it are huts of mud and straw surrounded by chickens and pigs, and beyond them lie deep green rice paddies where bullock carts bump along rough tracks. The road leads from Rajagriha to the village of Nalanda and some men in mud-yellow robes walk along it, slowly and in silence, resting their eyes on the track ahead of them. They wear an air of self-possession, especially their leader: Gautama.

A few minutes later two more figures appear, also in robes. The older man is called Suppiya and the younger is his student, Brahmadatta. They are disciples of Sanjaya Belatthaputta, and it is not long since Maudgalyayana, Shariputra and their students defected to Gautama and Sanjaya died of fury. They have seen Gautama and his followers ahead of them and this has sparked a furious argument – perhaps former fellow-disciples are in the group. Suppiya criticises Gautama, but Brahmadatta defends him, and their arguments circle round and round. When dusk falls, Gautama's group pitch camp and meditate together in the dying light before lying down to sleep. But the silence is broken by the arguing voices of Suppiya and Brahmadatta.

This incident, which is related at the very start of the Discourses as they are traditionally organised, suggests the turmoil Gautama had caused among the shramanas. His teaching differed from both the Brahminical tradition of ritual power and the drastic asceticism of the Jains; but it also challenged sceptics like Sanjaya, who told his students that they couldn't even trust their senses. Challenged to say whether life continued after death, Sanjaya declared: 'I don't say it's so, I don't say it's otherwise; I don't say it's not so and I don't say it's *not* not so.'[1] Gautama called such people 'eel-wrigglers',[2] because he thought their slippery words played with ideas and evaded life's central questions. Shariputra and Maudgalyayana had become Sanjaya's students in their search for 'the deathless', perhaps hoping to find the truth by scrupulously noting the extent of their ignorance. But Gautama's teaching of dependent arising cut through all that. Like Sanjaya, Gautama didn't ask followers to trust blindly in something beyond their experience; but he also said that liberation came from *paying attention to that experience* in a new way.

The dramatic arrival of Gautama and the Shakyaputras on the wanderers' scene seems to have provoked bemused, curious, and sometimes envious or angry responses from men like Suppiya. Their world was a continual tumult of opinion, fashion, reputation and controversy, and as Gautama developed his movement, he had to be careful how he engaged with the shramanas. He could hardly ignore them or ask his followers to do so: they were his natural constituency. The 'wise and discerning'[3] Arada Kalama and Udraka Ramaputra had been the first people he thought of when he wondered who might understand his teaching, and, although he rejected many of their beliefs, he respected yogis and mystics like them. He also felt an affinity with honest seekers like the five former companions to whom he addressed his first teaching. From the time Gautama left home until his death he was proud to call himself 'a wanderer'* and loved the life of renunciation and homelessness. Like most shramanas, he was celibate, refused to handle money and had few possessions. Despite images from later art that depict a resplendent figure draped in immaculate, flowing saffron, the robes Gautama wore were usually stitched together from scraps scavenged from rubbish heaps or removed from corpses in cremation grounds (though sometimes robes were donated). He settled in one place for the rainy season when travel was virtually impossible; but for the rest of the year he was on the road, wandering from place to place and usually sleeping rough – living beneath a canopy of tree roots or in the open at the edge of a town or village. The discomfort didn't bother him. A man who came across Gautama sleeping on a spread of leaves by a cattle track in the middle of winter, probably when he was quite old, anxiously remarked: 'The winter nights are cold and this is a week of frost. Cattle have trampled the ground making it hard and there are few leaves covering it – just as there are few leaves on the trees. Your yellow robe is thin, too, and the cold Verambha wind is blowing.'⁴

Gautama replied that he slept even better than a householder with an exquisite bed and four wives to attend him because he had 'removed care deep in my heart'. By contrast with his own life, Gautama often said, household life seemed narrow and troubled.

Gautama wanted the Shakyaputras to help reform the shramana world by carrying the practice of non-attachment into their

* The term translated as 'wanderer' is *parivrajika*. Wanderers were, in effect, a subset of the shramanas.

emotions and beliefs. A wanderer called Sabhiya, who had grown weary of gurus who failed to live up to their principles, asked Gautama who truly deserved to be called 'a wanderer'. Gautama responded with his favourite tactic of infusing an old category with a new meaning by drawing out the inner values it implied. 'When you move from place to place and never lose your power to understand, then you are a wanderer. And when you lose your hating, craving, delusion, pride and your sense of [separate selfhood], then you are truly a wanderer.'[5] Conversely, he once said, 'You don't truly become a wearer of a patchwork cloak merely by dressing in one.'[6] In other words, the wanderer's renunciation of the household life needed to become a psychological and existential attitude of contentment and simplicity. Gautama argued that when people craved they constructed a fixed self, like a man building a house; liberation meant ceasing to identify with the house and eventually destroying it altogether by removing the 'ridge-pole'.[7] Gautama himself was called the Great Shramana and was considered the wanderer par excellence: 'a slender hero with antelope calves, greedless, subsisting on little food, wandering alone like a lion or serpent, without concern for sensual pleasures'.[8]

For Gautama's message to be heard both he and the Shakyaputra monks needed to exemplify his values in their interactions with other shramanas, and he counselled the monks to stay out of the shramana debates. The encounter with Suppiya and Brahmadatta was a case in point. Having spent a night listening to their argument, the monks discussed the controversy they had stirred up, concluding rather weakly, 'How great Gautama must be to arouse such conflicting views!' But Gautama remarked that the opinions of both Suppiya and Brahmadatta just reflected their biases; he was more concerned with the way the monks themselves responded to praise or criticism. 'If anyone should disparage me, the Dharma or the Sangha, you should not feel angry, resentful or upset – that would be a hindrance to you. Just explain what is incorrect. And if others praise me, don't feel elated. Just acknowledge whatever is true.'[9] If there was nothing to say, the monks should say nothing. 'Listen to the sound of water in the clefts and in the gullies. The tiny streams gurgle loudly; mighty waters flow in silence.'[10]

For Gautama, the problem with praise, blame and controversy was that the version of reality they express is unavoidably distorted by angry and selfish emotions. How can a person overcome his own views, he asked, if he is 'led on by desire, bent by his own inclination? For as he knows, so shall he speak.'[11] In his talk to the monks who overheard Suppiya and Brahmadatta, Gautama analysed the intellectual landscape of his day, including the Brahmins' philosophies as well as the shramanas'. He identified sixty-two views of life and said they were all elaborate rationalisations of underlying emotions: 'merely the feeling of those who do not know and see, the worry and vacillation of those immersed in craving'.[12] Behind even the subtlest mystical beliefs Gautama detected an emotional bias, and he once identified the psychological state underlying belief as the desire to be right as opposed to being wrong: '"It is pleasant, it is unpleasant," so people speak in the world; and based upon that, arises desire. Having seen the appearing and disappearing of material things a man makes his judgements in the world. Anger, untruth and doubts, these states arise merely because of the existence of this duality.'[13]

This was one of Gautama's most original insights. He saw that feelings of attraction and aversion didn't shape just the way shramanas discussed their ideas; they shaped the ideas themselves.

Gautama offered teachings of his own and saw that these, too, could become objects of attachment. We hear, for example, of Shakyaputra monks who had formerly been shramanas of other sects, who used Gautama's ideas as new ways to score points in the old debates. But Gautama believed that the Dharma he taught was fundamentally different from what other teachers offered. In one sense, Gautama plainly believed it was better, and he sometimes told his followers that truly Awakened people were only to be found in the Shakyaputra community. He called such declarations his 'lion's roar'.[14] But, paradoxically, the nature of that superiority lay in the fact that practising Gautama's Dharma meant letting go of clinging or grasping, including the tendency to consider oneself superior, inferior or equal to others. In other words, *what* one believes cannot be separated from *how* one believes it. He taught only what he knew to be true from his own experience, and was not attached to that knowledge because he was free from attachment in general. In that sense, he sometimes said, he had no 'views' at all in the sense of a 'false theory or groundless, unfounded opinion'.[15]

For their part, some wanderers thought Gautama simply wasn't up to the cut and thrust of debate. Nigrodha, for example, told one of Gautama's followers: 'The ascetic Gautama's wisdom has been destroyed by his solitary life. He is unused to gatherings and no good at conversation. He's out of touch, like a bison that circles around the herd but stays at the edge. If Gautama were to join us, we could confound him with a single question!'[16]

In many of the discourses various shramanas try to do just that, and (if we can believe the Buddhist accounts) the Jains, sometimes egged on by Mahavira himself, were most intent on humiliating Gautama. Both teachers claimed to be fully Enlightened and they competed for the support of the same householders and the allegiance of the same shramanas. One day, a Jain called Saccaka decided to test his belief that he could reduce any opponent in debate to a quivering heap, and declared he would take on Gautama. His arguments would 'drag [Gautama] to and fro, shake him up and thump him'.[17] Saccaka posed his question and Gautama posed one in return, which Saccaka couldn't answer. We are told that a spirit wielding a thunderbolt hovered above Saccaka, ready to split his head into seven pieces if he said nothing.* Saccaka shamefacedly admitted he was wrong. Stories like this probably served a propaganda purpose for the later Buddhists who compiled them to show their teacher's superiority to his rivals, but their drama also suggests the importance in shramana culture of defending one's position.

In a more relaxed vein, Gautama would sometimes just walk over to a shramana meeting ground if he was staying nearby. If a wanderer who respected Gautama saw him coming he might tell his companions to stop their arguments because 'Gautama likes quiet.'[18] But others showed no such sensitivity and harangued him with their views. 'A dogmatist is hard to train',[19] sighed Gautama; and he told one interlocutor, 'You regard what I am saying as foolish, but in fact you don't have the slightest understanding of what I'm telling you. That's because you are obsessed by your preconceived notions.'[20] He once compared communicating with shramanas to pouring water into a cracked pot, but he persevered in the belief that 'if they understand even a single sentence, that will lead to their welfare and happiness'.[21] Observing the tricks the shramanas used to win debates, he told his followers that a person was 'incompetent to discuss'[22] if they wandered from one thing to another, pulled the discussion off the subject, got angry, put down the questioner, ridiculed him, or seized on little mistakes.

The challenge for Gautama was to cut through the wanderers'

---

* This is the first appearance in Buddhist scriptures of Vajrapani, the 'holder of the thunderbolt', who evolved into one of the most important Mahayana Bodhisattvas. Here he is a humble *yaksha*.

ideas and opinions. In place of debate he suggested that the best method for dialogue was to seek common ground: 'Let us leave aside matters where there is no agreement. But where there is agreement, wise people should take up the matter at hand and investigate and explore it with their teacher.'[23] That common ground lay in experience, rather than ideas; but Gautama still needed to show the wanderers a way to approach their experience that got them to set their ideas aside and look at it directly. Then they would see dependent arising for themselves. Gautama clearly thought hard about how to do this, and many of his ideas seem to have been worked out in conversations with shramanas such as his searching dialogues with the wanderer Vacchagotta.

Unanswerable Questions

Gautama was staying in the Jetavana just outside Shravasti, the Shakyaputras' most important base. He finished his daily meal and sat in a small, shaded space, enclosed by palm-fronds, called the Gandhakuti ('The Fragrance Hall') where he received visitors. Vacchagotta had come to see him. Their paths had already crossed on the shramanas' circuit around the Ganges Valley, and on their previous meeting Gautama had introduced himself to Vacchagotta in a shramana park in Vaishali. Vacchagotta had heard that Gautama claimed to be omniscient and asked if it were true. Gautama told him: 'Those people misrepresent me.'[24] His most important insight, he said, was into the underlying pattern of experience.

Vacchagotta had been impressed, but on this visit he felt he must pin down what Gautama really believed about what Vacchagotta considered the fundamental issues of life. He put to Gautama the questions that were the focus of the shramana philosophies: 'Do

you believe that the world is finite? Or do you think it is infinite?'
'Vaccha, I do not hold either of those views,' replied Gautama.
'Then, do you believe that the soul and the body are the same, or
that they are different?' Gautama again said that he held neither
position. Vacchagotta asked about the nature of an Awakened person.
'Does a Tathagata exist after death? Or does he not exist? Or perhaps the answer is both of these, or neither of them?'* Again, Gautama said that he held none of the views Vacchagotta had mentioned.
Eventually, Vacchagotta exclaimed, 'I am completely bewildered by
your answers, Master Gautama, and I am losing the clarity that I
gained in our previous discussions.'[25]

Vacchagotta wasn't alone in his confusion. The shramanas passionately wanted to discover the essence of human identity, and,
by extension, the essence of existence. It seemed evident that any
dharma worth the name must cast light on the nature of the *atman*,
the eternal essence of selfhood. *That*, after all, was the key to realisation and liberation. What kind of wisdom had nothing to say
about the nature of the world when it was well known that a yogi
could discover in meditation whether or not it was infinite? And
how could they take seriously Gautama's claim to Awakening if he
couldn't answer their questions about it? Some wanderers 'sneered
and jeered'[26] at Gautama's refusal to answer these questions, and a
Shakyaputra monk called Malunkyaputta threatened to disrobe
unless he provided answers. Gautama sympathised with Vacchagotta's bewilderment and agreed that his own teaching was 'hard

---

* Vacchagotta may have been alluding to the Upanishadic belief that full liberation could only be found after death. Gautama believed that it could be found in
this life, and that the status of an Awakened person after death could not be expressed.
As Chapter 10 discusses, this became an important issue after Gautama's own
demise.

to understand', especially as 'you hold another view, pursue a different training and follow a different teacher'.[27] To grasp Gautama's meaning, Vacchagotta would need to think about spiritual life in an entirely new way.

Gautama discussed the questions Vacchagotta had asked in a reflective, even philosophical, way and sometimes analysed the ways in which the self could be understood: 'Some declare that the self is material and limited, some that it is immaterial and limited, some that it is immaterial and unlimited and some that it is material and unlimited.'[28]

More simply still, he said that the different views could be summed up as 'eternalism' and 'nihilism'. Gautama had probably learned eternalist ideas from Arada Kalama and Udraka Ramaputra, along with meditation techniques that aimed at realising the *atman* and thereby contacting the ultimate basis of all existence. Many wanderers thought this way, while others, the 'nihilists', declared that nothing had any meaning. Gautama met and engaged in dialogue with both eternalists and nihilists, but, as the eternalists were the more important force, he concentrated his attention on them.

Among the eternalists were self-mortifiers like the Jains and Ajivakas, who thought they would find salvation by regulating their actions. They were a prominent, if grisly, presence in the shramana world. In Rajagriha, for example, Gautama encountered a group of Jains who practised 'continuous standing . . . experiencing racking, piercing feelings'.[29] He had a certain respect for their efforts, which echoed his own emphasis on overcoming selfishness, and he once called their beliefs 'the highest of the views held by other sects'.[30] But he still considered self-mortification 'the wrong way . . . a state beset by vexation, despair and fever'.[31] The real challenge, for him, was not to endure pain but to discipline the mind, 'abandon the corruptions', and develop 'non-enmity, non-ill-will and a heart full of loving-kindness'.[32] Having been a self-mortifier himself, Gautama detected a buried vanity in their extravagant austerities and noted, with some amusement, that when the agonies of their rivals were praised, they complained that 'I, who am the real ascetic and self-mortifier, get no such treatment!'[33]

Gautama detected a similar vanity in the accomplishments of the yogis, even though he knew from the time with his two teachers that some were powerful meditators whose subtle ideas grew from deep experience. In his view they failed to realise that, profound though their experience was, it was partial and not a sound foundation for their philosophies. He compared them to a group of blind men who are asked to describe an elephant.[34] Each man feels only one part of the animal's body, and their descriptions match the impression this gives him – the one who has touched the tail declares that an elephant is like a broom; the man who has touched the foot says it is like a post, and so on. Not knowing what it is to see something properly, the blind men don't realise how their blindness affects them, and they draw unwarranted conclusions. This parable isn't quite the argument for the relativity of all religious views it is sometimes made out to be. Gautama considered that he had his eyes wide open, and that his dharma was reliable because it accurately described the reality he saw.

Alongside the Jains and the mystics were those who reached their eternalist conclusions through philosophy. Such a person declares his viewpoint, 'hammering it out by reason, following his own line of thought',[35] as Gautama said. Many of these speculative thinkers argued that 'that which is called a "mind" or "mentality" or "consciousness" is a Self that is permanent, stable and not subject to change and will remain so eternally'. Gautama explained the mistake made by those who sought the eternal *atman* in one of his subtlest allegories. A king hears music for the first time, drifting on the air, and is entranced. 'Bring this "*music*" to me!',[36] he commands his servants. So they hurry off and return with a lute, which they hesitantly place before him. 'That's not what I want!' the king exclaims. 'Fetch me just the sound.' 'But the lute is made of many parts,' say the servants, 'and the sound is produced when these parts are put together in the proper combination and a person plays on it.' Perplexed, the king splits the lute into a hundred pieces, then sets fire to the wood and searches among the ashes. The music must be there somewhere! The ashes blow away, and the king cries: 'What a sorry thing this lute is – whatever a lute may be. It has thoroughly tricked and deceived people.'

The king's mistake, like the wanderers' approach to the self, is the attempt to isolate the essence of something that is really a *process*. Although many wanderers valued renunciation and non-attachment, they failed to see that they still clung to things – their views, the 'rules and observances' of their sects and, above all, to the subtlest form of attachment – 'belief in self'.[37] Some, who believed the *atman* stood apart from the flux of experience, thought: 'The world and the self are the same, and after death this is what I shall be: permanent, enduring, eternal, not liable to change, and I shall remain like that for all eternity.'[38] In rejecting this belief, Gautama separated himself fundamentally from the majority of religious practitioners of his time. Once, when addressing his followers, Gautama scratched the ground, showed a piece of dirt beneath his fingernail, and declared: 'There is not even this much individual existence that is permanent, stable, eternal and not subject to change, and that will remain the same!'[39] For most shramanas this was heresy, or at least nihilism, and Gautama made his point even more dramatically when he said the same thing while holding a pellet of cow dung. Cow-worshipping Brahmins would have been deeply shocked.

Many of Gautama's contemporaries assumed that if he denied the existence of the *atman* he must identify the mind with the body and therefore be a materialist who denied karma and rebirth. He was 'a destroyer of growth',[40] they said, who taught that individuals 'don't exist' at all. This was tricky territory. According to one account, when Vacchagotta asked Gautama, 'Is there no self?' Gautama remained silent. He explained to Ananda, 'If I had answered, "There is no self," then Vacchagotta, who is already confused, would have fallen into even greater confusion. He would have thought, "*It seems that the self I once had does not now exist!*"'[41]

This was the last thing Gautama wished to communicate. He believed that in this life we inherit the karmic consequences of our actions in past lifetimes, and that when we die, our future existence will depend on our moral state in this one. Having been brought up to believe implicitly in rebirth, this didn't raise for Gautama or his listeners the metaphysical problems it brings to many who hear these ideas today. He was trying to get away from metaphysical abstractions and point people towards the kind of experience they could detect and observe. Of course, Gautama was saying, every person, including a Buddha, thinks, feels and experiences; the point is that *how* we think and feel shapes the kind of people we become in the future. The self, therefore, is a *process* and the task is to shape it. The wanderers should stop asking of life, '*What is it?*' or '*Where is the true self?*' They should look, instead, at their actual experience and ask, '*How does it work?*' Sue Hamilton succinctly encapsulates Gautama's approach: 'That you are is neither *the* question or in question: you need to forget even the issue of self-hood and understand instead how you work in a dependently originated world of experience.'[42]

That is exactly what Gautama had done before his Enlightenment. It meant forgetting the metaphysical questions that obsessed

shramanas like Vacchagotta and concentrating on the true challenge of the human condition: the difficult truth that everything
is impermanent, shifting and dependently arisen. Far from being
nihilistic, realising this shows that every instant of experience is
morally significant and offers an opportunity for liberation.

Gautama's clarity about the nature of experience contrasted
starkly with the prevailing confusion. Potthapada turned to Gautama after days of intense discussion about the nature of perception in the Shravasti debating hall between 'shramanas and Brahmins
of different schools'. He reported:

> Some said, 'A person's perception arises and ceases without any cause.
> When it arises, one is aware. When it ceases, one is not.' Then someone
> else said, 'That's not right. Perception is a person's self, which comes
> and goes. When it comes, one is aware. When it goes, one is not.'
> Someone else said, 'There are powerful holy men who can draw per-
> ception in and out of a person.' But another person argued that only
> the gods did that to people.[43]

For Gautama, all these attempts to explore consciousness were laden
with assumptions. He proposed the radical alternative of simply
paying careful attention to what perception actually felt like. When
Malukyaputta threatened to disrobe unless Gautama answered the
four questions, Gautama asked him to imagine a man who had
been shot by a poisoned arrow. This man declared that he would
not allow the arrow to be pulled out until he knew the name, family,
appearance and caste of the person who had shot him. He wanted
to know what the feathers were made of and what kind of animal
gut was used to make the string. Gautama's point was that this
information wouldn't solve the man's problem: he just needed to
pull the arrow out. By analogy, someone wanting to find a mean-

ingful response to life's unsatisfactoriness didn't need a definition of the world, the self, or even a Buddha. He or she just needed to know what would help in finding liberation. Gautama warned Vacchagotta (in images drawn from the wandering life) that the result of puzzling over his questions would be like getting lost in the wilderness or caught in a 'thicket'.[44] They would engross him in speculations that would not help with the task of transforming the mind. In fact, he once said, thinking too much about an 'unconjecturable'[45] question like the origin of the world or the extent of a Buddha's power would eventually drive you mad.

Gautama regarded belief in *atman* as a reassuring illusion, just like belief in a creator god or conviction that one is superior or inferior to others because of one's caste, intelligence or beauty. The problem with the teachings of all the rival groups, he said, was that even when their teachings claimed to counteract clinging they failed to get to grips with its most basic manifestations: 'Clinging to sense pleasures, clinging to views, clinging to rules and observances, and clinging to a doctrine of self.'[46]

All are distorted perceptions produced by an inability to face life's impermanence and contingency and the need to bolster the sense that one exists as a solid, fixed self. 'Normal experience', therefore, is a state of denial. People ignore the inevitability of death, which advances, Gautama said, like 'a mighty mountain range, scraping the sky with rocky crags . . . crushing everything before it'.[47] However real such a life might seem, it is actually an illusion, like a mass of foam floating on the Ganges, a bubble on the surface of the water, a mirage at noon, or an 'illusion at a crossroads'[48] created by a travelling magician. His task as a teacher was to puncture such illusions, which 'make us babble like fools',[49] to explain how they produce suffering and to show a way to live that accords with reality.

The best image Gautama found to describe consciousness was a fire – the image he used in preaching to the Uruvilva priests. Although we can give it a name, a fire is clearly not fixed: it changes continually as it burns. Consciousness, too, is not a thing, Gautama suggested. More precisely, he identified five elements (*khandas* or *skhandas*) that make up what we call a person's 'experience', each of which is a process in its own right. There are the physical processes that comprise 'form' and the mental processes of feeling, perceiving, volition and being conscious. Gautama called these processes 'blazing masses of fuel'[50] (*upadana-khanda*) and said that experience emerges from them just as a fire flickers up from whatever is burning. Gautama also noted that how a fire burns depends on what is burning – a log fire is one that 'burns dependent on logs',[51] and so on. A moment of consciousness also depends on the conditions from which it has arisen. We suffer because of the past conditions – the fuel – from which our minds have grown, but other conditions (especially morally worthy intentions) enable them to develop in a more positive direction.

If consciousness is a flame, then the relationship between one life and the next is like one flame lighting another. As there is no *atman* to be reincarnated, nothing substantial is transferred to the new being, but old tendencies and volitions ignite new ones, Gautama said, through the mechanism of karma. Only an Awakened person is different because he or she does not respond with craving and does not generate fresh karma. When Gautama responded to Vacchagotta's question about the fate of a Tathagata after death he again used the image of a fire, and may have pointed to a real fire beside which they were sitting.* What would Vacchagotta say if

---

* Buddhist monks are forbidden by the Vinaya to sit beside a fire, but that does not mean that Gautama was bound by such rules. In *What the Buddha Thought* Richard Gombrich identifies another passage (MN 260) in which Gautama indicates, or perhaps lights, a fire.

someone asked where the fire had gone once it was extinguished? 'The fire burns in dependence upon grass and sticks. When that's used up, if it gets no more fuel, it is reckoned as extinguished,'[52] replied Vacchagotta. The same applies to a Buddha, Gautama said. The fire of craving, which fixes identity and selfhood, is 'blown out' in the process called Nirvana.

Seeing human experience like this – as a shifting flame-like process – is a Middle Way between the views of the eternalists and the nihilists. Gautama told the wanderer Kaccanagotta: '"All exists": Kaccana, this is one extreme. "All does not exist": this is the second extreme. Without veering towards either of these two extremes, the Tathagata teaches the Dharma by the middle.'[53]

His alternative means seeing how things arise and pass away without clinging to appearances or 'taking a stand about "my self"'. A second application of the Middle Way was to offer an alternative response to pleasure and pain, which was another prominent concern of the shramanas. In 'Turning the Wheel of Truth' Gautama spoke of the Middle Way as a path between the 'devotion to sensual pleasure with regard to objects of sensual desire' – the typical preoccupation of an 'inferior, vulgar worldling', and the 'devotion to self-torment' in which the Group of Five were themselves engaged. The first was an expression of craving, and the second of aversion, but neither was a realistic response to life. However, there was an alternative: 'Not approaching either of these two extremes, the Tathagata has thoroughly understood that it is the middle way of practice that brings insight and knowledge, that conduces to peace, to direct knowledge, to awakening, to Nirvana.'[54]

In many of his dialogues with other wanderers, Gautama needed to address their ideas about identity, belief and scepticism, the appropriate response to pleasure and pain, or some other preoccupation. He did so with stories, metaphors and concepts. Faced with Saccaka's

Jain view that pain is to be cultivated and overcome in order to gain 'mastery',[55] Gautama described his own practice of self-mortification and his discovery of an alternative. And when the Brahminical wanderer Magandiya argued for the value of sense pleasures, Gautama told him of his life in the palace, his understanding of the pleasures he enjoyed there, and asserted that there is 'a delight apart from sensual pleasures . . . which surpasses divine bliss'.[56] In comparison, mere sense delight is like the relief a leper receives from cauterising his wounds, he said. He told wanderers of inner qualities that are more valuable than outer observances, and states of realisation that made their vaguely defined ideals seem paltry.

Some wanderers were overwhelmed by these ideas and embraced them wholeheartedly. Vacchagotta, for example, glimpsed a way of perceiving the world that revealed the fallacy of his prior views and understood why Gautama had refused to answer his questions. This new Dharma wasn't about beliefs, its path to realisation had nothing to do with God, its meditation practice didn't consider mystical experiences to be ends in themselves and its wisdom wasn't concerned with secret mantras and initiations. Gautama was asking Vacchagotta to abandon altogether the idea of timeless essences and the soul, and to absorb the disruptive truth that what we call 'ordinary experience' arises and passes away in dependence upon conditions.

Others were baffled. Gautama's ideas challenged the most basic assumptions of his contemporaries and many wanderers saw them as an attack. He told one such group:

You may think: 'Gautama says this to get disciples!' But let your teacher remain your teacher! Or you may think: 'He wants us to abandon our rules!' Well, let your rules remain as they are . . . There are unwholesome things that have not been abandoned and these will produce suffering in the future. I teach for the sake of abandoning such things and if you do so you will grow and develop and through your own insight and realisation you will find the fullness of perfected wisdom in this very life.[57]

When another group of self-mortifiers accused Gautama of being 'a nihilist who doesn't declare anything',[58] he replied that he was simply interested in practical results:

I don't say that all asceticism is to be pursued, or that it is not to be pursued. If, when asceticism is pursued, unskilful qualities grow and skilful qualities wane, then I tell you that that sort of asceticism should not be pursued. But if unskilful qualities wane and skilful qualities grow, then it should be pursued.

The challenge this posed to these wanderers was so different from their usual debates that they were often at a loss for a response and 'sat silent and upset, their shoulders drooped and they hung their heads, downcast and bewildered'.[59] Others, like Potthapada, felt that even if they couldn't quite make sense of Gautama's teaching in terms of their old way of thinking, they nonetheless admired it:

I don't know whether the world is eternal or not, whether the soul and body are identical or different, or what happens to an Enlightened One after his death. But the ascetic Gautama teaches a genuine, authentic, and accurate practice, grounded in the Dharma and consonant with it. Why shouldn't a knowledgeable person like me rejoice in Gautama's well-spoken words?[60]

Following the Path

When Gautama moved from explaining what he *didn't* teach to offering his distinctive message, his subject shifted from what a person *is* to what they should *do*. Gautama's favourite image for this was 'the path'. One could *follow* a path by practising his teachings; more suggestively still he said the path was something to be 'cultivated'.[61] It meant living in accordance with dependent arising by finding the Middle Way between unhelpful beliefs and attitudes. Then one's life, itself, could be a path. Gautama formulated the path in many ways, but the most fundamental version has three great stages. The first, ethics, addresses an individual's actions in the world; the second involves developing certain qualities of the mind, especially through practising meditation; and the third is wisdom – learning to see reality directly.

ETHICS

Considering behaviour in terms of dependent arising means seeing that actions have consequences. Their effects on other people and the world are easy to observe, and the simplest level of Gautama's ethical teaching is his advice that people should follow the five precepts of not killing living beings, not taking anything that has not been freely given, and avoiding sexual misconduct, untruthful speech, and intoxicants. When Gautama spoke to householders, whether they were farmers or kings, he often just advised them to practise these precepts and fulfil their responsibilities to others. One who does so, he said, 'dwells happily both in this world and the other world'.[62] The same precepts applied to his monastic followers, although many additional rules shaped the lifestyle to which they committed themselves.

But there is more to Gautama's ethical teaching than this. He inherited the idea that actions, or karma, had consequences for the individual, and most religious teachings identified these actions with external behaviour. Brahmins taught that certain ritual actions, like a fire sacrifice, are inherently good and conducting them properly brings happiness, while others are bad. Among the shramanas, the Jain teacher Mahavira taught his followers: 'You have done evil actions in the past. Exhaust them now with the performance of piercing austerities.'[63] Gautama commented on the Jain position that people didn't know whether they had existed before this lifetime, whether they had done evil in past lives, how evil karma might be eradicated, or whether they had already eradicated it. He added (rather mischievously, it seems) that if Jains feel pain now they 'must surely have done bad deeds in the past'. Or perhaps 'an evil Supreme God'[64] had created them.

Gautama's approach to karma was fundamentally different from the Brahmins' or Mahavira's and he proposed a radical redefinition of established ideas in terms of his new understanding of the dynamics of being. For him, karmic effects depended not merely on the action itself, but on the *intention*, or state of mind, with which a person acts. In fact, Gautama said, the operation of the mind is itself a kind of action. If one acts from craving, hatred or ignorance (or even dwells on such states), these tendencies grow stronger until they etch themselves into one's character, like 'a rock carving'.[65] Conversely, a generous or honest action reinforces the tendency to be a generous or honest person.

To practise ethics in this expanded sense means not just regulating one's actions but knowing and 'purifying' one's motivations. This is a 'skill', like those of the craftsmen Gautama admired, so he called actions rooted in states such as contentment, kindness and wisdom 'skilful', and those rooted in craving, hatred and ignorance 'unskilful'. Unskilful actions, Gautama considered, are misguided efforts to achieve happiness that in fact lead to suffering because they prioritise selfish concerns and set one at odds with reality. Skilful actions, however, bring positive consequences, whether one wants to be happy in this life, gain a fortunate rebirth, or find Enlightenment. As Gautama suggested in one of his best-known sayings:

> If one speaks or acts with an impure mind, suffering follows even as the cartwheel follows the hoof of the ox drawing the cart . . .
>
> If one speaks or acts with a pure mind, happiness follows like a shadow that never departs.[66]

The precepts (which are formulated in various lists and versions) describe how a person who is wholly skilful naturally acts. Such people are 'seers of dependent origination, skilled in action and its results'.[67] For others, the precepts are 'training principles' that educate the ethical sensibility until one automatically recoils from unethical behaviour 'just as a young, tender infant lying prone at once draws back when he puts his hand or foot on a live coal'.[68] To some shramanas, this focus on mental states suggested that Gautama believed that *any* action is permissible if one's motivation is correct. Parodying the Buddhist position, a Jain text proposes that 'if someone puts a child on a spit and roasts it on a fire . . . it would be fit for Buddhists to [eat]'.[69] In fact, Gautama expected people to use their intelligence to assess their motivations and understand the situation. Gentle though this sounds, Gautama thought ethics the most demanding of all practices, and he told one group of monks that whatever happened to them – 'even if bandits were to sever you savagely with a two-handed saw' – they should reflect: 'Our minds will remain unaffected and we will not speak any harsh words. We shall regard that person with a mind suffused with compassion and loving-kindness, without any hostility.'[70]

Gautama disagreed with those of his contemporaries who taught that 'Whatever a person experiences ... is caused by what happened in the past.'[71]* A success or a disaster may be the result of past karma, but one cannot say for sure; that is more than 'one knows by oneself [or] what is considered to be true in the world'. But he was certain that unskilful actions committed now bring future suffering. In that sense, while the precepts aren't commandments, Gautama did consider his ethical principles 'an eternal law'.[72] To behave ethically, he said, is to act in accordance with Dharma on many levels, from fulfilling one's responsibilities to matching the underlying nature of reality.

DEVELOPING THE MIND

The specific definition of the second stage of Gautama's path – 'samadhi' – is the process known in English as 'meditation'. This means the various yogic techniques Gautama taught, some of which he seems to have borrowed from other traditions and some of which he devised himself. But meditation itself is an aspect of a broader undertaking: developing the mind so that it becomes increasingly skilful.

When a wanderer called Kundalayi, who knew the shramana

---

* He would also have disagreed with those later Buddhists who believe that everything that befalls a person can be ascribed to the karma of a previous life. Buddhaghosha developed this idea in his notion that there are five *niyamas*, or orders of conditionality.

teachings well, asked Gautama 'What benefit do you live for?'[73] Gautama replied by explaining the path to knowledge and liberation. First one needs to act ethically and live simply without getting excited by agreeable experiences, or dejected because of disagreeable ones. Then comes a process of inner cultivation that includes seven 'factors of Awakening' (*bojjangas/bodhiyangas*) which 'conduce to direct knowledge, Enlightenment, Nirvana'. These factors are mindfulness, investigation of the mind, energy, joy, tranquillity, absorption and equanimity. The list appears frequently in the Discourses and shows how Gautama understood the process of mental development.

Mindfulness

Following Gautama's path essentially means becoming more aware and therefore making more skilful choices. To this end he instructed his followers in a rigorous training programme:

> In moving forwards and turning back, a monk acts in full awareness; in looking ahead and looking around . . . in bending and straightening his limbs . . . in wearing his inner and outer robes and carrying his alms bowl . . . in eating, drinking, chewing, swallowing . . . defecating and urinating . . . walking, standing, sitting, falling asleep, waking up, speaking and keeping silent . . . a monk acts in full awareness.[74]

A visitor to the Jetavana (or a similar Shakyaputra centre) would encounter monks sitting quietly or pacing to and fro with quiet deliberation, creating an atmosphere that was quite unlike the gatherings of other shramanas who, Gautama noted, make 'a great clamour when they come together and engage in all kinds of unedifying conversation'.[75] Gautama often advised the monks to 'guard the sense doors', by which he meant avoiding distractions and reducing stimulation.

These were all ways to develop the first Awakening Factor of mindfulness: the simple activity of paying attention to what is happening in one's immediate experience and setting aside one's likes, dislikes and ideas about reality. Gautama clarified 'immediate experience' by dividing it into four areas – the body, feelings, thoughts, and what he called 'dharmas'. Mindfulness of the body means paying attention to the input of the senses through breath awareness and the physical sensations of walking, eating and so on. Awareness of feelings means noticing whether an experience or sensation 'feels' pleasant, or unpleasant, or neutral – and the emotions such as excitement, sadness, anxiety and fear that arise in response to those feelings. Awareness of thoughts simply means noting the thoughts that arise and recognising one's mental condition. And mindfulness of dharmas means seeing thoughts and feelings in terms of the underlying patterns that Gautama identified and explained in his teachings, and their map of how the mind works and how it can change.

Mindfulness of feelings is the key to guiding experience in Gautama's view, and this is the core of his approach to what we would call 'psychology'. Everyone experiences both pleasure and pain, and the ordinary human condition is to pursue one and avoid the other. For example, he once explained, when an ordinary person experiences pain, they just want it to go away, and they typically 'worry and feel distraught' when it doesn't. As a result, they experience a second 'mental' pain in addition to the physical sensation. 'It is as if they were pierced by an arrow, and then immediately afterwards by a second.'[76] The second arrow comes because people 'resist and resent' their pain until, eventually, resistance and resentment become 'underlying tendencies' that are part of one's character. But this isn't inevitable. Mindfulness can enable one to accept pain for what it is – an unpleasant sensation. When Gautama visited a 'ward' for sick monks he told the patients that if they felt pain they should simply reflect: 'There has arisen in me a feeling of pain.'[77] One who can practise mindfulness in such circumstances 'does not sorrow, grieve, or lament, does not beat his breast or become distraught', Gautama said, and consequently, 'he feels one feeling: a bodily one, not a mental one'.[78]

Awareness of pleasant experiences allows one to notice and even enjoy them without becoming attached or intoxicated. That goes against the mind's tendency to follow the pulls of the senses and seek distraction, and Gautama compared the discipline of remaining mindful to tying a wild animal to a post. He once suggested that the monks imagine themselves in the position of a man carrying a bowl of oil on his head when someone calls out, 'Over here! The most beautiful girl in the land is singing and dancing!'[79] Meanwhile another man, holding a sword, follows behind ready to cut off his head if he spills a drop.

Although mindfulness is the first of the Awakening Factors, it is a key to the whole path, and in his most important discourse on mindfulness Gautama called it 'a path leading directly to the purification of beings, the disappearance of pain and discontent, to finding the proper way, to the direct experience of Nirvana'.[80] Just as salt is always useful in preparing food, said Gautama, 'mindfulness is always useful'[81] at every stage and whatever is happening. It allows one to practise in a balanced way, navigating like a careful chariot driver rather than being pulled off course by temperamental preferences, and it brings understanding of the truth 'without reference to faith, personal preferences, oral tradition, reasoned reflection or abstract theoretical pondering'.[82]

Investigating Experience

It is likely that Gautama practised mindfulness before his Enlightenment, but the Discourses only describe it in passing. However, as we have seen, they do describe how he had explored his consciousness, learned to identify the emotional colouring of his thoughts and feelings, and noted their effects on his state of mind. He urged his followers to do the same in developing the second Awakening Factor by 'inspecting, distinguishing and investigating [the mind] with wisdom'[83] (*dharma-viccaya*). This investigation particularly involves identifying one's states of mind as skilful or unskilful, and Buddhist tradition developed an entire literature, the Abhidharma, devoted principally to analysing mental states in this way.* However, it also entails being sensitive to emotions and honestly admitting what they are, which requires what we would call 'self-awareness'. Here and there, we encounter remarkable instances of this quality, such as the monk Talaputa's dialogue with his mind:

> Not now will you deceive me again and again, time after time showing me a masque . . . you sport with me as though with a madman. And yet, how have I ever failed you, mind?
>
> Formerly this mind wandered where it wished, where it liked, as it pleased. Now I shall control it, as the hook-holder controls an elephant rut.[84]

---

* Buddhist tradition made the Abhidharma (Sanskrit), or Abhidhamma (Pali), the third division of the Buddhist scriptures, along with the Discourses (the Sutta Pitaka) and the monastic Discipline (the Vinaya Pitaka). It is traditionally said that Gautama devised the Abhidharma in the period following his Enlightenment, but as the Abhidharma isn't mentioned in the Discourses scholars conclude that it was compiled in later centuries.

Such passages are striking because they evoke a modern way of relating to experience. More commonly we find that the process of self-examination is supported by the social context in which the monks lived and practised. They learned about themselves and developed an ethical measure by listening to their teachers, sharing their lives with their friends and confessing to groups of monks.

Energy

The focus on mindful observation and investigation of experience gave Gautama's approach to mental development a new subtlety. Unlike the 'fatalistic' Ajivakas, Gautama thought people could change their states of mind if they were 'moved by a sense of urgency' and made 'a suitable effort'.[85] The Shakyaputras were famed for their persistence and determination, and Gautama's aunt Prajapati describes seeing 'the disciples all together, putting forth energy, resolute, always with strong effort'.[86] But Gautama intended the Shakyaputra lifestyle to be a Middle Way between the self-torture of the Ajivakas and Jains, for whom the mind and the body were enemies, and the self-indulgence of men like the Brahminical wanderer, Magandiya, for whom Nirvana meant no more than realising that 'I am healthy and happy and nothing afflicts me.'[87]

Sometimes the practitioner needs to engage in 'determined striving' to overcome a problem, and sometimes he should just 'look on with equanimity'.[88] Gautama explained this to Sona, a former lute-player, who came to him one day having practised walking meditation so intensively that the soles of his feet were split and bleeding. Using an image from Sona's former life, Gautama reminded him that his lute had been unplayable if the strings were too taut or too loose: 'Similarly, Sona, if energy is applied too forcefully it will lead to restlessness, and if energy is too lax it will lead to lassitude. Therefore, keep your energy in balance, penetrate to a balance of the spiritual faculties, and there seize your object.'[89]

Joy

The realisation that a certain kind of 'non-sensual' happiness could support spiritual development was a key insight on Gautama's own journey, and he taught that, far from being an enemy to spiritual practice, it was a natural result. One who develops the first three Awakening Factors and works skilfully with his or her mind will experience a deep sense of satisfaction and joy. The term used here is *priti*, which is the 'bliss' associated with meditative concentration, and later Buddhists described it in considerable detail: 'The lesser thrill is only able to raise the hairs of the body; the momentary rapture is like the production of lightning moment by moment; like waves on the seashore, the flooding rapture descends on the body and breaks; the transporting rapture lifts the body into the air.'[90]

More generally, *priti* suggests a range of deeply positive states that can be experienced outside meditation as well as within it. Gautama warned that ordinary enjoyments that are prompted by sense pleasures bring suffering in their wake, and in their place he praised non-sensual happiness: the 'bliss of renunciation, seclusion [and] peace'[91] that springs from the mind itself. The higher happiness drove out the lesser, 'just as a carpenter uses a sharper peg to drive out a blunt one',[92] he said. He told the Rajagriha Jains that in his early life he had been able to let go of the attraction of sensual pleasures only when he had experienced deep meditation and tasted 'the rapture and pleasure that is apart from sensual pleasures'.[93]

The practitioner could pass from the 'blameless bliss'[94] of a clear conscience, to the 'unsullied bliss' of living contentedly, and then progress through the increasingly refined happiness that flowed from mindfulness, leaving behind distractions, experiencing deep meditation and understanding the nature of reality. Gautama compared a mind that is free from attachment to 'a forest deer wandering in the forest wilds: he walks . . . without fear. Why is that? Because he is out of the hunter's range.'[95]

Gautama's disciples often spoke of their deep joy. The monk Pakkha declared that he had 'reached happiness through happiness',[96] while the nun Sumangalamata, having 'destroyed desire and hatred with a sizzling sound', simply meditated with the thought, 'Oh, the happiness!'[97] Observing a Shakyaputra gathering, another king (Prasenajit) declared that their happiness distinguished them from the 'lean and wretched' wanderers of other sects: 'Here I see monks smiling and cheerful, sincerely joyful, plainly delighting, their faculties fresh, living at ease, unruffled, subsisting on what others give and abiding with minds as aloof as a wild deer's.'[98]

Tranquillity

After joy comes *prashrabdi*: a sense of 'calmness, tranquillity, repose and serenity'[99] that suffuses both the mind and the body, and brings mental refinement, sensitivity and malleability. Gautama compared this mental ease to the experience of a cowherd who has put in the effort needed to keep his cattle safe and fed and can 'simply relax under the shade of a tree or out in the open, quietly paying attention to his cows'.[100] The energy produced in earlier stages is channelled in ways that suggest psychological integration, or perhaps the unification of the body's subtle energies discussed in traditions like yoga and tantra.

'When the mind is joyful, the body becomes tranquil, and when the body is tranquil one experiences happiness',[101] Gautama said, and as the practitioner gathers momentum, 'effort' becomes less important:

> It is a natural law that joy will arise in one who is glad at heart. For one who is joyful, there is no need for an act of will. It is a natural law that the body will be serene in one who is joyful ... that one who is serene will feel happiness ... for one who is happy that the mind will be concentrated ... for one with a concentrated mind to know and see things as they really are.[102]

Concentration

While the early Awakening Factors can occur at any time, the later ones apply to the realm of meditation which, for Gautama, meant the conscious development of concentrated and skilful states of mind. He often instructed his disciples to 'sit down cross-legged, holding body erect and keeping mindfulness to the fore',[103] but he was a flexible and creative meditation teacher who constantly devised new practices and adapted old ones, always conscious that their aim was liberation from craving and awakening to reality. In time, his senior disciples 'taught and instructed'[104] novices themselves.

The Discourses describe Brahmins and shramanas who follow a vast range of beliefs and practices, but only a handful mention that they engage in something that could be termed 'meditation', and one listener remarks of Gautama's meditation teaching: 'I do not see this division of Aryan concentration fulfilled thus anywhere among the ascetics and Brahmins of other schools.'[105] This leads scholars like Johannes Bronkhorst to conclude that, at least in its principal features, 'Buddhist meditation was introduced by ... the historical Buddha',[106] rather than being drawn from an earlier spiritual tradition.

One feature of meditation that probably wasn't original to Gautama is the practice of concentrating the mind, which Buddhist tradition termed *samatha*. But the way Gautama discussed concentration reflects the distinctive role he gave to mindfulness: he avoided philosophical or metaphysical ideas and carefully described what was happening in the mind. He noted the tendency for attention to jump from one thing to another and get lost in a torrent of discursive thoughts, and said this was because it was being driven by craving, aversion and associated 'hindrances'. Like others, he advised meditators to focus on an object such as the breath, and return the mind to it again and again, until the hindrances died down; and in teaching breath awareness and loving-kindness meditation Gautama probably drew on existing techniques. But he taught them with a distinctive psychological subtlety, directing meditators to focus on an object that suited their temperaments or addressed unhelpful propensities. Attitudes and motivations were always more important for Gautama than techniques or experiences, and perhaps the most distinctive feature of his teaching was the advice that meditators should avoid being distracted by the 'bark' of powerful meditative states from the 'heartwood'[107] of liberation.

The early stages of concentration involve stabilising attention. Then, in Gautama's meditation teaching, come deepening levels of concentration as the mind passes through the absorptions – the four dhyanas. He compared the integration and concentration of dhyana to 'a swiftly running river flowing down from the mountains . . . in which the channels leading water away from the main current had been closed off and the current is undiffused',[108] and noted that in these states, powerful and highly skilful 'faculties' and 'powers' become available to the mind, such as faith, energy, mindfulness and wisdom. Whether or not the very idea of dhyana was original, Gautama certainly stressed its importance and gave it a vital role in his account of the path to Awakening.

A second class of practices – 'insight' or *vipassana* meditation – accompanies concentration and connects it to Awakening. Vipassana practices involve examining experience to discern its true nature, and, by extension, the nature of all conditioned things. Many of these practices explore experience in the light of one of Gautama's analyses of consciousness, but at the root of all of them is contemplation of the unsatisfactory, impermanent or insubstantial nature of existence. In some later Buddhist traditions, concentration and insight were seen as separate endeavours and one was stressed at the expense of the other; but in the Discourses they go together. Gautama teaches concentration as a way to clear the mind and look deeply into it, while insight reflection is a way of seeing its true nature.

Equanimity

Gautama suggested that progress at each stage of the path follows a distinctive pattern: becoming aware of thoughts and feelings foreshadows awareness of reality, and stilling the mind in dhyana anticipates the complete stilling of Nirvana. As Rupert Gethin puts it: 'The laws that govern such progress are the same at any point along the path, for the principles that underlie the workings of the mind are always the same'.[109] Thus, the practice of being mindful and clearly aware involves seeing things for what they are and leaving aside partial responses. That is the seed of even-mindedness or 'equanimity' (*upeksha*), which is to the capacity to encompass a situation fully and unselfishly, maintaining composure whatever happens: 'Like a solid rock [that] cannot be shaken by the wind, so the spiritually mature person is unmoved by praise or blame.'[110]

Equanimity is far from indifference. Gautama presented it as a state of poise in which the Awakening Factors are perfectly balanced, and the culmination of a process of emotional maturation which starts with the cultivation of loving-kindness. In contrast to the trance-like states taught by Gautama's yogic teachers, in the third and fourth dhyanas the mind is acutely clear and sensitive, mindful and equanimous. The mind reaches a point of stillness and clarity, beyond clinging, in which one lets experiences arise and fall like 'raindrops on a slightly sloping lotus leaf'.[111]

WISDOM AND REALISATION

Equanimity prepares for and merges into wisdom, the third stage of Gautama's Threefold Path: 'Purified by equanimity and mindfulness, preceded by investigation of phenomena, I say, is the release through understanding, the destruction of ignorance.'[112]

Cultivating wisdom is in itself a path that accompanies and completes those of moral practice and mental development. Gautama told his followers to start by simply listening to his account of reality, which is so different from the familiar one. Then they should reflect on it, take in its implications and explore ways of thinking and acting that accord with it. Finally, they should meditate on it, turning over the teachings when they were deeply concentrated, looking directly at their experience to see for themselves that it was dependently arisen and therefore impermanent, insubstantial and unsatisfactory.

This means reflecting on actual experience, examining motivations, and rooting out beliefs and attitudes that spring from selfish emotions. Even advanced practitioners should continually ask them-

selves: 'Is there any obsession that might so consume my awareness that I cannot know or see things as they really are?'[113] Gautama's teachings, then, suggest new ways of seeing the world, and
the practitioner learns to look at life in this way. It's a matter of
'seeing through' the Buddha's eyes until one perceives reality directly,
at which point the teachings are simply descriptions of the practitioner's own experience. At that point, Gautama said, a person is
'independent in the Dharma'.

How *do* wise people see the world? What is it like to live entirely
free from craving or attachment? This is what Gautama conveyed to
Bahiya in the meeting that opened this book. For many years Bahiya
had meditated in a cave overlooking the Arabian Sea and was revered
as an accomplished holy man. He had practised with great intensity
and at last thought, 'Perhaps I have finally gained Awakening.' The
ghost of a deceased relative whispered to him, 'Bahiya, you haven't
found Awakening, and you aren't even on the path that leads to it.'
Gautama had come to the same realisation when he trained under
the two teachers. Bahiya asked: 'Does anyone in the world know the
path?' The ghost replied: 'In a distant country, in the city of Shravasti,
lives an Fully Enlightened One, who teaches dharma for realisation.'

The teaching Bahiya eventually received from Gautama transformed him:

Bahiya, you should train yourself thus: in the seen will be merely
what is seen. In the heard will be merely what is heard. In the sensed
will be merely what is sensed. In the cognised will be merely what is
cognised. In this way should you should train yourself . . . Then, Bahiya,
you are not 'in that' then. When you are not 'in that', then you will
be neither here nor beyond nor between the two. Just this, is the end
of suffering.[114]

Elsewhere, Gautama explains his meaning more fully. Driven by craving, aversion and delusion, an ordinary person 'perceives the seen, the heard, the sensed [and so on], and identifies himself with what he perceives. He thinks the objects of his sense are "mine" and takes delight in them.'[115] But this distorts experience because 'in thinking of an object in egotistical terms it becomes otherwise'.[116] The alternative is to let the seen be the seen and the heard be the heard, free from a restrictive sense of 'you', and to live happily as part of an impermanent, shifting reality. This is not so much a matter of 'living in the present' as engaging with the whole of experience, including sensations, memories and imaginings, without clinging to it: 'Let go of the past, let go of the future, let go of the present, transcending becoming.'[117] *That* is wisdom and the end of suffering.

If that sounds straightforward, the result is mysterious because it leaves behind familiar ways of being. Gautama said that following his Awakening his experience was 'free from craving, free from hatred, and free from ignorance' and in that sense 'unconditioned'.[118] His experience no longer depended on the senses, the elements, space or time, and flowed in a stream of skilful states. Being free of clinging, a wholly skilful person also ceases to create fresh karma, and even difficult experiences leave no impression, like a 'carving in water',[119] rather than an etching in rock. As Gautama's explanation to Vacchagotta suggests, he was now beyond the forces that led to rebirth and thereby rendered mysterious. He told Upasiva, 'There is no way of measuring one who has gone out. When all conditions are removed, all ways of telling are removed.'[120]

Another dimension of Awakening is also important. The Discourses often use negative language to describe the path: eradicating craving, overcoming hatred, destroying ignorance and so on. Many later Buddhists, in the movement called Mahayana, felt that this way of speaking failed to match the powerful emotional positivity of Gautama and other Enlightened masters, whose lives were a creative flow of generosity, kindness and energy. Mahayana teachings stressed that, in addition to wisdom, compassion could be a path to Awakening, and Richard Gombrich argues that, in fact, some discourses also declare 'love, compassion, empathetic joy and equanimity to be direct routes to Nirvana'.[121] Their message was misunderstood and then ignored, he thinks, but isolated texts retain the memory of Gautama's teaching that 'The monk who dwells in kindness, with faith in the Buddha's teaching, may attain the peaceful state, the blissful cessation of conditioning.'[122]

The third time Vacchagotta met Gautama was in Rajagriha. Their previous encounter had been overwhelming, but he could scarcely believe that others had achieved the depth of insight he had seen in Gautama. He asked: 'Apart from you, have any of those who follow your teachings achieved this liberation for themselves, through their own direct knowledge, so that they live within it right now?'[123] Gautama replied that many people (nuns as well as monks, and householders as well as renunciants) had realised his teachings. Vacchagotta was astounded by the scope of this new movement. 'Magnificent, Master Gautama! Magnificent! ... Just as the river Ganges flows towards the sea, your whole community slopes towards Nirvana.'

Finally, Vacchagotta decided to become a Shakyaputra and, despite his years as a shramana, he was happy to be a probationary monk for even longer than the usual period. Eventually he became an arahant and expressed his experience in a verse: 'I possess the triple knowledge. I am a great meditator, skilled in the calming of the mind. I have obtained the true goal. The Buddha's teaching has been done.'[124]

So far as we know, Vacchagotta never met Gautama again, but

he once asked some monks who were on their way to visit Gautama to pass on his overwhelming gratitude:

> 'Pay homage in my name and with your heads at the Blessed One's feet; say, "Venerable sir, the monk Vacchagotta pays homage." Then say, "The Blessed One has been worshipped by me, the Sublime One has been worshipped by me."'[125]

6

The Homeless Community

Sons of the Shakyan

As Gautama neared death, an important discourse relates, Mara reminded him of a conversation that occurred shortly after his Awakening. Mara tried to dissuade him from teaching, but Gautama declared that he had work to do. He would not attain Parinirvana ('final Nirvana') until his followers included monks, nuns, and male and female householders who were

> realised disciples, accomplished, experienced, learned . . . bearers of the Truth, practised in the teaching and its subtleties, conducting themselves properly and living in accordance with the Truth . . . learning what their teachers say and proclaiming it, teaching it, making it known, substantiating it, demonstrating it, explaining it, making it clear . . . refuting contrary teachings . . . and teaching the Truth and its wonders . . . And this spiritual practice has become successful and prosperous, spreading far, popular, widespread [and] renowned among men.[1]

Gautama called his movement 'the community of the four quarters' because its scope extended universally to the four great continents of the world, each with its territory, gods and king. Unlike the Brahminical teachers who only shared their teachings with an inner circle of disciples, Gautama re-imagined how everyone could live, not just religious specialists. But intensive meditation requires seclusion, and the 'noble' life Gautama advocated meant renouncing mainstream values. So most who were serious about realising his teachings 'went forth' from household life and took up a 'monastic' life under his tutelage. They became men or women 'of the four quarters' in the further sense of travelling wherever they wished, living without conflicts and being 'pleased with whatever came [their] way'.[2] This chapter will explore the monastic wing of Gautama's movement, while the lives of his householder followers and the movement's wider social impact are the subject of the next.

It isn't easy to get a clear picture of the early monastic community, as distinct from what it later became. Gautama's conversation with Mara gives the impression that he was establishing a carefully regulated body with clear structures and systems geared to training disciples in a correct understanding of the teaching and passing it on accurately. The same impression comes from the Vinaya, which lists the monastic rules and relates the circumstances in which Gautama laid them down. However, scholars are convinced that many of the rules were introduced long after Gautama and that the Vinaya's compilers projected their own regulated lifestyles onto those of Gautama's immediate disciples.

We get a different impression of how the early monks lived from some of the discourses that were set down earliest. In a famous passage from the Sutta Nipata collection, Gautama urges the monks to follow a life of solitary wandering and meditation:

> Affection comes into being for one who has associations; following on from affection, this misery arises. Seeing the peril which is born from affection, one should wander solitary as a rhinoceros horn . . .

As a deer which is not tied up goes wherever it wishes in the forest for pasture, an understanding man, having regard for his independence, should wander solitary as a rhinoceros horn . . .

As an elephant with massive shoulders . . . may leave the herds and live as it pleases in the forest, one should wander solitary as a rhinoceros horn.

It is an impossibility for one who delights in company to obtain even temporary release. Having heard the voice of the sun's kinsman [i.e. Gautama], one should wander solitary as a rhinoceros horn.[3]

These evocative verses suggest that the early Shakyaputras were more individualistic, less institutionalised and less regulated than later Buddhist monks. Other passages in the Sutta Nipata give the same impression, and we also have the *Theragatha*: an extraordinary collection of verses composed by Gautama's Enlightened male disciples that offers glimpses of their daily existence.

Gautama urged the monks and nuns to be their own 'islands of refuge'.[4] Being ordained was a freely chosen personal commitment and the community was an association of self-reliant individuals who initially needed relatively few rules to govern them. In the early days, the Shakyaputras probably just followed the conventions of shramana life. Not being married, they were celibate; having left the household life, in which rank and property were so important, they had no possessions or careers; and they did not observe caste distinctions or household rituals. Over and above this common lifestyle, Gautama seems to have decided for himself how to live, and his disciples probably followed his example.

One discourse represents Gautama looking back ruefully on the simplicity of these arrangements at a time when the rules had multiplied: 'At one time I just said to the monks, "I eat only one meal a day and that leaves me healthy, strong and contented. Do the same yourselves, and you will enjoy those benefits, too." There was no need for me to say any more; I just had to raise the issue.'[5]

Perhaps it was never quite that simple. We read elsewhere that when Gautama proposed this rule the monk Bhaddali was so upset that he refused to follow it.[6] Nonetheless, in this founding period Gautama probably just told the monks that they should own nothing beyond the 'four requisites' that addressed their basic needs for clothing (three simple robes); food (an alms bowl); shelter (they should live outdoors); and medicine (only cow's urine was allowed). Over the years, Gautama defined more precisely what he had in mind for each of these areas, but the guiding principle remained that Shakyaputras should be as free as possible to practise his teachings. Having a robe differentiated them from wanderers who went naked, but Gautama insisted that it should be a patchwork of discarded rags; and he told them to cut their hair off rather than letting it grow in thick, matted locks (like Brahmin ascetics), and to shave it with a razor rather than plucking it out (like the Jains).

The Shakyaputra lifestyle was intended to support non-attachment, and homelessness was especially important. Gautama constantly encouraged the monks to live on the road, travelling from place to place and, at least to start with, sleeping rough rather than staying in buildings. Here, too, Gautama struck a balance. Monks stayed put during the rainy season and could remain near a village for a period of time, rather than moving on every day as Jain wanderers did. It was still a tough existence. The 'shaven-headed, unsightly, reviled'[7] monks were separated from mainstream society, yet still dependent on it, and they could easily find themselves worrying, 'Where shall I find food, and what shall I be given? How badly I slept last night – I wonder where I will sleep tonight?'[8] But this was all part of the training, Gautama explained:

A monk who stands firm in the ancient traditions of the Noble Ones should be content with whatever lodging he finds. He doesn't do anything unseemly or inappropriate for the sake of a comfortable place to stay. If he finds nowhere he doesn't become agitated. If he does find somewhere he uses it without intoxication or regrets and doesn't become tied to it, because he sees the drawbacks of attachment.[9]

The rule that monks should only eat food they were given rather than gathering their own (which Jain monks could do), was another aspect of renunciation. Usually, villagers donated cooked rice, barley, wheat, beans, rye, fruit and vegetables, and wealthier householders might give food they enjoyed themselves such as 'pork cooked in jujube fruit juice', or 'cooked rice with dark seeds picked out, served with various soups and sauces'.[10] Strict vegetarianism wasn't an option, as meat was popular, and the monks were permitted to accept it provided they had not 'seen, heard or suspected'[11] that the animal was slaughtered specifically for their benefit. The basic principle was that they should eat what they were given, and the arch-renunciant Mahakasyapa took this to an extreme when he received food from a leper whose finger fell into the bowl. 'I ate the morsel and did not feel the least disgust',[12] he recalled. As monks could eat only food donated by householders they had to stay near villages, or at least farmsteads, instead of disappearing into the wilds and leaving society altogether. That made 'the welfare of the multitude'[13] a natural part of their concerns. A monk might teach the villagers after eating and then re-enter the jungle or clamber up to his cave and plunge back into meditation.

Wilderness

Gautama loved wilderness living all his days, and he loved the open road. 'When I am travelling along a road and see no one in front or behind me, then I feel at ease, even when I am urinating or defecating',[14] he once said. King Prasenajit remarked that Gautama had been 'a remote forest dweller for a long time'[15] and he was known for his affinity with wild animals, trees and forest spirits. But his teaching work took him away from the forest. Gautama once remarked that the two things he most often found himself thinking about were the 'the welfare of beings' and 'solitude'.[16] These are seemingly contrary impulses and he sometimes seems tugged in different directions by his love of wilderness living and his desire to share the Dharma. Gautama became a public figure who was accompanied on his travels by 'a multitude of followers'[17] and drew crowds of householders wherever he went.

But he kept contact with wilderness life through periods of solitary retreat lasting three or four months in which he told the monks that he 'should not be approached by anyone except the one who brings the alms food'.[18] Retreats helped Gautama maintain the freshness of his experience and at the end of one he said that he had been 'inhabiting the region in which I dwelt when I had newly realised Awakening'.[19] However, as time went by, even the retreats were disrupted. Once, when Gautama was meditating in a forest grove, he was disturbed by the noise of a large crowd of visitors. When his attendant explained that they had come to pay their respects, Gautama sternly replied, 'I have no interest in homage; my concern is with renunciation!'[20]

To get away, Gautama sometimes just 'set out on tour, without a companion', telling no one what he was doing. Ananda commented: 'Whenever the Blessed One sets out like that he wishes to be alone [and] should not be followed.'[21] As the Discourses record Gautama's talks and conversations they offer few glimpses of these times, but we do hear of people who just stumbled across him. Once, some boys were collecting firewood when they saw Gautama and ran to fetch their Brahmin teacher, who arrived to find a figure rapt in unearthly concentration. The Brahmin may have sat watching for many hours and when Gautama emerged from his absorption he said:

> Deep in the bowels of the terror-filled forest,
> Immersed in the empty and desolate woods,
> Without flinching at all, steadfast, compelling
> You meditate, monk, in an exquisite way.
> Where nothing is sung and nothing is sounded,
> Alone in the forest, a wood-dwelling sage,
> This appears to me something remarkable:
> That you live in the woods – alone – glad-minded!

The Brahmin asked if Gautama was seeking to 'attain Brahma', like a yogi of his own tradition. But Gautama replied that he needed no one – not even 'God' – to keep him company:

> Having gained the sublime, highest Awakening,
> I meditate, priest, in ripened seclusion.[22]

Gautama thought the experience of wandering and solitude was vital for every monk who could manage it, even novices. Gautama had made his breakthrough in the wilderness and associated it with the peace, clarity and freedom from distractions he considered necessary for intensive meditation and the attainment of Nirvana.

Sometimes, after a talk in which he outlined the theory of dharma practice, he exclaimed: 'There are these roots of trees; these empty huts. Meditate, monks, do not delay or else you will regret it later!'[23]

The 'seclusion' of the forest life didn't necessarily mean complete isolation. Gautama encouraged the monks to travel with a friend if they could find 'a zealous companion, an associate of good disposition'.[24] For some, that was a viable alternative to either complete solitude or the distractions of communal living; but, as the monk Yasoja remarked: 'One monk alone is like Brahma, two together are like two gods; three are like a village; more than this are a tumult.'[25] The distractions of the village were a greater problem, and a monk who entered a village on his alms round was expected to look down at the ground one plough-length ahead of him and be on his guard for distractions, as if he were 'walking barefoot on thorny ground'.[26]

Alone or with a friend, the wilderness contained many hardships and dangers, and Gautama told the monks to reflect:

> While I am living in the wilderness a snake or a centipede might bite me, or a scorpion might sting me. That would be how my death would come about. I might fall. My food might trouble me. I might find myself coughing up bile or phlegm. I might encounter a lion, a tiger, a leopard, a bear or a hyena, and they might kill me. I might meet youths on their way to committing a crime, and they might take my life. And the wilderness also contains vicious spirits who could kill me.[27]

The main difficulties of wilderness life the monks mention in the *Theragatha* are gnats, mosquitoes, hunger and discomfort. 'Brought low by colic, dwelling in a grove in a forest where there is little food and the conditions are harsh, how will you manage, monk?' Vakkali is asked. He replies, 'I shall live here come what may, filling the body with joy and happiness and enduring what is difficult.'[28] The struggles of wilderness living were part of the monks' training and, as Godakka put it, 'The pain springing from seclusion is better than the happiness arising from sensual pleasure.'[29] These hardships were, after all, of a piece with the rest of their lifestyle. Vanganaputta believed that

> A monk should live in a place that is secluded, quiet and haunted by wild beasts for the sake of solitary meditation. Having gathered odds and ends from the rubbish-heap he should wear a coarse robe. Making his mind humble, he should wander for alms from family to family, guarding the doors of his senses. And he should be content with rough food – the mind of one who is greedy for tasty food does not delight in meditation.[30]

Less accomplished monks, like the former Vajjian prince who lay alone outside Vaishali one night, could feel lonely. When he heard the music of a festival, he lamented that he found himself 'in the forest all alone, like a log rejected in the woods . . . On such a night as this, who is there worse off?'[31]

But the true wilderness monks were tough, self-sufficient individuals who had ceased to fear the wild and discovered its peace and beauty. The monks' verses contain wonderfully evocative descriptions of nature, often entwined with the experience of meditation. 'The call of the crested, blue-necked peacocks in the Kauraviya forest, urged on by the cool breeze, awakens the sleeper to meditation', declares Cittaka.[32] Culaka reflects that it is easy to renounce worldly pleasures when one is surrounded by 'peacocks with lovely feathers, lovely wings, lovely blue necks and lovely faces calling out a lovely song with a lovely sound'.[33] If the natural environment supported meditation, its fertility reflected the fruition of their practice in

Nirvana. 'When the sky-deva has rained, when the grass is four fingers high, when the grove is in full flower, I shall lie in the forest like a tree. It will be soft for me, like cotton. But I shall act as master',[34] says Talaputa. And Bhaddali tellingly remarks to Gautama in the Vinaya that his forest existence has left him 'with a mind become as a wild animal's'.[35] Sympathy with nature blended with the 'boundless heart towards all beings'[36] cultivated though loving-kindness meditation, and Revata declares: 'I am a friend to all, comrade to all and sympathetic to all beings, and develop a mind full of love.'[37]

Bhuta's verses show that, for all their delight in the beauty of nature, the monks still experienced its discomforts and terrors. But by meditating deeply, they found peace.

> When the thundering storm cloud roars out in the mist,
> And torrents of rain fill the paths of the birds,
> Nestled in a mountain cave, the monk meditates.
> – No greater contentment than this can be found.
>
> When along the rivers the tumbling flowers bloom
> In winding wreaths adorned with verdant colour,
> Seated on the bank, glad-minded, he meditates.
> – No greater contentment than this can be found.
>
> When in the depths of night, in a lonely forest,
> The rain-deva drizzles and the fanged beasts cry,
> Nestled in a mountain cave, the monk meditates.
> – No greater contentment than this can be found.
>
> When restraining himself and his discursive thoughts
> (Dwelling in a hollow in the mountains' midst),
> Devoid of fear and barrenness, he meditates.
> – No greater contentment than this can be found.[38]

Deep meditation directed at Awakening was the heart of the wilderness experience, and the verses often express the monks' yearning to plunge into the jungle, 'thrust aside kusa grass and bulrushes' and devote themselves to absorption. But meditation could be difficult. Before taking ordination Kappatakura had been a beggar dressed in rags who scavenged for rice grains, and his name means 'rag and rice'. His verse plays humorously on his name and the struggle to become concentrated: 'This fellow Kappatakura is truly a rag. In a clean jar of the death-free, filled to overflowing, a measure of the dharma has been put; a place has been made to heap up meditations. Don't nod off to sleep, Rag, lest I strike you on the ear!'[39]

The monks were filled with an urgent determination to master Gautama's teaching and gain insight: 'Let us, living in the forest, subsisting on alms food, delighting in the scraps that come into our bowls, tear apart the army of death,'[40] urged Maudgalyayana. Sirimanda told himself: 'Your final night is drawing near, you have no time to be lazy.'[41] Others, like Paccaya, were still more extreme and vowed: 'I shall not eat, I shall not drink, nor shall I go forth from my cell. I shall not even lie down on my side while the dart of craving is not removed.'[42] He is alluding to the *dhutangas* – a set of optional practices for intensifying wilderness life that include eating only one meal a day, refusing invitations to eat with a householder, and sleeping sitting up.*

Staying focused on Enlightenment meant steadfastly resisting the lures of the world – especially in the shape of women (who

---

* Paccaya's determination to avoid eating is reminiscent of the practices of Jains and other self-mortifiers. The tensions between hard-core renunciants such as himself and the mainstream, whose practice was less extreme, seems to have come to a head in the later years of Gautama's career, and continued to be an issue in subsequent years.

receive rough treatment in the monks' verses). Consider, for example, the plight of a solitary monk who is meditating beneath a tree when a woman approaches him. 'She sits down close beside him, lies down beside him and cuddles up to him.'[43] This monk, Gautama said, should show the courage of the warrior who does not tremble in the heat of battle when he sees the terrors of hand-to-hand combat. Keeping a cool head, he should extricate himself from the woman's embrace and walk away.

The body was another source of revulsion, and some monks stayed in cremation grounds amid the ghosts and rotting bodies. Practitioners observed the corpses carefully and noted ten stages in their decomposition, from swelling with gases and turning blue to filling with worms. Eventually only a skeleton was left, and they reflected that one day this would be their own fate. When the monk Rajadatta gazed at a female corpse, he recalled: 'Lust appeared in me, as if I were blind to the oozings.'[44] He was so shocked at his response that he gained Insight on the spot.

By living in the wilderness the monks entered the primal, chaotic space that was home to everything their culture excluded and feared. Townspeople and villagers believed that the wilds were home to spirits and demons, especially the powerful *yakshas*. Some *yakshas* were said to be the ghosts of deceased ancestors, who inhabited the tree above their funeral mound (the *cetiya* or *stupa* that became their shrine). A sympathetic *yaksha* could protect a town or village, and in Indian art they look like kings or queens who carry themselves with a dignified, regal bearing. However, a hostile *yaksha* was the enemy of settled life, and its desire for destruction or human flesh was propitiated with offerings to the ubiquitous *yaksha* shrines.

Yakshas sometimes tried to scare Gautama, as Ajakalapaka did when he uttered the blood-curdling cry: 'There's a goblin for you, recluse!'[45] Gautama told Ajakalapaka that he had 'surpassed [his] reach' because he was free from craving; but other monks needed help. One discourse describes a visit to Gautama by the Four Great Kings, the mightiest of all the *yakshas*, who admired Gautama but worried that lesser spirits would attack monks living in the 'remote recesses of forest and woodland wilderness'.[46] The *yakshas* in such places resented the monks' intrusion and were offended that Gautama disapproved of the pastimes they enjoyed, like killing and stealing. The Kings said they had no more control over such spirits than a human monarch had over bandits, and they proposed that if hostile *yakshas* attacked a Shakyaputra monk he should chant protective verses (*paritti*) and cry out: '*This yaksha is attacking me and will not let me go!*' Then the Four Kings and their allies would come to the monk's aid.

Other spirits were friendly. Sometimes a spirit visited a monk because it was curious to know what kind of being was so bright and serene, and some wished to hear Gautama's teachings and learn how to master the powerful passions that tormented them. A female *yaksha* listened eagerly to Gautama as he taught at the Jetavana, and hushed her children so she could find 'release from all the knots'[47] of her life. Others watched over monks and nuns to protect them, or to spur them on if they slacked, crying: 'Get up, monk! What need do you have of sleep!'[48] According to the Vinaya, a naga who hated his serpent form decided to become a Shakyaputra monk to win the merit that would allow him to be reborn as a human. The naga was ordained, but when he fell asleep his true form was revealed, and Gautama told him: 'You nagas are not capable of practising the Dharma.'[49] Gautama suggested he practise regular fasts instead. 'Pained, afflicted and shedding tears', the naga departed, we are told, and to this day candidates for Buddhist monkhood must declare that they are in fact human, not a spirit in disguise.

Like Gautama's battle with Mara and his victory over the nagas of the Gaya fire-shrines, these confrontations with wilderness spirits took place on a plane far removed from concepts, and reveal the deep intermingling in Gautama's world of the natural and the supernatural, the individual and the environment. In the lonely places of the wilderness a monk faced the dangerous elemental forces that drove the seasons and brought storm or famine. By exposing himself to them and withstanding the whirlwind of terror they provoked, he confronted the same forces in his own consciousness and brought their power under his control. He became a kind of a spirit himself – at least in the eyes of the awestruck villagers who filled his bowl, just as they might make an offering to a god. Gautama told the monks that when they mastered their minds sufficiently to enter dhyana or dwell within the 'divine abode' of loving-kindness, they inhabited a sphere that was equivalent to the god-realms.

Such a person feared no one. When robbers captured Adhimutta his calmness astonished them. 'You show no fear and your complexion brightens,' they exclaimed. 'Why aren't you trembling and babbling like others we have attacked?' He replied: 'There is no fear for one who sees things as they really are. Do whatever you like with this carcass, my body. I will feel neither hatred nor love as a result.'[50] The nuns were especially at risk in the wilderness, and the *Therigatha* describes several attempted rapes. Subha deterred a seducer who was entranced by her 'long eyelashes ... pure gaze ... [and] pleasant eyes' by telling him, 'You run after an empty thing ... like a golden tree at the end of a dream.'[51] Then she tore out one of her eyes and handed it to him.

Community

Gautama knew that wilderness living and solitude weren't for everyone. He recommended that a monk should stay in the wilderness if doing so helped his efforts to practise the Dharma, even if food and shelter were hard to come by. Otherwise, he should leave. Occasionally, a monk went mad or committed suicide in the wilderness, and Gautama stressed the need to be psychologically prepared for its rigours. That meant imbibing the lessons of renunciation, kindliness and non-violence, and being a 'purified' and 'discerning' person. A monk was free to decide for himself what conditions were best, but someone more experienced (like Gautama himself) might intervene. When Upali asked Gautama's permission to live in the wilderness, Gautama wryly remarked that, while a full-grown elephant could swim in a deep lake, a hare or a cat would drown if it tried to do so, and on that principle Upali should remain among his fellow monks.[52] But when Gautama saw Nanda, his half-brother with a taste for luxury, wearing neatly ironed robes, eye make-up and carrying a glazed bowl, he roared, 'When will I see you living in the forest, wearing robes stitched from rags, surviving on scraps given by strangers and paying no attention to sensual pleasures?'[53] He sent Nanda off to the jungle, where he quickly gained Insight.

The monks also needed moral support, especially when they spent a lot of time alone, so Gautama told the monks to meet with others in their locality on the *uposatha* days of the full moon and the new moon, which had long been considered sacred. Gautama based these meetings on the Kshatriya assemblies in which people spoke freely and decided things together while showing particular respect to elders. The monks or nuns made decisions by consensus and deferred to those more senior in years of ordination. This decentralised and fraternal arrangement reflected the distinctive principles that distinguished the community from mainstream society, and Gautama advised the monks to reflect on differences between their lives and those of ordinary citizens. The first reflection was, 'I am now come to the state of being an out-cast',[54] and Gautama remarked that the monks left behind their caste identity on ordination, just as 'the great rivers give up their former names on reaching the ocean'.[55] Then the monks should reflect: 'I myself am responsible for my deeds, I am heir to my deeds ... he to whom my deeds come home.'[56] They should ask if they can find any faults in themselves and consider if they had made enough spiritual progress that 'they might answer confi-dently if their fellows questioned them when they were on their deathbed'.

Uposatha meetings were also a vital ingredient in making the community effective in practising and preserving the Dharma. To start with, the monks probably chanted versions of Gautama's teach-ings, perhaps along the lines of the ceremony described in one dis-course in which monks recite verses from the Dhammapada:

> Not to do evil, but cultivate the good,
> To purify your mind. This the Buddhas teach.[57]

Communal recitation reinforced the practice of memorising certain texts which seems to have started in Gautama's time: in one dis-course Gautama asks a young monk to demonstrate what he knows of the teaching by 'reciting Dhamma',[58] and he responds by chanting sixteen discourses right through. In time, *uposatha* ceremonies also became opportunities to reinforce the monks' ethical conduct, adapting the practice of Jain monks and nuns, who confess their failings to their teacher. Shakyaputras recited the community's basic rules – the *patimokkha* (Pali) or *pratimoksha* (Sanskrit) – and then the most senior monk asked if those present were 'pure'. If any had broken a rule, he confessed his failing to the group (or he may have already confessed it in a smaller gathering or to a friend). The aim was for the monk to become conscious of his shortcomings and move on from them; but in the case of more serious breaches a further penalty applied. The community's main sanction was disapproval – a serious matter among people who prized the respect of their elders, and householders might be unwilling to feed a monk who 'does not fulfil his training'.[59] In more serious cases, a monk could be excluded from communal activities, and the ultimate sanction was expulsion.

Most historians believe that in Gautama's day the number of rules in the disciplinary code was far fewer than the 227 or more it eventually included. They must have included the four reliances, the five basic precepts followed by all Buddhists, and other basic prohibitions such as avoiding entertainments, wearing jewellery and handling money. Other rules were probably added as circumstances warranted them. The Vinaya relates a story purporting to describe the circumstances in which Gautama laid down each rule, but most are clearly apocryphal. However, they do indicate the problems the community encountered, from infringements of dining etiquette to the case of a monk who copulated with a female monkey. One discourse relates a rather more credible account by Udayin of the difficulties that had prompted Gautama to rule that they should only beg in the mornings.

> Sometimes monks wandering for alms in the pitch dark fell into a cesspool, stumbled into a thorn patch or tripped over a sleeping cow. Once, a woman saw me by a lightning flash and screamed out: 'I'm done for! A demon is after me!' I said, 'I'm no demon. I'm a monk waiting for alms.' She yelled back, 'It would be better if your belly was slit open by a butcher than you should go prowling in the dark in order to fill it!'[60]

Gautama wanted the Shakyaputras to be a community, not just a collection of individuals, and he considered living communally in a spirit of loving-kindness an important practice. In later years, perhaps following an earlier tradition, a monk started each period of meditation by radiating loving thoughts to fellow monks, then to the local gods and then to villagers. This encouraged others to feel 'tender-hearted' towards him.[61] Loving-kindness was also an important aspect of the profile of the exemplary monk envisaged by Gautama:

> He who is skilled in his good, who wishes to attain that state of calm [Nirvana], should act thus: he should be able, upright, perfectly upright, of noble speech, gentle, and humble!
>
> Contented, easily supported, with few duties, of light livelihood, with senses calmed, discreet, not impudent, not greedily attached to families.
>
> He should not pursue the slightest thing for which others might censure him. May all beings be happy and secure, may their hearts be wholesome.[62]

Gautama's praise of these qualities doesn't mean that Shakyaputras always embodied them, and a telling story from the Vinaya shows what was at stake when the community fell short. Arriving at a monastic settlement, Gautama and Ananda saw a monk with dysentery who was lying on the ground in his own urine and excrement. They brought the monk water, washed him, put him to bed, and then Gautama asked how he came to be in this condition. 'I am of no further use to the monks, so they do not tend me,'[63] the monk replied. Gautama gathered the other monks. 'You have no mother or father to tend you,' he told them. 'If you will not tend one another, who will? . . . Whoever would tend me, he should tend the sick.'

Loving-kindness naturally expressed itself in friendship, and once again Gautama was the model in his communication with Ananda. Gautama needed an assistant to manage the press of people wanting to see him, and to help with his day-to-day activities. Several monks, including Meghiya and Nagita, filled the role, but none was happy do whatever he needed and able to live with him in an easy rapport. Twenty years into his ministry (i.e. in c.429 BCE, when Gautama was fifty-five) Gautama asked his cousin Ananda to take on the role, and Ananda agreed on certain conditions. He wanted no special treatment and no perks, but he wished to be present whenever Gautama gave a teaching. If he wasn't, Gautama should repeat it to him later. The reason was Ananda's phenomenal memory. He could recall whatever he heard, and that made him a living archive or repository of everything Gautama said.

Ananda also looked after all Gautama's practical needs. He 'brought water for washing [Gautama's] face and tooth-wood for cleaning his teeth . . . arranged his seat, washed his feet, massaged his back, fanned him, swept his cell and mended his robes'.[64] People wanting to see Gautama usually had to see Ananda first, and sometimes he told them that Gautama was meditating or tired. Gautama sometimes asked Ananda to teach in his place, and, even though Ananda was not yet Enlightened, Gautama was confident of his ability to explain advanced matters such as his teachings of 'no self'. Ananda's final condition was the most touching of all. He asked Gautama if he could discuss with him any personal doubts and struggles about the teaching and the practice. Gautama agreed, and he wasn't just Ananda's master – he was his friend, and assured Ananda that such friendship was 'the whole of the spiritual life'.[65] Over the years, Gautama sometimes rebuked Ananda for his excessive sociability and fondness for spending time with the nuns, but he thought Ananda was resilient enough to take his criticism. 'The sound core will stand the test.'[66]

After a period of retreat Ananda exclaimed: 'Spiritual friendship is half the holy life.'[67] (The other half being a person's own efforts.) 'Not so,' replied Gautama. 'It is the whole of it!' The guidance, encouragement and friendship of someone who possessed 'faith, moral discipline, generosity and wisdom'[68] was the chief 'external'[69] support in following the path, just as 'proper attention' was the chief internal support. A true friend, Gautama said, 'gives what is hard to give. He does what is hard to do. He endures what is hard to endure. He reveals his secrets to you. He keeps your secrets. When misfortunes strike, he doesn't abandon you. And when things are going badly he doesn't look down on you.'[70] Such a friend would never let you down and would even 'sacrifice his life for you'.[71]

Before Ananda became Gautama's attendant, a succession of others performed the role. One of these was a young monk called Meghiya, who saw a beautiful mango grove on his way back from gathering food one day. Thinking, 'This is an excellent place for meditation', he asked Gautama's permission to meditate there. Gautama asked him to wait as no other monks were around to help him, but Meghiya replied that he still needed to practise while Gautama had no need to accomplish anything. 'What can I say, Meghiya, if you speak of endeavouring?' said Gautama. 'Do what you think it is time to do.' When Meghiya got to the grove he was surprised to find his mind filled with angry and greedy thoughts. Sheepishly, he returned to Gautama, who told him: 'Five things are conducive to freeing the mind – good friends, living virtuously, helpful discussion, directed energy, and wisdom.'[72] He added that, as friendships with the right people led to the other four, they underpinned the whole path.

Teacher and Disciples

Gautama was the centre of the Shakyaputra community, and even monks who were considered realised masters in their own right held him in immense esteem. The lives of many had been transformed by meeting Gautama. Vangisa, for example, had been a travelling poet:

Drunk with skill in composing poetry, formerly we wandered from village to village, from city to city. Then we saw the Enlightened one, who had reached the far shore of all phenomena. That sage . . . taught me the doctrine. Hearing [it] we believed; faith arose in us. Hearing his utterance . . . I went forth in the houseless state.[73]

Gautama did not merely teach. Surrounded by disciples, Vangisa said, he 'shines revered by the Order of [monks]', and his Dharma was like rain falling from 'a great cloud'.[74] Even though many of the monks had gained insight themselves, Gautama remained their inspiration, guide and 'refuge', and to hear Gautama's voice with the receptivity of a true *shravaka* was to hear the sound of the Deathless. 'I long for your voice as one longs for water when burned by the heat in summer; rain on our ears,'[75] Vangisa pleaded. Monks often simply meditated on Gautama's qualities, and felt his presence even when they were separated from him. Pingiya, who lived far away and was too old to travel, said: 'With constant vigilance, I see him with my mind as if with my eye and I spend the night revering him, so there is not a single moment in which I am apart from him.'[76] In such remarks we see the origins of the devotional practices, and even the visualisations, of later Buddhist tradition.

Gautama often sat together with the monks late into the night, 'completely silent, like a still pool'.[77] Then a brave individual might stand up and say: 'Venerable sir, I would like to ask a question, if you are willing to grant me an answer.'[78] Or Gautama might just start to speak, prompted by his reflections, a recent incident, or a wish to explain a topic in more detail. Most discourses purport to be 'transcripts' of such talks, and it is reasonable to think that some, at least, are genuine records of what he said.

Gautama once said that he was not 'tight-fisted in matters of Truth',[79] meaning that he had not held back from teaching all that he understood; but he also adjusted his teaching according to the receptivity and experience of his listeners. Once (probably late in his career) he looked around the 'silent Sangha of monks', and, feeling they were making good progress, announced that he would give a special teaching. In the meantime they should 'rouse more energy to attain the unattained'.[80] Monks gathered from across the district, and when the designated night came Gautama taught a version of the mindfulness of breathing meditation practice that was also a contemplation of reality: a complex practice that went far beyond the capacity of a beginner.

Gautama didn't expect blind faith from his disciples. He encouraged people to observe him closely 'in order to find out whether or not he [was] fully Enlightened'.[81] Even when they had committed themselves, he told the monks that one of the duties of a pupil to his teacher is to correct him when he is wrong or in danger of saying something unsuitable.[82] But he expected them to make a wholehearted effort, and, as well as inspiring and instructing, he sometimes urged, advised and scolded them. When a monk called Sudinna had intercourse with his former wife to provide his family with an heir, Gautama told him: 'Worthless man, it would be better that your penis be stuck into the mouth of a poisonous snake or a pit of burning embers than into a woman's vagina.'[83] According to tradition, this was the origin of the rule that forbade monks to have sexual intercourse, and Gautama's sternness was buttressed by his belief that the act would lead to rebirth in 'the bad destination, the abyss, hell'. In a similar vein, he insisted that monks should be self-contained and mindful, and when a group of novices arrived where he was staying and excitedly greeted the residents, Gautama asked Ananda: 'Who are these noisy people? They sound like fishermen selling their fish.' He told the new arrivals: 'I dismiss you. You cannot live with me!'[84] and only relented when householders and gods prevailed on him to show compassion. Gautama compared his rebukes to the actions of a woman looking after a baby that puts a stick in its mouth:

> If she were unable to remove it immediately, she would hold his head with her left hand and, hooking a finger of her right hand, remove it, even drawing blood ... It causes the boy pain, that I don't deny. Yet the nurse has to act in this way if she desires the boy's good ... and is motivated by kindness.[85]

Gautama could also be satirical – though translations often flatten the turns of phrase expressing his humour. Once, noting the temptation for monks to settle near families that provided a regular supply of food, Gautama declared: 'Suppose there was a dung beetle that was gorged with dung and had a huge pile of dung in front of him. He would look down on other beetles and declare, "Yippee! I'm a dung-eater with a huge pile of dung in front of me!"'[86]

A particular problem was literalism. Gautama's insistence that the concepts he used were a means to an end, and therefore not 'absolute truth', is one of the most remarkable characteristics of his teaching. He wished each of his disciples to become a liberated arahant who 'no longer clings to sensual pleasure, views, rules and observances

[or] a doctrine of self',[87] and urged them to hold his teachings lightly and 'relinquish them easily'.[88] But he commented (perhaps a little wearily) that some of his students knew his teaching very well but failed to achieve realisation because they 'put the words first'.[89] Gautama told one particularly literal-minded follower that grasping his meaning was like picking up a snake – the only way not to be bitten was to carefully 'hold down its head with a cleft stick and grasp it by the neck'.[90] The key is to recall the purpose of a teaching. Having become a nun, Prajapati prepared to leave for the wilderness and worried that she might not know which of Gautama's teachings to focus on. He told her to consider the effect a teaching had on her. If she could confidently say that it 'led to dispassion, not to passion; to being unfettered, not to being fettered' then she could conclude: 'This is the Dharma ... this is the Teacher's instruction.'[91] Gautama was rigorously consistent in his teachings in focusing on liberation. He once picked up a few simsapa leaves and asked the monks: 'Which is more numerous: these few leaves that I have taken in my hand or those in the simsapa grove overhead?' Similarly:

> Those things that I have directly known but have not taught you are numerous, while the things I have taught you are few. And why haven't I taught those many things? Because they are unbeneficial, irrelevant to the fundamentals of the holy life, and do not lead to revulsion, to dispassion, to cessation, to peace, to direct knowledge, to enlightenment, to Nirvana.[92]

As well as speaking publicly, Gautama also taught his disciples individually, and his method is illustrated by several discourses that trace the training of his son, Rahula. While Rahula was still a child, the boy washed his father's feet. Then Gautama pointed to the water that was left in the cup:

Do you see the leftover water in the cup, Rahula? That's how much
of a monk you are if you deliberately tell lies and then feel no shame
... Imagine a huge royal elephant with tusks like chariot poles. It
throws itself into battle, as it has been trained, but protects its trunk.
The elephant trainer sees that and trains the elephant not to defend
itself at all. In the same way, if someone feels no shame in telling a
deliberate lie, there is no evil he will not do.[93]

When Rahula was eighteen, Gautama gave him a more advanced
teaching, telling him that whatever he experienced, he should reflect:
'This is not me, this I am not, this is not my self.'[94] He taught his
son to navigate through the elements, to 'develop a meditation like
the earth', and then like water, air, fire, air and space. When Gautama was convinced that Rahula had understood impermanence
he explained that his attitude to this impermanent reality should
be one of non-attachment. Eventually, Rahula understood for himself that 'all that is subject to arising is subject to cessation'[95] and
became an arahant.

Gautama gave individual practitioners meditation practices that
suited their temperaments and matched their needs. He had many
successes, but some monks left the order unhappily, some failed
to make progress, and one striking account seems to show his
teaching going badly wrong. Having instructed a group of monks
in Vaishali to meditate on the decomposition of the corpse, Gautama went into strict retreat. In his absence the monks were
'repelled, humiliated and disgusted with this body'[96] and 'twenty
or thirty' of them committed suicide. It seems clear that this out-
come was far from what Gautama had intended. Emerging from
his retreat he remarked, in one version: 'The park seemed ablaze
with [monks]. But now ... the Sangha has become diminished,
thin, scanty, like sparse foliage ... Where have [they] gone?'[97]

However, no one suggests that Gautama had made a mistake, and he admits no error.

Gautama wasn't the only focus of veneration and instruction. According to the Vinaya, senior monks trained the novices from the Shakyaputras' earliest days. A 'preceptor' conducted a new monk's ordination and was responsible for his training over the next five years. The trainee helped his preceptor practically and was obliged to show him both respect and kindness. This system meant that senior monks and nuns had their own disciples, making Gautama 'the teacher of the teachers of many'.[98] In matters of monastic protocol, monks deferred to those who had been ordained before them, but a parallel hierarchy ranked people according to their level of attainment. Alongside the formally categorised stages of realisation, individuals were recognised as possessing distinctive qualities, and men like Maudgalyayana, Shariputra, Mahakasyapa and perhaps Devadatta developed large followings. These realised elders were an elect group among the monks: a Noble Community that was 'worthy of sacrifice, worthy of hospitality, worthy of offerings, worthy of reverence with folded hands, the unsurpassed field of merit for the world'.[99]

Mahakasyapa, for example, kept strictly to the four reliances, lived in the wilderness and was renowned as a meditation master with many psychic powers. When Mahakasyapa was old Gautama suggested that he ease up a little, for instance allowing himself to wear robes made by householders. Mahakasyapa insisted that he was setting an example for later generations and continued his austere way of life.[100] Mahakasyapa was eventually seen as the most senior disciple, but in Gautama's lifetime that place was held by Shariputra, whom Gautama called 'the son of the Blessed One, born of his breast, born of his mouth . . . an heir in the Dharma'.[101] The chief of Shariputra's gifts was the depth and clarity of his insight, and Gautama praised his 'quick, wide, penetrative wisdom'.[102] He was an exceptionally able teacher who stimulated 'quick-wittedness'[103] in his students. Gautama often asked him to elaborate his own Discourses, and seventy-five discourses given by Shariputra alone are included in the Buddhist canon. When Shariputra died, Ananda said he had been 'an adviser and a counsellor who instructed, exhorted, inspired and gladdened me'.[104] A stupa (or sacred funeral mound) containing his relics was constructed in Shravasti and Shariputra's cult continued through worship of the stupa. In the centuries after Gautama many such shrines sprang up across India, commemorating other realised masters who were thought, at least in popular belief, to be literally present in the stupas and continued to offer a 'refuge for many'.[105]

The devotion of both householder and monastic disciples to these elders brought the danger that sects might form within the order. This may have happened in the case of Devadatta, but the Discourses present a general image of harmony between the elders. One delightful discourse records a discussion between the senior disciples, who seem to have been on retreat together in the Gosinga sal-tree forest. It was a beautiful evening: 'The Gosinga Wood is delightful, the night is moonlit, the sal trees are in blossom and heavenly scents seem to be floating in the air,'[106] said Shariputra. The elders discussed what kind of monk they most admired. For Ananda it was one who was learned; for Revata it was the master of meditation; Anuruddha praised psychic powers above all; Mahakasyapa praised wilderness living; and Maudgalyayana spoke of two monks whose 'talk rolls on in accordance with the truth' as they discussed the Dharma. For Shariputra, the ideal monk was one 'who masters his mind rather than letting his mind master him'; and when the discussion was reported to Gautama, he said that this was his opinion as well.

Settled Living

When the Indian monsoon breaks in June or July, rivers swell to torrents and burst their banks, and travel on foot is difficult or impossible. Even Jain ascetics sought shelter in this season, but, according to the Mahavagga, the Shakyaputras kept travelling. Magadhan householders complained to Bimbisara that the monks were 'trampling down the crops and grasses and bringing many small creatures to destruction'.[107] For Jains, who believed that all matter was alive, this was unthinkable, and their example had already shaped how householders expected shramanas to behave. Gautama instituted an annual three-month-long rains retreat. Perhaps he had no choice (he told the monks, 'I instruct you to obey the commands of kings'[108]) but the retreat also gave him a way to cement the monastic community. Soon, monks gathered for rains retreats wherever they were living, and the monsoon 'vassa' became an important part of their year.

In rural areas monks found a cave where they could live together, or else they marked out a piece of ground called an *avasa*. The monks managed everything themselves and built simple shelters of branches and broad tropical leaves. They stayed there until the rains abated, unless the site turned out to be unsuitable, and lived on alms food from a nearby village. At the end of the retreat came a special ceremony in which each monk told his companions: 'If I have made any mistake or offended anyone here in the last three months, please accept my apologies.'[109] Then householders donated fresh robes – the one occasion in the year when they could do so.

Rains retreats held in or near towns were similar, but lay supporters looked after the monks' needs, built the accommodation and provided the food. Sometimes monks just stayed in thatched huts in a patron's garden, but another model existed from the community's first year (according to the Mahavagga's version of its history) thanks to Bimbisara's donation of the Venuvana outside Rajagriha. This was the Shakyaputras' first *sangharama* – a permanent monastic park – and similar bases were eventually started around all the region's major cities. These sangharamas allowed large numbers of monks and nuns to stay with Gautama or his senior disciples, and novices could be trained more effectively. The sangharamas also gave the Shakyaputras a profile in the cities, and therefore a role in society as a whole.

Gautama ruled that monks should leave the sangharama when the rains retreat was over; but it seems they gradually stayed longer and longer, and eventually the parks became permanent residences. As portrayed in the Discourses, the sangharamas of Gautama's time seem to have been open ground with trees and a few buildings; but the largest grew into extensive monasteries that eventually housed thousands of monks, complete with refectories, libraries and permanent staff. The distinction between sangharamas and monasteries is blurred in the Vinaya, however, which is the principal early source describing the community's development. It tells us that, at first, the Venuvana in Rajagriha contained no buildings, and monks slept 'here and there: in a forest, at the root of a tree, on a hillside, in a glen, a mountain cave, a cemetery, a forest glade, the open air, on a heap of straw'.[110] Then a wealthy merchant offered to build some huts and Gautama gratefully accepted, telling him: '[These dwellings] protect us from heat and cold, beasts of prey and creeping things, gnats and rain, in the wet season and the hot winds of summer.'[111]

The Jetavana in Shravasti was donated by Anathapindika, a member of the Ganges Valley's super-rich business elite and reportedly one of just seven Indians with over 500 servants. The Mahavagga tells us that Anathapindika found parkland just outside Shravasti owned by Prince Jeta, and therefore called 'Jeta's Grove' – the Jetavana. Like the Venuvana, it was conveniently near to the city but far enough away to be peaceful, and Anathapindika bought it at incredible expense. The Mahavagga tells us that he constructed a large monastery with 'dwelling-rooms, cells, porches, fire-halls, privies, places for pacing up and down, wells, bathrooms, lotus ponds [and] sheds'.[112] However, excavations on the site suggest it is unlikely that such a structure was built in Gautama's time, and the many discourses set in the Jetavana do not mention these grand buildings.

Taken as a whole, the Discourses suggest that Shakyaputra monks (and Gautama himself) alternately dwelled alone in the wilderness, travelled from village to village and lived communally for the rains – perhaps in a sangharama. The basic elements of the monastic code provide for life in all three environments. No doubt individual monks specialised in certain aspects of Shakyaputra life, and, in time, these became distinct vocations. A text that probably dates from the first century BCE describes a visitor to a monastery identifying 'the learned monk, the Dharma-preacher, the Vinaya-holder, the wilderness dweller, the yogi, the monk in charge of repairs and the administrator'.[113] They all coexist happily.

Gautama sometimes spoke of 'wilderness' and 'settlement' as states of mind rather than locations, and told the monks that by withdrawing from worldly concerns their minds could 'enter into the perception of forest'.[114] One discourse relates that Gautama was staying at the Venuvana, meditating outside in the 'thick darkness', when a giant snake appeared. He recognised the snake as Mara and understood that he was luring him back to more comfortable conditions. Gautama told Mara:

One who lives in empty huts is a self-controlled sage. It is right for him to live there, having given up everything. Though creatures crawl around him, terrors, flies and snakes, the sage in his hut does not stir one hair. Even if the sky splits open, the earth trembles, terrifying all, and men come and stab him in the heart, the Enlightened takes no shelter in possessions.[115]

Awakening was possible wherever one was, and the verses of Patacara, a senior nun, evoke her own Enlightenment in the midst of what seems to be a settled life and a steady routine: 'I took a lamp and I inspected my cell. I inspected the bed and sat on the couch. Then I took a needle and drew out the wick. The complete release of my mind was like the quenching of the lamp.'[116]

The community's most serious crisis in its early years was a split among the monks of Kausambi, the capital of the kingdom of Vamsa. The origins of the dispute are obscure, though later sources say the trouble started when a senior monk was accused of committing an offence under the disciplinary code. A chapter of monks expelled this monk when he refused to acknowledge his fault. Then the banished monk enlisted the support of his friends and disciples, and factions formed. By the time Gautama arrived the two parties 'had taken to quarrelling and brawling and were deeply at odds, stabbing each other with their words'.[117] Gautama reminded the monks of their duty to 'act towards one another with loving-kindness'[118] and suggested the warring groups meet separately until the matter was settled. But members of the groups 'came to blows',[119] nonetheless. Again Gautama called for restraint, but one participant told him: 'The responsibility for these quarrels is ours alone.' In the end Gautama just walked away, reflecting that such people 'do not realise that we are all heading for death. Those who do realise it will compose quarrels.'[120]

The Kausambi dispute seems to suggest that Gautama's authority diminished as his movement spread. It also illustrates potential fault lines in the Shakyaputra community. These included loyalty to an individual preceptor rather than to the order as a whole, and focus

on the minutiae of monastic observance rather than dharma practices. According to the Vinaya version of this story, Gautama left
Kausambi altogether and visited another group of monks that
included his cousin Anuruddha. The harmony between them, as
described by Anuruddha, showed communal monastic life at its best:

> We are united like milk and water, friendly, and have no quarrels. I
> am fortunate to live with such fellows, so I act, think and speak to
> them with loving-kindness. Sometimes I reflect: 'What if I put aside
> my own wishes and follow the wishes of my companions?' Conse-
> quently, although we have several bodies, we are one in mind.[121]

This spirit of cooperation extended to practical aspects of running
their household.

> Whoever returns first from the alms round in the village prepares
> the seats, pours out water for drinking and washing and places the
> spittoons. Whoever comes last puts away the seats and the water
> vessels, washes the spittoons and sweeps the refectory. If any of us
> sees that the toilets or the containers of water for drinking or washing
> are empty, he fills them up. And on every fifth day we discuss the
> Dharma late into the night.

Eventually Gautama returned to Kausambi, where the monks
were finally compelled to reason with each other when the householders refused to feed them. Gautama found a formula that allowed
both sides to save face, but he never returned to Kausambi again
or stayed with its monks, who were 'makers of strife, quarrels, disputes, brawls and legal questions in the order'.[122]

A final story suggests Gautama's response to the community's institutional problems such as the Kausambi dispute. In the middle of the

crisis, Gautama just walked off into the forest, telling no one where he was going. One version says that that he felt 'hemmed in by monks and nuns, men and women householders, kings, ministers, and other religious teachers and their disciples'.[123] Meanwhile, a bull elephant living nearby was also feeling hemmed in. Baby elephants and calves ate the fresh tips of the grass, and even if he pulled branches down from the trees they chewed them up before he could enjoy them himself; and when he went into the water for a drink the she-elephants had already muddied it. So the bull elephant also walked away from his group and came to a forest grove where Gautama was meditating. The two stayed together contentedly and the elephant brought Gautama drinking water in his trunk. Gautama reflected:

> This unites mind with mind,
> The Perfected One and the bull elephant,
> With tusks as long as chariot poles.
> That each delights in being alone in the forest.[124]

Daughters of the Shakyan

This book has so far focused on male members of the Shakyaputra community, and women have been mentioned only in passing. The Discourses and the Vinaya have relatively little to say about Gautama's contact with the nuns – the *Shakyadhitas*, or 'daughters of the Shakyan' – which is regrettable as what we do know of Gautama's attitude to women practitioners was remarkable for its time. The Brahminical view, as expressed in 'The Laws of Manu', was that a woman 'should do nothing independently, even in her own house. In childhood subject to her father, in youth to her husband, and when her husband is dead to her sons, she should never enjoy independence.'[125] Attitudes in the Ganges Valley seem to have been more relaxed, but there, too, women were expected to be wives and mothers. Mahavira founded an order of Jain nuns and we hear of other female wanderers, but Jainism's two main sects were divided over whether women could gain realisation. Gautama was certain that women could do so, and he may have been the first teacher ever to regard women as spiritual equals to men in this respect.

The nuns thrived during Gautama's lifetime, multiplying 'in diverse villages, towns, country districts and royal residences',[126] according to a late source; and vivid insights into their lives come from the post-Realisation verses of the Therigatha, which Kathryn Blackstone calls 'the only canonical text in the world's religions that is attributed to female authorship and focuses exclusively on women's experiences'.[127] Both the *Therigatha* and the Discourses testify that many nuns gained realisation and felt confident in their capacities. As Soma says: 'What harm could the women's state do to us, when the mind is well concentrated [and] knowledge exists?'[128] Blackstone's study of the Therigatha concludes that the nuns had a distinctive approach to dharma practice. While the monks' verses value 'peacefulness and quietude', the women's path to Enlightenment was 'fraught with difficulties that must be faced',[129] and, while the monks stress detachment, the women's lives after Awakening show 'a transformation of their emotional response to others'.[130] For one thing, they no longer needed men. When Mara appeared before one Theri she declared that 'men . . . are in that past for me. I do not grieve, I do not weep, and sir – I'm not afraid of you.'[131]

The success of the nuns' community is also obscured by the traditional account of its establishment. The Vinaya relates that in the early years of Gautama's ministry only men were ordained; but when Suddhodana died, Prajapati (his widow and Gautama's stepmother) requested that Gautama 'allow women the opportunity'[132] to go forth as well. Gautama refused, and Prajapati departed in tears. She and 500 Shakyan women cut off their hair, donned monastic robes and followed Gautama all the way to Vaishali. Ananda found her with 'her feet swollen, her limbs covered with dust, with tearful face',[133] and promised to take up her case. When Gautama refused him, too, Ananda asked: 'Can women attain Enlightenment?' 'Yes, they can,' replied Gautama. 'Then why don't you allow them to be ordained and practise your teachings?' He added that Prajapati had nourished Gautama and given him 'milk from her own breast'. Gautama relented, but insisted that nuns must accept eight additional rules. They should receive instruction from monks, and even the most senior nun should defer to and 'perform all proper duties towards'[134] the most junior monk.

Modern readers often see these rules as evidence of misogyny, and the impression is reinforced by discourses in which Gautama compares a woman to an 'unclean, bad-smelling, timid, fearful and treacherous'[135] snake, and so on. But Gautama's comments need to be read in context. His unflattering descriptions of women are addressed to monks to encourage them in their celibacy, and the Vinaya tells us that the extra rules were pragmatic precautions to guard against real dangers for the community: 'Those households which have many women and few men easily fall prey to robbers [and] when women can go forth from home, the holy life does not last long . . . I have set out the eight vows as a man might make a dyke around a reservoir, so the waters do not overflow.'[136]

Gautama doesn't say *how* the community would be weakened, but the nuns' presence clearly affected attitudes towards it in the general population. The sight of unattached women wandering freely, and perhaps encouraging other women to leave their families, threatened normal society more directly than male renunciation. Nuns were sometimes abused as 'shaven-headed strumpets', and the *Therigatha* describes the intense opposition faced by women like Sumedha, who only convinced her family to let her go forth when she threatened to starve herself to death and 'threw her hair on the ground'[137] before her prospective husband.

As they were social outsiders, the nuns' community became a refuge for society's female casualties – women who had lost their husbands, been turned out of their homes, or worked as prostitutes – which may have reinforced the view that they weren't quite respectable and that their motives for joining the community were dubious. Canda, for example, relates that, as a childless widow without friends or relatives, she had begged her food for seven years. 'Then I saw a nun who had obtained food and drink and approaching her I said, "Send me forth into the homeless state."'[138]

The purpose of the eight rules may, therefore, have been to placate mainstream society, but the sources also suggest that some monks shared society's concerns. The Vinaya tells us that Ananda was reprimanded after Gautama's passing for having pressed the women's case. Some scholars believe that this indicates a difference between the monks' view of the nuns and Gautama's, and one notes: 'There is considerable debate today about whether these eight rules were actually pronounced by the Buddha or were later inserted by monks.'[139] Others, like Richard Gombrich, also believe that 'the story of the Buddha's reluctance to allow women into the Sangha does not date from his lifetime'.[140]

While there is much we do not know about the nuns' situation, it does seem to locate the boundary between what Gautama believed – that they were capable of Enlightenment – and what society deemed acceptable. This introduces a broader theme in Gautama's career. For all his stress on the value of leaving society, both he and his monastic community remained deeply involved in it, and had to negotiate the constraints and opportunities that brought.

7

A Holy Man in the World

Finding a Place

One day, not long after his Awakening, Gautama was walking through the swamplands near the River Mohi when he fell into conversation with a herdsman called Dhaniya. Dhaniya told Gautama that he had been preparing for the rains. 'I've cooked my rice and milked my cows. My family live nearby in a well-thatched house and the fire's been lit. So, I say, *let the rain come down!*'[1] Gautama replied: 'I'm spending the night on the riverbank and the only house I have is my own body, but I am free of any anger or craving. So I also say, *let the rain come down!*' Looking askance at the wanderer's rags, Dhaniya remarked, 'I support myself by what I earn through honest labour. My sons are all healthy and I never hear a bad word about them.' 'I serve no one,' Gautama replied. 'Having found liberation I wander through the world with no need to earn anything!' With that, the monsoon broke, drenching the two men.

Gautama's dialogue with Dhaniya shows one version of his message to mainstream society: a complete rejection of its worldly values and the 'cramped and dusty' householder lifestyle. At the end of the discourse Mara pops up to defend possessions, but Gautama tells him: 'One with sons grieves because of his sons and one with cattle grieves because of them. A person's grief comes from possessions, and someone with no possessions does not grieve.' Some historians think this radical message of renunciation was all Gautama taught, and that his only concern when he spoke to ordinary people was persuading them to leave household life. But the Discourses suggest that Gautama's ideas evolved over time. At first, as 'The Noble Quest' relates, he considered not teaching at all because he couldn't see how people 'impassioned by greed, enveloped in a thick darkness'[2] could grasp the profound and difficult truth of dependent arising. At Sarnath he succeeded triumphantly in communicating with shramanas who had already rejected the world and had 'little dust in their eyes'. But subsequently, according to the Mahavagga, he taught everyone he met, embarking on an urban mission that took him to Rajagriha, Kapilavastu and eventually Shravasti. Most of the householders he taught at Sarnath became renunciants, but he also met some who were unwilling (or unable) to take that step. The inability of Dhammadinna – the layman who still lived 'in a home crowded with children'[3] – to understand his deeper teachings suggests that it took Gautama time to learn how to address people according to their situations and capacities.

The meeting with Dhaniya probably occurred early in Gautama's ministry when he still wandered freely during the rains, and the herdsman's response gives a clue to how his teaching would develop. Speaking for himself and his wife, Dhaniya declared: 'The gains are not small for us who have seen the Blessed One. We come to you for Refuge . . . Be our teacher.'[4] Gautama's qualities somehow met a deep need in Dhaniya. The holy man connected Dhaniya to a dimension that his domestic satisfactions did not encompass – the Dharma – which was a safer 'refuge' than a well-thatched hut. Someone who responded to Gautama like this might not renounce his or her worldly life (though the discourse tells us that Dhaniya did), and most householder followers probably regarded Nirvana as a distant and perhaps incomprehensible ideal. But they still wanted a connection to Gautama and aspired to apply his teachings on their own level.

The challenge for Gautama was to show what the Dharma meant within the concrete reality of people's daily activities, and that meant engaging with the issues and concerns that shaped ordinary lives in the Ganges Valley. Some of those concerns have modern parallels, but others belong to a pre-modern society. These include acute fear of the spirit world and anxiety about what lay ahead after death. So Gautama also engaged with folk religion and came into contact (and sometimes competition) with other religious teachers. Meanwhile, for their part, the Shakyaputras couldn't survive without householders to feed them, and the support – or at least the toleration – of those who wielded power.

Shravasti

Jain monks and forest hermits separated themselves from society; urban Brahmins were immersed in it; but the lifestyle Gautama crafted for the Shakyaputras trod a middle way between the settlement and the wilderness. The Jetavana outside Shravasti offered a model. Like the Venuvana it was 'neither too far from the village, nor too near, suitable for coming and going, accessible to people whenever they want, not crowded by day, having little noise at night . . . secluded from people [and suitable] for meditation'.[5] The Jetavana became Gautama's principal base and he spent twenty-five rains retreats there or elsewhere in Shravasti, and over 800 discourses are set in the area. As Gautama's fame spread, people travelled to the city from across India to hear his teaching. In later years, the Chinese traveller Fa-hsien visited the Jetavana and noted 'the clear water of the ponds, the luxuriant groves and numberless flowers of variegated hues'.[6] That landscape must have been a later creation, but the Discourses also evoke a tranquil scene in which monks practised Gautama's teachings intensively in a relaxed, natural environment.

Traditional sources, notably the commentary written by the Sri Lankan monk Buddhaghosha in the fifth century CE, tell us that Gautama followed a regular daily routine. He rose early, having slept for just one hour 'lying on his right side after the manner of a lion',[7] he rinsed his mouth and then meditated. Before the heat became overwhelming he went on his alms round, sometimes alone and sometimes with other monks. When he was in Shravasti he walked from the Jetavana through the fields of wheat and rice towards the city's ramparts, entering through its massive gates. On the other side was a gaggle of grocers' stalls and the noises typical of such a city: 'elephants, horses, carriages, kettle-drums, side-drums, lutes, singing, cymbals and gongs and cries of "Eat, drink and be merry."'[8]

Gautama once said that he liked to meditate after his meal: 'When I return from my alms round and have eaten my meal I make for the edge of a forest. There I gather together whatever grasses or leaves there are into one place and sit down cross-legged, holding my body straight and setting mindfulness in front of me.'[9]

The Discourses say that in meditation, Gautama would 'abide in voidness'[10] or in compassion. But dhyana clearly remained important, and he also practised the mindfulness of breathing, commenting that even for those who have achieved realisation, it 'leads to a pleasant dwelling in this very life and to mindfulness and clear comprehension'.[11] Buddhaghosha outlines a slightly different schedule according to which Gautama meditated in the early

morning and evening. In the afternoon he returned to the Jetavana, washed his feet and sat in the Gandhakuti (the 'Fragrance
Hall'), where he answered questions from monks and assigned meditation practices 'suited to their individual characters'.[12] In the hot
season he sometimes took a mid-afternoon nap, which brought the
accusation from the more ascetically minded shramanas that he
was lazily 'abiding in delusion'.[13] Gautama responded that ignorance was the real laziness and that when he napped he did so
'mindfully and fully aware'. What's more, he always 'slept well'.[14]

Towards evening, visitors dressed in 'their best tunics and robes'
came to see Gautama, bringing 'perfumes, flowers' and other offerings.[15] There were wanderers, local dignitaries, laymen and women,
spiritual seekers, as well as the curious, the sick and the desperate.
Sometimes people wanted to become his followers, and Gautama
led them in reciting the verses of dedication to the three Refuges
and five precepts. His public talks usually concerned matters relevant to householders' lives, but sometimes he touched on more
advanced aspects of the path.

Gautama bathed and then 'came out of the water (and) stood
in one robe, drying his limbs'.[16] Then he meditated, and in the
evening received visits from monks. Then the gods came to see
him, and observers sometimes reported an eerie light shining from
Gautama's chamber. He spent some time pacing mindfully up and
down, and then surveyed the world with 'the eye of a Buddha',
seeking those who were open to his teaching. A monk named Sona
Kutikanna, who says he lived with Gautama, reports that he 'spent
much of the night in the open air'[17] practising meditation with the
monks; then, 'spreading his outer robe, Gautama made his bed,
like a lion in a rocky cave'[18] and, briefly, he slept.

These accounts mix the concrete with the mythic, but they add
up to a plausible portrait of a busy public figure who was nonetheless

set apart by the sense that he partook of a greater reality: a human and a more-than-human being whose message was both 'visible here and now'[19] and sublimely elusive. This combination also tells us something about the needs of the society to which Gautama ministered. People wanted a teacher to embody virtues they could develop on their own level; but they also wanted contact with a holy man who transcended the world and through whom they could be in relationship with the fundamental forces of life.

Competing Forces

Gautama's claim that he was fully Enlightened inevitably placed him in competition with other religious figures, both shramanas and Brahmins, and his dialogues with them are less an attempt to forge amicable community relations than a battle of ideas. Householders observed these debates with keen interest because they wanted to know which of the holy men would bring them more merit and improve their fortunes in the afterlife. Of course, some people resented all shramanas as lazy good-for-nothings who 'don't like to work [and] live off what's given by others',[20] but supplying shramanas with their daily meal was a long-established tradition in the Ganges Valley, and on special occasions a wealthy householder would feed an entire shramana community. The result was competition for support between shramana groups and we hear, for example, that when the Shakyaputras were favoured and received plentiful 'robes, alms food, lodgings and medical requisites',[21] other shramanas went without. The followers of Susima urged their teacher to become a Shakyaputra so that they could win donations by 'mastering [Gautama's] Dharma and preaching it to laypeople'.[22] Further problems arose when wealthy benefactors switched allegiance, and Gautama advised important converts from Jainism to continue giving to the community they had 'long supported'.[23]

Without householders to support them, the shramanas could not survive, but dependence on donations brought dangers and the Discourses are full of stern warnings that Shakyaputra monks shouldn't become attached to what they received. 'It is better to swallow a flaming, red-hot ball of iron than to be an immoral, uncontrolled man living on the alms food of the land',[24] said Gautama. He insisted that the monks must make themselves worthy recipients of offerings by practising true renunciation. For their part, householders' gifts won them karmic 'merit' bringing benefits in both this life and the next.

Gautama often said that giving to true holy men was the best way to acquire merit. This may appear self-serving, but a less cynical interpretation is that Gautama saw respect for shramanas as a positive element in his society which connected people to important values. We hear, for example, of an unruly group of young men of the Licchavi clan: 'quick-tempered, rough and greedy fellows' who liked to rob messengers and 'slap women and girls on the back'. When they encountered Gautama in the Mahavana forest, 'They cast aside their bows, called off their dogs . . . saluted him and stood with hands upraised in silence, revering him.'[25] Gautama remarked to a bemused Licchavi elder who witnessed the scene that acting respectfully had a mellowing and maturing effect. When a son shows respect to a parent, the parent 'fondly regards him with loving thoughts', and venerating a holy man prompts his 'compassion, benevolence' and blessing. He added that those who act respectfully become 'lovely in their actions' and 'worthy of praise'.[26]

Supporting *any* shramana was an alternative to sponsoring Brahminical sacrifices, but that was just the outward sign of a much wider competition between the two groups. Whether Brahminism was long established in the Ganges Valley or a new arrival, the Discourses suggest that the Brahmins were carving out a distinctive role during Gautama's lifetime. In the west, Brahmins favoured rural life, but those who migrated eastwards, probably drawn by the region's wealth, became wealthy and influential residents of Ganges Valley cities. We hear of land grants by kings to Brahmins, perhaps in payment for consecration rituals, and learn that the most important Brahmins were significant landowners.

Through their mastery of the Vedas and the power of sacrifice, Brahmins performed a quasi-magical role. Then, as now, they were fortune-tellers who practised 'palmistry, foretelling a person's lifespan . . . knowledge of animal cries . . . predicting an eclipse of the moon, or good or bad rainfall' and magicians who conjured 'charms against arrows' and 'spells to bind the tongue or jaw or make the hands jerk'.[27] Johannes Bronkhorst suggests that the Brahmins' arrival in the Ganges Valley prompted a clash of cultures:

> The spread of Brahminical culture implied, at least to some extent, the imposition of the Brahmins' view of the world, combined with the belief that they had more access to supernatural powers than anyone else. The battle for hearts and minds of people, and of their rulers in particular, was fought, so far as the Brahmins were concerned, on this level rather than on an intellectual, 'philosophical' level.[28]

Gautama said that he refrained from 'such base arts and wrong means of livelihood'[29] as astrology and fortune-telling, and defined the true shramana as 'one in whom the power of omens such as shooting stars, dreams and signs has been destroyed'.[30] His teaching did address the needs and fears to which folk religion and Brahminism ministered, but it also brought freedom from a certain kind of 'magical thinking'.

In the accounts of Gautama's meetings with Brahmins he is always well-mannered and remains calm and reasonable even when a Brahmin interlocutor becomes angry or dogmatic. Nonetheless, he fundamentally rejects their caste-based view of society and themselves:

> For name and clan are assigned
> As mere designations in the world;
> Originating in conventions,
> They are assigned here and there.[31]

Gautama praised the idealised Brahmins of the Vedas who extolled 'the holy life and virtuous conduct, uprightness, mildness, austerity, meekness, non-violence and forbearance'.[32] But he said that as society had become richer, Brahmins had grown envious of 'the splendour of kings' and fallen prey to the allure of magnificent chariots, sumptuous buildings and beautiful women. Having grown wealthy on their patrons' gifts, 'their craving increased' until they became the worldly urban priests of Gautama's day, whom he considered hypocrites for claiming spiritual authority while failing to embody their ancient ideals. Brahmin renunciants were different. Gautama said they were worthy recipients of offerings, but he still suspected that their austerity was merely an outward show:

> What's the use of your matted hair, you man of evil understanding? What's the use of your deerskin garment? Within you are a dense jungle of passions, yet you touch up the outside.
>
> The man who wears rags from a dust heap – who is lean, whose veins stand out all over his body, and who, alone in the forest, is absorbed in [meditation], *him* I call a Brahmin.[33]

In speaking like this Gautama inverted the Brahminical rhetoric that had such powerful resonance for the Brahmins themselves and the Ganges Valley citizens who were drawn to them. Going a step further, Gautama declared that 'the true Brahmin' was one who acted ethically and possessed the inner qualities of 'truth and principle'.[34] This redefinition of the term 'Brahmin' was the most concerted element in a campaign to subvert Brahminical language altogether by reinterpreting socially ascribed roles in terms of inner qualities. 'Aryan' may not have been a strictly racial term in the Ganges Valley, but it still connected the idea of 'nobility' with the prestige of ancient ancestry. However, when Gautama called his Four Truths and Eightfold Path 'aryan' he used the word in a way that jettisoned racial connotations and made nobility a matter of personal qualities alone.

Gautama's criticisms touched a nerve because the Brahmins already half acknowledged the gulf between their ideas of what a Brahmin should be and the reality of their lives.* Their faith depended on the inspired sages who had composed the Vedas and yogis who were destined for union with Brahma; and meeting a realised holy man was considered a great blessing. Some, at least, saw Gautama as a modern embodiment of their ideals and even accepted his claim to be the true heir of the 'Brahmins of old', but they were perplexed that he also taught the dangerously democratic notion of 'purification for all four castes'[35] which rendered Brahmins redundant. Consequently, Brahmin audiences regarded Gautama with varying degrees of admiration and mistrust. 'Some made obeisance, some exchanged courtesies with him, some saluted

---

* We need to be a little cautious in reading these accounts of Gautama's victories over the Brahmins. They are, among other things, Buddhist propaganda designed by monks of a later period to show the superiority of their faith to that of their Brahmin rivals.

him with joined hands, some announced their name and clan, and some sat down at one side in silence.'[36]

Even senior Brahmins were intrigued by Gautama and his movement. Seeing crowds of Brahmin families on their way to visit Gautama, Sonandanda decided to join them, despite his colleagues' protests that this was 'not proper'. Sonandanda compared Gautama's qualities with his own, and admitted that, while they were both well-born and respected, Gautama was superior because he had renounced worldly life and was 'free from sensual lust and without personal vanity'.[37] When Brahmins overcame their reservations and recognised Gautama as a realised spiritual master, they felt intense devotion and responded like Brahmayu who 'prostrated himself with his head at the Blessed One's feet, covered them with kisses and caressed them with his hands'.[38]

Brahmins mythologised Gautama as the 'Great Agent' foretold in the Vedas, and therefore a worthy recipient of devotion from 'one looking for merit'.[39] But Gautama sometimes undermined such ways of thinking by playing with Vedic myths and Brahminical ideas and making fun of Brahminical literalism. When Assalayana repeated the belief that Brahmins were 'born of Brahma's mouth', Gautama wryly replied, 'You know, Brahmin women have been seen having their periods, becoming pregnant, giving birth and suckling their babies.'[40] In one remarkable discourse Gautama even satirised Brahma himself by telling a story of a monk who made his way to the highest heaven and enquired of Brahma: 'Where do the four elements end?' He was asking how one could get beyond mundane existence, and the question echoes the idea of the spiritual quest as union with Brahma. Brahma declares, rather like the old man who masqueraded as the Wizard of Oz: 'I am the Great Brahma, the all-seeing, all-powerful lord, creator, ruler, appointer and Orderer, father of all that have been and shall be.'[41] When the monk points out to Brahma that he hasn't answered his question, the god takes him aside and confides that, although he cannot admit it in front of the lesser gods, he only knows about 'creation', not how to escape it. Only Gautama could answer *that* question.

Some scholars suggest that Gautama's presentation of his Dharma systematically inverted Vedic and Brahminical doctrines in order to give them new meanings.* One day, two young men asked Gautama to help them resolve the conflicting advice of their gurus about how to achieve union with Brahma. 'Are these different paths to Brahma like the paths to our village – all leading to the same destination?' they asked. Gautama posed a question in return: 'These teachers know the Vedas and can recite them exactly, but have any of them actually seen Brahma face to face?'[42] Of course, they hadn't. Gautama told the youths that their gurus relied on the authority of tradition, like a file of blind men who each stumbled forward by following the person in front. For Gautama, salvation was something you had to achieve for yourself, and Brahmins who thought God would save them reminded him of a crow who wanted to cross a river but just sat beside it crying out, 'Come here, other bank!'

Such teachings spoke powerfully to those Brahmins who felt (as Pingiya put it) that the underlying message of Vedic tradition was 'This is how it has always been, and this is how it will always be.'[43] The Brahmins of Sala told Gautama that they had questions about ethics, karma, rebirth, the gods and the nature of realisation; and yet, they said, 'There is no teacher in whom we have acquired faith that is backed up by reasons.'[44] Such people were willing to listen to Gautama and even become his followers. While these accounts

* The British Pali scholar Richard Gombrich is the leading exponent of this approach in his various books.

may be tinged with Buddhist propaganda, the impression that some Brahmins were questioning their tradition (perhaps under the impact of urban life and Ganges Valley ideas) has echoes in the slightly later Brahminical text, the *Mahabharata* and it is reinforced by the evidence that many Shakyaputra monks were of Brahmin birth.

Perhaps Gautama chose satire as his method because it allowed him to criticise Brahminism without stoking antagonism. The danger that relations could turn unpleasant was real enough. Brahminism was deeply chauvinistic, convinced of its superiority and a growing force in the Ganges Valley. Brahmins who joined the Shakyaputras were told: 'You have given up the best class and joined . . . those pathetic, shaven-headed, extravagant ascetics, the dark descendants of our ancestors' feet.'[45] By living and eating with people from all castes the monks made themselves no better than *shudras*, in Brahmin eyes, and their wandering lifestyles probably made them as dark-skinned and weatherbeaten as field workers. Ambattha added that Shakyans were especially unworthy, 'being of menial origin'.[46]

Throughout Gautama's life we hear of debates and disputes, of Brahmins spreading rumours against him, and of his criticisms in return. Gautama sometimes suggested that Brahminism could reform itself if 'butter, ghee, curds, honey and molasses' were used in sacrifices rather than the animals; but he added that a better sacrifice still was supporting Shakyaputra monks. Better than that was going for refuge to the Buddha, Dharma and Sangha; then came practising the ethical precepts; and the highest sacrifice of all was taming the mind: 'That sacrifice is simpler and yet more profitable than all the others.'[47] This was a fundamentally different view of religion, the individual and society.

The Living and the Dead

Anathapindika is the emblematic householder disciple in the Discourses, and the stories associated with him offer a starting point for considering the 'occult' aspect of Gautama's role in society.

In the first year of Gautama's ministry, the Mahavagga relates, Anathapindika, who had not yet met Gautama, was in Rajagriha on business when he visited his brother-in-law, the merchant who was building the monks' accommodation at the Venuvana. The household was a tumult of activity:

'Are you preparing for a marriage feast or a sacrifice or a visit from the king?' Anathapindika asked. The merchant told him, 'I have invited Gautama the Buddha and his monks for tomorrow's meal.'
'Did you say "Buddha"?' asked Anathapindika.
'I did,' replied the merchant.
'You say "Buddha"?'
'I say "Buddha".'
'You say "Buddha"?'
'Yes, I say "Buddha".'
'Even this sound is hard to come by in the world. "Buddha", "Buddha". Can I go to see him right now?'[48]

Buddhahood was a long-established ideal within the Ganges Valley, and held a powerful mythic resonance. Although Anathapindika was a millionaire householder who presumably knew little about holy men or religion, just hearing of someone who had gone beyond the perplexities of ordinary existence was a profound blessing that convulsed him with excitement.

The Mahavagga says that Anathapindika wanted to meet Gau-

tama immediately, but was told it would be impolite to turn up
unannounced in the middle of the night. He decided to wait till
morning, only to find he was so excited that he woke three times
thinking it was light. Eventually, he set out to meet Gautama, even
though his route took him through a cremation ground. Indians
believed that terrifying spirits such as *yakshas* and *rakshasas* haunted
such places, and no one in their right mind (yogis aside) went there
at night. The gates swung open, and when Anathapindika stepped
inside 'the light vanished and darkness appeared'. He was overwhelmed by terror, but a *yaksha* who was devoted to Gautama
whispered words of encouragement: 'A hundred thousand elephants,
horses, chariots, maidens or earrings are not worth a sixteenth part
of a single step forward.'[49] Light appeared, and Anathapindika overcame his fear enough to continue. He arrived as dawn was rising,
and saw Gautama pacing back and forth in mindful meditation.

In presenting Gautama as an alternative source of power to the
spirits of the cremation ground, this story echoes Gautama's battle
with Mara and his triumph over the Gaya nagas, which make him
a powerful protagonist in the ancient battle between settled society
and its ghostly shadows. A legend from the commentaries which
shows his importance as a master of the spirit realm tells that five
years after Gautama's Awakening a drought brought famine to
Vaishali, the capital of the Vrijian Federation. The earth was parched
and cracked, rivers dwindled to a sluggish trickle and corpses were
piled high. A powerful stench attracted evil spirits and the city
seemed cursed. The despairing citizens knew they needed a mighty
spiritual force to save them. They could have asked a magician to
conjure spells, a Brahmin to perform a sacrifice or a shaman to
intercede with the spirits. Instead, they sent for Gautama, and the
moment he set foot on Vrijian land 'a severe storm came up and
there was a heavy fall of rain. Streams of water flowed waist deep

and washed the corpses into the Ganges, and the whole region round about was cleansed.'[50] Then Gautama recited verses that became famous across the Buddhist world:

> Whatever spirits are assembled here, earthly or celestial, may
> every one be happy, and may they listen attentively:
> O spirits, listen closely. Show kindness to human beings. Day
> and night they bring offerings, so protect them carefully.
> The greatest treasure in the world and the greatest jewel in the
> heavens do not compare to the Tathagata. This precious jewel
> is Gautama. May this truth bring peace.[51]

Hearing these words, the hostile spirits fled in terror. The sick were cured and the friendly spirits joined the population in acclaiming Gautama.

Encounters between Gautama and *yakshas* in the Discourses are early examples of the same phenomenon. Typically, the spirit feels Gautama's power or glimpses his wisdom, agreeing to act ethically and support the Dharma. Leaving the wilderness, it takes up residence on the edge of the village or in a monastery, and Gautama encourages the villagers to continue to make offerings to it, provided these involve no alcohol or violent sacrifices, and regard his own Enlightened qualities as superior. Recent archaeological discoveries showing that important monasteries were often built above megalithic burial sites suggest that early Buddhist monks inherited from older religions a role in tending the spirits of the dead, and to this day visitors to a Buddhist temple may notice a shrine near the entrance dedicated to local gods and perhaps other deities. The popular Buddhism that is still found in many Asian countries has always incorporated, and even rejoiced in, worship of god and spirits, while subordinating it to Buddhist ideals.

From the perspective of normal society, Gautama was a saint who had engaged the frightening supernatural forces ruling the wilderness, absorbed their power and learned to control them. Having done so, his protective influence could assuage the unquiet dead who hovered around the living. Spirits were said to populate the hills around Rajagriha, for example, and psychically attuned monks like Maudgalyayana witnessed a Dantesque phantasmagoria at Vulture's Peak. He reported seeing a skeleton flying through the air pursued by vultures, a figure pierced by body hairs formed into needles, and another – the ghost of 'a corrupt magistrate'[52] – with testicles like water pots. Hsuan Tsang reported that 'strange forms, as of nagas, serpents and lions' still emerged from another Raja-griha cave, and that 'those who see such sights lose their reason and become dazed'.[53]

Some *yakshas* were the reborn spirits of ancestors, while *pretas* were the anguished ghosts of departed humans (usually relatives) who couldn't relinquish their unsatisfied cravings. Gautama's pres-ence naturally subdued the spirits, and we read that when he stayed in a town or village 'that place [was] not troubled by non-human beings'.[54] But the spirits turned hostile if they didn't receive offer-ings, and when Bimbisara first gave alms to Gautama, one discourse reports, they 'set up a dreadful wailing outside the palace walls in the dead of night'.[55] Gautama explained that the ghosts of departed relatives were complaining that the King had deprived them of their sustenance in giving food to the monks instead of making offerings to their shrines. Henceforth, Gautama said, the merit gained through donations to monks should be 'transferred' to the spirits.

Just as Gautama's victory over the death-demon Mara drama-tised his attainment of the 'deathless', his mastery of the spirit realm was connected to his mastery of death. The meaning of Gautama's

Enlightenment was probably mysterious to most householders, but his triumph over death had a deep resonance. Hell and the demonic realms were vividly real, and everyone wanted to know how to ensure a happy rebirth. One of Gautama's powers was knowledge of where the deceased had been reborn, and people constantly asked him about the fate of dead friends or relatives. Gautama eventually grew weary of this role, and preferred to motivate people to practise his Dharma by reminding them of their mortality. If they did that, he said, they would not be powerless victims of death. Acting skilfully would bring a good rebirth while, conversely, he told one group of householders, 'It is by reason of unethical conduct ... that some beings are reborn after death ... in the lower world of hell.'⁵⁶

At least some of Gautama's listeners understood his teaching that karmic results depend on the state of mind with which one acts, and that morality involves training the mind. A good rebirth, therefore, follows from developing a positive state of mind, and Gautama sometimes taught a hierarchy of meritorious actions starting with 'giving and acting ethically' and culminating in 'developing the mind through meditation'.⁵⁷ His cousin Mahanama worried that he might die in a moment of unawareness and his merit would be swept away; but Gautama reassured him that the accumulated influence of his positive actions would remain:

Suppose a man submerges a jar of ghee or oil in a deep pool of water and breaks it. Its shards and fragments would sink downwards, but the ghee or oil would rise upwards. So, too, when a person's mind has been fortified with faith, virtue, learning, generosity and wisdom, then when various creatures eat his body ... his mind ... goes to distinction. Don't be afraid, Mahanama! Your death will not be a bad one.⁵⁸

Still more attentive listeners understood that Gautama denied the existence of an *atman* or soul, but, like later generations of Buddhists, they sometimes struggled to understand what was reborn, or even how rebirth was possible.

Gautama's power over the spirit world made him, in some respects, like the gods themselves – the devas who (according to popular belief) dwell in a heavenly realm and often appear as a radiant presence in the background of the Discourses. Observers reported that Gautama sometimes broke off in mid-conversation to address an unseen deity, and we learn that devas instinctively recognised Gautama's qualities. His teaching delighted them so much that sometimes, 'elated and full of joy, they shone with many lustrous colours, like a beryl gem that radiates when placed on a brocade'.[59] But Gautama explained that, for all their glory, the gods were still part of ordinary existence; their lives in the heavens, though long-lasting, were not eternal; and they were as baffled by the ultimate nature of existence as human beings.

Gautama accepted worship of the gods among householders, though not Shakyaputra monks, but it seemed to him a distraction from the real concerns of life. He told those who looked for a protective force outside themselves that they could also rely on his mastery of the spirit realms, and that the Awakened state he embodied would help them in the face of whatever mysteries they feared. This made Gautama a worthier and more profitable focus of devotion than the gods, and he told people: 'If you revere those worthy of worship – Awakened Ones and their disciples . . . there's no measure for reckoning your merit.'[60] The source of his strength was the freedom from craving, hatred and delusion that he had attained through his Enlightenment. The spirits had no hold over him, and he was a true refuge because he was beyond samsara entirely.

The Art of Living

When he was out walking near the Venuvana in Rajagriha one day, Gautama came upon a sight that is common in India even today. A young man called Sigala was propitiating the gods and powers of the universe by praying to the Six Directions (the four points of the compass, plus upwards and downwards). In these directions, according to Indian cosmology, lie the four cosmic continents with their divine and demonic inhabitants and the forces of life, death, creation and destruction they represent. Gautama called Sigala over and suggested another way of understanding what it meant to protect the Six Directions. For him, 'the world' meant the things one actually experienced, so Gautama told Sigala that the true meaning of the Six Directions lay in human relationships: 'the East should be seen as one's mother and father, the South as one's teachers, the West as one's wife and children, the North as one's friends and companions, the direction below as servants and workers, the direction above as ascetics and brahmins'.[61] The ethical person protects the Six Directions, he suggested, by honouring the responsibilities these relationships brought in a spirit of kindness. This binds people together in the network of reciprocal obligations we call 'society'.

The story once again shows Gautama inverting a person's belief in the value of an external ritual by revealing a meaning that connects the ritual action to the moral state of the person performing it. It's not so much that Gautama considered psychology more important than ritual but that, for him, the universe was inherently moral. The law of karma operates everywhere, he stressed, so every action and thought has a moral weight and shapes a person's future. That was a powerful message and of a piece with Gautama's general philosophy. Dependently arisen reality isn't just a matter for holy men: it is the life that unfolds each moment in every person's experience and actions. So morality really means understanding the motives that lie behind an action, and intelligently anticipating its consequences. That, *in itself*, connects a person to the underlying patterns of existence. Serving others in the ways Gautama suggested to Sigala, and feeling gratitude for what one receives in return, aligns a person with the true character of human society.

On the special *uposatha* days that mark the phases of the moon Jain householders adopted aspects of monastic life, and these days may already have had a status in Magadha comparable to the Jewish Sabbath. Gautama adapted the custom for his own householder disciples. When monks gathered to confess they should spend the day living simply: not eating after noon and abstaining from sex, entertainments, cosmetics and comfortable beds. In a similar vein, Gautama also offered householders advice on acting skilfully in a marriage, in work and in managing money. Perhaps reflecting the number of business-minded merchants among his listeners, he suggested that a man should divide into four parts the wealth he had 'amassed by the strength of his arms, earned through the sweat of his brow'.[62] He should spend a quarter to maintain his happiness and that of his dependents; save a quarter as provision for the future; give a quarter to friends; and donate the final quarter to holy men. The proportions suggest a society awash with surplus wealth and a fast-growing economy.

Gautama sometimes explicitly said that wealth was a sign of merit:

Someone who is virtuous ... accumulates great wealth on account of his lack of negligence; his good reputation spreads around; whenever he enters a company, whether of nobles, Brahmins, householders or ascetics, he does so with confidence; he dies untroubled; and at the breaking up of the body after death he is reborn in a happy destiny, a heavenly world.[63]

Brahmins and others who equated status with birth resented this praise of wealth (which anyone could gain). But it legitimised the position of merchants like Anathapindika who had won or sustained their social positions through their efforts, and associated it with an underlying pattern of reward and punishment. The most prominent figures in the Discourses are Kshatriyas and Brahmins, followed by Vaishyas, and some historians suggest that Gautama's movement appealed to the social elite. Often in later Buddhist history, monks bolstered the standing of rich benefactors on whom they depended, and there are hints in the early sources that some poor people thought the monks paid the wealthy more attention. However, inscriptions on shrines from the early centuries of Buddhist history show that donors came from many sections of society, especially artisans, guilds of craftsmen, traders, fishermen and gardeners, small-scale landowners, and monks and nuns themselves – in fact, all sections that could afford to make donations.* This reflects the pattern in the Discourses, in which Gautama teaches publicly to anyone who will listen – rich or poor, male or female – and sometimes singles out an outcast like the leper Suppabudda or the bandit Angulimala.

All Gautama's teaching expressed his understanding of life, but it is hard to know how many of his subtler insights he shared with

---

* This does not mean that Gautama did not appeal to poor people as well, who *couldn't* afford to sponsor an inscription. Most disciples mentioned in the Discourses come from relatively affluent backgrounds, but that may simply reflect what the monastic tradition considered worth recording. Enough poor people are mentioned to imagine that there were many more.

householders. He told Vacchagotta that he had numerous lay followers who 'carry out my instruction, respond to my advice, have
gone beyond doubt and become independent in [the Dharma]'.[64]
But teachings in the Discourses that are addressed to groups of
householders (as opposed to individuals) usually confine themselves to praise for ethics and giving. When Anathapindika was
dying, Shariputra told him: 'Do not cling to what is seen, heard,
cognised, encountered, sought after and examined by the mind and
your consciousness will not be dependent on that.'[65] The instruction not to cling to experience was one of Gautama's basic teachings, but Anathapindika burst into tears and told Shariputra:
'Although I have long attended the Teacher and other worthy monks,
I have never before heard such a talk.' He urged Shariputra to make
such teachings more widely available because some householders
had 'little dust in their eyes and are wasting away through not
hearing the Dharma'.

Prasenajit

One day – it can't have been many years after Gautama's Awakening
– Prasenajit, the Kosalan Maharaja, visited him at the Jetavana. He
arrived resplendent atop the white state elephant, accompanied by
soldiers and members of his court, and his sister rode quietly behind
him. The meeting changed the lives of both men. Prasenajit was
the same age as Gautama, but he was a connoisseur of the pleasures of 'each of the five senses'[66] and had a substantial collection
of beautiful wives. However, he lived in an atmosphere of intrigue,
suspecting that the courtiers were insincere, the judges corrupt and
the generals plotting against him. In his world, Prasenajit later told
Gautama, 'kings quarrel with kings, Brahmins with Brahmins,

householders with householders, mothers with sons, brother with brother and friend with friend'.[67]

Prasenajit seems to have regarded Gautama with a mix of curiosity and wariness. The new guru was Prasenajit's subject by birth and Gautama's father may have attended assemblies of provincial chieftains. But Gautama was also a man of considerable influence. If the Mahavagga is to be believed, he had already won the support of Prasenajit's brother-in-law and sometime rival, the mighty Bimbisara, and in Shravasti he was backed by Anathapindika's money. Gautama's claim that he was not just wise but had attained supreme Enlightenment set him apart from most shramana gurus; and the establishment of the Jetavana must have shifted the balance of Shravasti's religious world. His teachings challenged worldly values, yet Anathapindika, who had more money than anyone, was devoted to him, and many gifted young Kosalan men had joined the Shakyaputras. Prasenajit's chief wife, Mallika, had become a devotee and quoted Gautama's sayings so often that Prasenajit eventually exclaimed: 'No matter what Gautama says, you applaud it!'[68] But the young teacher's predictions had a disconcerting way of coming true, and Prasenajit at last decided to see Gautama for himself to judge if he were a saviour or a charlatan, an opportunity or a threat.

Prasenajit's first words expressed his wariness. 'Master Gautama, do you claim, "I have awakened to unsurpassed perfect Enlightenment"?'[69] 'Great king,' Gautama replied, 'if you could rightly say that of anyone, you could say it of me.' 'But, Master Gautama, when I have asked other teachers, who are leaders of their own communities, if they were perfectly Enlightened they did not claim to be so. And yet you are still young and newly gone forth.' Gautama responded with a blistering declaration.

Great king, there are four things you should not look down on for
their youth: a warrior, a snake, a fire and a perfect monk.

Do not underestimate a young warrior. One day he will gain the
throne and punish you with his royal might. So avoid him if you
value your life.

Do not look down on a young snake. It slithers along, shimmering
with vibrant colours, and one day it may bite the fool who scorns it.

Do not disparage a fire that is newly lit. Some day it may burn
you. If it grows it will become a great mass of flame that feeds on
everything and leaves a blackened trail behind it.

When a fire burns down a forest the shoots grow up again; but if
a perfect monk burns you with his potency, you will not acquire sons
or cattle, and your heirs will not enjoy wealth. They will be barren
and heirless, like the stumps of palm trees.[70]

In this searing proclamation of spiritual authority Gautama challenged Prasenajit by his sheer personal force (just as he had presented himself to Bimbisara as the conqueror of the Gaya serpent
gods). It was the language of power. As well as threatening Prasenajit, Gautama's declaration challenged the promises of the Brahmins who clustered around his court. Gautama was claiming that,
in his own way, and without the help of verses or rituals, he too
could channel the forces on which life depends. More than that:
he embodied an equivalent authority, and by supporting Gautama,
Prasenajit would join himself to it. Prasenajit was overwhelmed by
Gautama's words and became 'a lay-follower who has gone for Refuge
for life', while his sister decided to become a nun.

Prasenajit needed a religious sanction of some sort. Kosala was
a loose collection of disparate provinces that were separated by
bandit-infested badlands, and for most of its citizens the king was
a distant figure. If his power were to be based on more than the

brute force of his armies and spy networks, his subjects must respect him. One source of support came from the Brahmins. The Buddhist commentaries say that as a young man Prasenajit studied at the great Brahmin centre of Taxila in modern-day Pakistan, and the Discourses say that as king he commissioned sacrifices and granted land to Brahmins. Brahmins were numbered among his courtiers and advisers, and insight into their counsel comes from the *Arthashastra*, a Brahminical manual of statecraft written a few generations later. It suggests numerous stratagems for maintaining power that include spying on subjects and deceiving enemies, as well as a whole chapter concerning secret poisons and curses. In this world, magic and the occult were woven into politics, warfare and state occasions. Grand Brahminical sacrifices, especially grand events like the horse sacrifice, were, in effect, elaborate spells to bring prosperity and victory to the entire state.

From the standpoint of Gautama's pragmatism, Brahminical pretensions seemed hollow superstition, and he countered the claims they made for their rituals with hilarious descriptions:

> A king or clan-leader builds a new assembly hall. Shaving off his hair and beard and putting on a rough hide, he smears his body with ghee and oil, scratches his back with a deer's horn, and enters the hall. He lies down on the bare grass and milk is drawn from the first nipple of a young cow to feed the king, from the second to feed his queen, from the third to feed his chief adviser. Then he orders people to kill bulls, cows, goats and sheep for the sacrifice, trees are felled for the sacrificial post, and grass is cut. Meanwhile, his terrified, tear-stained servants are threatened with punishment and made to do the work.[71]

Gautama added ruefully that in this way people tormented both themselves and others. And yet, in his first meeting with Prasenajit,

Gautama made his own claim to supernatural power. As a realised holy man he was part shaman, part teacher and part divinity, embodying an archetype that touched the deepest needs of both Prasenajit and the society he ruled – their fear of death and the spirits of the departed, their awe of the divinities with power in the spirit realm and their desire for happiness and success in this life. In this role, Gautama could communicate his understanding of life.

If Prasenajit was impressed by Gautama's spiritual power, he also appreciated his personal qualities, contrasting the atmosphere among the Shakyaputras with the corruption and intrigue of the court. The king often officiated in Shravasti's Judgement Hall, where he arbitrated in disputes between members of Kosala's wealthy elite. Each day he had the wearying experience of listening to people 'speaking deliberate lies for the sake of their own selfish pleasures'.[72] By contrast Gautama had no hidden agenda, no interest in money or sex, and he offered straightforward, honest advice, rather than 'reciting charms, interpreting dreams or practising astrology'[73] like the Brahmins. The qualities Gautama valued and encouraged his monks to develop also made him someone the king could trust – an invaluable quality. Gautama said of the ideal monk: 'He keeps his eyes from wandering restlessly, his ears are deaf to chatter and gossip and he has no desire for possessions. He isn't troubled by criticism or impressed by praise. When he speaks to householders he doesn't hope for a reward . . . He doesn't tell lies, avoids treachery, and even if he is provoked he doesn't retaliate.'[74]

The Shakyaputras may have had their own interests and rivalries, but Gautama tried not to fuel them, and his discretion and neutrality made him an ideal counsellor. As Gautama put it, Dharma practice brought maturity and independence along with 'a sense of meaning, a sense of oneself, a sense of moderation, a sense of time, and a sense of social gatherings'.[75] The last quality was the capacity to move easily between different groups and act appropriately in each – a rare virtue in India's divided society Prasenajit ruefully mused that, even though he could order people to be exiled or executed, they still barged in when he was sitting in council. Gautama's disciples treated him with far more respect. Listening to Gautama teach one day, Prasenajit noticed that when a monk cleared his throat 'one of his companions nudged him with his knee to indicate: "Be quiet, venerable sir," Prasenajit reflected. 'It is wonderful that an assembly can be so disciplined without force or weapons.'[76]

Prasenajit faced spiritual challenges as well as political ones, and realised that 'Very few people who acquire great wealth do not become intoxicated and negligent, succumb to greed or act cruelly.'[77] Gautama told him that to make progress he would need 'spiritual friendship'[78] and, according to some accounts, when Gautama was in Shravasti Prasenajit visited him every day, and they made a point of meeting when their paths crossed elsewhere. Gautama offered the king honest advice, and in return he asked Prasenajit to be 'honest and sincere', as well as to 'show himself to his teacher'[79] as he actually was. His guidance ranged from reflections on high matters of state to lifestyle advice. One day Prasenajit came to see Gautama having eaten 'an entire bucketful of rice and curry'. Gautama told him:

> When a person is constantly mindful,
> And knows when enough food has been taken,
> All their afflictions become more slender.[80]

Prasenajit asked his attendant to repeat these lines at every mealtime and before long he grew slim and 'stroked his limbs' with satisfaction. Gautama told the king that paying careful attention to *whatever* was happening was both a spiritual quality and a worldly advantage, and that 'diligence' or 'heedfulness'[81] was the one quality that brings benefits in both this life and the next.

Prasenajit slowly learned from Gautama that it wasn't enough to buttress his material fortunes: he also needed to develop inner qualities. 'Those who engage in misconduct of body, speech and mind leave themselves unprotected', he reflected, 'even if they're protected by an entire company of soldiers. That protection is merely external.'[82] There is no mention that Gautama explained his more philosophical ideas to the king or taught him to meditate, but the pair repeatedly discussed the inevitability of death and the need to prepare for it. Gautama didn't hold back. Late in their lives Gautama told Prasenajit that old age and death advanced towards living beings like 'a mountain range as high as the clouds',[83] crushing everything in its path. Kings fight off their enemies by sending armies against them, employing advisers adept at subterfuge or buying them off with money, he said, but such methods are futile when ageing and death come rolling in. Gautama reminded the king of this lesson when Mallika died and Prasenajit was struck dumb with grief. Gautama told him that even the gods couldn't escape decay, illness, death, disappearance and destruction and suggested that he reflect:

It's not just me: wherever beings are born their nature is to decay. If I were to lament and become distraught, my food would not agree with me, my body would become unattractive, my affairs would go untended, my enemies would be gratified and my friends unhappy.[84]

'Perform meritorious actions,' he added. 'There is nothing else to do.'

Prasenajit became deeply devoted to Gautama, and by the end of their lives he felt a strong, abiding affection for his teacher. He stood up for the Shakyaputras when they were criticised, reported misbehaving monks to Gautama and paid homage as a faithful disciple by 'placing his head at Gautama's feet'.[85] But this didn't mean that Prasenajit ruled according to Gautama's principles. State violence was a fact of Kosalan life, and one day monks returning to the Jetavana from their alms round reported seeing 'a great mass of people bound in ropes, clogs and chains'.[86] The Discourses list a range of tortures used against criminals including 'beating them with canes or clubs, cutting off their hands or feet, hanging them from meat hooks, splashing them with boiling oil, feeding them to dogs and impaling them alive on stakes'.[87] Prasenajit still performed state sacrifices where many animals were killed, and Gautama told the monks not to attend.

Gautama had to deal cautiously with Prasenajit and others who wielded power. The *Arthashastra* frankly encourages rulers to exploit holy men for their own ends by counselling them to

provide all ascetics with subsistence, clothing and lodging, and send on espionage such among those under his protection as are desirous to earn a livelihood, ordering each of them to detect a particular kind of crime committed in connection with the king's wealth and to report of it when they come to receive their subsistence and wages.[88]

Prasenajit once pointed to a group of shramanas and asked Gautama whether he thought any of them had achieved Realisation. Gautama replied that a person's character could only be known after a long time and through careful observation and discussion. Prasenajit told him who the wanderers really were: 'They are informers who are returning after spying on the country and I will make them tell me what they have learned. Then they will wash off the mud and dirt, trim their hair and beards and dress in clean clothes.'[89]

Gautama seems to have preferred the collective government of the clan-republics to that of the kingdoms and modelled Shakya-putra life on clan meetings. He sometimes voiced his disapproval of royal injustice, but he balanced that by criticising criminals for their crimes. His closest approach to suggesting a radical political philosophy comes in the form of a myth about the legendary First King, who deals with disorder through economic development rather than punishment:

> The king should supply seed and feed to those who are working at agriculture and animal husbandry; he should supply capital to those who are working at commerce; he should organise food and wages for those working in his own service. Then those people will be keen on their jobs and will not harass the countryside, the king will acquire a great pile. The country will be secure, free from public enemies. People will be happy and dance their children in their laps.[90]

This is a strikingly modern perspective on government, and an equally radical philosophy is found in the Agganna Sutta, in which Gautama reimagines the origins of society in a way that subverts Brahminical ideas. Caste roles, he says, aren't divinely ordained: they just reflect the lifestyles chosen by distant ancestors. And kings were originally appointed by the populace, not the gods, to 'show anger where anger was due, censure those who deserved it and banish those who deserved banishment'.[91]

In describing these mythic societies Gautama was suggesting that there is a natural order that was very different from the actual state of affairs in Kosala and Magadha. But Gautama was neither a social commentator nor an other-worldly figure with no relevance to social realities. Gautama's contemporaries identified him as a figure of cosmic significance, a 'Great Agent'[92] for whom two possible destinies were open: that is the significance of the unusual physical characteristics he is said to have possessed. If such a person renounces household life he will become 'a fully enlightened Buddha, who has drawn back the veil from the world'. But if he remains a householder he will be a Universal King and rule according to dharma. Here, dharma primarily means the reality that is the natural order of things and the natural laws that underlie society. For 'a just and righteous king' to 'rule by Dharma only'[93] therefore means cutting through man-made conventions (such as caste divisions) and manifesting righteousness, virtue and justice.

In his final existence Gautama chose Buddhahood, but several discourses relate that in previous lives he had been a Universal King who had governed the earth 'as far as its ocean boundaries, a land open, uninfested by brigands, free from jungle, powerful, prosperous, happy and free from perils'.[94] In this sense, Gautama was a kind of monarch as well as a spiritual teacher, and his Dharma was a blueprint for a cosmic golden age, as well as a description of the path to Nirvana.* By embodying and describing a different order of reality, Gautama established a measure against which a living monarch could be judged.

The social ideal that Gautama evoked probably had little effect in his lifetime, but a century and a half later the Emperor Ashoka reformed his pan-Indian Empire in the light of Gautama's teach-

---

* Gautama's association with the figure of the Universal Monarch is explicit in the claim that he was descended from one and in his instructions that his funeral follow the elaborate rituals associated with one. The figure of the Bodhisattva, which is central to the Mahayana Buddhism of the first millennium CE, inherited many features from the Great Agent, and also has a social meaning.

Stone seal from Mohenjo-Daro showing a mysterious figure who may be meditating. Indus Valley, Pakistan, 3000–1500 BCE.
© Harappan National Museum of Karachi, Karachi, Pakistan / The Bridgeman Art Library

Limestone relief panel depicting Gautama's departure from the palace.
© The Trustees of the British Museum

The ruins of Shravasti, capital of Kosala in Gautama's time.
© Eye Ubiquitous / Alamy

Gautama's birth, springing miraculously from the flank of his mother, Maya. Stone relief sculpture from East India, 10th century CE. © The Art Archive / British Museum

Gautama's life in Suddhodana's palace, as imagined by a Tibetan artist, 18th century.
© The Art Archive / Musée Guimet Paris / Gianni Dagli Orti

Gautama in the period between his departure from the palace and his Enlightenment. Fourth-century figure in schist or shale from Mekha-Sanda near Shabaz-Garhi, Pakistan.
© Musée Guimet, Paris, France / Peter Willi / The Bridgeman Art Library

Gautama's Awakening. Fifth-century CE image, found at Sarnath. © Delhi, National Museum / R. & S. Michaud / akg-images

Mara and his army attack Gautama, Tibet, 18th century. © The Art Archive / Musée Guimet Paris / Alfredo Dagli Orti

Gautama's first teaching to the group of five ascetics, Pakistani, 2nd century CE. © Fred Jones Jr. Museum of Art, University of Oklahoma, USA / Wentz-Matzene Collection, 1936 / The Bridgeman Art Library

Following his Enlightenment and his first teaching, Gautama returned to Gaya and tamed the local serpent gods. Here he presents the snake's lifeless body to the awed Brahmans. Stone relief in Greco-Buddhist style, 1st–4th century CE. © National Museum of Karachi, Karachi, Pakistan / Giraudon / The Bridgeman Art Library

Gautama teaching: a limestone relief panel showing the conversion of Sundarananda. © The Trustees of the British Museum

Gautama's return home. This fresco from the Ajanta caves (c. 5th century CE) shows Gautama's return to Kapilavatsu after his Enlightenment and his reunion with his wife and son.
© Lindsay Hebberd / CORBIS

Gautama seated under the Bodhi tree, worshipped by monks and princes. Stone relief carving BPA2# 4094, 2nd century CE, Indian Museum of Sarnath. © Bettmann / CORBIS

Ananda, Gautama's personal attendant.
© The Granger Collection / TopFoto

A yaksha (male) and yakshi (female): dangerous spirit figures.
© Orissa Museum. Photo: akg-images

Gautama flanked by his chief
disciples Shariputra and
Maudgalyayana, Tibetan
thangka image.
© Tibet Ancient Art &
Architecture Collection

Gautama's miraculous descent from heaven. © Christie's Images / CORBIS

Gautama's Parinirvana. Gautama is lying on his bed surrounded by noblemen, beggars and followers. Ananda, Gautama's companion and Subhadra, his last disciple, are in front of the bed. Grey slate relief. © akg-images / Erich Lessing / British Museum

The division of the Gautama's relics, schist relief panel.
© The Trustees of the British Museum

Bodh Gaya today.
© TopFoto

Marble Slab inscribed with Pali discourses, Maha Lawka Marazein Pagoda, Madalay, Burma.
© 2006 Alinari/TopFoto

Theravadin monks and laypeople worshipping at the Sarnath stupa (site of Gautama's first teaching).
© Dinodia / The Bridgeman Art Library

The Buddha meditating just after his Enlightenment, shaded by Mucalinda the serpent-god.
© Werner Forman Archive / Musée Guimet

The god Indra disguised as a woodcutter offers grass to the Buddha while Vajrapani looks on,
Gandhara, 1st century CE. © Peshawar Museum, photo by Sylvia Sax

ings and attempted to rule it according to 'dharma'. That idea, more than any specific proposals for reform, was Gautama's abiding contribution to Indian civilisation and the Buddhist civilisation that eventually spread far beyond India.

The Killer

Shravasti today is largely unexcavated. The huge earthen ramparts still stand, but within their confines just a few substantial constructions rise above the scrub and bushes. There are stupas, or memorial monuments, to Prasenajit, Anathapindika ... and to the city's most notorious murderer. The story of his encounter with Gautama touches on many of the themes explored in this chapter.

Several versions of the story have come down to us, including one in Pali and another in Chinese translation that is simpler and probably older. This version tells us that Gautama was wandering through the Dhavakjalika forest, some distance south of Shravasti, mixing with the 'cowherds, shepherds, wood gatherers and grass gatherers',[95] and pacing mindfully along the road through the forest. They warned him: 'Do not continue to walk on this path. Further ahead is the robber Angulimala. Avoid this fearsome man.' It tells us nothing more about Angulimala, though other texts say a great deal. His name means 'finger necklace', and we hear that his fetish was to sever a finger from his victims' corpses. At first he hung them from a tree and birds pecked off the flesh, but when he saw the fingers rotting on the ground he threaded them together into a garland that he wore round his neck. Angulimala incarnated the terrors of the wilderness, and the Pali text says that terrified citizens fled towns and villages in fear of him.

According to the Pali commentary, Angulimala had been ordered to kill by his Brahmin guru, who wrongly believed that Anguli-mala had seduced his wife. The teacher considered murdering him but decided against it because Angulimala was 'as strong as seven elephants'.[96] Besides, killing a student was bad for the guru's business. Instead, he ordered Angulimala to bring a necklace made of fingers from a thousand victims. Central to all versions of the story is the suggestion that Angulimala kills from compulsion: perhaps a weird sense of religious duty that anticipated the Hindu ritual murderers of later times, perhaps a psychopathic bloodlust, or perhaps the mixture of need and circumstance that leads people to banditry in all ages.

Gautama told the labourers, 'I am not afraid', and continued walking down the road mindfully and in silence. Angulimala watched as the solitary, robed figure approached, and the Pali version relates that he strapped on his sword and shield, buckled his bow and ran towards Gautama. Then something strange happened. Angulimala ran till his heart pounded and sweat poured from him, but however fast he ran he came no closer to the robed figure before him. Exhausted and confused, he halted: a few yards from Gautama but separated by an unbridgeable gap. 'Stand still, stand still, don't go,' he cried. Gautama continued to walk on calmly and told Angulimala: 'I am always standing still; but you are not standing still yourself.'

Some commentaries explain the 'miracle' of Angulimala's failure to catch Gautama as a display of his psychic powers – one source even explains that Gautama magically expanded the earth he walked on and contracted the ground beneath Angulimala. However it happened, the meaning of Gautama's 'miracle' lies in his mysterious statement 'I am standing still', even though he was walking. What did he mean, Angulimala demanded. Was he lying?

Angulimala, I say that I always stand still in the sense that I have put down the weapons that might be directed towards other beings. You, however, are terrifying others ... and for a long time have been inflicting suffering on them. I am established in my own Dharma ... but because you do not have the vision of the Four Truths you have not ceased to be negligent.

These words had a shattering effect. Angulimala cried out: 'At long last I see the sage whose tracks I pursued earlier. Having heard your true and sublime words I will forsake my prolonged evils.' He threw away his sword and shield, and laid himself at Gautama's feet. 'May I be granted the going forth.' Gautama smiled, 'his mind full of loving-kindness and compassion and with the pity of a great spirit for the manifold sorrows of beings'. 'Come, monk,' he said, and through that simple ceremony Angulimala became a Shakyaputra monk.

Gautama's miracle may have stunned Angulimala, but the teaching that revealed its meaning transformed him. The image of a man running but failing to catch another who is moving more slowly dramatises the contrast between Angulimala's state of mind and Gautama's. Whether his motive was blind hatred or pernicious vows, the effect was the same. Driven by a compulsion to kill, Anguli-mala was out of control, while Gautama had mastered his mind and was no longer driven by unconscious emotions. His instruction to Angulimala to 'stand still' was shorthand for his entire teaching – as he suggests by mentioning the Four Noble Truths. To be still was to stop craving, stop killing, stop fighting the world and stop being directed by unconscious compulsions.

The texts do not delve far into the emotions behind Angulimala's dramatic transformation, but they hint at its cause. Angulimala operated through power, yet Gautama showed no hint of the fear

Angulimala was used to seeing in his victims. In a similar situation, the monk Adhimutta told the bandits who attacked him, 'I have no fear of death',[97] and that stopped them in their tracks. Gautama had escaped the realm of desire in which he was vulnerable to fear or force, and Angulimala – like the *yakshas* – had no hold on him. Instead, Gautama gave the murderer his complete, untroubled, loving attention, and the Pali version poignantly relates that Angulimala cried out: 'Oh, at last this recluse, a venerated sage, has come to the forest *for my sake*.'[98]

Both the Chinese and Pali versions of the story include the verses that Angulimala composed during the solitary retreat in which he gained Enlightenment. In a few luminously calm stanzas we sense the relief of a man who had left behind the dark places of his mind:

> Who checks the evil deeds he did
> By doing wholesome deeds instead,
> He illuminates the world
> Like the moon freed from a cloud.[99]

Through his realisation Angulimala became a holy man like Gautama, who illuminated society and healed its troubles. The Pali text expands this theme with a dramatic encounter on the road to Shravasti with Prasenajit, who was leading a large military force to track Angulimala down. When Gautama reveals that the cloaked figure beside him is none other than the fearsome killer, Prasenajit is amazed: 'We could not subdue him with all our weapons, yet you have tamed him without using force!' The conversion dramatises Gautama's alternative form of power and his counterintuitive teaching that 'not by hatred are hatreds ever pacified ... They are pacified by love.'[100] He represents a completely different way of doing things.

Taken as a fable, Angulimala's conversion shows that no one is beyond redemption, and as the story evolved his transformation became an emblem for the capacity of spiritual change to heal society as a whole. According to the Pali account, when Anguli-mala stayed with Gautama in Shravasti angry citizens pelted him with rocks as he made his alms round. 'Bear it,' Gautama told him. 'You are experiencing the results of your actions.' One day, Anguli-mala saw a woman in agony during a breech birth and returned to the Jetavana, his heart heavy with compassion for her suffering. This showed the extent of his transformation. Gautama told Anguli-mala to return to her and say: 'Sister, since I was born I do not recall intentionally killing a living being.'[101] Angulimala protested that he could not truthfully say this, so Gautama told him to say: 'Since I was born in the Noble Life I do not recall intentionally killing a living being. Through this act of truth may there be well-being for you and well-being for your child.'

An 'act of truth' was powerful magic in Gautama's world – the statement of a deeply felt fact that implied a new way of seeing things – and the mother and her child returned to health. Anguli-mala's conversion had turned him from a destructive force to one that sustained life, like Gautama himself; and even today Buddhist monks recite this verse as a blessing at the time of a woman's delivery.

8

Crisis

Seeds of Conflict

The decades following Gautama's Enlightenment were a time of relative peace and stability in the Ganges Valley. One of the few wars we know of was an inconclusive conflict between the minor kingdoms of Avanti and Kausambi. The major powers, Magadha and Kosala, became allies when Bimbisara and Prasenajit married one another's sisters, and Bimbisara received a village in Kasi as a dowry. But the economic and military power of Magadha was rising inexorably. The village brought access to the Ganges, and Magadha prospered through its combination of trade and natural resources. A second marriage allied Bimbisara to an important family in the Vaishali nobility, and, having secured his northern and western borders, he attacked Anga to the south-east. That won Maghada the important city of Campa and access to the Ganges delta. It now controlled important points on the Ganges trade route, and competition intensified with the Vrijian Federation which governed much of the river's northern bank. Bimbisara used the kingdom's growing wealth to boost the power of the state by improving administration, holding large meetings of regional chieftains, and establishing the region's first standing army. By the end of Bimbisara's reign, Magadha was a thriving nation 300 miles in circumference, and the Vinaya tells us that 'Bimbisara ruled with supreme authority over eighty thousand villages',[1] while Rajagriha overflowed its boundaries, and a new city was built further down the valley.

One discourse looked back on this period as a golden age in which 'the holy life waxed mightily and prospered and spread widely as it was proclaimed among mankind'.[2] The peripatetic existence of the Shakyaputras was intended to help spread Gautama's teaching, and the nun Baddha reported that for fifty-nine years she had 'wandered over Anga and Magadha, Vajji, Kasi and Kosala'.[3] Gautama's own travels were just as extensive, and the setting of several discourses is Kuru, beyond the central Ganges Valley. We also hear of a monk called Punna who tells Gautama he was travelling to Sunaparanta (the modern Indian state of Maharashtra in central western India), notwithstanding its 'fierce and rough'[4] inhabitants. And a Maharashtran Brahmin living 'on the bank of the Godhavari'[5] sent sixteen of his pupils to question Gautama. One of them reportedly founded a community in Aurangabad on his return.

Gautama based himself in Shravasti where he was accepted as the leading teacher of his time, and he was the supreme influence on the Shakyaputra community. The senior disciples established followings of their own, especially in Rajagriha, where Shariputra, Maudgalyayana and Gautama's cousin Devadatta were acclaimed as realised masters. But tensions were building that threatened both the region and the Shakyaputras, and the last eight years of Gautama's life saw crises for both.

Gautama was growing old. Ananda, by now a very old friend and Gautama's long-time companion, told him, 'It's strange. Your skin is no longer clear and radiant, your limbs are flabby and wrinkled, your body is stooped, and all your senses are weaker.' Ananda's frankness evokes their years of intimacy, and Gautama was philosophical. 'That's the way it is, Ananda. When young, one is subject to ageing; when healthy, subject to illness; when alive, subject to death.' But he continued less phlegmatically:

I spit on you, old age –
old age that makes for ugliness.
This charming puppet, the body
is crushed by advancing age.
Even one who lives to a hundred
is headed towards death,
which spares none along the way,
but tramples everything.[6]

Later commentators suggested that Gautama dismissed old age because he had transcended death, but the note sounded in these lines is not quite the equanimous acceptance he suggested to the monks when he told each of them to 'await his time mindful and clearly comprehending'.[7] Gautama's vehemence suggests the visceral abhorrence for the sufferings of the human condition that had prompted his flight from the palace so many years earlier.

Some years after Gautama's death a monk called Phussa lamented that his contemporaries were a pale reflection of the heroes of the Shakyaputras' early years. In the old days, Phussa said, monks had lived 'in the forest, at the root of trees, in caves and grottoes, devoting themselves to seclusion'.[8] But the mighty elders had passed away, and Phussa considered the monks of his time a worldly, degenerate group: 'They practise medicine as if they were doctors; they have many duties, just like a householder; they dress themselves up as if they were courtesans; and they are as fond of exercising authority as a nobleman. Chasing after opportunities, excuses and stratagems, they build their careers and accumulate wealth.'

Several passages in the Discourses suggest that these developments started in Gautama's own lifetime. In one, Mahakasyapa, the epitome of forest renunciation, complains that the newer monks don't listen to him when he urges them to practise intensively. Gautama agrees:

> In the past, elder monks were forest dwellers, alms food eaters, and rag-robe wearers. They had few desires and were content; they lived alone, remaining aloof from society and made tremendous efforts. But now the monk who is well known, who loves to receive fine robes, lodgings, alms food and medicine and is fond of company is the one who is offered an honoured seat.[9]

Such comments suggest a growing tension between a hard core of Shakyaputras devoted to wilderness practice, and an increasingly settled monastic community with an acknowledged place in society. The more successful Gautama and the Shakyaputras became, the more temptations they faced; and Gautama repeatedly warned the monks against succumbing to 'gains, honours and praise'.[10] He once warned the monks that if they chased high social status they would resemble 'an old jackal afflicted by mange':[11] wherever they went they would not feel at ease. Some discourses suggest that these dangers were the reason for the growing body of rules that constrained the Shakyaputras' lives. One monk asked Gautama, 'Why is it that previously there were fewer training rules and more monks who gained liberation, but now there are more rules and liberation is rarer?'[12] Gautama replied, 'There are more training rules when beings are deteriorating and the true Dharma is disappearing.' That happens, he said, when the monastic community gains 'greatness, worldly fame and long-standing renown' and risks contamination.

We know that the monastic community became increasingly institutionalised and rule-bound in the centuries after Gautama, and
it may be that in such passages monks of a later time projected the
struggles of their era back to Gautama's day. But the monks who
compiled the Discourses were probably the very monastery-dwelling
scholars these passages criticise, and we should take seriously their
testimony that the process was under way in Gautama's lifetime.
Any collective endeavour develops an institutional aspect, bringing
inherent problems, and the Discourses suggest that the Shakyaputra community's institutional problems came to a head in Gautama's last decade.

Schism

Some time in Gautama's later years, Mahavira, the definitive teacher
of Jainism, died aged seventy-two by starving himself to death, and
the Jain monks split into two warring factions: 'They were brawling,
squabbling, and wounding each other with verbal arrows. It seemed
as if there was internecine strife among [them]. And the white-
robed lay disciples were as disappointed, dismayed and disgusted
with his pupils as they were with his Dharma . . . They were left
without a refuge.'[13]

The dispute was serious: 'You would have thought the [Jains] were
bent on killing each other',[14] and it must have sent shockwaves through
the shramana world. Ananda told Gautama about the dispute and
said he feared the same could happen among the Shakyaputras. Gautama was reassuring. Shakyaputra monks might well disagree about
the correct observance of the monastic code, as the Kausambi monks
had. But such matters were trifling, and the real danger was 'a dispute
about the path or the way'.[15] The Jain monks could not agree on what

Mahavira had actually taught, but Gautama was confident that he had expressed his teachings clearly, that the monks understood them and that there was little disagreement on fundamental doctrines. He added that disputes usually started for emotional rather than intellectual reasons and it was within the monks' power to check such tendencies. 'If you see any such root of dispute, either in yourselves or in others, you should strive to abandon it', Gautama urged.[16] What's more, he had confidence in senior teachers 'who have attained freedom from bondage, are able to refute opposing doctrines, and can give a grounded exposition of the Dharma'.[17]

But what *would* happen to the community when Gautama died? Gautama had, in effect, made Shariputra his deputy, ably backed by his close friend, Maudgalyayana. Shariputra was 'the captain of the Dharma' and 'the chief among those of great wisdom [in the Shakyaputra community]'.[18] According to the traditional account, he had made great strides in systematising Gautama's teaching and developing ways to train the monks. Did that make Shariputra Gautama's heir? The possibility was never tested as Shariputra died before Gautama, but the Discourses contain hints that his appointment might have caused problems. Gautama's recognition of Maudgalyayana and Shariputra as his 'chief disciples' countered the principle that monastic seniority went according to the time of ordination, and the Discourses record a string of complaints against the pair. 'They have come under the control of evil wishes',[19] one monk protested, perhaps concerned at the extent of their influence. Some resented Shariputra's strict discipline, and one complained that Shariputra had beaten him. When Gautama asked Shariputra about this he declared, unapologetically, that he had a 'heart that is like the earth, vast, exalted and measureless, without hostility and without ill will'.[20] Gautama admiringly called this 'Shariputra's lion's roar'.

There is no mention of a proposal to make Shariputra Gautama's successor, but we do hear of an alternative plan that in future the Shakyaputras would be guided by the Dharma and the monastic code. That fitted Gautama's inclination to deflect displays of devotion by saying that the Dharma was important, not him, and that the best way to follow him was by practising his teachings. He saw monks and nuns as self-reliant individuals striving to realise a transpersonal truth, and had faith in institutions and doctrines as receptacles of his Dharma. But Gautama was also an Enlightened Buddha who inspired people personally and whose communication was as much 'transmission' as instruction, and a second element in his legacy was the lineage of teachers who traced their realisation back to his own.

The Vinaya relates that the issue of future leadership came to a head when Gautama visited Rajagriha some years before his death. In its account, Gautama's cousin Devadatta addresses him at a large formal gathering including many monks and King Bimbisara himself: 'Lord, you are now advanced in years and have come to the last stage of your life. You should rest now and enjoy happiness. Hand over the community of monks to me and I will lead it.' Gautama replies: 'Enough, Devadatta. Do not aspire to govern the community. I would not hand on its leadership to Maudgalyayana or Shariputra. How could I do so to a wretch like you, who should be vomited out like a ball of spit?'[21] Then Gautama asks Shariputra to announce in Rajagriha that Devadatta has changed and in no way represents Gautama's teaching or community.

The rejected monk responds furiously to his humiliation. He approaches Bimbisara's son Ajatashatru with a proposal: 'You kill your father and become the king, and I will kill the Blessed One and become the Buddha.' Devadatta launches a series of attempts on Gautama's life – dispatching murderers, hurling a rock as

Gautama climbs the path to Vulture's Peak and loosing a rampaging elephant in his path. Each attempt fails because Gautama is immune to such assaults, just as he had been invulnerable to Mara's army. When anxious monks set a guard around Gautama he tells them, 'It is impossible to take the life of a Perfect One through aggression.'[22] Next, Devadatta tries to split the monastic community by proposing five new rules for the Shakyaputras, which Gautama rejects, and Devadatta finally declares that he and his 500 monastic followers will no longer regard Gautama as their Buddha Refuge or the Shakyaputras as their sangha. Shariputra and Maudgalyayana reduce the impact of the schism by persuading the 500 monks to return, and when Devadatta hears of their defection he vomits blood and dies.

This story became prominent in the legendary versions of Gautama's life, which make Devadatta an archetypal villain and Gautama's rival even since childhood. But the story raises many questions. Why did Gautama respond to Devadatta with such extreme language? How could Devadatta have been in a position to propose changes to the Shakyaputras *after* a campaign against Gautama that would surely have led to his expulsion? Scattered references to Devadatta in the Discourses, anomalies in the legends and scholarly analyses of the sources allow us to suggest an alternative account of who Devadatta really was.

In a discourse called 'The Elders' Gautama includes Devadatta among eleven monks who, he says, are all 'arahants who have destroyed the fetters'.[23] This seems to recall a time in which Devadatta was considered an exemplary monk, and in the Vinaya Shariputra responds to Gautama's request that he denounce Devadatta by saying that he had previously praised him as being 'of great power and great majesty'.[24] Buddhist tradition offered numerous explanations of this contradiction, the simplest being that Devadatta was once virtuous – 'regarded as wise, composed, incandescent with honour' – and fell from grace when he was seduced by 'evil desires' and 'obsessed by evil friends'.[25]

A clue to an alternative explanation is the five rules Devadatta proposed. The Vinaya relates that Devadatta reminds Gautama of his praise for 'desiring little, contentment, expunging evil from the mind, graciousness, overcoming obstructions and making a great effort'.[26] He proposes that all monks should undertake the practices that he and his friends already follow, and maintain them throughout their lives. Henceforth, Devadatta suggests, the monks should live in the wilderness; beg for alms and not accept invitations to eat in supporters' houses; wear only cast-off rags rather than robes given by householders; sleep at the foot of trees, not under a roof; and be vegetarian.

Some scholars believe that these new rules are the core of the Devadatta legend while other elements are later additions. The Vinaya tells us that Devadatta's motive for proposing these changes was that he knew Gautama couldn't possibly accept them and was deliberately engineering a dispute. A more plausible explanation is that Devadatta's proposals were a sincere attempt by the leader of a group of hard-core wilderness monks to halt the community's drift from its forest origins towards communal and settled living. Devadatta's rules would have dramatically altered the Shakyaputras' future course and ensured that every monk practised extreme renunciation, like the Jains. His view that wilderness living was the only authentic form of renunciation echoes the sentiments of Phussa, Mahakasyapa and other wilderness monks, who also opposed the way the community was going.

A thousand years later, the Chinese pilgrim Fa-hsien reported meeting a community of Devadatta's disciples near Shravasti who revered three previous Buddhas, but not Gautama; and in 700 CE

Hsuan Tsang met monks who lived in three monasteries in Bengal and 'do not take thickened milk, following the instructions of Devadatta'.[27] This strongly suggests that Devadatta's split with the Shakyaputra mainstream was real and that there was more to it than mere villainy. The Vinaya tells us that Gautama responded to Devadatta's rules by explaining that he preferred choice to coercion and diversity to conformity:

> Let those who wish to live in the wilderness, and those who wish to live near a village. Let those who wish to beg for alms, and those who wish to accept invitations. Let those who wish to dress in rags, and those who wish to accept of robes from laymen. I have permitted monks to sleep beneath the trees for eight months of the year; and fish and meat may be eaten provided a monk has not seen, or heard, or suspected that it has been caught for that purpose.

This also has the ring of authenticity. It accords with the accommodating approach we find in the Discourses. Gautama's movement could include ardent renunciants, those who thrived through communication and friendship, and those who wanted a more settled life. He urged his monastic followers to practise intensively, whatever their lifestyle, and encouraged those who remained in lay society to apply his teachings as well.

Ajatashatru

As well as being a tale of religious politics, the Devadatta legend is a story of court intrigue. The Vinaya relates that Devadatta persuaded Ajatashatru to murder Bimbisara and that the prince crept, Macbeth-like, into his father's bedroom feeling 'afraid, anxious, fearful, and alarmed'[28] as he prepared to kill him. Unlike Macbeth, Ajatashatru was stopped before he could act, and his father asked, 'Why did you want to kill me?' 'Because I need a kingdom,' replied Ajatashatru. 'Then let it be yours!' With that Bimbisara abdicated, but tradition records that Ajatashatru, now king himself, imprisoned his father and deprived him of food. Only Bimbisara's wife was allowed to visit, and he survived by licking syrup that she had smeared on her body. The ruse was discovered, and, even as Bimbisara wasted away, his son had his feet cut with razor blades so that he died in agony. No one expected Gautama to save Bimbisara, but they did ask him to declare Bimbisara's fate in the afterlife. Gautama 'meditated in solitude' and saw a vision of a *yaksha*, now in the court of the great *yaksha* king, who cried out to him: '*I am Bimbisara! I am Bimbisara!*'[29]

Ajatashatru threw himself into the task of developing Magadha's military power and set the country on its way to control of an empire that, some generations later, stretched across India. Bimbisara had sponsored the education of Magadhan youths in the Brahminical colleges of Taxila in the north-east, where the students (who may have included Ajatashatru) would have learned of the vast power of the Persian Empire that stretched all the way to Egypt.* An age was approaching in which great empires vied for supremacy, and when Ajatashatru became king his thoughts turned to conquest. He overhauled Maghada's administration, increased taxes and put the country on a war footing. His military build-up created a powerful, professionally trained army and new weapons which, Jain sources inform us, included powerful catapults and a chariot fitted with a huge mace. The status quo in the Ganges Valley was shattered.

---

* In 518 BCE Taxila was annexed to the Persian Empire by Darius the Great, and it may have remained part of the empire in Gautama's day.

After Bimbisara's death his widow also died of grief, and, as she was Prasenajit's sister, the Kosalan king declared that the village in Kasi that had been ceded to Magadha in her dowry should revert to Kosala. When Prasenajit occupied the village, Ajatashatru mobilised his army and drove the Kosalans out. But after several more battles Ajatashatru was captured and brought before Prasenajit. 'He is still my nephew', Prasenajit reflected, so he decided to 'confiscate Ajatashatru's elephants, cavalry and infantry',[30] but spare his life. The commentaries add that Ajatashatru swore an oath never to attack Kosala again, and to seal the pact he married Prasenajit's daughter, Vajira. They add that Gautama commented, watching the shifting fortunes of the two sides, 'Victory brings hatred, for the defeated one experiences suffering. The tranquil one experiences happiness [by] giving up both victory and defeat.'[31] He also remarked that Ajatashatru was experiencing the effects of his actions:

> The killer begets a killer
> One who conquers a conqueror . . .
> Thus by the unfolding of karma
> The plunderer is plundered.[32]

However, fate had several more twists in store for all of them.

A discourse called 'The Fruits of the Ascetic Life' describes the only meeting between Gautama and Ajatashatru, setting the scene with rare eloquence. Ajatashatru was sitting on the roof of his palace, surrounded by his ministers, when he declared: 'Delightful is this moonlit night! What ascetic or Brahmin might we visit tonight so that our heart might be at rest?'[33] The ministers mentioned the names of several gurus, but the king was silent. Then Jivaka, Ajatashatru's doctor, suggested a visit to Gautama who was staying nearby with a large group of monks. 'If my lord were to visit the

Blessed One his heart would certainly be set at rest.' 'Then prepare the riding-elephants!' cried Ajatashatru, and soon the royal party set off.

They approached the mango grove where Gautama was staying with his community and heard ... nothing. Fear swept through Ajatashatru. 'Are you deceiving me, Jivaka?' he asked. 'Are you perhaps going to hand me over to my enemies? For how can it be that from a great company of 1,250 monks there is not a sneeze, not a cough, not a murmur?' Jivaka swore there was no trick, and the party proceeded until the elephants could go no further. Continuing on foot, they came upon hundreds of robed figures, sunk in meditation, 'completely silent, like a still pool'. The king sighed with wonder, 'May my son come to possess such calm!' Jivaka pointed out Gautama in their midst and when Gautama stirred Ajatashatru addressed him. 'I have something I would like to ask the Blessed One.'

Ajatashatru's question expressed his personality and perhaps his situation. He listed the trades and crafts pursued by his subjects: 'These people enjoy the evident fruits of their labour here and now: they bring happiness and joy to themselves, to their mother and father, to their wives and children, and to their friends and acquaintances. Is it possible to point out a fruit of the ascetic life that is similarly evident here and now?'[34] When Ajatashatru described the answers other teachers had given to his question he expressed his frustration that their ideas about the world lacked any clear sense of the relationship between actions and their consequences. Because they offered no moral compass, we may infer, they did not help him make sense of his own tortured conscience.

Gautama responded with a masterful exposition of the path that showed how one could take responsibility for one's life and develop the mind into unimaginable dimensions of wisdom and power.* Ajatashatru was deeply moved. 'I transgressed . . . when foolishly, in confusion, and unskilfully seeking to dominate, I deprived my father, the good and just king, of his life.'³⁵ He asked Gautama to accept his 'confession' for the sake of 'future restraint'. Gautama replied that it was good Ajatashatru had seen his error and wished to counteract it through the Dharma so that he might behave differently in future. But he also believed that 'Actions willed, performed and accumulated will not become extinct as long as their results have not been experienced, be it in this life, in the next life, or in subsequent future lives.'³⁶ According to his way of thinking, an action cannot be expiated through confession alone; its karmic effect has to play itself out. When Ajatashatru left, Gautama told the monks that the King would not escape the karmic effects of killing his father and would suffer intensely in his next life. Had it not been for this act, he added, 'the pure and spotless Dharma eye would have arisen to him.'³⁷

The End of the Shakyans

Even as Magadha transformed itself into a military state with a ruthless young ruler, trouble was stirring in Kosala. The Jataka collection and the commentaries to the Discourses tell a powerful and complicated story of deception, intrigue and violence that caught up Prasenajit, Gautama's Shakyan relatives and, eventually, Gautama himself.³⁸ We cannot vouch for its authenticity with any certainty, but scattered hints in the Discourses and the Vinaya suggest that there is more to it than legend, and it is possible to combine

---

* This discourse – the Sammanaphala Sutta – is one of the classic expositions of the Buddhist path.

the sources into a compelling narrative that frames the more familiar story of Gautama's final years.

The seed of the crisis was the status-laden custom of making lavish donations to monks. The monks could find themselves beholden to the donor if they accepted but cause offence if they refused. Prasenajit offered to feed Gautama and all the monks staying with him at the Jetavana, and for seven days he personally served them food. When Prasenajit suggested that this should become a regular arrangement Gautama declined, sending Ananda and other monks in his place. Prasenajit forgot to give any food at all for three days, and when he resumed only Ananda was there to receive the great feast he had prepared. The King complained to Gautama, who explained that the monks were not obliged to follow the wishes of householders, and, ashamed of himself, Prasenajit decided to make amends. From such small origins, disaster grows.

Prasenajit decided to take a Shakyan princess for his wife and sent an envoy to ask Gautama's cousin Mahanama (who had succeeded Suddhodana as chieftain) to find a suitable girl. But if Prasenajit thought he was bestowing an honour on the Shakyans, he reckoned without their lingering resentment at Kosalan rule and their intense racial chauvinism. Shakyan nobles believed they were descended from the Sun God, which made Prasenajit their inferior, and marriage to him would have disgraced any well-born Shakyan family. Mahanama devised a ruse to avoid either contaminating Shakyan blood or offending the king. He sent Prasenajit his own daughter, the beautiful Vasabha, as his bride, and informed the king that the young woman was the child of Shakya's chieftain and a close relative of Gautama's. Prasenajit was delighted to accept her, but what he didn't know, and Mahanama didn't mention, was that Vasabha was illegitimate and her mother was one of Mahanama's slaves.

Prasenajit and Vasabha had a son, Vidudabha, and as Prasenajit's only male child he was the heir to the Kosalan throne. When Vidudabha was sixteen the boy paid a visit to his Shakyan relatives. They received him politely, but the day after the formal reception in the meeting hall, one of Vidudabha's attendants observed a servant scrubbing the seat on which the prince had sat, ritually purifying it and cursing his master as the son of a slave. When Vidudabha learned of this, the whole story came out. He was furious and vowed to wash the seat with 'the blood of Shakyan throats'. Appalled to discover his son's lowly forebears, Prasenajit stripped Vidudabha and his mother of their royal gifts and reduced them to slaves. He relented when Gautama himself interceded, restoring Vidudabha as his heir, as well as making him the commander of the army.

Meanwhile, a court intrigue resurfaced that was rooted in the earlier years of Prasenajit's reign. Weary of trying court cases, he had passed the responsibility to an old friend and former fellow student called Bandhula, a Vrijian who had sought refuge in Shravasti. 'Let Bandhula be known for his judgements!'[39] declared the King. Bandhula's personal wealth made him immune to the bribery that was endemic in the system, and he soon offended vested interests by overturning unjust decisions and removing corrupt judges. The judges told Prasenajit that Bandhula was planning an insurrection, and, believing them, Prasenajit had Bandhula and his sons murdered. Prasenajit regretted what he had done and appointed Bandhula's nephew Digha-karayana as his new general; but Digha-karayana never forgave Prasenajit for Bandhula's murder and, like Vidudabha, he nursed his grievance.

One of the most moving scenes in the Discourses is the final meeting between Gautama and Prasenajit (described in a discourse called 'Monuments of the Dharma'). Prasenajit was travelling with Digha-karayana through Shakya – we don't know why, but the suspicion must be that their presence was connected with the coming storm. Prasenajit visited a peaceful woodland and the spreading tree roots seemed 'lovely and inspiring, quiet and undisturbed by voices, with an atmosphere of seclusion, remote from people and suitable for retreat'.[40] They evoked the Jetavana and other places in which Prasenajit had met Gautama and his disciples in years gone by. A desire to see Gautama once more filled the King. Digha-karayana, who commanded the royal guard that accompanied Prasenajit, told him that Gautama was staying nearby, and the company set off to see the king's old friend and teacher.

Arriving at park near Medalumpa, Prasenajit was delighted to find himself once again surrounded by Shakyaputra monks and immersed in the unique atmosphere they created. Gautama was in a small dwelling, and before entering Prasenajit handed Digha-karayana the royal insignia he wore on his person: his ceremonial sword and the royal turban adorned with the dazzling octagonal Verocanamani jewel, which legend declared was a gift from the god Sakka himself. Prasenajit cleared his throat and tapped on the door-frame. Gautama came to the door and the king entered, closing the door behind him. 'So the king is going into secret session now, and I have to stand here alone!' thought Digha-karayana. Then he looked down at the emblems of power that were in his hands.

Prasenajit was deeply moved to see Gautama. He 'covered the Blessed One's feet with kisses' and poured out everything he admired about Gautama and the Shakyaputras. Other holy men lost their commitment to spiritual practice and became worldly, he said, 'but here I see monks leading the pure and perfect holy life as long as their breath and their lives last'. For years, Prasenajit had endured the intrigues and quarrels of the court, 'but here I see the monks living in concord, with mutual appreciation, without arguing, blending like milk and honey and viewing each other with kindly eyes'. What's more, the monks seemed happy, and he inferred that they had made genuine spiritual progress. He had also seen the immense respect in which Gautama's disciples held their teacher and his growing influence among shramanas, many of whom had become his followers. Prasenajit frankly admitted that people respected Gautama more than they respected him, and recalled how, during a military campaign, two court officials had slept 'with their heads in the direction in which the Blessed One was staying, with their feet pointed towards me'. Finally, Prasenajit said, 'the Blessed One is a Kshatriya and I am a Kshatriya; the Blessed One is a Kosalan and I am a Kosalan; the Blessed One is eighty years old and I am eighty years old.' Prasenajit's words expressed the deep bond he felt with Gautama, whose mere presence and example brought respite from the burden of ruling.

Gautama was moved by Prasenajit's eloquent words, which he said were 'monuments of the Dharma'. But when Prasenajit left the hut the king discovered that his entourage had left, too. Digha-karayana had taken the royal bodyguard and the insignia, and left behind only a single woman servant and a horse. It was a coup.

The accounts of what happened next are brief and stark, as if they recount a grand, epic tragedy in précis. Digha-karayana hurried back to Shravasti where he proclaimed Vidudabha king. Hearing this, Prasenajit fled on horseback south-east to Rajagriha to seek refuge with Ajatashatru. He arrived late at night and the gates of the city were already closed. Alone and exhausted, Prasenajit found rough lodgings at an inn, and that night he died. The servant in whose arms he perished cried out, 'My lord, the King of Kosala, who ruled two countries, has died a pauper's death and is now lying in a common pauper's rest house outside a foreign city!'[41]

Ajatashatru performed solemn funeral rites over his uncle's body and was so furious that he wanted to march immediately against

Vidudabha. But Ajatashatru, the murderer of his own father, could hardly criticise others for disloyalty, and he had sworn not to invade Kosala. Ajatashatru's ministers dissuaded him from attacking and an uneasy peace settled between the two kingdoms. Meanwhile Vidudabha marched east, determined to fulfil his oath to destroy the Shakyans.

In some versions of this story Gautama tries to avert the coming slaughter. According to one, Vidudabha's army came upon him seated beneath a withered tree beside the road. The king asked why he didn't find better shelter, and Gautama replied: 'The shade of my kin keeps me cool.'[42] Understanding that Gautama still felt close to his relatives, the army turned back, but they returned and eventually Gautama saw that the Shakyans' fate was sealed by their past karma. One senses the perplexity of the devout authors of these accounts, struggling to understand how the mighty Buddha could have failed to deter a king or protect his kinsmen. In fact, the account of Gautama's failed intervention is almost certainly a late addition to the main story, and the truth behind the whole narrative is hard to discern. But the tradition that some dark fate overcame the Shakyans is strong. We know that a town which might have been Kapilavastu was burned down around this time, and that afterwards the Shakyas disappear from history. However, it is quite possible that Vidudabha's campaign came after Gautama's death, and that its aim was to subdue a rebellious region and cement Kosalan control of a vital trade route, rather than to avenge the king's wounded pride.

The sources present Vidudabha's assault as a brutal campaign of ethnic cleansing. He gave orders that all those calling themselves Shakyans should be killed, starting with the babies. According to one account, after an easy victory over the ineffectual Shakyan army, the king chose 500 young Shakyan women for his harem. They refused him – not for the sake of their honour but because of his low birth. 'Hearing this,' the text continues, 'the king was filled with rage and ordered that all the women be killed. At the king's orders the executioners cut the sinews of their arms and legs and threw the women into a ditch.'[43] Mahanama alone was spared, but he killed himself soon after the massacre. Vidudabha marched back to Shravasti, pitching camp in a dry riverbed. During the night a sudden flood overwhelmed the army, and the King and many of his followers were washed into the sea.

Numerous legends tell of Shakyan survivors. One relates that some escaped the slaughter by denying they were Shakyans, and the Burmese people trace their ancestry from this group. Meanwhile, Sri Lankan kings claimed descent from other Shakyans who had founded a city south of the Ganges. A problem with the whole story that the Shakyans were wiped out is the mention in the account of Gautama's last days that a portion of his relics were sent to Kapilavastu, and some speculate that after Vidudabha's attack they built a new city nearby to which the relics were sent. Hsuan Tsang wrote that the relics were claimed by a refugee who had become a prince in what is now Pakistan; but the most eloquent testimony to Shakya's fate comes from his fellow pilgrim Fa-hsien who saw Kapilavastu around 500 CE: 'In this city there is neither king nor people; it is like a great desert. There is simply a congregation of priests and about ten families of lay people.'[44]

The Deaths of the Chief Disciples

The disciples closest to Gautama were those who had been with him longest, and they were all growing old. Shariputra returned to his birthplace in Magadha to see his mother one last time. He told her what he had learned from Gautama and made a final profession of faith: 'There has never been nor will there ever be a shramana or Brahmin who is more fully Enlightened than the Blessed One!'[45] He turned to the monks who attended him and said, 'For forty-four years I have lived and travelled with you, my brothers. If anything I have done or said was unpleasant to you, please forgive me.' The monks replied that, though they had followed him like a shadow, there was nothing to forgive. Then Shariputra entered deep meditation, ascending through the absorptions, before finally passing away.

A novice monk called Chunda took Shariputra's robe and bowl and travelled to Shravasti to tell Gautama the news. Ananda was overwhelmed. 'My body seems as if it had been drugged, I have become disoriented and the teachings are no longer clear to me.' Gautama gently chided him: 'Has Shariputra taken your share of virtue, concentration or wisdom?' 'No, he hasn't,' Ananda replied. 'But he was an adviser and counsellor who inspired and gladdened me.'[46]

In his own way, Gautama was affected as well. Some time later, he heard that Maudgalyayana was also dead. Maudgalyayana was celebrated for his psychic powers and, according to the commentaries, he declared that on his visits to the god realms he had learned that followers of Gautama were reborn in the heavens, but that followers of other teachers were destined for hell. This declaration went to the heart of the hopes that householders rested on their holy men, and rival monks – some versions say they were Jains – hired a 'brigand' to murder Maudgalyayana. Despite Maudgalyayana's powers, the brigand and his followers tortured him and 'crushed his bones'.[47] When Ajatashatru heard of the crime he had the killers arrested and buried alive up to their necks in a field, which was then ploughed over. It's a gruesome story that vividly evokes the vicious rivalries and brutal retribution of Gautama's world.

One day, Gautama looked around a gathering of monks and declared:

> This assembly seems empty to me now that Shariputra and Maudgalyayana have attained final Nirvana! It is amazing that disciples act in accordance with a teacher's instructions and become beloved by the whole community! It is impossible that what is born and is subject to disintegration should not disintegrate; and yet, it is as if the largest branches have broken off a great tree![48]

Gautama's own health was failing, his two leading disciples were dead and he had lost his haven in Shravasti. The time had come for one last journey.

9

The Final Journey

Vulture's Peak

In the wake of his homeland's calamity, Gautama travelled to the Ganges Valley's eastern power centre, Rajagriha, where he could stay in the hills he loved and enjoy the protection of his new supporter, King Ajatashatru. The account of Gautama's last days is the longest of all the Discourses – known in Pali as the Mahaparinibbana Sutta and in Sanskrit as the slightly different Mahaparinirvana Sutra.[1] The title is sometimes translated as 'The Discourse on the Great Decease', but *parinirvana* really means 'complete' or 'supreme Enlightenment' and a better rendition is 'Final Nirvana'. For Buddhist tradition Gautama's 'death' was the point at which his Enlightenment found its full fruition, and not an end or an occasion for grief but something to be celebrated. However, the discourse's vivid and detailed account powerfully mixes celebration with deep sadness.*

* The Discourses are unclear (or perhaps unconcerned) about the exact distinction between Nirvana in life and Nirvana after death, but later Buddhism distinguished them carefully: a living Enlightened person was still affected by 'the result of past clinging' but after death their Enlightenment was 'without remainder'. (*Visuddhimagga* XVI: 94 – Nanamoli 1991: 522.)

The story opens amid the stark rock formations of Vulture's Peak that loom menacingly above the winding path, like a bird of prey. Hsuan Tsang described the scene for his Chinese readers 1,200 years later: 'Touching the southern slope of the northern mountain, it rises as a solitary peak to a great height, on which vultures make their abode. It appears like a high tower on which the azure tints of the sky are reflected, the colours of the mountain and the heaven being commingled.'[2]

Mahakasyapa, who spent long periods in the Rajagriha mountains, evoked the experience in a beautiful set of verses:

> Strung with garlands of flowering vines,
> This patch of earth delights the mind;
> The lovely calls of elephants sound –
> These rocky crags do please me so!
>
> The shimmering hue of darkening clouds,
> Cool waters in pure streams flowing;
> Enveloped by Indra's ladybugs –
> These rocky crags do please me so!
>
> The lovely ground is rained upon,
> The hills are full of holy seers;
> Resounding with the cry of peacocks –
> These rocky crags do please me so!
>
> Not occupied by village folk,
> But visited by herds of deer;
> Strewn with flocks of various birds –
> These rocky crags do please me so![3]

Gautama was eighty, but despite his age and the stiffness of his limbs, he walked each day down the long track to the city to beg his food. Hsuan Tsang heard that Bimbisara had made a staircase 'about ten paces wide'[4] up to Gautama's abode; but visitors still had to dismount their horses or elephants and climb on foot to see him, however important they were. As ever, Gautama was accompanied by Ananda. The two men had shared their lives for twenty-five years and their friendship ran deep. Ananda had 'grey hairs'[5] of his own, and the two men understood one another instinctively, spoke frankly to each another, and lived together without friction. Ananda later said: 'For twenty-five years I served the Blessed One with loving deeds, loving words and loving thoughts, like a shadow that never left him. I paced up and down behind the Buddha while he paced up and down. When the Dharma was being taught, knowledge arose in me.'[6] Together they had seen triumphs and wonders, the tributes of kings and the steady growth of the community. Ultimately, they had witnessed the murder of their families and the deaths of their friends.

If Gautama had come to Rajagriha to find peace and escape politics, he was disappointed. Ajatashatru had promised not to attack Kosala, but his desire to expand Maghada was stronger than ever. Tensions were rising on his western border with Avanti, and he also cast his eyes northwards to the Vrijian Federation – the alliance of clans that rivalled him for control of the Ganges. Ajatashatru sent Vassakara, his chief minister, with a message telling Gautama that he intended to 'attack the powerful and mighty Vrijians, cut them down, destroy them and bring about their ruin and devastation'.[7] In one version of the discourse (which survives in a Chinese translation), Ajatashatru adds that this will be a war for economic gain: 'The Vrijis' country is rich, with many people. The land is fertile and the fields are rich. They want to extract those riches for themselves and do not bow their heads to me.'[8] The campaign would be another episode in the rise of the kingdoms and the downfall of the republics, whose bloody precursor Gautama had witnessed in Shakya. Ajatashatru wanted Gautama's opinion of his plans because, as he told Vassakara, 'the Tathagatas do not speak what is untrue'.[9]

Gautama didn't answer Vassakara directly: what could he say without offending the king or becoming party to a war of conquest? Furthermore, Ajatashatru was 'the son of the Queen of Videhi',* one of the main Vrijian territories, so, like Vidudabha, he was planning to attack his own relatives. Gautama turned to Ananda, who was fanning him in the time-honoured Indian fashion, and asked, 'Have you heard that the Vrijians meet together frequently and regularly to conduct their business?' 'I have heard this, Lord.'[10] 'As long as the Vrijians do so they can be expected to prosper and not to decline,' Gautama said. He asked six more questions that had the same implication. Did the Vrijians meet together and act in concert? Did they rule themselves according to their traditional laws, rather than making laws that had no precedent in the clan traditions? Did they honour and respect their elders and give weight to their recommendations? Did they refrain from abducting women and girls of good family? Did they honour and maintain ancient shrines and make offerings to them? And did they protect and support arahants – realised holy men? The answer in each case was that the Vrijians did act in these ways and that it was a source of their strength. These 'principles of a healthy society' suggest Gautama's belief that republican assemblies and popular participation in government supported social cohesion, and that the Vrijians' deep-rooted clan culture, with its ancient practices and respect for elders, brought them strength.

* The discourse alludes to this when Vassakara calls Ajatashatru 'Videhiputta' (Videha's son).

Gautama had often passed through the Vrijian lands as he walked the trade road between Kosala and Magadha. Perhaps his connection with their inhabitants had started with whatever events lie behind the story that he ended the drought, cured the plague and cleansed Vaishali of its demons. We hear that the Vrijians bestowed extravagant gifts on Gautama and his monks, and that he found it hard to conduct a solitary retreat within their borders because so many people wanted to see him. Gautama admired the renowned Kshatriya fortitude of both the Vrijians and the Licchavis. To call someone a 'Vrijian' was another way of saying he was a true warrior, rather like being a Roman or a Spartan. But Gautama told Ananda that he was concerned they would grow weaker:

> The Licchavis use blocks of wood as cushions and are diligent and ardent in training. That is why King Ajatashatru of Magadha cannot get hold of them. But in the future they will become delicate, with soft and tender hands and feet. They will sleep until sunrise on soft beds with cotton pillows and then Ajatashatru will control them.[11]

Gautama told Vassakara that he had already informed the Vrijians that the seven customs he had listed would ensure they remained strong, and Vassakara agreed that even one of them would be enough to maintain Vrijian strength. But the conclusion Vassakara drew cannot have been the one Gautama intended. He commented that 'King Ajatashatru will never overcome the Vrijians in war without some intrigue, without creating dissension among them.'[12] Then he made his excuses and left. It had occurred to him that victory might be achieved by destabilising the Vrijians, and he commenced a prolonged campaign to sow dissension among the clans.

The discussion of the sources of a nation's strength must have set Gautama thinking about the monastic community, as he asked

Ananda to summon all the Shakyaputra monks in the Rajagriha region to a meeting on Vulture's Peak. The discourse tells us they met in an assembly hall, but it is more likely that they gathered on the mountainside, their robed figures spreading up the slopes and among the rocks. Many must have sensed that this was Gautama's parting address. He spoke again of the seven principles, but adapted the list to show how they could prevent decline among the monks. They should 'meet together frequently and regularly',[13] he said, maintaining the balance between the solitary and the communal aspects of Shakyaputra life and guarding against factionalism. They should meet, act and follow the Shakyaputra life in concert, following the pattern of the republics rather than developing new power structures. The monks' common lifestyle also unified them, so Gautama told them not to 'make pronouncements that have not been agreed upon [or] revoke pronouncements that have been agreed'. Similarly, they should maintain the principle of seniority and 'honour, revere and worship those monks who are elders, possess pearls of wisdom, went forth into the holy life long ago [and] are the fathers and leaders of the community'. Whereas he had told the Vrijians to treat women respectfully, Gautama told the monks that they shouldn't be overcome by 'the kind of craving that leads to rebirth'. Stressing once again the vital role of wilderness-dwelling in Shakyaputra practice, Gautama urged the monks to 'have regard for living in the forest'. Finally, he reminded them that mindful awareness was the most vital ingredient of the harmonious Shakyaputra life. They should 'continue to establish mindfulness, such that well-behaved companions in the spiritual life who have not come are encouraged to come, and those that have come live easily'.[14]

'Final Nirvana' adds other aspects of Dharma practice to this list, but the seven factors are the core of Gautama's advice in all the versions that have come down to us. The discourse also relates

that Gautama gave a further talk in which he went over the basic
principles of the path, explaining:

> how concentration that is invested with good conduct is of great fruit
> and benefit, how wisdom that is invested with concentration is of
> great fruit and benefit, and how the mind that is invested with wisdom
> is fully released from the taints, namely the taint of sense desire, the
> taint of being, the taint of view, is of great fruit and benefit.[15]

Across the Ganges

Gautama left Rajagriha to start his final journey.* We don't know
why Gautama decided to leave – perhaps he was just continuing
to wander as he always had – and we don't know why he took this
particular path. He had probably walked these roads many times,
but it is striking that his route took him away from Rajagriha,
where Ajatashatru was building his armies, into the Vrijian lands
Ajatashatru was planning to attack, and towards his already devast-
ated homeland. 'Final Nirvana' tells us that Gautama set out with
'a large party of monks', but in most of the scenes it describes along
the way he seems to be accompanied only by Ananda and sometimes a few others. This was no grand progress, just the last journey
of an old wanderer and his faithful companion.

The land between Rajagriha and the Ganges in modern Bihar is
intensely fertile. Rice paddies and barley fields border the road to
Patna, and they are still speckled with ponds, water tanks, palm

---

* The discourse describes a meeting with Shariputra shortly after, but this is probably a later addition to the story.

trees and huts made from mud and brick, just as they must have been when Gautama walked through them. It was the end of the hot season when a muggy dust, scuffed by cattle, clouds the air, and the mud track would have been caked hard beneath Gautama's feet. Gautama was a seasoned traveller, and he travelled the same road he had first walked when he set out from Shakya to join the Rajagriha shramanas. But now he was walking in the opposite direction and he used a stick to support himself.

Gautama arrived at the small river port of Pataligama, where householders offered him a place in the travellers' rest house. 'They spread the floor, provided a jug of water, filled the oil lamp', and then told Gautama, 'All is ready.'[16] Gautama washed his dusty feet and sat down, resting his back on the central pillar while the monks sat against the west wall and the householders sat opposite. This intimate scene, in which Gautama was joined by perhaps a dozen listeners, evokes the modest reality of his teaching work. He repeated a familiar teaching on the benefits to householders of acting ethically and the dangers of immorality. Then he dismissed his audience, saying, 'It is now well into the night',[17] and retired to sleep.

When morning came, Pataligama was a less than tranquil scene. The village resounded with building work and Gautama asked what was happening. Ananda told him: 'Sunidha and Vassakara, the Magadhan ministers, are building a fortress against the Vrijians.' It was a defence against Vrijian incursions, but it also offered a base for Maghadan expeditionary forces in the war Ajatashatru was planning. Gautama elsewhere describes the plan of such a frontier fort:

The central pillar is deeply embedded, there is a moat, it has a great armoury of armour and spears, a large body of troops is stationed there – horsemen, bowmen, storm troops and slaves; and the rampart is high and wide and covered with plaster. There are stores of grass, wood, water, rice, corn, sesame beans and medicines.[18]

The Pataligama citadel must have been large, as Gautama realised it would be the focus of a city that would dominate the Ganges. Rajagriha, with its ring of mountains, had served Magadha well as a capital, but control of the Ganges was the key to future expansion. In time, Pataligama, renamed Pataliputra (the modern Patna), would become the capital of a great empire based on the river. Gautama saw a vision of a future in which the city ruled 'as far as the noble realm reaches and trade extends'. Freely mixing the natural and the supernatural, 'Final Nirvana' tells us that Gautama saw a crowd of spirits flocking to the site, choosing the spots where important houses were to be built and they would be the tutelary deities. But this grand metropolis would be subject to fate, Gautama said, and face the perils of 'fire, invasion and dissension among its people'.[19] All these things eventually came to pass.

When the Maghadan ministers provided Gautama and his companions with 'various fine foods' for their daily meal, he said nothing about the fate he foresaw for the city they were founding, and made no comment on Ajatashatru's plans for conquest. Instead he told them to make offerings to the gods as well as holy men: he could at least appeal to their reverence for another dimension of existence. Then he bade them farewell and walked down to the river, which was in full flood, and left Magadha forever by the ferry to the northern shore.

Gautama walked north from the Pataligama ferry to the village of Kotigama, where he stayed with a group of Shakyaputra monks. Everywhere he went on this last tour Gautama met the monks who were staying locally and gave a talk on a basic aspect of his teaching. In Kotigama his subject was the Four Noble Truths.

Travelling on to Nadika he found himself besieged, once again, by questions about the fate of the recently deceased. He obliged the questioners by relating that a certain nun would attain Nirvana without returning to the world, a householder would return once more and gain Awakening in his next life, and so on. A striking feature of these predictions is Gautama's belief that advanced states of realisation weren't restricted to monks and weren't the rarities that later Buddhism often considered them.

Gautama's comments to Ananda, who had passed on the requests, are also telling. 'That human beings should die is not out of the ordinary. But if you are going to come to the Tathagata and ask him this question every time someone should die, that will be a nuisance.'[20] He told Ananda, with surely more than a little irony, of a powerful method for telling someone's rebirth, called 'the mirror of Truth'. If someone had unwavering faith in the Buddha, Dharma and Sangha and exhibited virtues that were 'praised by the discerning, untarnished and conducive to concentration', they would have a good rebirth or even find Awakening after death; and if they didn't . . . they would have a worse one. There was no need to consult someone with special powers to know your future fate. You just needed to observe your behaviour, consider its likely consequences and draw your own conclusions.

Vaishali

Gautama walked on towards the Vrijian capital, Vaishali – a prosperous commercial town, but not a great city like Shravasti or Rajagriha – where he joined a group of monks on parkland outside the town, owned by the famous courtesan Ambapali. The commentaries say that as a baby Ambapali had been abandoned and left under a mango tree where she was found by a wealthy family who raised her in their household. There she mastered dancing, singing and music, and became 'beautiful, comely and glorious to look at, like a lotus-flower'.[21] Young noblemen vied for her favour and believed that her dazzling elegance and beguiling wit brought alive the goddesses and sultry heroines of romantic poetry. In the end, to prevent their competition turning to blows, the noblemen made her a courtesan. She was no common prostitute like Vimala – a nun who had once 'spread [her] snare for fools'[22] at the brothel door. Ambapali received fifty pieces of gold for a night; she was wealthy and esteemed, and counted Bimbisara himself among her admirers.

Ambapali had long revered Gautama but she had never met him, so when she heard he was staying at her grove she rode there straight away. His teaching affected her so deeply that she offered to host the monks the following day and provide them with a sumptuous meal. On the road back to Vaishali she met a group of Kshatriya youths of the Licchavi clan who were also riding to see Gautama. 'Ambapali came past, scraping the young Licchavis' axles, wheels and yokes with hers.'[23] She shouted across that the monks were to be her guests. The youths were incensed: 'Give up this meal for 100,000 pieces!' Ambapali said she would not lose this chance to feed Gautama for all the wealth of Vaishali, and the youths snapped their fingers: 'We have been cheated by the mango girl!' This competition to host Gautama illustrates the frenzy that the chance to feed a holy man could prompt – and, in this case, it was the Buddha himself. It also suggests the ambiguity of Ambapali's position as a celebrity courtesan who wasn't quite respectable, and the odd fact that it was considered unremarkable for celibate monks to be hosted in a mansion devoted to sensual pleasures.

Ambapali's meetings with Gautama affected her so deeply that she donated her park to the Shakyaputras and eventually joined the community. As an old nun, wizened by age, she looked back on her former life with sharpness and humour:

> My hair was as black as a bee, with curly ends;
> Now it's as rough as old hemp.
> Adorned with flowers, it smelled like a perfumed box;
> But now it reeks like a mangy dog.
> I had a sweet voice, like a cuckoo in a jungle thicket;
> Now it is cracked with age.
> My breasts were swollen, round, compact and high;
> Now they sag like empty water bags.
> Such was my body. Now it is a place of pain,
> Dilapidated, like an old house with the plaster falling off.[24]

The decay that awaited Ambapali had already caught up with Gautama. He taught the monks in the mango grove for several weeks, but when the monsoon started he decided to spend it meditating alone in a small village just outside Vaishali, accompanied only by Ananda. As the rain drummed down and damp seeped everywhere Gautama fell seriously ill, suffering 'severe pains, as if he were close to death'.[25] He endured it all without complaint and mustered his strength for one last effort: 'It is not right for me to pass away without addressing those who attended on me and taking leave of the monks. I must use my strength to suppress this illness and maintain the life force [*jivam*].' The disease abated, but Ananda was distraught and told Gautama, 'my body seemed to be drugged'.

Ananda was comforted only by the thought that Gautama wouldn't die until he had given the monks his instructions for the future. But Gautama didn't regard himself as a leader so much as the person who explained the truth, and he had established the

Shakyaputras as a decentralised community focused on dharma practice. Gautama responded:

> What does the community of monks want from me? I have taught the Truth without considering who is an insider and who is an outsider. The Tathagata is not the kind of teacher who is tight-fisted in matters of Truth. Surely if there is someone who thinks that it is he who should be in charge of the Community of monks or that the Community of monks is his particular concern, then it is he who should say something about [it].[26]

In any case, Gautama continued, at present he only felt comfortable when he withdrew his awareness from his decaying body through meditation. He no longer had the energy to concern himself with other people's worries and expectations:

> I am an old and aged man, Ananda, who has done his time and reached old age. I have turned eighty and just as a worn-out cart is kept going with the help of repairs, so it seems is [my] body only kept going with repairs. So, Ananda, you should live with yourselves as your island of refuge and not someone else, with the Truth as your refuge, not something else.[27]

The image of an island of refuge suggests the hillocks and sandbars that are the only dry land above the Indian plains when the rivers flood: a practitioner would find a refuge from the floods of life by truly making the Dharma his or her own. From now on Gautama's followers would have to be their own 'guides in the darkness'.

A few days after this charged exchange Gautama was well enough to walk into Vaishali to beg his food. He told Ananda to bring a mat because he wanted to visit the Capala shrine – a huge tree held sacred to a local spirit, probably with a funeral mound beneath it. Sitting below the shady branches and absorbing the energy of the place, Gautama mused, 'How delightful is Vaishali. How delightful are the shrines of Udena, Gautamaka, Sattambaka, Bahuputta and Sarandada. How delightful is the shrine of Capala.'[28] Gautama had told Vassakara that the Vrijians' respect for such places was a key to their strength, and something about its atmosphere and beauty stirred him deeply. He told Ananda, 'One who has developed the four bases of success and practised them often could undoubtedly live for a full age. Having developed those powers myself I could live on.' The bases of success are the qualities required to develop on the path, especially the psychic abilities of one who has 'developed a shining consciousness'[29] through meditation practice. Such capabilities, Gautama explained, allow a person to determine 'the length of their life',[30] though it isn't clear if the 'age' Gautama mentioned was the proverbial allotted span of 100 years (the Indian equivalent of the Bible's 'three score years and ten'), or the duration of an aeon (kalpa). In any case, Ananda missed Gautama's hint and left without asking him to go on living.

As Gautama meditated, Mara appeared before his old adversary. He reminded Gautama of his resolve not to die before he had established a community that could both practise and communicate the Dharma. Gautama had achieved everything he had wished, Mara said, so 'now is the time for the Lord's Parinirvana'. 'Don't worry, Mara,' Gautama replied. 'Three months from now I will enter Parinirvana.' With that, he let go of the life force and then, Ananda reported, 'the earth quaked violently, frightening, making my hairs stand on end, and claps of thunder rent the air.'[31] Gautama breathed a sigh:

Balancing the incomparable against existence, the sage gave up
    the force of becoming.
Concentrated deep within, he rent his existence like a coat of
    mail.[32]

Gautama explained that while the cause of an earthquake might
be the movement of the earth, earthquakes also accompanied great
events in the life of a Buddha. He told Ananda of Mara's visit and
his relinquishment of the life force, and at last Ananda understood what was happening. 'Live on for an aeon, for the good and
happiness of many, out of sympathy for the world, for the benefit, good and happiness of men and gods,'[33] he implored. But
Gautama told Ananda that he had missed the 'obvious hint' he
had given earlier. 'You were unable to understand . . . If you had
asked, the Blessed One would have twice refused your request, but
the third time he would have agreed. So it is you who are at fault,
Ananda, you who have failed.' However, Gautama's next words
seem to contradict the suggestion that his lifespan was under his
command: 'Ananda, have I not warned you about this before: we
must lose and be deprived of and separated from everything
pleasant and dear. That something is born, come into being, conditioned and of a nature to decay should not decay – this cannot
happen.'[34]

Gautama told the Vaishali monks, 'My life is over . . . [and] I
must leave you behind, acting as my own refuge.'[35] Rather than
grieving, they should devote themselves to Dharma practice. Then
Gautama left, allowing himself one last backward look at the beautiful city, turning his body around fully, as an elephant does. 'This
is the last time I will see Vaishali,'[36] he said.

Kusinagara

Gautama was in no hurry. The rains were over and the days grew cooler. He walked a few miles a day, going from village to village and meeting with the Shakyaputra monks staying near each one. Every evening he addressed them, repeating the message he had always given: explaining the nature of the path and the need for a sincere effort to practise it. We hear of no dramatic encounters or sudden breakthroughs, just a steady round of meetings and discussions.

Although Gautama was confident in his teachings, he knew that misunderstandings might arise once he had gone. One night, Gautama suggested criteria for judging the authenticity of a teaching. What would happen, he asked, if a monk declared that he had heard from Gautama himself that 'such is the practice, such the discipline, such the Teacher's instruction'?[37] He advised them to be cautious. 'Without being accepted or rejected, his words and expressions should be learnt and then compared against the Teaching and examined against the Discipline.' If these sources confirmed the monk's ideas, his words could be trusted; otherwise listeners should conclude, 'This is certainly not the word of the Blessed One but something the monk has mistakenly learnt.' In later years these words buttressed the views of those who mistrusted innovation, and some scholars think they have been interpolated into the text. Elsewhere, Gautama expresses a willingness to allow for variations in expression provided people understand and hold true to the essential meaning of his teachings.

Gautama's journey took him out of the Vrijian country and into the republic of the Mallas. He was well away from the bustle of the kingdoms and the cities, travelling towards the borders of the Ganges

Valley and towards Shakya. However, we cannot say whether he was heading for his homeland or just following the trade road. He arrived in Pava village and settled himself in a mango grove belonging to a metalsmith called Chunda (who was probably a wealthy man, as metal was a rarity and a forge was cutting-edge technology). Gautama had stayed with Chunda before and the smith was delighted to greet this distinguished visitor. The next morning, the monks went to Chunda's house where he had prepared a sumptuous meal of sweet rice and cakes with plenty of 'tender boar'.[38] A fierce debate has raged over what this meal contained between pro-vegetarian scholars, who argue that it was truffles, and those who believe that it was boar-meat; but it matters little as Gautama and his companions would have eaten whatever they were given. Gautama told their host: 'Serve me with the tender boar you have prepared, serve the community of monks with other sorts of food,' adding that Chunda should bury in a pit any of his food that was left over.

The meal (whatever it comprised) disagreed violently with Gautama, and he 'fell seriously ill, passing blood in his stools and suffering severe pain as if he were close to death'.[39] Though near, death hadn't yet arrived, and Gautama summoned his energy for one last leg. He walked on wearily towards Kusinagara, the Mallas' chief town. A convoy of trading carts rumbled past, and, overwhelmed with exhaustion, Gautama sat down to rest. 'Could you bring me some water, Ananda?' he asked. 'I am thirsty and must drink.' Ananda looked unhappily at the stream that had been turned muddy by the wagons and suggested they walk on a little to the River Kukuttha. Gautama told him not to worry and when Ananda looked at the water again it had cleared, as if by a miracle. This was the final appearance in Gautama's life of a symbol – the stream – that had shaped many of his descriptions of both the human condition and the spiritual path.

A conversation with another traveller brought back more memories. A local man called Pukkusa strode up to Gautama and offered
an anecdote. He was a disciple of Arada Kalama, as Gautama had
once been, and the convoy of carts and the sight of Gautama under
the tree had reminded Pukkusa of a time when Arada Kalama had
sat beside a road when a similar convoy rolled by. The old guru
had been so absorbed in meditation that he hadn't noticed a thing.
Gautama told Pukkusa of a time when he had meditated right
through an immense thunderstorm, which killed four cattle and
two farmers, without noticing a thing. An awestruck witness had
cried: 'How remarkable, how extraordinary that those who have
gone forth live life in such peace that, while conscious and awake,
they will neither see anything nor hear a sound!'[40] It's an odd story,
but Pukkusa clearly learnt something new from Gautama's account,
as he declared, 'What faith I had in Arada Kalama let the wind
blow away as chaff.' He went for refuge to Gautama instead and
offered him a set of robes stitched from golden cloth. When Gautama put them on Ananda exclaimed that, against his body, they
seemed dulled. 'This is remarkable, sir, this is extraordinary – [your]
skin is so pure and clear!' 'There are two occasions on which the
Tathagata's skin is very pure and clear,' said Gautama: the night on
which he reached 'highest perfect Enlightenment and the night he
attains Parinirvana . . . So tonight, in the last watch, at Upavattana,
between two sala trees, the Parinirvana of the Tathagata will occur.'[41]

Gautama bathed in the river, rested and walked back to Chunda's
grove, where he slept deeply. He told Ananda that, whatever
happened, no blame attached to Chunda for giving him the food.
In fact, it was a source of merit. This no doubt saved Chunda from
both guilt and opprobrium, and it says much for Gautama's sensitivity that he was aware of the smith's situation even in the midst
of a serious illness.

When the heat lessened, Gautama felt able to attempt the journey once again and set out for Kusinagara. He and Ananda crossed the River Hiranyavati and arrived at a grove of trees just outside the town. The Mallas had planted two rows of sala trees running from east to west, and at the eastern end was a platform that was used for meetings. 'I am tired and must lie down,' Gautama told his companion. 'Could you prepare for me a bed between two trees with the head to the north?'[42] Ananda placed a covering over the ground and Gautama lay down on his right side upon the platform, supporting his head with his hand. This 'lion posture' was Gautama's usual way of sleeping and depictions of his Parinirvana always show him resting in this position. We are told that the trees had bloomed early and their yellow flowers fell on Gautama, accompanied by celestial music. However, Gautama soberly commented that the best way to honour and revere him was by 'practising the teaching and its subtleties' and 'living in accordance with the Truth'.[43]

Nonetheless, the events that were unfolding had an inescapably mythic dimension. Gautama told one of the attendant monks to move, as the sky was filled for miles around with a gathering of 'most of the gods of the ten world systems [who have] assembled here to see the Tathagata'. The gods were complaining that 'we have come from afar to see the Tathagata and this monk is standing in front of the Blessed One preventing us getting a view!'[44] What's more, Gautama added, some of the less refined spirits were mourning his passing.

It was dawning on Ananda that the end really was near, and it occurred to him that he did not know what funeral arrangements to follow. 'How should we treat the Tathagata's body?' he asked. Gautama told him not to worry about such matters and concentrate on his own Awakening. 'There are knowledgeable rulers, Brahmins and householders, too, who are committed to the Tathagata

– they will take care of such things.'[45] But he also outlined elaborate arrangements for his cremated remains, which, he said, should be treated like those of the legendary Universal Ruler. A stupa – a circular ritual mound that was customary for special funerals in the Ganges Valley – should be erected at the crossroads where people could lay garlands and make other offerings, and rites should be enacted that were associated with a Universal Ruler.

Ananda went into the living quarters, leant against the doorpost and wept: 'I am a learner with much work still to do, but my teacher, who has been so kind to me, is about to pass away.' Gautama called Ananda back.

> Enough, Ananda. Do not grieve and lament. Have I not warned you about this before: we must lose and be deprived of and separated from everything pleasant and dear? How else could it be otherwise? For a long time, you have attended me helpfully, gladly and whole-heartedly. You have done well, Ananda. Keep on applying yourself and you soon will be free.[46]

Gautama encouraged this attitude with more than words. Throughout the discourse he faces his death with dignity, realism and acceptance. 'Take a person who has not done wrong, not acted cruelly and wickedly, but has done beautiful things', he once said. Faced by death, such a person 'does not grieve, fret, lament; he does not cry out beating his chest; he does not become deranged'.[47] In his final hours Gautama also showed a generosity that went beyond stoicism. He turned to the monks who were gathered there and praised Ananda. People were always happy to see him, Gautama said. When Ananda spoke about the Dharma they were pleased, and when he kept silent they were sad. This was a final expression of Gautama's affection for his friend.

Ananda looked at the humble surroundings. He told Gautama it was not fitting that he should die in this remote 'mud-wall town' rather than an important city such as Campa, Rajagriha, Shravasti, Saketa, Kausambi or Varanasi, where wealthy followers could provide a funeral of appropriate grandeur. Gautama had a different perspective. 'Don't call this town a miserable place in the back of beyond.' He conjured a vision of a bustling ancient city that had existed on the spot long before and had been 'successful and prosperous, with many inhabitants, full of people and well provided with food'.[48] Another discourse gives a fuller account of this city and his life there as Mahasudassana – 'a Universal Ruler, a righteous king of Truth, sovereign of the four quarters'[49] – in the last of his many lives before this one.

No less important to Gautama than this mythic past were the present-day inhabitants of Kusinagara – old friends and followers he would have met on previous visits. They would have been upset, and perhaps offended, if so momentous an event as the death of a great teacher had occurred near their city without their knowledge, so Gautama told Ananda to inform the Mallas that they had one last chance to see him. When Ananda passed the news to a gathering in the Mallas' assembly hall, the citizens were distraught and commenced what seems to have been a collective grieving ritual: 'With dishevelled hair some spread their arms wide and called out; they fell to the ground, broken, and rolled back and forth. "All too soon will the Blessed One attain final Nirvana! All too soon will the eye of the world disappear!"'[50]

That evening a procession of Malla families filed past Gautama to pay their respects, and news of Gautama's imminent death had also been spreading through the Shakyaputra community. Of the senior disciples only Ananda's half-brother, Anuruddha, arrived, but many more monks converged on the sala grove. Others came too and a wanderer named Subaddha, who happened to be in the area, approached Ananda and asked if he could put a question to Gautama. 'He's tired,' said Ananda. 'Don't disturb him.' But Gautama told Ananda to let Subaddha pass, sensing that he would listen receptively. Subaddha was steeped in shramana culture and wanted to know from Gautama if the other teachers of the age had reached the final goal of spiritual life: 'Have all of these gained the direct knowledge they claim, or has none achieved it, or have some achieved it and some not?'[51] The question was typical of the shramanas' obsession with competing teachers, and Gautama told Subaddha that his question could wait. The important thing was to follow a path of spiritual development that was based on the truth, not to involve oneself in philosophy and guru-obsession. Gautama added that where the Eightfold Path was taught many practitioners would attain realisation of one degree or another, but without it there would be no such success. He continued in verse:

> When I was twenty-nine years of age, Subaddha,
> When I went forth to search for what is good.
> Now it is more than fifty years
> Since I went forth, Subaddha.
> To abide in the realm of the way of Truth,
> Outside which there is no ascetic.[52]

Subaddha replied with the same cry of delight that is repeated in the Discourses by innumerable people when they were touched by Gautama's words: 'Excellent, sir! Excellent! As if someone were to set upright what had been knocked down, or reveal what had been hidden, or hold a lamp up in the dark so that those with eyes could see – just so the Blessed One has made clear the Truth.' Subaddha asked to go for refuge to the Buddha, Dharma and Sangha, but as

he was a wanderer of another sect Gautama set out the probationary period he should follow. He was Gautama's last disciple.

One final, painful duty remained for Gautama, and the suspicion must be that he had been putting it off to the last possible
moment. Chandaka, his charioteer in his days in the Shakyan palace
(whom he had known all his life), had become more and more
difficult. His devotion had spilled over into partisanship and he
had become embroiled in monastic politics between the monks
and the nuns. Gautama told Ananda that the monks should ignore
Chandaka. Whatever he said, 'monks are strictly not to speak to
him, nor give him advice or instruction'.[53]

Then Gautama turned to the monks gathered around him: 'It
may be that one of you has doubts or uncertainty about the Buddha,
the teaching, the community, the path, or the practice,' he said. 'Ask
your questions, monks. Do not later regret that, although your
teacher was right in front of you, you were not able to put your
questions.' The monks were silent. 'Perhaps you do not ask your
questions out of respect,' said Gautama. 'Let one companion tell
another his questions.'

The monks remained silent and Ananda said, 'This is extraordinary . . . There is not a single monk who has doubt or is confused.' Gautama remarked that, while Ananda said this out of faith,
he *knew* it to be so. Every one of the monks 'has entered the stream
and is beyond affliction, destined to full Awakening for sure'. Then
Gautama spoke his last words, which encapsulated his message.
'Well, monks. Now I take my leave of you: it is of the nature of
things to decay, but if you are attentive you will succeed.'[54]

Then Gautama passed into meditation and an unearthly stillness covered him, and the monks stayed beside him, absorbed in
a shared stillness. 'Final Nirvana' describes a complex process in
which Gautama ascends a meditative ladder culminating in the

mysterious 'stage of cessation'. But this seems to be a 'later version'[55] of the story. The earliest elements of the text tell us that Gautama simply ascended the four dhyanas. He entered the first and then: 'emerging from that he attained the second absorption. Emerging from that he attained the third absorption. Emerging from that he attained the fourth absorption. Emerging from the fourth absorption, the Blessed One directly attained final Nirvana.'[56]

Eventually, one account relates, Anuruddha broke the silence that settled upon the disciples who surrounded their departed master:

> With unshrinking mind
> He endured his pain;
> Like the quenching of a lamp
> Was the deliverance of his mind.[57]

10

Gautama's Legacy

Circling the Buddha

The land that was once ancient Maghada today comprises, in large measure, the Indian state of Bihar: one of the country's poorest states and a byword for corruption. Its name derives from the Sanskrit and Pali word *vihara* ('dwelling place'), the term for a Buddhist temple, because for 1,500 years it was filled with Buddhist monasteries. At its centre was Bodh Gaya's thriving complex of buildings. The earliest memorial construction there has long since been destroyed and so has the temple depicted in a beautiful early carving of worshippers at a simple shrine beside the Bodhi Tree. The tree was cut down twice, but according to Buddhist legend it miraculously sprouted again. It finally died of old age and was replanted in 1881 from an offshoot that had survived in Sri Lanka.

A century ago Bodh Gaya was crumbling and desolate, but today it is again filled with activity. The restored Mahabodhi temple is an ornate, tapering structure with a shrine in its base, and the Bodhi Tree spreads alongside. Pilgrims pace mindfully around its exterior or sit in meditation or prayer, and on special days Tibetan donors fill the entire compound with thousands of butter-lamps. But the pilgrims regard each other with a mixture of feelings including bemusement and confusion. Some monks are dressed in the orange or ochre robes of the Theravada school, which prevails in Sri Lanka and most of South East Asia; others wear the maroon robes of Tibet and the Himalayas; and others again the charcoal robes of East Asia. Coach parties from Japan and Korea mix with farmers from Bhutan and Ladakh and Indian 'new Buddhists', who have joined Buddhism to escape the burden of untouchability. There are Hindus who regard Gautama as an incarnation of the god Vishnu, and Buddhists from the West where the faith has grown steadily, as well as tourists, hawkers and the spiritually curious.

Language and culture separate the Buddhist pilgrims; they follow different scriptures and view Gautama in diverse ways. Until western scholars made the suggestion, Buddhists in Sri Lanka and Japan had little sense that they shared a single religion – at least as the word has been understood in modern times; and, until those same scholars coined the term 'Buddhism', the faith had no single name. But all the pilgrims believe they are true heirs to Gautama's teaching (or perhaps to the spirit that informed it), and come to Bodh Gaya because of him.

To understand his legacy we must trace the differing responses to Gautama that developed in the centuries after his death and the various ways in which people envisaged the Awakened state he attained. Then we must consider the attempt to manifest his values in Indian society, and, finally, his relevance in the modern world.

Dead or Alive?

According to 'Final Nirvana', Gautama's followers felt his absence acutely. The earth shared their grief, it says, and responded with a terrifying earthquake that shook the ground and made men's hair 'stand on end'.[1] 'Then there was terror, then there was excitement', recalled Ananda in his *Theragatha* verses, 'when the fully Enlightened one, possessed of all excellent qualities was quenched!'[2] He felt bewildered:

> All the directions are obscure,
> The teachings are not clear to me;
> With our benevolent friend gone,
> It seems as if all is darkness.[3]

He sat up all night talking with his brother Anuruddha and eventually composed himself enough to help arrange the funeral. But as more and more people arrived at Kusinagara, he withdrew to the jungle where the spirits urged him: 'Meditate . . . don't be negligent!'[4]

Gautama was unique and irreplaceable. When a Magadhan official asked Ananda how the monks would function without him, he explained: 'No single monk possesses in each and every way those qualities that were possessed by the Blessed One. He was the arouser of the unarisen path, the knower of the path and the one skilled in it. But his disciples now abide following the path and become possessed of it afterwards.'[5] But was Gautama really 'gone for good',[6] as Ananda said? In response to Vacchagotta's question about the fate of an Enlightened person after death, Gautama had told him that it was impossible to express. One in whom 'the link that bound him to becoming [has been] cut'[7] is 'profound, immeasurable, hard to fathom like the ocean',[8] even when he is alive. You can't say that he reappears after death, or that he does not reappear, or both, or neither – just that 'at the breaking up of the body and the exhaustion of the life-span, devas and humans will see him no more'.[9] And if Gautama wasn't exactly dead, then he might still be present in some way.

That possibility hovers around the events that followed Gautama's death (as 'Final Nirvana' describes them). Indian funerals are usually speedy affairs because bodies decay rapidly in the tropical climate, but the Mallas spent seven days 'honouring and revering [the body] and worshipping it with dances, songs and music, garlands and incense'.[10] As Gautama had instructed, his body was wrapped, perfumed and cremated, in keeping with customs associated with a Universal Monarch; and when the ash was cleared what remained were not charred bones but jewel-like stones. These were Gautama's relics: sacred objects that were 'endowed with life'[11] and inherited his power to heal and bless. The Mallas spent a further week honouring the relics with 'dancing, singing and garlands' and refused to part with them to the representatives of various states who arrived at Kusinagara demanding a share. A full-scale 'War of the Relics' was averted only when a priest reminded the factions that Gautama had taught 'tolerance'.[12]

Portions of Gautama's relics were installed in stupas in Kusinagara town and the spot where he died, as well as Rajagriha, Vaishali, Kapilavastu (which was presumably inhabited by Shakyan survivors) and four other towns. Further stupas were erected at Lumbini, Bodh Gaya and Sarnath. These weren't just memorials. In one version of 'Final Nirvana' Gautama says that a visitor to the major sites would be 'in my presence',[13] suggesting that he lived on in the stupas. He told Ananda that a faithful follower should witness and experience these stupas and that 'all those who die with faithful hearts while they are on pilgrimage will, at the breaking up of the body after death, be reborn in a happy realm, in a heaven world'.[14] Like the relics, the stupas became objects of intense devotion.

Some scholars suggest that the monks of a later era who gave 'Final Nirvana' its final form played down passages showing that monks and nuns were involved in these rituals, presumably wishing to minimise the devotional apect of Gautama's profile. In a similar vein, western commentators who are wary of 'religion' have also seen stupa and relic worship (as well as the mythic context in which the texts place Gautama's life) as superstitious intrusions. But ritual and devotion always surrounded Gautama. For devotees, forming a relationship with him through offerings and reverence involved them in a cosmic drama in which Gautama, as an Enlightened Buddha, was a central player. By participating in the drama, they touched the reality Gautama embodied and found a refuge from samsara.

Imagining the Buddha

In the differing responses to Gautama which we see at the time of the Parinirvana we can detect the seeds of the varying views of him that developed over the following centuries. Even for those who believed Gautama was 'gone for good', his continued guidance was essential if they were to follow his path and realise his teachings. Before he died Gautama told the monks that 'the teaching and discipline that I have taught you and explained to you – that is your teacher after I have gone.'[15] For many monks (though perhaps not all) this made it vital that Gautama's words be preserved and passed on as accurately as possible. According to the Vinaya, shortly after the Parinirvana Mahakasyapa heard a monk declare: 'We are well rid of this great recluse. He always bothered us by saying: "You should do this and you shouldn't do that." Now we can do whatever we like!'[16] Seeing that vigorous action was needed to establish a definitive version of the teachings, Mahakasyapa summoned the monastic elders – all Enlightened arahants – to 'chant together the Dharma and the Vinaya before what is not Dharma is spread abroad and what is Dharma is put aside; and before those who argue against the Dharma become powerful and those who hold to it become weak.'[17]

This meeting is known as the 'First Council' (though its name really means 'the first communal recitation'[18]), and it is said to have taken place during the rainy season that followed the Parinirvana in a hall erected on Mount Vebhara on the outskirts of Rajagriha. Upali, the barber who shaved the heads of ordination candidates, was the expert on the rules of monastic life, and the Vinaya tells us that Mahakasyapa asked him to recite each rule in turn and describe the circumstances in which Gautama had laid it down. Ananda was allowed in at the last minute, having become an arahant the previous night, and we are told that he recited the Discourses just as we encounter them now in the Pali canon. The Council is also said to have devised a system of communal recitation to pass on the teachings.

A group of leading monks probably did pool their recollections of Gautama's teachings shortly after the Parinirvana, but there is compelling evidence that the Discourses and the Vinaya developed gradually over several centuries. Stating that *all* 17,000 discourses were recited verbatim by Ananda is a way of claiming that they possess a unique authority as the authentic word of the Buddha. But from the outset there were alternatives to the 'orthodoxy' preserved in the canon. The Theravadin Vinaya itself relates that a monk called Purana refused to accept the First Council's version of Gautama's teachings, saying that he preferred to follow the Dharma 'in the way that I heard it from the Lord's presence and received it from him'.[19] This suggests that teachings not included in the canon may have been passed on through independent lineages.

Around a century after the Parinirvana, perhaps longer (i.e. *c.*300–260 BCE), the monastic community split between a majority party called Mahasanghikas and a minority of 'elders' called Sthavi-ravadins. In time, many more doctrinal schools, all focused on the Discourses, evolved from these two groups. The traditional number is eighteen, but there seem to have been more and their differences are often obscure, or else too complex to treat briefly. In any case, these groups were more like contending philosophical schools than the fractious sects of early Christianity. All members of the monastic community followed the same (or virtually the same) monastic code; and monks who followed different teachings often lived together happily in the same monastery. Among most Buddhists this tolerance persisted centuries later, even when the schools became formally independent of one another. One text declares:

> The Mahasanghikas diligently study the collected Discourses and teach their true meaning because they are the source and centre. The Dhar-maguptaka school master the flavour of the true way. They are guides for the benefit of all and their way of expression is special. The Sar-vastivada school quickly gain unobstructed knowledge, for the Dharma is their guide.[20]

This diversity reflects the way Gautama had taught. He spoke from experience, formulated the teachings in response to questions and shaped his movement by addressing practical issues as they arose. In his efforts to communicate, Gautama used numerous dialects and adapted others' terminology, and his words were sometimes ambiguous, ironic or metaphorical. The teachings were ways to help people develop 'peace not passion [and] contentment not attachment',[21] and progress towards Nirvana. It is no wonder that they were understood in different ways. Sectarian attitudes developed in later centuries, especially in outlying areas, but Tibetans, for example, inherited, relatively late in Indian Buddhist history, the view that the various schools and practices offered between them '84,000 gateways' to the Dharma.

Followers of these schools sought, in various ways, to maintain a relationship with Gautama. The Discourses give a powerful impression of the disciples' intense faith that Gautama was a living embodiment of ultimate reality; and he remained a vivid presence even when he was physically absent. Pingiya declared: 'Day and night, I see him with my mind, as if with my eye.'[22] After the Parinirvana, many Buddhists sustained that connection by reflecting on Gautama and his Enlightened qualities, and, in time, artists started to depict him. In the earliest friezes, which date from the second century BCE, they avoid depicting Gautama himself and represent him with an emblem such as a wheel. Or they left a space: a vacant throne, an umbrella without the person it shaded, or a footprint without the foot. But early in the first millennium CE, statues of Gautama, including the beautiful Greek-influenced Gandharan figures from Pakistan and Afghanistan, were created as 'reminder relics' to set people in mind of Buddhahood.

A legend recounted in the *Ashokavadana* (*c*.200 CE) suggests how imagining Gautama could become visionary contact with him. In this text a Buddhist sage called Upagupta converts Mara to the Dharma. Then, reflecting that Mara met Gautama many times, Upagupta asks him to assume Gautama's appearance. Mara manifests a Buddha form and Upagupta, entranced, prostrates at its feet. Realising that he has bowed before an illusion, Upagupta hurriedly explains: 'Of course I know that the Best of Speakers has gone to extinction ... Even so, when I see his figure, which is so pleasing to the eye, I bow down before that sage ... just as men bow down to clay images of the gods, knowing that they worship the god not the clay.'[23]

Others believed that through their practice of Gautama's teachings they contacted a level of reality in which he was still present. In

one discourse Gautama tells the monk Vasettha that if asked to identify himself he should reply: "'I am the Blessed One's own child,
born of his mouth, born of the Dharma, created by Dharma, heir
of the Dharma"; for Gautama himself is designated "Dharma-bodied,
Brahma-bodied, become-Dharma, become-Brahma."'[24] In saying that
he was 'Dharma-bodied' Gautama probably meant that he could be
identified with his metaphorical 'body' of teachings. But some believed
he was, in fact, disclosing the existence of a transcendent dharma-
body, or *dharmakaya,* which was perceived with the dharma-eye and
lived on when Gautama's form-body (the *rupakaya*) had perished.
That was the view of many Mahasanghikas, who believed that Gautama persisted as a transcendental presence. In a similar vein, some
Buddhist philosophers found new ways of understanding the world
that made Gautama's continued presence seem reasonable. The Sar-
vastivada school held that the past and the future were as real as the
present – they were just different 'modes' in which something could
be said to exist. And if the past was real, then the Gautama of the
past was still accessible. Others, again, pondered Gautama's teaching
that phenomena lack an abiding essence and asked what it means
to say that *anything* exists or does not exist – Gautama included.

Another way of kindling Gautama's presence was by telling stories
about him. Vivid reliefs decorating Buddhist monuments such as
the Great Stupa at Sanchi depict scenes from Gautama's life and
show that, three centuries after the Parinirvana, he was already the
subject of densely imagined legend. Many of the incidents recounted
in this book are portrayed, but their biography starts with Gautama's previous lives as a 'bodhisattva' and the countless virtuous
actions he performed as an animal, an ascetic, a god and finally a
Universal Ruler. Some of these tales (called *jatakas* or 'birth stories')
appear in the Discourses, and hundreds more were eventually gathered
into great collections such as the *Jataka-mala.*

From around the first century CE lengthy poetic biographies started to appear, filling a gap in the Pali canon, which contains no continuous narrative of Gautama's life. The first-century CE *Mahavastu* tells Gautama's story up to his Enlightenment, while Ashvaghosha's second-century CE *Buddhacarita* ('Acts of the Buddha') recounts his entire career. This is one of the masterpieces of classical Sanskrit literature and seems to be an attempt by a highly educated Buddhist poet to rival the *Mahabharata* and *Ramayana*, the mighty Hindu epics then capturing Indian imaginations. These biographies lack the naturalistic elements we find in the Discourses: quirky characters, shafts of humour and odd details that serve no polemical purpose. Instead, we find a vivid spiritual hero who starts in ignorance and suffering and becomes a consummate holy man (in Reginald Ray's summary: 'an accomplished being, superhuman in stature, recognised as fully realised by those in his environment, surrounded by miracles and in possession of magical powers, venerated by gods, human beings and the cosmos as a whole, one who compassionately leads others on the path to liberation'.[25] His every action possessed a symbolic meaning and his Awakening had a profound importance for the entire cosmos.

The Transcendent Buddha

Through a gradual process that cannot easily be traced, a new movement emerged within some of the early Buddhist schools that eventually came to be known as the *Mahayana* ('the Great Way'). The Buddha of the Mahayana is prefigured in a classical biography called the *Lalitavistara* ('Living out the Game') which presents him as a transcendental being – not an ordinary human at all – whose life is a drama enacted for the edification of living beings. At its start

Gautama is in the Tushita heaven teaching the Dharma to the gods, but he decides that the time is right for his final birth and enters his mother's womb fully conscious.

The Mahayana movement centred on new scriptures, the Mahayana Sutras, which portray Gautama as a transcendent figure, usually called *Shakyamuni* ('the Shakyan Sage'), who teaches in a cosmic setting to a host of gods, men and spiritual beings. As one Sutra explains: 'The body of the Tathagata is the Dharmakaya and does not come from the illusion of thought and desire. His body is above and beyond the three realms [of desire, form and beyond form] and is outside the stream of transmigratory suffering. The Buddha body is transcendental and is beyond destiny.'[26]

Adherents of these scriptures claimed they had been secretly passed down from Gautama and preserved by the gods or spirits who lived in the depths of the ocean. Other texts were inspired by visionary experiences or the cogent application of the *spirit* of Gautama's teaching at a time when it was in danger (from the Mahayana viewpoint) of being swamped by the *letter* of intellectual analysis. By the start of the first millennium CE, monks' wanderings had been curtailed, and their lives increasingly regulated and focused on large monasteries where the main activities were recitation and scholarship. Some monasteries became important intellectual centres where philosophy, logic and other disciplines were practised by the finest intellects of the age, and the largest, Nalanda, grew into a university-style campus that attracted students from across the Buddhist world. But many feared that non-scholarly activities were being frozen out and the true goals of Dharma practice forgotten.*

---

* There were many Mahayana philosophers and scholars, but the movement's followers insisted that intellectual pursuits should be subordinate to the goal of Awakening. Nagarjuna and his heirs, for example, practised philosophy with the aim of showing the limitations of rational understanding.

While some other strands of Indian Buddhism prided themselves on changing little, the Mahayana was, for many years, a fer-
ment of creativity and innovation. In principle, some Mahayana
texts argued, *any* doctrine or practice that leads beings towards
Awakening, whatever its source, could be deemed 'the word of the
Buddha'. This allowed Mahayana practitioners to embrace practices like stupa and relic worship and to address the aspirations of
householder Buddhists alongside those of the monks. It also explored
devotional rituals and visionary experiences, developed an expansive mythology and offered new insights into the mind. It wasn't
a single, unitary movement, and some Mahayana teachings are contradictory; but all were inspired by the stories of Gautama's countless lifetimes as a bodhisattva, acting selflessly for the benefit of
others. For Mahayana practitioners this 'bodhisattva path' was vastly
superior to that of his arahant disciples who found Awakening and
then disappeared. Guided by the resonant, transforming force of
bodhicitta – the 'mind or will to Awakening' – they vowed to put
off entering Nirvana in order to help all beings attain it. By comparison with the breathtaking spiritual ambition of this Great
Vehicle, its followers considered the older traditions cramped and
self-absorbed, calling them the *Hinayana*: the 'lesser vehicle'.

Some later Mahayana Sutras explain that the eternal Buddha
they portray is distinct from the form in which he appeared on
earth – his *nirmanakaya*, or emanation-body. The Buddha of the
sutras inhabits a glorious, subtle 'Body of Complete Enjoyment'
(*Samboghakaya*). Dwelling eternally in this transcendent domain,
the Buddha spreads his compassionate influence throughout the
universe (or, at least, the part of it that is his 'Buddha field') so
that all who are open may benefit. The form in which this eternal
Buddha was conceived rapidly multiplied into numerous figures
embodying particular qualities or dimensions of Enlightenment.

The five Conquerors (*Jinas*), including the radiant Amitabha and the 'unshakeable' Akshobhya, formed a *mandala*, or sacred pattern, of fully Enlightened Buddhas. Some texts describe the beautiful Pure Lands these Buddhas have created and say that after death the truly faithful and virtuous will be reborn there. Beside the Buddhas are archetypal bodhisattvas like the compassionate Avalokitesvara, the wise and majestic Manjushri and the radiant Tara ('the Saviouress'), who can be called on as sources of support and inspiration.

Beyond the archetypes of the Samboghakaya lies the Dharmakaya, the 'Body of Truth or Dharma', which in this context means the purified qualities of the Buddha and the primordial, signless reality he had realised. That reality cannot be conceptualised and the Mahayana 'Perfection of Wisdom' texts used the term emptiness (*sunyata*) to describe it. Gautama, himself, had used the word to evoke the insubstantiality of all phenomena, and now the great Mahayana philosopher, Nagarjuna, used it to cut through the mass of doctrines the early Buddhist schools had developed in their efforts to explain existence. Things cannot be defined or tied down, he said, because they arise and pass away in dependence upon conditions; therefore, they are empty and mysterious and magically alive, and realising this truth brings Liberation.

For the 'Mind-Only' (*Cittamatra* or *Yogacara*) school the Dharmakaya is a mysterious, luminous, non-dual consciousness at the heart of existence, which one can reach through meditation and from which everything else arises. According to a further group of scriptures, if emptiness is the true nature of all beings and all beings have the capacity to realise that nature, then, in some sense, Buddhahood, or 'Buddha-nature' (*Tathagatagarbha*) is present within us, like a 'womb' or matrix: 'All living beings, though they are among the defilements of hatred, anger and ignorance, have the Buddha's wisdom, Buddha's Eye, Buddha's Body ... they are possessed of the Tathagatagarbha ... the Buddha preached the doctrine in order to remove the defilements and manifest the Buddha-nature within living beings.'[27]

A final movement, the Vajrayana, grew in Indian Mahayana circles from around the sixth century CE. If the Mahayana sought to assert what its followers considered the true meaning of the Dharma in the face of the early schools, the Vajrayana responded to the immense timescales envisaged by Mahayana scriptures, which made full Buddhahood a very distant goal. 'Vajrayana' means 'the Diamond Vehicle' or 'the Way of Reality', and texts called Tantras set out an intensely demanding method of practice that was said to lead quickly to Awakening. These esoteric teachings were passed in secret from master to disciple and required utter devotion to the teacher, or *guru*, who gave it. For such a disciple, the tantric guru *is* the Buddha (or, more precisely, he or she is an 'esoteric Buddha refuge'). The various schemes of tantric practice involve elaborate rituals and devotions as well as visualisations and meditations on chosen Buddhas and bodhisattvas, and at the higher levels meditation involves transforming the body's subtle energies and identifying with the Buddhas at the level of ultimate reality.

If early Mahayana imaginings resolved the uncertainty over whether the Buddha lived on by focusing on his timeless and archetypal aspect, these movements restored him as an immediate presence. In the Buddha-nature perspective he is the essence of all beings – even their 'True Self' – that waits, womb-like, to be reborn in each of us. For Vajrayana practitioners, he resides in the magical potentiality of each moment to reveal the vibrant, essence-less nature of existence. Paradoxically, while these movements clearly develop aspects of Buddhist practice, they all claim that they are merely reasserting teachings that were there right from the start. In some cases, their approach is prefigured in the earliest scriptures; in others the differences seem more fundamental. Believers in Buddha-nature, for example, have often been criticised for slipping into the very belief in *atman* that Gautama took such pains to avoid. But it is quite possible that at least some of them preserve traditions dating back to Gautama that were excluded or marginalised in the texts that became normative.

The Reign of Dharma

Paralleling the efforts of the various schools to engage with Gautama and his teachings were efforts to manifest those teachings in society as a whole. Telling the story of the vast Buddhist civilisation in which Gautama's teachings and example had a central place would take this chapter too far from Gautama himself, so that is left to the Appendix. However, the reign of the Emperor Ashoka has a special place in this story.

In the years following Gautama's death Ajatashatru and his heirs conquered the Vrijians, then Kosala and the rest of the Ganges Valley, and in time their territory stretched far beyond the lands Gautama had known. They successfully beat back the invading army of Alexander the Great, only to be ousted from within by a challenger called Chandragupta Maurya (c.322 BCE). The Mauryan Empire, ruled by Chandragupta from Pataliputra, soon extended all the way to Afghanistan, and, in time, it spread southwards to include most of the Indian subcontinent.

Chandragupta's grandson Ashoka came to the throne in c.272 BCE, 132 years after the approximate date of Gautama's death, and ruled until his death in 231 CE.* In his youth Ashoka probably studied the *Arthashastra*, the ruthless manual of gaining and keeping power written by the Brahmin who was Chandragupta's chief adviser. In keeping with its view of how a ruler should act, Ashoka struggled viciously with his brothers to win the throne and launched a campaign to expand the empire that culminated in an attack on Kalinga, a wealthy nation on India's eastern seaboard. Ashoka (referring to himself as 'Piyadassi') takes up the story in one of the Edicts he had inscribed on rock faces around the empire:

> Beloved of the Gods, King Piyadassi, conquered the Kalingas eight years after his coronation. 150,000 were deported, 100,000 were killed and many more died [of other causes]. After the Kalingas had been conquered, he felt a strong inclination towards the Dharma, a love for the Dharma and for instruction in Dharma. Now [he] feels deep remorse . . . [and] is deeply pained because of the killing, dying and deportation that take place when an unconquered country is conquered.[28]

Legends tell that Ashoka was struck by the calm and integrity of Shakyaputra monks, which spoke to his condition more directly than Brahminical ideas about his roles and duties. It showed what his own life lacked. In another inscription from two and a half years after the Kalinga war, Ashoka says he is making a strenuous effort to improve himself with the help of Buddhist monks and urges his subjects to do the same.

Henceforth, Ashoka sought to rule his vast empire according to 'Dharma'. The word carried Buddhist associations, but it also

---

* This is a rare piece of fairly solid dating in the uncertain chronology of ancient India, although the date of Ashoka's birth is less certain.

expressed the universal ethical values of 'little evil, much good, kindness, generosity, truthfulness and purity'.[29] More broadly, it embodied Gautama's teaching that a moral order underpinned the world through the action of karma, and Ashoka's agenda unmistakably echoes the example of the Universal Monarch. In place of further military expansion, Ashoka launched a campaign of 'Dharma conquest' to reform the empire. He built monuments, expanded education, reformed the justice system, enhanced provision for the destitute and improved the roads. 'Dharma Officers' fanned out across the empire to implement justice, clemency and equity, and see that state institutions followed the emperor's principles.

Ashoka redefined the monarch's role as that of a father, rather than a sanctified semi-deity, and acknowledged the limits of his power: 'Progress among the people through Dharma has been done by two means, by Dharma regulations and by persuasion. Of these, Dharma regulation is of little effect, while persuasion has much more effect.'[30] This echoed Gautama's belief that individuals create a society, rather than the ruler, and that its health depends on their virtue and the networks of healthy, respectful relationships they establish. At the same time, it was a prudent and realistic policy for the ruler of a sprawling empire that was tugged by contending national, religious and cultural forces, and where regional governors influenced people's lives more directly than the distant emperor. Following Gautama's principle of exemplifying the virtues he proclaimed, Ashoka became a vegetarian and tried to get his court to follow suit. Where previous rulers had devoted much of their time to hunting, Ashoka worked constantly to promote the moral welfare of the realm, conducting 'Dharma tours' of the regions that combined pilgrimage to Buddhist holy places with inspections of the local administration and addresses urging his subjects to make a moral effort.

Ashoka distinguished his personal faith in Gautama's teaching from his responsibilities to subjects of all faiths, and there were no forcible conversions. Nonetheless, the remains of large Buddhist monasteries and stupas dating from Ashoka's time show that Buddhism expanded dramatically during his reign right across the empire. In fact, the monks prospered so much that Ashoka had to intervene in the community's affairs by expelling 'false monks' who took robes in order to share its privileges, and recommending texts that all monks should know. Dharma officers, 'occupied with various good works among the ascetics and householders of all religions',[31] monitored religious groups to ensure they set aside their rivalries, moderated their speech and became allies in the emperor's campaign of moral development. 'If there is cause for criticism, it should be done in a mild way', one edict urges. 'But it is better to honour other religions ... One should listen to and respect the doctrines professed by others.'[32]

As our information about Ashoka comes from Edicts which the emperor issued himself, we must be cautious in appraising him. But his story has been a powerful inspiration. Buddhists of later centuries regarded Ashoka's reign as the golden age of a real-life Universal Monarch: a rare example of a ruler putting Buddhism's implicit social teachings into effect on a large scale. And when India became an independent country in the last century its founders invoked Ashoka's empire as a model, regarding it as a tolerant and multicultural state in which moral and spiritual values had an esteemed place and state machinery was dedicated to social altruism, education and, where feasible, non-violence. The example of Ashoka's India vividly demonstrates that Gautama's Dharma does not just have a bearing on the minds of individuals. It implies a different way of ordering the world.

Gautama's Heirs

The phases of Indian Buddhism (the early schools, the Mahayana and the Vajrayana) created the framework for subsequent developments, and their differences, along with the impact of the cultures to which Buddhism travelled, underlie the diversity of the Buddhists one sees in a setting such as Bodh Gaya. Globalisation has thrown together schools that have been separated by culture, language and sometimes belief, each of which has its own scriptures, saints and forms of practice, as well as critiques of one another dating back millennia. But these Buddhists also share a great deal. The commonest Buddhist ritual is the act of going for refuge to the Three Jewels: the Buddha, the Dharma and the Sangha. Becoming a Buddhist involves making an act of commitment to the Three Jewels and in many countries Buddhists recite the verses of going for refuge each day.

For all their philosophical differences, the schools broadly share Gautama's understanding of reality: his Dharma. They teach that everything we experience is impermanent, insubstantial and dependently arisen and that human beings, being prone to craving for pleasure and security, set themselves at odds with reality and thereby create the seeds of their suffering. Like Gautama, the schools teach ways for people to change their condition, sometimes speaking of the need to follow a 'path', but always stressing the importance of manifesting qualities such as generosity, faith, energy, mindfulness, wisdom and compassion. Buddhists also agree on the importance of living by ethical principles such as non-violence and contentment, and most offer methods of mental development, especially in the grand tradition of Buddhist meditation practice.

Sangha means the community of Buddhists, and its centrality

contradicts the view that Buddhism is simply a path of individual practice and personal development. All the schools have full-time practitioners at the heart of their communities and value a way of life that is dedicated to realising Buddhist ideals. These full-time practitioners are usually monks (and sometimes nuns) who follow the Vinaya, but some are priests, renunciants or others who do not take monastic vows. Monastic institutions have sometimes been rigid, and dependence on patronage has made the monks vulnerable to political change, but as Robert Thurman comments, the monastic movement started by Gautama has been remarkably successful. It 'swept throughout Asia, transforming the landscapes, the cultures and the politics of all its nations, as well as countless individuals. It is quite likely that it influenced West Asia, North Africa and Europe by lending its institutional style to Aramaic and Egyptian Christianity as well as to Manichaeism.'[33]

The traditions also focus on the lineages of teachers, yogis, saints and philosophers who inspired and led their schools: Nagarjuna, Vasubandhu and Asanga, Padmasambhava, Tsongkhapa and Milarepa, Hui Neng, Kukai and Dogen. These remarkable individuals (and many others), who continue to inspire millions of devotees, are another aspect of Gautama's legacy, perhaps the most important. Modelling themselves on Gautama, they set out to attain Awakening themselves, and their followers, at least, believe that they succeeded.

The Buddha Jewel is Gautama himself and the ideal of Buddhahood he embodied. In some traditions the historical Gautama is lost in a crowd of transcendental Buddha figures, and his life story is often mixed with legend or reformulated as mythology. But time and again in Buddhist history the tradition has revived by returning to Gautama or re-emphasising the importance of the Awakening he embodied.

The shared commitment to the Three Jewels links Buddhists to one another and to the very earliest followers of Gautama. In reciting the verses of going for refuge, they repeat the words of the people in the Discourses who speak with Gautama and are overwhelmed by the vision of existence he reveals. Each of them prostrates before Gautama and declares that he or she will go for refuge to the Buddha, Dharma and Sangha.

Gautama, Our Contemporary

Gautama remarked that, like everything else, his teaching was subject to the universal law of impermanence: in time, it would cease to be a living force in the world and eventually be forgotten. A case can be made that over the last century, this has been happening to traditional Asian Buddhism. Its time-honoured institutions flourished in stable societies in which monks represented a link with a higher order of reality. But when Asian countries encountered the array of hostile, alien forces of modernity, Buddhism had few defences.

First came colonial rule which was sometimes hostile to Buddhist practice, especially when the colonial powers brought aggressive Christian missionaries with them. Then, as imperial and feudal governments faltered and communism swept Asia, Buddhist monks were murdered in their tens of thousands. That's what happened in Stalin's Siberia, Mao's China and Pol Pot's Cambodia. The story of Tibetan Buddhism's suppression by the Chinese forces who took full control of the country in 1959 is well known, but it is less often seen as part of the wider suppression of religion by the Chinese authorities and the assault on Buddhism by communists in general. These events truly deserve to be called 'the Buddhist Holocaust'.

Traditional Asian Buddhism is not dead. Many centres of intensive practice survive, the faith has re-emerged in formerly communist countries like Mongolia and China, and some traditions flourish. The troubles of Burma, North Korea and Tibet still fill the headlines, but most Buddhist countries enjoy relative political stability. However, even in countries where Buddhism is thriving – Thailand, Japan, Taiwan and South Korea – the strongest forces are consumerism and the drive for economic growth. To many young people, Buddhism is associated with dusty traditions that have little connection with their lives.

The surest sign than Buddhism has a continuing relevance, even in modern culture, is its ever-growing appeal in the West.* Western Buddhists are diverse, but they all engage with Buddhism because they feel it is relevant to their needs, rather than for reasons of tradition or culture. Some follow the teachings of particular schools more or less as they have been practised for centuries. Others adapt the tradition and attempt to separate Asian culture from the aspects of the Dharma that are relevant to them. According to Joseph Goldstein, such Buddhists are informed by a 'pragmatic' engagement with 'a very simple question: "what works?" What works to free the mind from suffering? What works to engender a heart of compassion? What works to awaken?'[34]

This pragmatism echoes that of Gautama himself in his desire to communicate his insights in whatever ways people could understand, but it also means that westerners tend to interpret Buddhism according to their own needs and agendas. For some, Buddhism is a quintessentially modern faith: a rational religion that suits people who have rejected God but still desire a source of values and

---

* This doesn't mean that western Buddhism is necessarily more important than what is happening in Asia. Asia is also changing dramatically and many Asian Buddhists are trying to adapt to the new conditions, without losing what is most valuable in their traditions.

meaning. For others (especially followers of Tibetan Buddhism), its appeal is that it contains the very things that rationalism lacks and its teachings open a magical dimension that is better expressed through symbols than concepts. For a third group, Buddhism means stripping away beliefs, interpretations and myths and focusing on what is happening in the present moment.* Finally, 'engaged Buddhists' see it as a vehicle for social change and find the meaning of Buddhist practice in its practical effects in the world.

None of these approaches does full justice to Gautama's teaching, although each reflects an aspect that has continuing resonance. In the early sources we find a rational Gautama – as great a demystifier as his contemporary, Socrates – who urged people to think for themselves and look to their own experience rather than accepting the beliefs that were passed down to them. But he was also at home using mythic language and communicating with the gods. Meditation was a central part of Gautama's path and he told his disciples to be aware of their experience as fully and deeply as possible. But he also encouraged his followers to develop communities and friendships and to cultivate the virtues that make for a good society.

Much could be written about the ways in which western scientists, artists, contemplatives, philosophers and activists have engaged with Buddhism.† But it would be a mistake to identify

---

* This description applies to many western Buddhists including Vipassana practitioners and followers of Zen.

† The recent wave of interest in Gautama's view of consciousness among psychologists and neuroscientists is an example. Many neuroscientists are exploring parallels between recent insights into the brain's neuroplasticity (its capacity to change) and neurogenesis (the development of fresh neural pathways as a result of using the brain in new ways) and Gautama's view of the mind (see www.mindandlife.org). Meanwhile, psychologists are using mindfulness as a key to helping their patients relate differently to their experience (see www.mindfulexperience.org).

Gautama's legacy with certain ideas or particular religious institutions, texts, myths, archetypes or meditation practices. Gautama's vision of human life contains all these elements, but its focus is the most fundamental dynamics of being. His continuing significance ultimately rests on his insights into the nature of experience, and a way to approach these is to focus on his time meditating in the forest as he sought Awakening.

The accounts of this time start with Gautama's recognition that his childhood experience beneath the rose-apple tree had shown him the 'path to Awakening'.[35] Understanding that his mind was capable of the intense concentration, bliss and refinement of dhyana, Gautama abandoned the shramanas' mistrust of pleasure, and rejected the ideas of God that had framed other approaches to meditation. He was free to address his experience directly and discover how it worked.

The heart of his realisation was the discovery that consciousness is a process, not a thing. He saw that skilful states (such as contentment and loving-kindness) brought happiness for himself and others, while unskilful ones caused suffering, and he learned to mould his consciousness by cultivating the former and discouraging the latter. He realised that values, meaning and ethics grow from the nature of the mind itself and don't depend on divine revelation, and concluded that karma (the key element of his culture's religious world view) depends on the intention with which one acts, not just the action one performs.

Gautama applied his insights most dramatically in confronting the fear and dread that was stirred by Gaya's demonic spirit shrines. In that way, he confronted death, the spirit world and the instinctual fears they roused in him, as a shaman might, and mastered them by practising mindful awareness of his experience. Through this practice, and with the power unleashed in intensely concentrated meditation, he freed his mind from limitations. Having seen the processes shaping his consciousness, Gautama understood that the same principles are at work in the whole of existence. All phenomena arise in dependence upon conditions; everything is process, including the natural world and human society. After his Awakening, Gautama applied these principles in guiding his disciples, formulating the path and developing the monastic community.

Perhaps we can say that Gautama's legacy is, fundamentally, an orientation to life and a vision of existence. It is something to be felt, experienced and developed. So I will conclude not with a definition but with images of Gautama that draw me towards him and make him a reference for the deepest hopes and fears of my own life.

I think of the young Gautama learning the tangled ways of Kapilavastu life, seeing that his companions were like fish struggling for space in a drying river and realising that his heart was wounded, just like theirs, by a thorn lodged deep within it. I think of Gautama burning with fiery realisation in his forest meditation, and resting in the afterglow of Awakening in the deep satisfaction of primordial awareness; then setting out on the dusty road to Sarnath, with no reason to think anyone would understand his message beyond the compassionate apprehension that people are like lotuses waiting to burst into flower. I think of him hammering out his ideas through dialogue with shramanas and his wary meetings with Brahmins and kings. I see him sitting amid the community of monks, sharing with them a silence as deep as a lake, and then returning to the wilderness where he sat impassive as a mountain. Finally, I think of him resting at the end of an exhausting journey, lying down on his side and passing into a state beyond life, for which his followers had no words.

The encounter with Bahiya has a special resonance. It stands for his many meetings and communications, but it has a unique drama. Its heart is the teaching that describes not just how Bahiya should train himself but how Gautama experienced the world. He was a man for whom the seen really was just the seen, the heard was the heard and the cognised was the cognised. What could be simpler than that? Yet, somehow, that made him a man who was 'neither here nor beyond nor between the two', whose experience was constructed in an entirely novel way and who possessed a key to life, as if he had woken up after a long sleep filled with endless compassion and wisdom.

What does this mean? Perhaps the best explanation is not a philosophy or a myth, or even an image. It is the example of Gautama's remarkable life.

APPENDIX

An Outline of Buddhist History

Ashoka's reign marked the start of Buddhism's impact on Indian society as a whole, and its effect on the world beyond India. One of Ashoka's Edicts states that the Emperor sent Dharma missions to people living beyond the borders of his realm, 'even as far as 600 yojanas'[1] (about 3,000 miles), listing the kings of Sri Lanka, Egypt, Syria and Macedonia among their recipients. Hinduism also spread beyond India to South East Asia, but it remained the religion of a particular culture and drew people who were attracted to that culture. Buddhists, in contrast (like Christians and Muslims after them), said that their teachings held true everywhere and for everyone. At its height the Buddhist world spread from Persia in the west to Indonesia in the east, and from Korea in the north to Sri Lanka in the south. A traveller like Hsuan Tsang could rightly feel that he was participating in a world religion that touched most of humanity. Above all, Buddhism deeply affected China and India, the two great Asian civilisations.

Buddhism in India after Ashoka

Ashoka's reign, which lasted thirty-seven years, marks an early high point of Buddhism's impact on Indian society. His regime depended on central power and his own impact as a charismatic leader who commanded exceptional loyalty. Soon after he died the empire started to break up, probably because of economic difficulties and the strength of the regions relative to the centre. Fifty years after Ashoka's death, the last of the Mauryas was assassinated by his general, Pushyamitra, whose first act was to perform the Vedic horse sacrifice. The new emperor devoted his reign to restoring Brahminical influence, and Buddhist chronicles tell us that Pushyamitra 'burned down numerous monasteries . . . killed a number of vastly learned monks . . . and within five years the Doctrine was extinct in the north'.[2] That almost certainly exaggerates what happened, but for the time being Buddhist fortunes had turned.

Victorian archaeologists unearthed the buried monuments of a Buddhist civilisation that recovered from Pushyamitra's persecution and spread across the subcontinent in the centuries after Ashoka. Hsuan Tsang's account of his travels through the subcontinent in the seventh century shows that while Buddhism had declined in some regions, it thrived in others. Everywhere, it competed for influence with Jains and the priests of the Brahminical 'deva temples'. Monarchs usually supported all the major faiths, and there are no further examples of rulers who tried to manifest Gautama's Dharma as a social reality, as Ashoka had done.

Buddhism remained associated with the merchant class, who supported Buddhist monks even when the state was hostile or indifferent, and helped it to spread along the trade routes. Buddhist teachings supported the open, entrepreneurial culture in which commerce thrived, whereas Brahminism stifled it, and some historians regard Buddhism's 1,500-year history in India as a forgotten battle between two very different visions of life. Some sources hint at competition for patronage between Buddhists and Brahmins, as well as fierce debates and occasional persecution of the Buddhists.

The Linga Purana, for example, relates that a king named Pramitra 'destroyed barbarians by the thousand, killed all the kings born of Shudras and cut down the heretics'.[3]

Brahmins sought new ways to embed their vision of existence in the fabric of Indian life by fostering a feudal economy and turning existing social divisions into a rigid caste system that assigned people a group within which they lived, worked, ate and married. Brahminism also allied itself with the cults of popular deities like Shiva and Vishnu; the great mythic cycles of the *Ramayana* and the *Mahabharata* were formed according to Brahminical perspectives; yogic traditions found a place in the Brahminical mainstream; and, partly in response to the intellectual challenge of Buddhism, Brahmin theologians and philosophers found subtler ways to articulate their tradition. The elements that comprise what we now call 'Hinduism' slowly coalesced.

The Brahminical model of society shaped the lives of ordinary Indians, and its amalgam of caste, deity worship and a resurgent priesthood increasingly commanded their religious imaginations. Developments in Indian Buddhism, such as Mahayana devotions and Pure Land teachings, show that the tradition found new ways to connect with popular religious needs; but, eventually, Buddhists found themselves frozen out by caste regulations while royal patrons were drawn to the Brahminical consecration rituals that sanctified their rule. In return, the kings built huge temples in regional capitals across India that became centres of the new deity cults.

The Muslim invaders who swept across India in the thirteenth century destroyed the already weakened remnants of Indian Buddhism when they razed Nalanda, Vikramasila and other Buddhist centres. Barring a few remnant groups in Orissa and some border areas, the faith disappeared from India. The motivation of the Muslim attackers was probably loot and conquest rather than

Taliban-style religious hatred, but a degree of hostility to Buddhism per se may have fuelled their aggression.

Although Buddhism became India's greatest cultural export, it was forgotten in the land of its birth. Its reverberations are evident in the devotional traditions around some Hindu deities and Muslim saints, as well as in Hindu meditation, art and yoga. But Buddhism itself was written out of Indian history, and until colonial archae-ologists took an interest its temples lay ruined or buried or were converted into Hindu shrines. Indians forgot Ashoka and the Hindu texts do not mention him. Indeed, Brahminical sources are largely silent about Buddhism, and the little they do say is set within a narrative of 'Hindu' triumph. Modern Hindu thinkers sometimes describe Gautama as a 'rebel child'[4] of the mainstream faith and his teachings as a 'branch' of that tradition; and Brahmins long ago recast Gautama as an 'avatar', or incarnation, of the great god Vishnu. And while the nations that inherited Indian Buddhism preserved the scriptures and philosophies relevant to their schools, the texts of the Indians themselves were destroyed.

Sri Lanka

We have no record of the reception Ashoka's missionaries received in Europe or Asia Minor, but Sri Lanka's king enthusiastically greeted the mission to the island, led by Ashoka's sons, and set about making it a Buddhist nation. From the outset, the state supported Sri Lankan Buddhism and the monastic establishment eventually commanded enormous wealth and influence, burgeoning as nowhere else in the Indian subcontinent. In the fifth century Fa-hsien reported finding 60,000 monks on the island. The price of state patronage was that, from its inception, Sri Lankan Buddhism supported the state in whatever it did – a pattern that continues in the island's current ethnic conflicts. Ashoka's envoys belonged to a precursor sect of the Theravada school that still dominates Sri Lankan Buddhism, whose adherents believed they were preserving the Buddha's original teaching. That view led an important Theravadin chronicle called the *Dipavamsa* to declare: 'The seventeen sects [of Indian Buddhism] are schismatic. Only one sect is non-schismatic . . . Like a great banyan tree, the Theravada is supreme.'[5]

The principal Sri Lankan monasteries competed for royal favour, and monks split into factions. The question for the Sri Lankans was which form of Theravada was supreme. Sri Lankan monks also focused on literary work. They wrote down the canon of early scriptures in the Pali language, produced chronicles and commentaries, and eventually, through the immense labours of the fifth-century monk Buddhaghosha, gave the texts the form in which they have been passed down ever since. Sri Lankan Buddhism's fortunes have fluctuated along with those of the island itself, which was invaded from India and later colonised by Portugal and Britain. The monastic order died out and had to be reintroduced from Burma, and on several occasions it needed to be reformed and revived. But unlike its Indian counterpart, Sri Lankan Buddhism survived and preserves to this day the practices and teachings of at least some early Buddhists.

South East Asia

Ashokan missionaries also travelled to the Mon territories of lower Burma and northern Thailand, and by the turn of the millennium Theravada was firmly established there. Eventually it dominated the whole of Burma, as it has to the present day. An important part of Buddhism's appeal was its connection to Indian culture, whose literature and philosophy was far more sophisticated than that of the indigenous people. But that culture contained many strands, and in Cambodia and Thailand, Mahayana Buddhism was embraced along with elements of Hinduism, and the two faiths replayed the competition for influence and royal favour that occurred in India itself. The spectacular Angok Wat temple, which now rises in extraordinary crumbling grandeur from the tangle of Cambodian jungle, was built in the twelfth century as a Hindu temple and became a Theravadin shrine when the country adopted the faith. Neighbouring Thailand also became solidly Theravadin only in the fifteenth century, and all these countries (and Laos as well) adopted the Sri Lankan model in which Buddhism supported the state in return for patronage and regulation.

'Official' histories of Buddhism in these countries tend to emphasise the Theravada school and the institutions that created the grand temples and influenced affairs of state. But alongside that, the unofficial Buddhism of practice and popular belief contained other elements that are sometimes overlooked. Mahayana and even tantric practices were adopted in some of these countries, and even in Indonesia, as the magnificent Borobudur temple complex testifies. Mahayana vestiges lived on in South East Asian countries, even when they became officially Theravadin, and in the villages a monk will often act as a shaman and healer as well as a priest, educator and spiritual guide. Wonderfully evocative accounts also survive of the experiences of wilderness monks, whose lifestyle dated back to Gautama himself. Development, centralisation and war have limited the scope to live this way today, but in remote regions of forests and mountains some still do.

The Silk Road

Even more significant than centrally directed missionary efforts to spread the faith outside India was its gradual diffusion along trade routes. To the north and north-east are the virtually impassible Himalayas; but the passes on the north-west were no such barrier, and traders, migrants and armies travelled them continually. Kashmir was an important focus for Mahayana Buddhism, and the Kushan Empire, founded in the first century CE, joined it to the lands to the north and west. Kashmiri Buddhist influence spread through Pakistan and even made long-forgotten inroads into Persia. The Jataka Tales of Gautama's previous lives were translated into Persian in the sixth century and became known in western lands, where they influenced Aesop's fables, the tales of Sinbad and the *Arabian Nights*, while in distant Europe the 'bodhisat' – the name of the Buddha-to-be – transmuted into the Christian Saint Josephat.

Buddhism reached Afghanistan during Ashoka's reign, and until their destruction by the Taliban in 2001 the towering Buddhas of Bamiyan were the most visible remnants of a thriving Buddhist culture. The caves around the statues were home to 2,000 monks, and the world's oldest oil paintings have been found inside them. Further north, the huge, arid territories of Central Asia were less hospitable. But this region was a vital part of the network of trade routes connecting China and the Middle East, with a southern spur that led to India. Marco Polo, who went from Italy to China in the fourteenth century, was the most famous trader to travel the 'Silk Road', but the route he followed was already many centuries old. Much earlier, Buddhist monks had joined the trading caravans, and Buddhist texts describe the perils that confronted them. Some settled in oasis towns where Chinese and Indian culture converged, along with Persian and even Nestorian Christian influences. Buddhism flourished in this fertile environment until the Muslim invasions of the eighth century. By the fourteenth century, little was left to show for Buddhist culture, but when the Hungarian archaeologist Aurel Stein entered a cave in Dunhuang at the eastern end of the Silk Road, he discovered 40,000 scrolls containing Buddhist texts dating from the ninth century or earlier. They include the earliest known versions of important Buddhist scriptures, the first-ever printed book (a copy of the Mahayana Diamond Sutra) and Buddhist-influenced Nestorian texts entitled the Jesus Sutras.

China

In the first century Buddhists reached China, at the eastern end of the Silk Road, where they found a civilisation at least a match for India's. Confucianism and Taoism were deeply established indigenous faiths, and Buddhism initially made little impact, though many scriptures were translated. The country changed in 220 CE when the Han dynasty collapsed, and in the subsequent period of turmoil the religion took off spectacularly. By the fifth century, northern China boasted 30,000 monasteries housing an astonishing two million monks and nuns, principally following the Mahayana – more than in India itself. Meanwhile, in southern China, which was still ruled by the old dynasty, Confucian influence declined and Buddhism appealed to members of the relocated court. Cut off from India and Central Asia, new and characteristically Chinese forms of Buddhism started to emerge that showed Taoist or Confucian influences. When the two regions were reunited under the Sui and T'ang dynasties of the sixth to tenth centuries, the two streams of Chinese Buddhism mingled, and immensely accomplished teachers and scholars founded new schools that drew on Indian Buddhism (often basing themselves principally on a single scripture), but with a distinctly Chinese cast.

A byproduct of the fertility of the Indian Mahayana, with its succession of teachings, philosophies, schools and practices, all piled on top of the earlier scriptures, was that later generations faced an overwhelming profusion of material. Only dedicated scholars could become familiar with even the main aspects of the tradition, and even they were left asking what was most important and how they could practise it. Indian teachers had their own solutions, which Tibetan Buddhism inherited, but the Chinese were cut off from India by this time. The approach of the Hua-yen and the T'ien-t'ai schools was to consider one sutra the key to the whole tradition and to arrange the rest in a hierarchy of importance beneath it. An alternative was to focus on a single practice that cut through the complexity and offered a direct path to Nirvana. Some schools taught ways to be reborn in Amitabha's pure land, while Ch'an focused principally on meditation and made the heart of its teachings: 'a special transmission outside the scriptures; no dependence on words and letters; direct pointing to the mind; [and] seeing into one's nature and realising Buddhahood'.[6]

The fortunes of Chinese Buddhism changed abruptly in 845 when a Taoist emperor launched a massive campaign to suppress it. In the most intense of four separate persecutions in this era monasteries were dissolved and the monks and nuns forcibly disrobed. The great scholastic sects, which depended on large monastic institutions, never recovered. Buddhism remained a potent force in Chinese culture, and experienced periods of significant revival, but it was never again the virtual state religion it had been in its heyday.

East Asia and Japan

China was the dominant civilisation of East Asia, just as India dominated South Asia, and Chinese Buddhism was exported throughout the region. It reached Vietnam (where it eventually mixed with South East Asian Theravada), and in the sixth century it reached Korea and Japan. The Japanese aristocracy wanted to civilise their turbulent subjects and looked to Buddhism as the embodiment of Chinese virtues that also offered distinctive ethical teachings. By the eighth century, Japanese Buddhism was the state religion and there were temples in every province. T'ien-t'ai lived on in Japan after its demise in China as the Tendai school, and tantric traditions were introduced with the Shingon school. Characteristically Japanese forms of Buddhism developed during the Kamakura period (1185–1333) when a series of charismatic Japanese teachers founded schools and movements that bypassed the existing, allegedly corrupt, monastic establishment. The new schools shared a stress on the redemptive power of faith, devotion to a single practice and a belief that the world was passing through a dangerous period of decline. From this turbulent time emerged the traditions of Japanese Zen (a development of Ch'an); Jodo-shin-shu, which taught surrender to the 'other-power' of Amitabha (called Amida in Japan); and Nichiren Buddhism. Nichiren was a Tendai monk who became deeply disillusioned with the state of Japanese Buddhism and declared that only a particular form of devotion to the Mahayana scripture the Lotus Sutra would be effective. Both Nichiren Buddhism and Jodo-shin-shu offered simple practices that won a popular following.

Tibet and Mongolia

Buddhism travelled to Tibet directly from India, with Nepal as an important staging post (though there was also some early influence from China). It arrived in two waves, in the seventh century and the tenth century, which was relatively late in Indian Buddhist history, and the Tibetans inherited Indian Buddhist traditions virtually in their entirety. They made sense of them in terms of the systematised schemes the Indian Mahayana had developed, and like many of their Indian Buddhist contemporaries they considered Vajrayana the highest form of practice. But the Buddhist civilisation that developed in Tibet was also unique because the shamanistic and magical aspects of Vajrayana enabled it to absorb the indigenous beliefs of the Tibetans themselves. A founding myth of Tibetan Buddhism tells of the conversion of the nation's demon-spirits by the great tantric sage Padmasambhava. That echoed Gautama's battle with Mara and his battles with other Indian demons, but it also suggests that, in Tibet, the most primal and barbaric forces of the culture were united with the higher pursuits of Dharma practice. One historian calls Tibetan Buddhists 'civilised Shamans'.[7]

Tibetan Buddhist history includes great thinkers who grappled with the ancient problems of Buddhist philosophy and made new and liberating syntheses; vast monastic colleges that echoed the lost universities of India; and a unique system of identifying the children, or 'tulkus', in whom great teachers were thought to be reborn. In the seventeenth century the Mongol Khan made an important teacher the country's head of state with the title 'Dalai Lama', and children identified as his tulku succeeded him in the role. The Dalai Lama led a Buddhist school that competed with others, so feelings towards him were often mixed; but on another level he was considered the manifestation of Chenrezig, bodhisattva of compassion and the nation's embodiment.

The Revival of Indian Buddhism

The struggles of Buddhism in the modern era have already been touched on. This has been one of the most difficult periods for Buddhism in its entire history. However, it seems fitting to conclude this sketch of Buddhist history with its dramatic return to India as a mass movement.

Each year on 14 October a million pilgrims flood into a vast area of open ground known as Diksha Bhumi (the 'Conversion Ground'), dominated by a huge modern stupa. A casket at its centre contains the ashes of Dr Ambedkar (1891–1956), India's first Law Minister and the focus of the pilgrims' reverence. Portraits, which appear everywhere on banners and placards, show a thickset, bespectacled man in a western business suit who seems an unlikely focus for a religious movement. But for his followers, the two hundred million Indians considered 'untouchables' under the Hindu caste system, he is a saviour for two reasons. He framed newly independent India's constitution which outlawed untouchability, and in 1956, just before his death, he initiated a wave of mass conversions to Buddhism.

Under Dr Ambedkar's inspiration, Buddhism has returned to India as a mass faith. Ambedkarite Buddhists number twenty to thirty million, and many more are drawn to the movement. But most of Dr Ambedkar's followers do not follow Buddhism in one of its traditional forms. His conversion was driven by an urgent need to find an alternative to the Hindu world view, and the aspects of Buddhism that he valued most highly addressed his community's need for 'social uplift' and education as well as affirming the meaning and dignity of human life. To find them, he turned to the life and teachings of Gautama, the historical Buddha.

Select Bibliography

TEXTS (PALI, SANSKRIT, CHINESE AND GREEK)

Anguttara Nikaya   Nyanaponika Thera and Bhikkhu Bodhi, *Numerical Discourses of the Buddha: An Anthology of Suttas from the Anguttara Nikaya* (New Delhi, 2001).
Gradual Sayings of the Buddha   5 vols: 1, 2 and 5, F. L. Woodward (Oxford, 1932, 1992, 1994); Vols 3 and 4, E.M. Hare (Oxford, 1988 and 1999).

Ashokan Inscriptions   Ven. S. Dhammika, *The Edicts of King Ashoka: An English Rendering* (Kandy, 1993).

Ashokavadana   John Strong, *The Legend of King Ashoka, A Study and Translation of the Ashokavadana* (Princeton, 1983).

Brahmajala Sutta   Bhikkhu Bodhi, *Discourse on the All Embracing Net of Views: Brahmajala Sutta and its Commentaries* (Kandy, 1998).

Buddhacharita   E. H. Johnston, *Asvaghosha's Buddhacharita or Acts of the Buddha* (Delhi, 1984).

Dhammapada   Sangharakshita, Dhammapada: *The Way of Truth* (Birmingham, 2001).

Digha Nikaya   Maurice Walshe, *Thus Have I Heard: The Long Discourse of the Buddha* (London, 1987).

Indika   E. A. Schwanbeck and J. W. McCrindle, *Ancient India as Described by Megasthenes and Arrian* (London, 1877).

Ituvittaka   John Ireland, *Udana & Ituvittaka: Two Classics from the Pali canon* (Kandy, 2007).

Jataka   E. B. Cowell *et al.*, *Jataka Stories*, 6 vols (London, 1895).

Lalitavistara   Gwendolyn Bays, *The Voice of the Buddha: The Beauty of Compassion*, 2 vols (Berkeley, 1983).

Mahabharata   John D. Smith, *The Mahabharata* (London, 2009).

Majjhima Nikaya   Bhikkhu Nyanamoli and Bhikkhu Bodhi, *The Middle Length Discourses of the Buddha: A New Translation of the Majjhima Nikaya* (Boston, 1995).

Manusmriti   G. Buhler, *The Laws of Manu* (Oxford, 1886).

Milindapanha   I. B. Horner, *The Questions of Milinda*, 2 vols (Oxford, 1890, 1894).

Nidana Katha   N. A. Jayawickrama, *The Story of Gotama Buddha*, (Oxford, 1990).

Samyutta Nikaya   Bhikkhu Bodhi, *Connected Discourses of the Buddha: A Translation of the Samyutta Nikaya* (Boston, 2000).

Satapatha Brahmana   Julius Eggeling, *Satapatha Brahmana*, 5 vols (London, 1882–1900).

Si-Yu-Ki   Samuel Beal, *Buddhist Records of the Western World*, 2 vols (London, 1906).

Sutta Nipata   K. R. Norman, *The Rhinoceros Horn and Other Early Buddhist Poems* (Oxford, 1986).

———Ven. Saddhatissa, *Sutta Nipata* (London, 1985).

Theragatha   K. R. Norman, *Poems of the Early Buddhist Monks* (Oxford, 1997).

Therigatha   C. A. F. Rhys Davids and K. R. Norman, *Poems of the Early Buddhist Nuns* (Oxford, 1997).

Udana   John Ireland, *Udana & Ituvittaka: Two Classics from the Pali canon* (Kandy, 2007).

Ugrapariprccha   Jan Nattier, *A Few Good Men: The Bodhisattva Path According to the Enquiry of Ugra* (Honolulu, 2005).

Upanishads   Valerie Roebuck, *The Upanishads* (London, 2004).

Vimalakirti Nirdesa Sutra   Charles Luk, *Vimalakirti Nirdesa Sutra* (Boston and Shaftesbury, 1990).

Vinaya-Pitaka   I. B. Horner, *Book of the Discipline*, Vol. 4 (Oxford, 1993), Vol. 5 (Oxford, 1992).

Visuddhimagga   Bhikkhu Nyanamoli, *The Path of Purification* (Kandy, 1991).

ANTHOLOGIES

Bhikkhu Bodhi, *In the Buddha's Words: An Anthology of Discourses from the Pali canon* (Boston, 2005).

Gethin, Rupert, *Sayings of the Buddha: New Translations from the Pali Nikayas* (Oxford, 2008).

Bhikkhu Nyanamoli, *The Life of the Buddha According to the Pali canon* (Kandy, 1992).

Wallis, Glen, *Basic Teachings of the Buddha: A New Translation and Compilation with a Guide to Reading the Texts* (New York, 2007).

Warren, Henry Clarke, *Buddhism in Translations: Passages Selected from the Buddhist Sacred Books and Translated from the Original Pali into English* (Boston, 1896).

ONLINE RESOURCES

Translations from the Pali Nikayas by Thanissaro, Andrew Olendzki and Buddharakkhita are at www.accesstoinsight.org.

OTHER WORKS

Allchin, F. R. *et al.*, *The Archaeology of Early Historic South Asia: The Emergence of Cities and States* (Cambridge, 1995).

Analayo, *Satipatthana: The Direct Path to Realisation* (Birmingham, 2003).

——*From Craving to Liberation: Excursions into the Thought-world of the Pali Discourses* (New York, 2009).

Armstrong, Karen, *Buddha* (London, 2000).

——*The Great Transformation: The World in the Time of Buddha, Socrates, Confucius and Jeremiah* (London, 2006).

Aronson, Harvey, *Love and Sympathy in Theravada Buddhism* (Delhi, 1980).

Bailey, Greg, and Mabbett, Ian, *The Sociology of Early Buddhism* (Cambridge, 2004).

Basham, A. L., *The Wonder That Was India* (New York, 1963).

Batchelor, Stephen, *Living with the Devil: A Meditation on Good and Evil* (New York, 2004).

Battacharya, N. N., *Buddhism in the History of Indian Ideas* (Delhi, 1993).

——*The Awakening of the West: The Encounter of Buddhism and Western Culture* (Berkeley, 1994).

Bloom, Harold, *Jesus and Yahweh: The Names Divine* (New York, 2005).

Bechert, Heinz (ed.), *The Dating of the Historical Buddha* (*Die Datierung des historischen Buddha*), 3 vols (Gottingen, 1991, 1992, 1997).

Blackstone, Kathryn R., *Women in the Footsteps of the Buddha: The Struggle for Liberation in the Therigatha* (Richmond, 1998).

Bronkhorst, Johannes, *Two Traditions of Meditation in Ancient India* (Stuttgart, 1986).

Buddhist Teaching in India (Boston, 2009).

——*Greater Magadha: Studies in the Culture of Early India* (Leiden and Boston, 2007).

Collins, Steven, *Selfless Persons* (Cambridge, 1982).

——*Nirvana and Other Buddhist Felicities: Utopias of the Pali Imaginaire* (Cambridge, 1998).

Crystal Mirror Series, *Holy Places of the Buddha* (Berkeley, 1994).

DeCarolli, Robert, *Haunting the Buddha: Indian Popular Religions and the Formation of Buddhism* (Oxford, 2004).

Dundas, Paul, *The Jains* (London and New York, 2002).

Dutt, Sukumar, *Buddhist Monks and Monasteries of India* (London, 1962).

Eliade, Mercea, *Yoga: Immortality and Freedom* (Princeton, 1969).

Foucher, A., *The Life of the Buddha According to the Ancient Texts and Monuments of India* (New Delhi, 2003).

Gethin, Rupert, *The Foundations of Buddhism* (Oxford and New York, 1998).

——*The Buddhist Path to Awakening* (Oxford, 2002).

Gombrich, Richard, *Theravada Buddhism: A Social History from Ancient Benares to Modern Colombo* (London and New York, 1988).

——*How Buddhism Began: The Conditioned Genesis of the Early Teachings* (Oxford and New York, 1996).

——*What the Buddha Thought* (London, 2009).

Hamilton, Susan, *Early Buddhism: A New Approach* (Richmond, 2000).

Hare, E.M., *Woven Cadences of Early Buddhists* (London, 1945).

Harvey, Peter, *Selfless Persons: Personality, Consciousness and Nirvana in Early Buddhism* (Richmond, 1995).

Jinananda, *Warrior of Peace: The Life of the Buddha* (Birmingham, 2002).

Keown, Damien, *Oxford Dictionary of Buddhism* (Oxford, 2004).

Ling, Trevor, *The Buddha* (New York, 1973).

Malasakare, G. P., *Dictionary of Pali Proper Names*, 2 vols (London, 1974) and online: www.palikanon.com

Masefield, Peter, *Divine Revelation in Pali Buddhism* (London, 1986).

Mishra, Pankaj, *An End to Suffering: The Buddha in the World* (London, 2004).

Morrison, Robert, *Nietzsche and Buddhism: A Study in Ironic Affinities* (Oxford, 1997).

Murcott, Susan, *The First Buddhist Women: Translations and Commentary on the Therigatha* (Berkeley, 1991).

Bhikkhu, Nananada: *Concept and Reality in Early Buddhist Thought* (Kandy, 1971).

——*The Magic of the Mind: An Exposition of the Kalakarama Sutta* (Kandy, 1974).

Nakamura, Hakjime, trans. Gaynor Sekimori, *Gotama Buddha: A Biography Based on the Most Reliable Texts*, 2 vols (Tokyo, 2000 and 2005).

Nyanaponika Thera and Hecker, Helmuth, *Great Disciples of the Buddha: Their Lives, their Works, their Legacy* (Boston, 2003).

Olendzlci, Andrew, 'Lions in the Wilderness: Early Buddhist Appreciation of Nature' (1996) at www.dharma.org

Omvedt, Gail, *Buddhism in India: Challenging Brahminism and Caste* (Delhi and London, 2003).

Penner, Hans, *Rediscovering the Buddha: Legends of the Buddha and their Interpretation* (Oxford, 2009).

Rahula, Walpola Sri, *What the Buddha Taught* (Oxford, 1997).

Ray, Reginald, *Buddhist Saints in India: A Study in Buddhist Values and Orientations* (New York and Oxford, 1994).

Rhys Davids, T. W., and Stede, W., *Pali–English Dictionary* (New Delhi, 2001).

Ryan, P. D., *Buddhism and the Natural World* (Birmingham, 1998).

Samuel, Geoffrey, *Civilised Shamans: Buddhism in Tibetan Societies* (London, 1993).

——*The Origins of Yoga and Tantra: Indic Religion to the Thirteenth Century* (Cambridge, 2008).

Sangharakshita, *A Survey of Buddhism: Its Doctrines and Methods through the Ages* (Calcutta, 1957).

——*The Three Jewels: An Introduction to Buddhism* (Purley, 1967).

——*Who is the Buddha?* (Birmingham, 1994).

——*Living with Kindness: The Buddha's Teaching on Metta* (Birmingham, 2004).

Schopen, Gregory, *Bones, Stones and Buddhist Monks: Collected Papers on the Archaeology, Epigraphy and Texts of Monastic Buddhism in India* (Honolulu, 1997).

——*Buddhist Monks and Business Matters: Still More Papers on Monastic Buddhism in India* (Honolulu, 2004).

Schumann, H. W., *The Historical Buddha: The Times, Life and Teachings of the Founder of Buddhism* (London, 1989).

Skilton, Andrew, *A Concise History of Buddhism* (Birmingham, 1994).

Spiro, Melford, *Buddhism and Society: A Great Tradition and its Burmese Vicissitudes* (London, 1971).

Strong, John S., *The Buddha: A Short Biography* (Oxford, 2001).

Subhuti, *Buddhism and Friendship* (Birmingham, 2004).

Sujato Bhikkhu, *Sects and Sectarianism: The Origin of Buddhist Schools* (lulu.com, 2006).

Thapar, Romila, *Ancient Indian Social History: Some Interpretations* (Hyderabad, 1978).

——*Early India from the Origins to AD 1300* (Berkeley, 2002).

Thomas, Edward, *The Life of the Buddha as Legend and History* (London, 1927).

Tiyanavich, Kamala, *The Buddha in The Jungle* (Chang Mai and Seattle, 2003).

Tweed, Thomas A., *The American Encounter with Buddhism: Victorian Culture and the Limits of Dissent* (Chapel Hill and London, 2000).

Wijayaratna, Mohan, *Buddhist Monastic Life* (Cambridge, 1990).

Williams, Paul, *Mahayana Buddhism: The Doctrinal Foundations* (London, 1989).

Wynne, Alexander, *The Origins of Buddhist Meditation* (Abingdon, 2007).

Glossary of Terms, Names and Places

Ajatashatru (Pali: Ajatasattu) King of Magadha, son of Bimbasara

Ajivaka a sect of self-mortifiers led by Mahali Gosala who believed that man's fate is predetermined

Ambattha a proud Brahmin youth

Ananda Gautama's cousin and his personal attendant for many years

Anathapindika a wealthy lay disciple who donated the Jetavana monastery

Angulimala a murderer who was converted by Gautama

Anuruddha cousin and important disciple of Gautama

Arada Kalama (Pali: Alara Kalama) Gautama's first teacher, who taught 'the sphere of Nothingness'

Arahant (Pali: arhat) one who has found Awakening or realisation by following the Buddha's teaching

Aryan either 'a noble one', or a member of the Aryan race

aryavarta the lands deemed 'pure' by Aryans

Ashoka third-century BCE monarch, who ruled over most of India and converted to Buddhism

Ashvajit (Pali: Assaji) one of the Group of Five self-mortifiers

atman (Pali: atta) the unchanging eternal essence of selfhood sought by yogis, thought by some to be identical to Brahman

Bimbisara King of Magadha

Bodh Gaya the site of Gautama's Enlightenment

Bodhi Tree the tree under which Gautama sat when he gained Enlightenment

Bodhisattva (Pali: Bodhisatta) one destined for Enlightenment, such as the Buddha before his Awakening, or, in the Mahayana, one who defers realisation for the sake of others

Brahma   the highest class of divinities, and sometimes an individual member of this class

Brahman   the divine heart of existence, described in the Upanishads and elsewhere

Brahminism   the religion of the Aryans and the precursor of Hinduism

Brahmin   a member of the priestly caste of Aryan society

Buddha   literally 'the Awakened', Gautama's principal title after his Enlightenment

Chandaka (Pali: Channa)   Gautama's groom, who helped him leave the palace and later joined his order

commentaries   texts expounding the Buddhist Discourses, compiled in later centuries

dependent arising   the Buddhist teaching of conditionality or causality

deva   a class of divine being

Devadatta   Gautama's cousin and eventual rival

dharma (Pali: dhamma)   the nature of reality and how one should act to be in accordance with it. The teaching of the Buddha

dharmakaya   'The body of truth or dharma', the purified qualities of the Buddha and the primordial, signless reality he realised

dhyana (Pali: jhana)   a state of meditative absorption

Digha-karayana   a Kosalan general

Discourses   the body of suttas/sutras of the Buddhist canon

dukkha   the 'suffering' or 'unsatisfactoriness' that characterises conditioned existence

Fa-hsien   Chinese pilgrim who described his visit to India early in the fifth century CE

Four Sights   the encounter with an old man, a sick man, a corpse and a religious wanderer, ascribed to Gautama

gana community   a clan-based oligarchy or republic, such as Shakya

Ganges Valley   the region in which Gautama lived, roughly equivalent to the Central Ganges Basin

Gautama (Pali: Gotama)   the Buddha's clan-name

Group of Five   the five men who practised self-mortification with Gautama and to whom he addressed his first teaching

Hsuan Tsang   Chinese pilgrim of the seventh century CE

Jainism   an important religious movement of Gautama's day, led by Mahavira

Jatakas   tales of Gautama's previous lives

Jetavana   a monastic park in Shravasti where Guatama spent many rainy seasons

kalpa   an aeon: a measure of time variously defined as 1051, 1059 or 1063 thousand years

Kapilavastu (Pali: Kapilavatthu)   the capital of Shakya, where Gautama grew up

karma (Pali: kamma)   actions or thoughts whose results are felt in this or future lives

Kausambi (Pali: Kosambi)   the capital of the kingdom of Vatsa, situated on the Yamuna river, near the confluence with the Ganges. Local monks engaged in a serious dispute

Koliya   a clan closely related to the Shakyas

Kosala   one of the major kingdoms of the Ganges Valley, with Shravasti as its capital

Kshatriya (Pali: Khattiya)   the warrior and aristocratic caste of Aryan society

Kusinagara (Pali: Kusinagara)   a small town in Malla, where Gautama entered Parinirvana

Lumbini   Gautama's birthplace

Magadha   a major kingdom of the Ganges Valley, with its capital in Rajagriha

Mahakasyapa (Pali: Mahakassapa)   a leading disciple of Gautama's, famed for his austerities, who presided over the First Buddhist Council

Mahanama   cousin of Gautama and leading Shakyan noble

Mahavagga   a section of the Vinaya that contains an extended account of the start of Gautama's teaching career

Mahavira   'Great Hero': teacher of the Jains

Mahayana   'the great vehicle'. A broad Buddhist school or movement

Malla   the land (including Kusinagara) inhabited by Great Vehicle Mallas: members of the Malla clan

Mara   chief god of the 'realm of desire', who challenged Gautama on the night of his Enlightenment

Maudgalyayana (Pali: Moggallana) one of Gautama's two chief disciples, famed for his psychic powers

Maya (or Mahamaya, or Mayadevi) Gautama's mother

naga a class of serpent-like spirits

Nanda Gautama's brother

Nikaya a division of the sutta collection of the Pali canon

Nirvana (Pali: Nibbana) the 'blowing out' of craving, hatred and ignorance, the goal of the Buddhist path

Pali the north Indian dialect in which the best-known versions of Gautama's Discourses are recorded

Parinirvana (Pali: Parinibbana) the death of a Buddha or arahant, and their 'complete Nirvana' because they will not be reborn

Prajapati (Pali: Mahapajjapati) Gautama's aunt and stepmother

Prasenajit (Pali: Pasenadi) King of Kosala

Rahula Gautama's son

Rahulamata Gautama's wife, sometimes named as Yashodhara, Bimba, etc.

Rajagriha (Pali: Rajagaha) a mountain-fortress city, the capital of Magadha, ruled by Bimbasara and Ajatashastru

Rohini the principal river of Shakya

sangha the 'spiritual community' of the Buddha's followers and the order of Buddhist monks and nuns

Sanjaya Belataputta a teacher of scepticism and leader of a community of shramanas

Sanskrit India's 'holy language' in which many Buddhist scriptures are recorded

sangharama a monastic park

Shakya the tribe to which Gautama belonged, and the territory in which they lived

Shakyamuni 'Sage of the Shakyans': a title given to Gautama and his principal epithet in Mahayana Buddhism

Shakyaputra (Pali: Shakyaputta) 'the sons of the Shakyan', the name by which Gautama's monastic followers were known

Shariputra (Pali: Sariputta) one of Gautama's two chief disciples, famed for his understanding

shramanas 'strivers': wandering spiritual seekers of the Ganges Valley

Shravasti (Pali: Savatthi) capital of Kosala where Gautama spent many rains retreats

Shudra the servant class of Aryan society

Siddhartha (Pali: Siddhattha) Gautama's personal name according to later tradition, meaning 'he who achieves his aim'

stupa circular funeral mounds which developed into Buddhist monuments

Suddhodana Gautama's father

sutta (Sanskrit: sutra) a discourse attributed to the Buddha

Tantra a class of esoteric texts and traditions of Hinduism and Buddhism

Tathagata 'the thus gone' or 'thus come': a title given to Gautama following his Awakening

Taxila an important centre of Brahminical study and training in the modern Pakistani Punjab

Theragatha/Therigatha collections of verses composed by the early monks/nuns

Theravada the Buddhist school now found in Sri Lanka and South East Asia, which preserves the Pali scriptures

Udraka Ramaputra (Pali: Uddaka Ramaputta) Gautama's second teacher, who taught the attainment of 'the sphere of neither perception nor non-perception'.

Upanishads a set of Brahminical texts

uposatha days on which monks meet to recite and confess, and lay people practise extra precepts

Uruvilva (Pali: Uruvela) the village near to which Gautama gained Enlightenment

Uruvilva Kasyapa (Pali: Uruvela Kassapa) the priest of a temple in Uruvilva, and one of three brothers Gautama visited after his Enlightenment

Vacchagotta a shramana who engaged in several dialogues with Gautama and eventually joined his order

Vaishali home of the Licchavi clan and chief city of the Vajjian confederation

Vajrayana the 'Diamond Vehicle' tradition of esoteric Buddhism, commonly called 'tantra'

Vedas sacred texts of Brahminism

Venuvana (Pali: Veluvana) the 'Bamboo Grove' – a monastic park in Rajagriha

Vidudabha son of King Pasenadi and a Shakyan slave-girl, who slaughtered the Shakyans on becoming king

Vinaya the Buddhist monastic code, whose texts make up one of the three divisions of the ancient Buddhist canon

vipassana 'insight' meditation practices

Vrijjian Federation (Pali: Vajjian) an alliance of eight or nine clans, all ruled as republics

Vulture's Peak a mountain on the outskirts of Rajagriha, where Gautama often stayed

yaksha (Pali: yakkha) a class of 'worldly' spirits, often hostile to human life

Yoga spiritual practice, e.g. meditation

Notes

NOTE ON PALI QUOTATIONS

Most of the quotations in this book come from the suttas (or Discourses) of the Pali canon. Where possible I have included the name of the sutta from which the quotation is taken; then comes the collection, or Nikaya, of which it is a part, and then the sutta's number in that Nikaya. References in brackets are to the volume and page number of the Pali Text Society edition. References to the shorter collections are by PTS verse number or sutta number as applicable.

Numerous translations are available of the best-known suttas. In some cases (where no translator is cited) I have compared translations and made a fresh version, which should therefore be read as a rendering or paraphrase rather than an exact quotation.

ABBREVIATIONS

AN – Anguttara Nikaya
DN – Digha Nikaya
MN – Majjhima Nikaya
SN – Samyutta Nikaya
Sn – Sutta Nipata
Ud – Udana
Dhp – Dhammapada
It – Ituvittaka
ATI – Access to Insight: online quotations at www.accesstoinsight.org

INTRODUCTION: GAUTAMA AND THE BUDDHA

[1] Vidhurapandita Jataka: *Jataka 545* – Cowell 1895, 6: 276.

[2] Bahiya Sutta: *Udana* 1: 10 (Ud 6) – Ireland 1997: 20.

[3] This is Richard Gombrich's rendering of the term in *What the Buddha Thought*, p.151.

[4] Bahiya Suttu: (Ud 6) – Ireland 1997: 21.

[5] Ariyapariyesana Sutta: *Majjhima Nikaya* 26 (I 167) – Gethin 2009: 186. Quotations from the Ariyapariyesana Sutta and the Mahasaccaka Sutta are drawn from Gethin's translation of the same passages (where parallels exist) in the context of the Bodhirajakumara Sutta – *Majjhima Nikaya* 85.

[6] Stephen Collins, 'On the Very Idea of the Pali canon', *Journal of the Pali Text Society* 15 (1990): 89.

[7] This date is proposed by Richard Gombrich in *The Dating of the Historical Buddha*, Vol. 2.

[8] Sangharakshita, *Living with Awareness: A Guide to the Satipatthana Sutta* (Birmingham, 2004), p.61.

[9] Harold Bloom, *Jesus and Yahweh: The Names Divine* (New York, 2005), p.1.

[10] Dona Sutta: *Anguttara Nikaya* 4: 36 (II 45) – Nyanaponika and Bodhi 2000: 88.

[11] Mahapadana Sutta: *Digha Nikaya* 14 (II 13) – Walshe 1987: 203.

[12] Ray, 1994: p.62.

[13] Bahiya Sutta (Ud 6) – Ireland 1997: 21.

[14] Ibid.

[15] Rohitassa Sutta: *Samyutta Nikaya* 2: 26 (I 62) – Gethin 2009: 210.

1: A WORLD IN FERMENT

[1] *Samyutta Nikaya* 55: 21 (V 369).

[2] *Si-Yu-Ki* – Beal 1906, 2: 13–14.

[3] Cullavagga 7.1.1–2.

[4] *Si-Yu-Ki* – Beal 1906, 1: l.

[5] Mahaparinibbana Sutta: *Digha Nikaya* 16 (II 74).

[6] Ambattha Sutta: *Digha Nikaya* 3 (I 91) – Walshe 1987: 114.

[7] *Nidana Katha* – Jayawickrama 1990: 69.

[8] Acchariya-abbhuta Sutta: *Majjhima Nikaya* 123 (III 122) – Nyanamoli and Bodhi 1995: 982.

[9] Cullavagga 10.1.3 Vinaya – Horner 1992, 5: 354.

[10] Sukhamala Sutta: *Anguttara Nikaya* 3: 38 (I 145) – Nyanaponika and Bodhi 2000: 53.

[11] *Kama Sutra* 2: 1, trans. Richard Burton.

[12] Sukhamala Sutta: *Anguttara Nikaya* III 3: 38 – Nyanaponika and Bodhi 2000: 54.

[13] Samannaphala Sutta: *Digha Nikaya* 2 (I 65) – Gethin 2009: 21.

[14] Ibid.

[15] Magandiya Sutta: *Majjhima Nikaya* 75 (I 504) – Nyanamoli and Bodhi 1995: 609.

[16] Sakkapanha Sutta: *Digha Nikaya* 21 (II 267) – Walshe 1987: 323.

[17] *Anguttara Nikaya* 2: 230 (II 237) – Woodward 1932: II: 37.

[18] Mahadukkhakkhanda Sutta: *Majjhima Nikaya* 13 (I 87) – Nyanamoli and Bodhi 1995: 181–2.

[19] Dhammapada 103 – Sangharakshita 2001: 43.

[20] Ibid. 80 – Sangharakshita 2001: 35.

[21] Mahasaccaka Sutta: *Majjhima Nikaya* 36 (I 246) – Gethin 2009: 183.

[22] *Atharva Veda*: 3: 17, 4, trans. W. D. Whitney.

[23] Mahasaccaka Sutta: *Majjhima Nikaya* 36 (I 246) – Gethin 2009: 183.

[24] Samannaphala Sutta: *Digha Nikaya* 2 (I 74) – Gethin 2009: 28.

[25] Pabajja Sutta: *Sutta Nipata* 422–3 (adapted).

[26] Ambattha Sutta: *Digha Nikaya* 3 (I 92) – Walshe 1987: 114–15.

[27] Agganna Sutta: *Digha Nikaya* 27 (III 83) – Gethin 2009: 120.

[28] Samannaphala Sutta: *Digha Nikaya* 2 (I 51) – Gethin 2009: 10.

[29] Mahadukkhakkhanda Sutta: MN 13 (I 85) – Nyanamoli and Bodhi 1995: 180.

[30] Bhaddiya Thera: *Theragatha* 863, trans. Andrew Olendzki, *Insight Journal*, 31 (winter 2009): 32.

[31] Cullavagga 7. 1. 6.

[32] Attadanda Sutta: *Sutta Nipata* 936 – Olendzki: ATI.

[33] Ariyapariyesana Sutta: *Majjhima Nikaya* 26 (I 163) – Gethin 2009: 176.

[34] Mahaparinibbana Sutta (DN II 151) – Gethin 2009: 87.

[35] Devadutta Sutta: *Majjhima Nikaya* 130 (III 178–80) – Nyanamoli and Bodhi 1995: 1030–32.

[36] Sukkhamala Sutta: *Anguttara Nikaya* 3: 38 (I 145).

[37] Analayo, *Satipatthana*, p.244.

[38] Arakenanusasani Sutta: *Anguttara Nikaya* 7: 70 (IV 136–7) – Gethin 2009: 261–2.

[39] Ariyapariyesana Sutta (MN I 162) – Nyanamoli and Bodhi 1995: 255.

[40] Sukhamala Sutta (AN 146) – Nyanaponika and Bodhi 2000: 54.

[41] Ibid.

[42] Attadanda Sutta (Sn 935–9) – Olendzki: ATI.

[43] Jeremiah 31: 33, King James Bible.

[44] Acchariyaabbhuta Sutta: *Majjhima Nikaya* 123 (III 123).

[45] Tinakattham Sutta: *Samyutta Nikaya* 15: 1 (II 177) – Bodhi 2000: 651.

[46] Pabbata Sutta: *Samyutta Nikaya* 15: 5 (II 181) – Bodhi 2000: 654. The setting in which these words were spoken is imagined.

[47] Puggala Sutta: *Samyutta Nikaya* 15: 10 (II 185) – Bodhi 2000: 657.

[48] Assu Sutta: *Samyutta Nikaya* 15: 3 (II 180) – Bodhi 2000: 653.

[49] Dhammapada 188 – Sangharakshita 2001: 68.

[50] Mahapadana Sutta: *Digha Nikaya* (II 29) – Walshe 1987: 210.

[51] Kautilya, *Arthashastra* 1: 3.

[52] Bharandu Kalama Sutta: *Anguttara Nikaya* 3: 124 (I 267).

[53] *Satapatha Brahmana* 13. 8. 1. 5.

[54] *Sankhalikhitadharmasutra* 7, quoted in Bailey and Mabbett 2004: 44.

[55] Patanjali: *Maha-bh* in Bronkhorst 2007: 1.

[56] *Satapatha Brahmana* 13. 8. 1. 5.

[57] *Rig Veda* 10: 136, quoted in Eliade 1969: 102.

[58] Kutadanta Sutta: *Digha Nikaya* 5 (1 127) – Walshe 1987: 133.

[59] Puggalo Sutta: *Samyutta Nikaya* 3: 21 (I 93–4) – Bodhi 2000: 185.

[60] *Rig Veda* 10: 90, trans. Basham in *The Wonder That Was India*, p.241.

[61] Madhura Sutta: *Majjhima Nikaya* 84 (II 84).

[62] Assalayana Sutta: *Majjhima Nikaya* (II 149) – Nyanamoli and Bodhi 1995: 764.

[63] Romila Thapar, *Early India from its Origins to 1300 AD*, p.148.

[64] Ambattha Sutta: *Digha Nikaya* 3 (I 92–3) – Walshe 1987: 113.

[65] *Mahabasya* 2. 4. 12 vt.2, quoted in Bronkhorst 2007: 84.

[66] *Udana* 7. 9.

[67] Ambattha Sutta (DN I 104–5) – Walshe 1987: 121 (abridged).

[68] *Indika*: Schwaben and McCrindle 1877: 98.

[69] Ariyapariyesana Sutta (MN I 163) – Nyanamoli and Bodhi 1995: 256.

[70] Ariyapariyesana Sutta (MN I 163) – Gethin 2009: 176.

[71] Pabbajja Sutta: *Sutta Nipata* 405–6 – Saddhatissa 1985: 46.

[72] Udaya Sutta: *Samyutta Nikaya* 7: 12 (I 174) – Olendzki: ATI.

2: THE SEARCH FOR WISDOM

[1] Andhakavinda Sutta: *Samyutta Nikaya* 6: 13 (I 333–4) – Olendzki: ATI.

[2] Bhayabherava Sutta: *Majjhima Nikaya* 4 (I 16ff.).

[3] *Anguttara Nikaya* 1: 19. 1 (I 33) – Nyanaponika and Bodhi 2000: 38.

[4] Khaggavisana Sutta: *Sutta Nipata* 52 – Norman 1984: 8.

[5] Maha-Assapura Sutta: *Majjhima Nikaya* 39 (I 276).

[6] Ashokan Rock Edict 13.

[7] Bhaya Sutta: *Anguttara Nikaya* 3: 62 (I 177) – Woodward 1932: 161.

[8] *Satapatha Brahmana* 13. 2. 4. 4.

[9] Bhayabherava Sutta (MN I 17) – Nyanamoli and Bodhi 1995: 102.

[10] *Indika*: Schwaben and McCrindle 1877: 102.

[11] Ibid.

[12] Kumbhakara Jataka: *Jataka* (III 337) – Cowell 1895: 3: 229.

[13] Isigili Sutta: *Majjhima Nikaya* 116 (III 68).

[14] *Indika*: Schwaben and McCrindle 1877: 102.

[15] E.g. Samannaphala Sutta: *Digha Nikaya* 2 (I 63) – Gethin 2009: 19.

[16] Culadhammasamadana Sutta: *Majjhima Nikaya* 45 (I 305) –
       Nyanamoli and Bodhi 1995: 405.

[17] *Si-Yu-Ki* – Beal 2: 160.

[18] Ganakamogallana Sutta: *Majjhima Nikaya* 107 (III 5) – Nyanamoli
       and Bodhi 1995: 877.

[19] *Si-Yu-Ki* Beal 2: 9, p.156.

[20] Mahakassapa Sutta: *Udana* 1: 6 (Ud 4) – Ireland 1997: 17.

[21] Megasthenes in Schwaben and McCrindle 1877: 102.

[22] Kundaliya Sutta: *Samyutta Nikaya* 5: 46 (V 73).

23 Jatila Sutta: *Udana* 6: 2 (Ud 64) – Ireland 1997: 84.
24 Dhammacetiya Sutta: *Majjhima Nikaya* 89 (II 121) – Nyanamoli and
    Bodhi 1995: 730.
25 Kukkuravatika Sutta: *Majjhima Nikaya* 57 (I 387).
26 E.g. Sandita Sutta: *Majjhima Nikaya* 76 (I 513–14) – Nyanamoli and
    Bodhi 1995: 618.
27 Samannaphala Sutta: *Digha Nikaya* 2 (I 66) – Gethin 2009: 22.
28 Pasura Sutta: *Sutta Nipata* 826–30 – adapted from Norman 1984:
    138
29 Mahaparinibbana Sutta: *Digha Nikaya* 16 (II 149) – Gethin 2009: 86.
30 Samannaphala Sutta: (DN I 55) – Gethin 2009: 13.
31 Sabbasava Sutta: *Majjhima Nikaya* 4 (I 8).
32 Samannaphala Sutta (DN I 55) – Gethin 2009: 13.
33 Ibid. (DN I 52) – Gethin 2009: 11.
34 *Ayaramga* 1. 5. 6. 4, trans. Schubrung, quoted in Bronkhorst 2007: 34.
35 Ibid. 1. 8. 7. 227, p.16.
36 Dundas 2002: 2. Evidence for this comes from Jain inscriptions of a
    later period.
37 Isigili Sutta (MN I 92) – Nyanamoli and Bodhi 1995: 187.
38 Devadaha Sutta: *Majjhima Nikaya* 101 (II 214) – Nyanamoli and
    Bodhi 1995: 827.
39 Samannaphala Sutta: *Digha Nikaya* 2 (I 53) – Gethin 2009: 12.
40 Jambuka Thera: *Theragatha* 283–4 – Norman 1997, 1: 36.
41 Samannaphala Sutta (DN I 53). This amended translation is in
    Bronkhorst 2007: 47.
42 *Anguttara Nikaya* 1:18 (I 32) – Woodward 1932, 1: 92.
43 Kalama Sutta: *Anguttara Nikaya* 3: 65 (I 189) – Gethin 2009: 252
    (abridged).
44 Ibid. (I 190) – Gethin 2009: 254.
45 Khana Sutta: *Samyutta Nikaya* 35: 153 (IV 138) – Bodhi 2000: 1215.
46 Magandiya Sutta: *Sutta Nipata* 837.
47 Ariyapariyesana Sutta (MN I 164) – Gethin 2009: 176.
48 Ibid.
49 Ibid.
50 Brahmajala Sutta: *Digha Nikaya* 1 (I 38) – Bodhi 1998: 86.

[51] Ibid. (I 35) – Bodhi 1998: 80.

[52] Mokshadharma: *Mahabharata* 12. 212. 17.

[53] Ariyapariyesana Sutta (I 164) – Gethin 2009: 177.

[54] Upasiva-manavapuccha: *Sutta Nipata* 1070 – Norman 1986: 170.

[55] Attadanda Sutta: *Sutta Nipata* 938 – Olendzki (ATI).

[56] Ariyapariyesana Sutta (I 164, 165) – Gethin 2009: 177.

[57] Vassakara Sutta: *Anguttara Nikaya* 4: 187 (II 180) – Woodward 1992, 2: 187.

[58] Pasadika Sutta: *Digha Nikaya* 29 (III 126) – Walshe 1987: 431.

[59] Mandukya Upanishad 7 – Olivelle 2008: 289.

[60] Uddaka Sutta: *Samyutta Nikaya* 35: 103 (IV 83) – Bodhi 2000: 1182.

[61] *Anguttara Nikaya* 10: 190 (V 63) – Nyanaponika and Bodhi 2000: 246.

[62] Latukikopama Sutta: *Majjhima Nikaya* 66 (I 456).

[63] Mahasaccaka Sutta: *Majjhima Nikaya* 36 (I 240) – Gethin 2009: 179.

[64] Mahasihanada Sutta: *Digha Nikaya* 8 (I 165) – abridged.

[65] Mahasihanada Sutta: *Majjhima Nikaya* 12 (I 78) – Nyanamoli and Bodhi 1995: 173.

[66] Ibid. (MN I 79).

[67] Mahasaccaka Sutta (MN I 242) – Gethin 2009: 181.

[68] Ibid. (MN I 243–4) – Gethin 2009: 181–2 (abridged).

[69] Ibid. (MN I 245).

[70] *Ayaramga* 1. 8. 7. 7–8.

[71] *Mahabharata* 1. 81. 16 in Bronkhorst 1986: 46.

[72] Mahasaccaka Sutta (I 245–6) – Gethin 2009: 182–3 (abridged).

[73] Pancattaya Sutta: *Majjhima Nikaya* 102 (II 233).

[74] Mahasaccaka Sutta (MN I 246–7) – Gethin 2009: 183–4 (abridged).

[75] Ibid. (MN I 247) 184.

[76] Bhayabherava Sutta: *Majjhima Nikaya* 4 (I 17–18) – Nyanamoli and Bodhi 1995: 103.

[77] Nagara Sutta: *Samyutta Nikaya* 12: 65 (II 105) – Bodhi 2000: 603.

[78] *Si-Yu-Ki* – Beal 1906, 2: 115.

[79] Bhayabherava Sutta (MN I 21) trans. Ryan in *Buddhism and the Natural World*, p.69.

[80] *Samyutta Nikaya* 35: 117 (IV 97) – Bodhi 2000: 1191.

[81] Dvedhavitakka Sutta: *Majjhima Nikaya* 19 (I 114).

[82] Tevijja Sutta: *Digha Nikaya* 13 (I 251).

[83] Dvedhavitakka Sutta (MN I 115).

[84] *Samyutta Nikaya* 54: 8 (V 317) – Bodhi 2000: 1770.

[85] Mahasaccaka Sutta (MN I 247) – Gethin 2009: 184.

[86] Dvedhavitakka Sutta (MN I 116) – Nyanamoli and Bodhi 1995: 208.

[87] *Samyutta Nikaya* 54: 8 (V 317) – Bodhi 2000: 1770.

[88] Mahasaccaka Sutta (MN I 246) – Gethin 2009: 183.

[89] Samannaphala Sutta (DN I 75) – Gethin 2009: 29.

[90] Mahasaccaka Sutta (MN I 247) – Gethin 2009: 184.

[91] Samannaphala Sutta (DN I 75) – Gethin 2009: 29.

[92] Bodhirajakumara Sutta: *Majjhima Nikaya* 85 (I 92) – Gethin 2009: 176.

[93] *Samyutta Nikaya* 51: 11 (V 263) – Bodhi 2000: 1726.

[94] Upakkilesa Sutta: *Majjhima Nikaya* 128 (III 161) – Nyanamoli and Bodhi 1995: 1015.

[95] Dvedhavitakka Sutta (MN I 117) – Nyanamoli and Bodhi 1995: 209.

[96] Ariyapariyesana Sutta (I 167) – Nyanamoli and Bodhi 1995: 259.

[97] Atanatiya Sutta: *Digha Nikaya* 32 – Walshe 1987: 474.

[98] Ariyapariyesana Sutta (I 167) – Nyanamoli and Bodhi 1995: 259.

[99] Appativana Sutta: *Anguttara Nikaya* 2: 1, 5 (I 50).

[100] Mahagosinga Sutta: *Majjhima Nikaya* 32 (I 219).

3: NIRVANA

[1] Padhana Sutta: *Sutta Nipata* 425 – Saddhatissa 1985: 48.

[2] Ibid., Sn 426–8 – Saddhatissa 1985: 48.

[3] Godhika Sutta: *Samyutta Nikaya* 4: 23 (I 122) – Bodhi 2000: 214.

[4] Manasa Sutta: *Samyutta Nikaya* 4: 15 – Bodhi 2000: 205.

[5] Batchelor 2004: 21.

[6] Mahasamaya Sutta: *Digha Nikaya* 20 (II 262) – Walshe 1987: 320.

[7] Padhana Sutta: Sn 442 – Saddhatissa 1985: 49.

[8] Ibid. 434, 443 – Saddhatissa 1985: 48, 49.

[9] *Nidana Katha* 74: *The Story of Gotama Buddha*, p.98.

[10] *Lalitavistara* ch. 21: Bays 1983, O: 482.

[11] Maradhitu Sutta: *Samyutta Nikaya* 4: 25 (I 127).

[12] Ibid.

[13] Padhana Sutta: Sn 447 – Saddhatissa 1985: 49.

[14] Sattavassanubandha Sutta: *Samyutta Nikaya* 4: 24 (I 124).

[15] Maradhitu Sutta: *Samyutta Nikaya* 4: 25 (I 124) – Bodhi 2000: 217.

[16] Mahasaccaka Sutta: *Majjhima Nikaya* 36 (I 247–8) – Gethin 2009: 184.

[17] Dhatuvibhanga Sutta: *Majjhima Nikaya* 140 (III 243).

[18] Mahasaccaka Sutta (MN I 247) – Gethin 2009: 184.

[19] Potthapada Sutta: *Digha Nikaya* 9 (I 184) – Walshe 1987: 162.

[20] Ibid. (DN I 185) – Walshe 1987: 163.

[21] *Samyutta Nikaya* 12: 66 (II 107) – Bodhi 2000: 604.

[22] Maha Sakyamuni Gotamo Sutta: *Samyutta Nikaya* 12: 10 (II 10) –
     Bodhi 2000: 537.

[23] Ibid.

[24] *Samyutta Nikaya* 12: 69 (I 118) – Bodhi 2000: 611.

[25] Dhammapada 1 – Sangharakshita 2001: 13.

[26] *Samyutta Nikaya* 22: 26 (III 27–8), *Samyutta Nikaya* 14: 31 (II 31),
     Samyutta Nikaya 36: 23 (IV 222).

[27] Nagara Sutta: *Samyutta Nikaya* 12: 65 (II 104) – Bodhi 2000: 601.

[28] *Anguttara Nikaya* 3: 101 (I 258) – Nyanaponika and Bodhi 2000: 75.

[29] i.e. '*yathabhutanyanadassana*'.

[30] Madhupindika Sutta: *Majjhima Nikaya* 18 (I 111) – Nyanamoli and
     Bodhi 1995: 203.

[31] Mahasaccaka Sutta (MN I 249) – Gethin 2009: 186.

[32] Dhammacakkapavatana Sutta: *Samyutta Nikaya* 56: 11 (V 422) –
     Gethin 2009: 244.

[33] Mahasihanada Sutta: *Majjhima Nikaya* 12 (I 70) – Nyanamoli and
     Bodhi 1995: 166.

[34] Mahasaccaka Sutta (MN I 249) – Gethin 2009: 186.

[35] Pathamaparinibbana Sutta: *Udana* 8: 1 (Ud 81).

[36] Epithets collected by T. W. Rhys Davids, *Early Buddhism*, quoted in
     Sangharakshita 1957: 67.

[37] Sariputta Thera: *Theragatha* 1013 – Norman 1997, 1: 98.

[38] Paccaya Sutta: *Samyutta Nikaya* 12: 20 (II 25).

[39] Ibid.

[40] Pathamabodhi Sutta: *Udana* 1: 1 (Ud 13) – Ireland 1997: 13.

[41] Tatiyabodhi Sutta: *Udana* 1: 3 (Ud 14) – Ireland 1997: 15.

[42] Mucalinda Sutta: *Udana* 2: 1 (Ud 10) – Ireland 1997: 23.

[43] Garava Sutta: *Samyutta Nikaya* 6: 2 (I 139).

[44] I.e. *katthavatthuni* – Sangiti Sutta: *Digha Nikaya* (III 220) in Collins 1998: 162.

[45] Nava Sutta: *Sutta Nipata* 319 – Saddhatissa 1985: 35.

[46] *Samyutta Nikaya* 12: 23 (II 32) – Gethin 2009: 215.

[47] E.g. Culasakuludayi Sutta: *Majjhima Nikaya* 79 (II 32) – Nyanamoli and Bodhi 1995: 655.

[48] Pathamabodhi Sutta: *Udana* 1: 1 (Ud 1) – Ireland 1997: 13.

[49] This and following quotes: Ariyapariyesana Sutta (I 167–8) – Gethin 2009: 186.

[50] Naga Sutta: *Udana* 4: 5 (Ud 41) – Ireland 1997: 58.

[51] Catuma Sutta: *Majjhima Nikaya* 67 (I 458) – Nyanamoli and Bodhi 1995: 561.

[52] Sanankumara Sutta: *Samyutta Nikaya* 6: 11 (I 125) – Bodhi 2000: 247.

[53] Kosala Sutta: *Anguttara Nikaya* 10: 29 (V 58) – Woodward 1994: 41. Various views of Brahma are found in both Buddhist and Brahminical sources, offering a greater complexity than can be addressed here.

[54] Ariyapariyesana Sutta (MN I 168–9) – Gethin 2009 – p.187.

[55] Ibid. (MN I 169) – Gethin 2009: 187–8.

[56] Ibid. (MN I 170) – Gethin 2009: 188.

4: THE AWAKENING MOVEMENT

[1] *Ta-Tang Ta-tz'u-en-ssu San-tang fa-shih-chuan*, fasc. 3, quoted in Nakamura 2000, I: 194.

[2] Ariyapariyesana Sutta: *Majjhima Nikaya* 26 (I 171).

[3] Samannaphala Sutta: *Digha Nikaya* 2 (I 54) – Gethin 2009: 12.

[4] Nigrodha Sutta: *Udana* 1: 4 (Ud 15) – Ireland 1997: 15.

[5] Ariyapariyesana Sutta: *Majjhima Nikaya* 16 (I 171) – Gethin 2009: 190.

[6] Ibid.

[7] Ibid. (MN I 172) – Gethin 2009: 191.

[8] Gombrich, *How Buddhism Began*, p.61.

9 Sonadanda Sutta: *Digha Nikaya* 4 (I 115) – Walshe 1987: 126.

10 Sundari Theri: *Therigatha* 333 – Norman 1997, 2: 208.

11 Venaga Sutta: *Anguttara Nikaya* 1: 180 – Woodward 1932: 163.

12 Sela Thera: *Theragatha* 818–20: Norman 1997, 1: 83.

13 Jara Sutta: *Samyutta Nikaya* 48: 41 (V 216) – Bodhi 2000: 1686.

14 Brahmayu Sutta: *Majjhima Nikaya* 91 (II 138) – Nyanamoli and
   Bodhi 1995: 747.

15 Dhatuvibhanga Sutta: *Majjhima Nikaya* 140 (III 238).

16 Culasunnata Sutta: *Majjhima Nikaya* 121 (III 104).

17 Mahasihanada Sutta: *Majjhima Nikaya* 12 (I 83) – Nyanamoli and
   Bodhi 1995: 177.

18 Sakalika Sutta: *Samyutta Nikaya* 4: 13 (I 245–6) – Bodhi 2000: 203.

19 Acchariya-abhuta Sutta: *Majjhima Nikaya* 123 (III 124) – Nyanamoli
   and Bodhi 1995: 124.

20 Vassakara Sutta: *Anguttara Nikaya* 4: 35 (II 35) – Woodward 1992: 41.

21 Herman Hesse, trans. Hilda Rosner: *Siddhartha*, New York, 1951,
   p.22.

22 Jivaka Sutta: *Majjhima Nikaya* 55 (I 369) – Nyanamoli and Bodhi
   1995: 475.

23 Mahavagga 4. 36. 3 – Horner, 1993, 4: 341.

24 Umbarika-sihanada Sutta: *Digha Nikaya* 25 (III 38) – Walshe 1987:
   386 (adapted).

25 Kutthi Sutta: *Udana* 5: 3 (Ud 48) – Ireland 1997: 66.

26 Mahaparinibbana Sutta: *Digha Nikaya* 16 (II 109) – Gethin 2009: 62.

27 Sonadanda Sutta (DN I 116) – Walshe 1987: 127.

28 Brahmayu Sutta: *Majjhima Nikaya* 91 (I 369) – Nyanamoli and Bodhi
   1995: 748.

29 Aranavibhanga Sutta: *Majjhima Nikaya* 139 (III 231) – Nyanamoli
   and Bodhi 1995: 1085.

30 Gombrich, 1996: p.18.

31 Alagaddupama Sutta: *Majjhima Nikaya* 22 (I 135) – Gethin 2009: 160.

32 Pingiya-manavapuccha: *Sutta Nipata* 1120 – Saddhatissa 1985: 129–30.

33 Pingiya-manavapuccha Parayana Thuti Gatha: *Sutta Nipata* 1134, 1135
   and 1137 – Saddhatissa 1985: 131–2.

34 Erdosy, George: 'The Origin of Cities in the Ganges Valley', *Journal of*

Economic and Social History of the Orient 28: 81–109.

[35] Punnika Theri: *Therigatha* 240 – Norman 1997 II: 199.

[36] *Dhammapada* 165 – Sangharakshita 2001: 61.

[37] Jatila Sutta: *Udana* 1: 9 (Ud 7) – Ireland 1997: 9.

[38] Dhammacakkapavattana Sutta Samulta Nikaya (S6: II 424) – Gethin 2009: 245–6.

[39] Mahavagga 1. 6. 47 – Horner, 1993, 4: 21.

[40] Ibid. 1. 7. 2 – Horner, 1993, 4: 22.

[41] Madhupindika Sutta: *Majjhima Nikaya* 18 (I 111) – Nyanamoli and Bodhi 1995: 203.

[42] *Anguttara Nikaya* (II 52) trans. Masefield in *Divine Revelation in Pali Buddhism*, p.52.

[43] Dhammapada 165 – Sangharakshita 2001: 61.

[44] Dhotaka-manavapuccha: *Sutta Nipata* 1064.

[45] Ganakamoggallana Sutta: *Majjhima Nikaya* 107 (III 2) – Nyanamoli and Bodhi 1995: 874.

[46] *Samyutta Nikaya* 45: 91 (V 38).

[47] Katigiri Sutta: *Majjhima Nikaya* 70 (I 477) – Nyanamoli and Bodhi 1995: 580.

[48] Ibid. (abridged).

[49] Samannaphala Sutta: *Digha Nikaya* 2 (I 63) – Gethin 2009: 19.

[50] Nakhasikha Sutta: *Samyutta Nikaya* 13: 1 (II 134) – Bodhi 2000: 621.

[51] Dhammapada 290 – Sangharakshita 2001: 99.

[52] Upali Sutta: *Majjhima Nikaya* 56 (I 380).

[53] *Samyutta Nikaya* 35: 136 (IV 127) trans. Masefield in *Divine Revelation in Pali Buddhism*, p.7.

[54] Cakkhu Sutta: *Samyutta Nikaya* 25: 1 (III 225).

[55] Sangiti Sutta: *Digha Nikaya* 33 (III 227) – Walshe 1987: 491.

[56] *Samyutta Nikaya* 55: 2 (V 344).

[57] *Anguttara Nikaya* 2: 5, 4 (I 71) – Woodward 1932: 67.

[58] Kutthi Sutta: *Udana* 5: 3 (Ud 48) – Ireland 1997: 67.

[59] *Samyutta Nikaya* 55: 31–3 (V 391–2) – Bodhi 2000: 1821–2.

[60] *Samyutta Nikaya* 55: 38 (V 396) – Bodhi 2000: 1825.

[61] Agganna Sutta: *Digha Nikaya* (III 84) – Gethin 2009: 120 (adapted).

[62] Mahavagga 1. 11. 1.

63 Dhammadinna Sutta: *Samyutta Nikaya* 55: 53 (V 407) – Bodhi 2000: 1833.

64 *Si-Yu-Ki:* Beal 2: 145.

65 Jatila Sutta: *Udana* (Ud 64) – Ireland 1997: 63.

66 Mahavagga 1.15.7 – Horner, 1993, 4: 35.

67 Gaya Sutta: *Anguttara Nikaya* 8: 64 (IV 302) (abridged).

68 Samannaphala Sutta (DN I 78) – Gethin 2009: 31. See also the *Iddhisamyutta*: ch: 56 of the *Samyutta Nikaya*.

69 E.g. Sonadanda Sutta: *Digha Nikaya* 4 (I 110) – Walshe 1987: 125.

70 Uruvelakassapa Thera, *Theragatha* 375–7.

71 *Si-Yu-Ki* – Beal 2: 113.

72 Adittapariyaya Sutta: *Samyutta Nikaya* 4: 35 (IV 19–20) – Gethin 2009: 223.

73 Mahavagga 1. 22. 4 – Horner 1993, 4: 48.

74 Ibid. 1. 23. 5 – Horner 1993, 4: 54.

75 Ibid. 1. 24. 4.

76 Anupada Sutta: *Majjhima Nikaya* 111 (III 25) – the Sutta's title as rendered in Nyanamoli and Bodhi 1995: 899.

77 Ibid. (MN III 25).

78 Ibid. (MN III 29).

79 Mahavagga 1. 24. 6 – Horner, 1993, 4: 56.

80 Mahanidana Sutta: *Digha Nikaya* 15 (II 58) – Bodhi 2005: 36.

81 Dhammapada 15.

82 *Anguttara Nikaya* 8: 25 (IV 219) – Nyanaponika and Bodhi 2000: 208.

83 *Anguttara Nikaya* 6: 63 (III 414).

84 Mahavagga 1. 22. 17 – Horner 1993, 4: 51 (adapted).

85 Mahaparinibbana Sutta: *Digha Nikaya* 16 (II 115–16) – Gethin 2009: 66.

86 Kaludayin Thera, *Theragatha* 527–9 – Andrew Olendzki: ATI.

87 *Nidana Katha* 89 trans. Jayawickrama 1990: 121.

88 Ibid. 88: 119.

89 Theragatha commentary (I 15), quoted in the *Pali Dictionary of Proper Names* entry on Channa (i.e. Skt. Chandaka).

90 Nanda Thera, *Theragatha* 157–8.

91 Cullavagga 7. 1. 2 – Horner 1992, 5: 254.

92 Mahavagga 1.54.5.

[93] *Dhammapadathakatha* (III 354) 15:1 – Burlingame 1990 3: 70.

[94] Attadanda Sutta: *Sutta Nipata* 936, 938 – Olendzki: ATI.

[95] Ibid. 939 – Saddhatissa 1985: 109.

[96] *Dhammapadathakatha* (III 356) 3: 71.

[97] Ibid. (adapted).

[98] Dhammapada 197–9 – Sangharakshita 2001: 71–2.

[99] Cullavagga 7. 1. 1 – Horner 1992, 5: 253.

5: DIALOGUE

[1] Samannaphala Sutta: *Digha Nikaya* 2 (II 58) – Gethin 2009: 15.

[2] Brahmajala Sutta: *Digha Nikaya* 1 (I 27) – Walshe 1987: 81.

[3] Ariyapariyesana Sutta: *Majjhima Nikaya* 26 (I 169–70) – Gethin 2009: 188.

[4] Hatthaka Sutta: *Anguttara Nikaya* 3: 34 (I 136).

[5] Sabhiya Sutta: *Sutta Nipata* 537 – Saddhatissa 1985: 62.

[6] Cula-Assapura Sutta: *Majjhima Nikaya* 40 (I 281).

[7] E.g. Dhammapada 154.

[8] Enijhanga Sutta: *Samyutta Nikaya* 1: 30 (I 16) – Bodhi 2000: 104.

[9] Brahmajala Sutta (DN I 2–3) – Walshe 1987: 67.

[10] Nalaka Sutta: *Sutta Nipata* 720 – Olendzki: ATI.

[11] Dutthatthaka Sutta: *Sutta Nipata* 781 – Norman 1984: 130.

[12] Brahmajala Sutta (DN I 40) – Walshe 1987: 87.

[13] Kalahavivada Sutta: *Sutta Nipata* 867–8 – Ireland: ATI.

[14] Mahasihanada Sutta: *Majjhima Nikaya* 12 (I 70) – Nyanamoli and Bodhi 1995: 166.

[15] *Pali – English Dictionary*, p.321 – entry on 'ditthi'.

[16] Udumbarika-sihanada Sutta: *Digha Nikaya* 25 (III 38).

[17] Culasaccaka Sutta: *Majjhima Nikaya* 35 (I 228).

[18] Mahasakuludayi Sutta: *Majjhima Nikaya* 77 (II 2).

[19] Mahaviyuha Sutta: *Sutta Nipata* 910 – Norman 1986, II: 148.

[20] Magandiya Sutta: *Sutta Nipata* 841 – adapted from Saddhatissa 1985: 99.

[21] Desana Sutta: *Samyutta Nikaya* 42: 7 (IV 317) – Bodhi 2000: 1340.

[22] Kathavatthu Sutta: *Anguttara Nikaya* 3: 67 – Woodward 1932: 179.

[23] Mahasihanada Sutta: *Digha Nikaya* 8 (I 165).

[24] Tevijjavacchagotta Sutta: *Majjhima Nikaya* 71 (I 482).

[25] Aggivacchagotta Sutta: *Majjhima Nikaya* 72 (I 487).

[26] Potthapada Sutta: *Digha Nikaya* 9 (I 192) – Walshe 1987: 165.

[27] Aggivacchagotta Sutta (MN I 487) – Nyanamoli and Bodhi 1995: 593.

[28] Mahanidana Sutta: *Digha Nikaya* 15 (II 66) – Walshe 1987: 226 (abridged).

[29] Culadukkhakkhanda Sutta: *Majjhima Nikaya* 14 (I 92) – Nyanamoli and Bodhi 1995: 187.

[30] *Anguttara Nikaya* 10: 190 (V 63) – Nyanaponika and Bodhi 2000: 246.

[31] Aranavibhanga Sutta: *Majjhima Nikaya* 139 (III 231) – Nyanamoli and Bodhi 1995: 1081.

[32] Mahasihanada Sutta: *Digha Nikaya* 8 (I 170) – Walshe 1987: 154 (adapted).

[33] Udumbarika-sihanada Sutta: *Digha Nikaya* 25 (III 44) – Walshe 1987: 388.

[34] Pathamananatthiya Sutta: *Udana* 6: 4 (Ud 66).

[35] Brahmajala Sutta (DN I 21) – Walshe 1987: 78.

[36] Vina Sutta: *Samyutta Nikaya* IV 35: 246 (IV 195).

[37] Culasihanada Sutta: *Majjhima Nikaya* 11 (I 66) – Nyanamoli and Bodhi 1995: 161.

[38] Alagadupama Sutta: *Majjhima Nikaya* 22 (I 135–6) – Gethin 2009: 162.

[39] *Samyutta Nikaya* 22: 96 (III 144) – Bodhi 2000: 954.

[40] Magandiya Sutta: *Majjhima Nikaya* 75 (I 503).

[41] Ananda Sutta: *Samyutta Nikaya* 44: 10 (IV 401).

[42] Hamilton 2000: 23.

[43] Potthapada Sutta (DN I 180).

[44] Aggivacchagotta Sutta (MN I 485).

[45] Acintiya Sutta: *Anguttara Nikaya* 4: 77.

[46] Culasihanada Sutta: *Majjhima Nikaya* 11 (I 66) 38 – Nyanamoli and Bodhi 1995: 161.

[47] Pabbatopama Sutta: *Samyutta Nikaya* 3: 25 (I 101).

[48] Kalakarama Sutta: *Samyutta Nikaya* 22: 95 (III 140–41) – Gethin 2009: 221.

49 Ibid. (SN I 142) – Gethin 2009: 222.

50 Richard Gombrich's rendering of the term in *What the Buddha Thought*, p.114.

51 Mahadukkhasankhaya Sutta: *Majjhima Nikaya* 38 – Nyanamoli and Bodhi 1995: 351.

52 Aggivacchagotta Sutta (MN I 487) – Nyanamoli and Bodhi 1995: 488.

53 Kaccanagotta Sutta: *Samyutta Nikaya* 12: 15 (II 17) – Bodhi 2000: 544.

54 Dhammacakkappavattana Sutta: *Samyutta Nikaya* 56: 11 (V 421) – Gethin 2009: 244.

55 Mahasaccaka Sutta: *Majjhima Nikaya* 36 (I 239) – Nyanamoli and Bodhi 1995: 332.

56 Magandiya Sutta: *Majjhima Nikaya* 75 (I 504 and 507) – Nyanamoli and Bodhi 1995: 609, 613.

57 Udumbarika-sihanada Sutta: *Digha Nikaya* 25 (I 56–7) – Walshe 1987: 393–4 (adapted).

58 Vajjiyamahita Sutta: *Anguttara Nikaya* 10: 94 (V 190).

59 Udumbarika-sihanada Sutta (DN III 57) – Walshe 1987: 394.

60 Potthapada Sutta (DN I 190).

61 Dhammacakkappavattana Sutta (SN V 422) – Gethin 2009: 245.

62 Dhammapada 169 – Sangharakshita 2001: 62.

63 Devadaha Sutta: *Majjhima Nikaya* 101 (II 218) – Nyanamoli and Bodhi 1995: 829.

64 Ibid. (DN II 222) – Nyanamoli and Bodhi 1995: 833.

65 Lekha Sutta: *Anguttara Nikaya* 3: 130 (I 283) – Woodward 1932: 262.

66 Dhammapada 1–2 – Sangharakshita 2001: 13.

67 Vasettha Sutta: *Sutta Nipata* 653 / *Majjhima Nikaya* 98 (II 196) – Nyanamoli and Bodhi 1995: 807.

68 Kausambiya Sutta: *Majjhima Nikaya* 48 (I 324) – Nyanamoli and Bodhi 1995: 806.

69 Suyagada 2, 6, 26–8, trans. Bollee; quoted in Bronkhorst 2007: 19.

70 Kakaupama Sutta: *Majjhima Nikaya* 21 (I 129) – Nyanamoli and Bodhi 1995: 223.

71 Sivaka Sutta: *Samyutta Nikaya* 36: 21 (IV 230) – Bodhi 2000: 1279.

72 Dhammapada 5 – Sangharakshita 2001: 14.

[73] Kundaliya Sutta: *Samyutta Nikaya* 46: 6 (V 73–6) – Bodhi 2000: 1575.

[74] Sammanaphala Sutta: *Digha Nikaya* 2 (I 71) – Gethin 2009: 26.

[75] Udumbarika-sihanada Sutta: *Digha Nikaya* 25 (III 38) – Walshe 1987: 385.

[76] Sallatha Sutta: *Samyutta Nikaya* 36: 6 (IV 207–8).

[77] Gellanna Sutta: *Samyutta Nikaya* 36: 8 (IV 212) – Bodhi 2000: 1267.

[78] Sallatha Sutta (SN IV 209) – Bodhi 2000: 1264.

[79] Sedaka Sutta: *Samyutta Nikaya* 47: 20 (V 170).

[80] Satipatthana Sutta: *Majjhima Nikaya* 10 (I 63) – Gethin 2009: 151.

[81] *Samyutta Nikaya* 46: 53 (V 115) – Bodhi 2000: 1607.

[82] Khana Sutta: *Samyutta Nikaya* 35: 153 (IV 138).

[83] *Samyutta Nikaya* 46: 45 (V 111).

[84] Talaputa Thera: *Theragatha* 1129–30 – Norman 1997, 1: 108.

[85] Somanassa Sutta: *Itivuttaka* 2: 37 (It 29) – Ireland 1997: 176.

[86] Mahapajjapati-Gotami Theri, *Therigatha* 161 – Norman 1997, 2: 188.

[87] Magandiya Sutta: *Majjhima Nikaya* 75 (I 510) – Nyanamoli and Bodhi 1995: 510.

[88] Devadaha Sutta: *Majjhima Nikaya* 101 (II 223) – Nyanamoli and Bodhi 1995: 834.

[89] Sona Sutta: *Anguttara Nikaya* 6: 55 (III 374) – Nyanaponika and Bodhi 2000: 168.

[90] *Atthasalini* – trans. Pe Maung Tin, *The Expositor* (London, 1920), p.153, quoted in Sangharakshita 1967: 114.

[91] Aranavibhanga Sutta (MN III 236) – Nyanamoli and Bodhi 1995: 1085.

[92] Vitakkasanthana Sutta: *Majjhima Nikaya* 20 (I 119).

[93] Culadukkhakkhandha Sutta: *Majjhima Nikaya* 14 (I 92) – Nyanamoli and Bodhi 1995: 187.

[94] Kandaraka Sutta: *Majjhima Nikaya* 51 (I 346) – Nyanamoli and Bodhi 1995: 450.

[95] Ariyapariyesana Sutta: *Majjhima Nikaya* 26 (I 174) Nyanamoli and Bodhi 1995: 267.

[96] Pakkha Thera: *Theragatha* 63 – trans. Analayo, *From Craving to Liberation*, p.107.

[97] Sumangalamata Theri: *Therigatha* 24 – Norman 1997, 2: 167.

[98] Dhammacetiya Sutta: *Majjhima Nikaya* 89 (II 121) – Nyanamoli and Bodhi 1995: 730.

[99] *Pali–English Dictionary*, p.447.

[100] Dvedhavitakka Sutta (MN I 116–17).

[101] Sammanaphala Sutta: *Digha Nikaya* 2 (I 74) – Gethin 2009: 28.

[102] *Anguttara Nikaya* 10: 2 (V 2) – Nyanaponika and Bodhi 2000: 238.

[103] E.g. Anapanasati Sutta: *Majjhima Nikaya* 118 (III 80).

[104] Ibid.

[105] Subha Sutta: *Digha Nikaya* 10 (I 209) – Walshe 1985: 173.

[106] Bronkhorst 1986: 123.

[107] Mahasaropama Sutta: *Majjhima Nikaya* 29 (I 195) – Nyanamoli and Bodhi 1995: 228.

[108] Avarana Sutta: *Anguttara Nikaya* 5: 51 (III 63).

[109] Gethin 2002: 172.

[110] Dhammapada 81–2 – Sangharakshita 2001: 35.

[111] Indriyabhavana Sutta: *Majjhima Nikaya* 152 (III 300) – Nyanamoli and Bodhi 1995: 1148.

[112] Udaya-manavapuccha: *Sutta Nipata* 1107 – trans. Wynne, *The Origins of Buddhist Meditation*, p.101.

[113] Kausambiya Sutta: *Majjhima Nikaya* 48 (I 323).

[114] Bahiya Sutta: *Udana* 1: 10 (Ud. 6) – Ireland 1997: 21.

[115] Mulapariyaya Sutta: *Majjhima Nikaya* 1 (I 3).

[116] Dvayatanupassana Sutta: *Sutta Nipata* 757.

[117] Dhammadpada 348 – trans. Bhikkhu Analayo in 'The Verses on an Auspicious Night, Explained by Mahakaccana – a Study and Translation of the Chinese Version', *Canadian Journal of Buddhist Studies*, 4 (2008): 18.

[118] *Samyutta Nikaya* 43: 1 (IV 359) and repeated throughout the Asankhyatasamyutta.

[119] Lekha Sutta: *Anguttara Nikaya* 3: 130 (I 283) – Woodward 1932: 283.

[120] Upasiva-manavapuccha: *Sutta Nipata* 1076 – E. M. Hare: *Woven Cadences of Early Buddhists* (London, 1945).

[121] Gombrich: *What the Buddha Thought*, p.90.

[122] Dhammapada 368, trans. Gombrich in *What the Buddha Thought*, p.87.

[123] Mahavacchagotta Sutta: (MN I 491).

[124] Vacchagotta Thera: *Theragatha* 112 – Norman 1997 1: 17.

[125] Mahavacchagotta Sutta (I 497) – adapted from Nyanamoli and Bodhi 1995: 602.

6: THE HOMELESS COMMUNITY

[1] Mahaparinibbana Sutta: *Digha Nikaya* 16 (II 105–6) – Gethin 2009: 60.

[2] Khaggavisana Sutta: *Sutta Nipata* 42 – Norman 1984: 7.

[3] Ibid. Sn 36, 39 and 53–4 – Norman 1984: 7–8.

[4] Mahaparinibbana Sutta: Digha Nikaya 16 (II 101) – Gethin 2009: 58. See also Magga Sutta: *Sutta Nipata* 501 for the same instruction applied to the monks while Gautama was living.

[5] Kakucupama Sutta: *Majjhima Nikaya* 21 (I 124).

[6] Bhaddali Sutta: *Majjhima Nikaya* 65 (I 437–8).

[7] Talaputa Thera: *Therigatha* 1118: Norman 1997, 1: 107.

[8] Sariputta Sutta: *Sutta Nipata* 970.

[9] Ariyavamsa Sutta: *Anguttara Nikaya* 4: 28 (II 27).

[10] Manapadayi Sutta: *Anguttara Nikaya* 5: 44 (III 48).

[11] Jivaka Sutta: *Majjhima Nikaya* (I 369) – Nyanamoli and Bodhi 1995: 474.

[12] Mahakassapa Thera: *Theragatha* 1056.

[13] Mahavagga 1. 11. 1.

[14] Yasha Sutta, *Anguttara Nikaya* 8: 86 (IV 341).

[15] *Anguttara Nikaya* 10: 30 (V 65) – Nyanaponika and Bodhi 2000: 248.

[16] Vitakka Sutta: *Itivuttaka* 2: 38 (It 39).

[17] Sonadanda Sutta: *Digha Nikaya* 4 (I 116) – Walshe 1987: 128.

[18] E.g. *Samyutta Nikaya* 54: 11 (V 326) – Bodhi 2000: 1778.

[19] *Samyutta Nikaya* 45: 11 (V 13) – Bodhi 2000: 1531.

[20] Nagita Sutta: *Anguttara Nikaya* 6: 42 (III 342).

[21] Parileyya Sutta: *Samyutta Nikaya* 22: 81 (III 94) – Bodhi 2000: 921.

[22] Katthaharaka Sutta: *Samyutta Nikaya* 7: 18 (I 180–181) – trans. Olendzki: ATI.

[23] E.g. Dvedhavitakka Sutta: *Majjhima Nikaya* 19 (I 118) – Nyanamoli and Bodhi 1995: 210.

24 Khaggavisana Sutta: *Sutta Nipata* 45 – Norman 1984: 7.

25 Yasoja Thera: *Theragatha* 245 – Norman 1997 1: 32.

26 Parapariya Thera: *Theragatha* 946.

27 Anagata-bhayani Sutta: *Anguttara Nikaya* 5: 77 (III 100).

28 Vakkali Thera: *Theragatha* 350–51.

29 Goddaka Thera: *Theragatha* 669 – Norman 1997 1: 71.

30 Vanganaputta Thera: *Theragatha* 577–81.

31 Vajjiputta Sutta: *Samyutta Nikaya* 9: 9 (I 202) – Nyanamoli and
    Bodhi 1995: 300.

32 Cittaka Thera: *Theragatha* 22 – Olendzki (1996).

33 Culaka Thera: *Theragatha* 211 – Olendzki: ATI.

34 Talaputa Thera: *Theragatha* 1137–8 – Norman 1997 1: 109.

35 Cullavagga 7. 1. 6 – Horner 1993, 5: 258–9.

36 Karaniya Metta Sutta: *Sutta Nipata* 149 – Sangharakshita (2004), p.6.

37 Revata Thera: *Theragatha* 648 – Norman 1997, 1: 70.

38 Bhuta Thera: *Theragatha* 522–5 – Olendzki: ATI.

39 Kappatakura Thera: *Theragatha* 199–200 – Norman, 1997 1: 27.

40 Maha-Moggallana Thera: *Theragatha* 1146 – Norman, 1997 1: 111.

41 Sirimanda Thera: *Theragatha* 452 – Olendzki: ATI.

42 Paccaya Thera: *Theragatha* 223 – Norman 1997, 1: 30.

43 Yodhajiva Sutta (1): *Anguttara Nikaya* 5: 75 (III 89) – Woodward 1988:
    78.

44 Rajadatta Thera: *Theragatha* 316.

45 Ajakalapaka Sutta: *Udana* 1: 7 (Ud 5) – Ireland 1997: 17.

46 Atanatiya Sutta: *Digha Nikaya* 32 (III 195, 204).

47 Punnabbasu Sutta: *Samyutta Nikaya* 1: 10 (I 210) – Bodhi 2000: 310.

48 Upatthana Sutta: *Samyutta Nikaya* 9: 2 (I 198) – Bodhi 2000: 294.

49 Mahavagga 63. 3 – Horner 1993, 4: 111.

50 Adhimutta Thera: *Theragatha* 705–25.

51 Subha Jinakambavanika Theri: *Therigatha* 383 – Norman 1997, 2: 213.

52 *Anguttara Nikaya* 10: 99 (V 201).

53 *Samyutta Nikaya* 21: 8 (II 281) – Bodhi 2000: 719.

54 Dasadhamma Sutta: *Anguttara Nikaya* 10:48 (V 87) – Woodward
    1994: 62.

55 Uposatha Sutta: *Udana* 5: 5 (Ud 51) – Ireland 1997: 73.

[56] Dasadhamma Sutta (AN V 87) – Woodward 1994: 62.

[57] Mahapadana Sutta: *Digha Nikaya* 14 (II 49) – Walshe 1987: 219.

[58] Sona Sutta: *Udana* V 6 (Ud 57). The monk recites the *Atthakavagga* section of the *Sutta Nipata*.

[59] Bhaddali Sutta (Mn 1 439).

[60] Lakukopama Sutta: *Majjhima Nikaya* 66 (I 148–9).

[61] *Visuddhimagga* 3: 58.

[62] Karaniya Metta Sutta: *Sn* 143–5 – Sangharakshita (2004), p.5.

[63] Mahavagga 8. 261–4 – Horner 1993, 4: 431–2.

[64] Nyanaponika and Hecker, 2003: 148.

[65] Upaddha Sutta: *Samyutta Nikaya* 45: 2 (V 2).

[66] Mahasunnata Sutta: *Majjhima Nikaya* 122 (III 118) – Nyanamoli and Bodhi 1995: 979.

[67] *Samyutta Nikaya* 45: 2 (V 2) – Bodhi 2000: 1524.

[68] *Anguttara Nikaya* 8: 54 (IV 281).

[69] Samyutta Nikaya 45: 49 and 50 cf. Nyanaponika and Bodhi 2000: 308 n.3.

[70] Mitta Sutta: *Anguttara Nikaya* 7: 35 (IV 30) – Nyanaponika and Bodhi 2000: 220.

[71] Sigalaka Sutta: *Digha Nikaya* 31 (III 187) – Walshe 1987: 465.

[72] Meghiya Sutta: *Udana* 4: 1 (Ud 35) – Ireland 1997: 52 (abridged).

[73] Vangisa Thera: *Theragatha* 1253–5 – Norman 1997, 1: 119.

[74] Ibid. 1239 and 40 – Norman 1997, 1: 118.

[75] Ibid. 1273 – Norman, 1997 1: 121.

[76] Parayana Thuti Gatha: *Sutta Nipata* 1142.

[77] Samannaphala Sutta: *Digha Nikaya* 2 (I 51) – Gethin 2009: 9.

[78] Mahapunnama Sutta: *Majjhima Nikaya* 109 (III 15).

[79] Samannaphala Sutta: (DN 1 101) – Gethin 2009: 58.

[80] Anapanasati Sutta: *Majjhima Nikaya* 118 (III 79) – Nyanamoli and Bodhi 1995: 941.

[81] Vimamsaka Sutta: *Majjhima Nikaya* 47 (I 320) – Nyanamoli and Bodhi 1995: 415.

[82] Vinaya I 49. 20. 46.10. Cited in Gombrich, *What the Buddha Thought*, p.16.

[83] Suttavibhangha 3.11–21.

84 Catuma Sutta: *Majjhima Nikaya* 67 (I 458) – Nyanamoli and Bodhi
    1995: 561.

85 *Anguttara Nikaya* (III 5–6) – Gethin 2009: 259.

86 Pilahaka Sutta: *Samyutta Nikaya* 17: 5 (II 228–9).

87 Culasihanada Sutta: *Majjhima Nikaya* 11 (I 67) – Nyanamoli and
    Bodhi 1995: 162.

88 Sallekha Sutta: *Majjhima Nikaya* 8 (I 43) – Nyanamoli and Bodhi
    1995: 127.

89 *Anguttara Nikaya* 4: 133 (II 135).

90 Alagaddupama Sutta: *Majjhima Nikaya* 22 (I 135) – Gethin 2009: 160.

91 Gotami Sutta: *Anguttara Nikaya* 8: 53 (IV 280) and Satthusasana
    Sutta: *Anguttara Nikaya* 7: 80 (IV 123).

92 Simsapa Sutta: *Samyutta Nikaya* 56: 32 (V 439) – Bodhi 2000: 1858.

93 Ambalatthikarahulovada Sutta: *Majjhima Nikaya* 61 (I 415).

94 Maharahulovada Sutta: *Majjhima Nikaya* 62 (I 421) – Nyanamoli and
    Bodhi 1995: 528.

95 Cularahulovada Sutta: *Majjhima Nikaya* 147 (III 280) – Nyanamoli
    and Bodhi 1995: 1128.

96 *Samyutta Nikaya* 54: 9 (V 320) – Bodhi 2000: 1773.

97 *Samyutta Nikaya* commentary quoted in Bodhi 2000: 1952.

98 Canki Sutta: *Majjhima Nikaya* 95 (II 167) – Nyanamoli and Bodhi
    1995: 777.

99 Vatthupama Sutta: *Majjhima Nikaya* 7 (I 37), i.e. the traditional
    chant, the *sanghavandana*, in the *Tiratanavandana* – Nyanamoli
    and Bodhi 1995: 119.

100 *Samyutta Nikaya* 16: 5 (II 202–3) – Bodhi 2000: 666.

101 Anupada Sutta: *Majjhima Nikaya* 111 (II 29) – Nyanamoli and Bodhi
    1995: 902.

102 Ibid. (II 25) – Nyanamoli and Bodhi 1995: 899.

103 Vangisa Thera: *Theragatha* 1231: Norman 1997, 1: 117.

104 Cunda Sutta: *Samyutta Nikaya* 47:13 (V 162) – Bodhi 2000: 1642.

105 Magha Sutta: *Sutta Nipata* 503.

106 Mahagosinga Sutta: *Majjhima Nikaya* 32 (1 212ff.) – Nyanamoli and
    Bodhi 1995: 307ff.

107 Mahavagga 3. 1. 2 – Horner 1993, 4: 183.

[108] Ibid. 3. 4. 3.

[109] See Mahavagga 4.

[110] Cullavagga 6. 1. 1 – Horner 1992, 5: 204.

[111] Ibid. 6. 1. 5: 206 (adapted).

[112] Ibid. 6. 4. 10: 223.

[113] Ugrapariprccha 20 C; Jan Nattier (trans.) 2005: 274.

[114] Culasunnata Sutta: Majjhima Nikaya 121 (III 10) – Nyanamoli and
     Bodhi 1995: 965.

[115] Sappa Sutta: Samyutta Nikaya 4: 6 (I 106–7) – Bodhi 2000: 199.

[116] Patacara Theri: Therigatha 115–16 – Norman 1997 2: 183.

[117] Kausambiya Sutta: Majjhima Nikaya 48 (I 320).

[118] Ibid. (I 321).

[119] Mahavagga 10. 2. 1 – Horner 1993, 4: 488.

[120] Dhammapada 6 – Sangharakshita 2001: 14. See Dhammapa-
     datthakatha (I 58–65) for this ascription.

[121] Culagosinga Sutta: Majjhima Nikaya 31 (I 206–7) and Mahavagga 10.
     4. 2–5.

[122] Mahavagga 10. 4. 6 – Horner 1993, 4: 503.

[123] Naga Sutta: Udana 4: 5 (Ud 41).

[124] Ibid. – Ireland 1997: 59.

[125] Manusmriti V 147 trans. Basham in The Wonder That Was India,
     p.182.

[126] Dhammapala, Paramadipani, trans. Caroline Rhys Davids, in
     Norman 1997, 2: 4.

[127] Blackstone 1998: 9.

[128] Soma Theri: Therigatha 61 – Norman 1997, 2: 176.

[129] Blackstone 1998: 112.

[130] Ibid. p.109.

[131] Samyutta Nikaya 5: 3 (I 130), trans. Andrew Olendzki, Insight Journal,
     29 (Winter 2008): 32. The speaker is Kisagotami, whose story is
     well known.

[132] Cullavagga 10. 1. 1 V – Horner, 5 1992: 353.

[133] Ibid. 10: 1. 3.

[134] Cullavagga 10. 1. 4 – Horner 1992, 5: 353.

[135] Anguttara Nikaya 5: 260 (III 260).

136 Cullavagga 10. 1. 6 – Horner 1992, 5: 356 (adapted).
137 Sumedha Theri: *Therigatha* 514 – Norman 1997, 2: 227.
138 Canda Theri: *Therigatha* 124 – Norman 1997, 2: 184.
139 Anne Bancroft, 'Women in Buddhism', in *Women in the World's Religions*, ed. Ursula King (New York, 1987), p.83.
140 Richard Gombrich, *What the Buddha Thought*, p.53.

7: A HOLY MAN IN THE WORLD

1 Dhaniya Sutta: *Sutta Nipata* 18–30 (adapted).
2 Ariyapariyesana Sutta: *Majjhima Nikaya* 26 (I 167–8) – Gethin 2009: 186.
3 Dhammadinna Sutta: *Samyutta Nikaya* 55: 53 (V 407) – Bodhi 2000: 1834.
4 Dhaniya Sutta: *Sn* 31 – Norman 1984: 5.
5 Cullavagga 6. 4. 8 – Horner 1992, 5: 222.
6 *Si-Yu-Ki XX* – Beal I: lxliv.
7 *Sumangala-vilasini* 1: 45 (Buddhaghosa's Commentary on the Digha-Nikaya) in Warren, *Buddhism in Translations*, p.93.
8 Mahaparinibbana Sutta: *Digha Nikaya* 16 (II 147) – Gethin 2009: 84.
9 Venaga Sutta: *Anguttara Nikaya* 1:182 – Woodward 1932: 165.
10 Mahasunnata Sutta: *Majjhima Nikaya* 122 (III 111) – Nyanamoli and Bodhi 1995: 122.
11 Ibid.
12 *Sumangala-vilasini* 1: 46 in Warren, *Buddhism in Translations*, p.92.
13 Mahasaccaka Sutta: *Majjhima Nikaya* 36 (I 249) – Nyanamoli and Bodhi 1995: 342.
14 Sudatta Sutta: *Samyutta Nikaya* (I 212).
15 *Sumangala-vilasini* 1: 46.
16 Ariyapariyesana Sutta: *Majjhima Nikaya* 26 (I 161) – Nyanamoli and Bodhi 1995: 253.
17 Sona Kutikanna Thera: *Theragatha* 366: Norman 1997, I: 44.
18 Ibid. *Theragatha* 367.
19 Vatthupama Sutta: *Majjhima Nikaya* 7 (I 37).
20 Rohini Theri: *Therigatha* 273.

[21] Susima Sutta: *Samyutta Nikaya* 1: 70 (II 119–20) – Bodhi 2000: 612.

[22] Ibid.

[23] Upali Sutta: *Majjhima Nikaya* 56 (I 379) – Nyanamoli and Bodhi 1995: 484.

[24] Dhammapada 308 – Sangharakshita 2001: 105.

[25] *Anguttara Nikaya* 5: 58 (III 75) – Hare 1989, 3: 62.

[26] Ibid. (III 77), 3: 64.

[27] Brahmajala Sutta: *Digha Nikaya* 1 (I 9–11): Walshe 1987: 71–2 (abridged).

[28] Bronkhorst 2007: 271.

[29] Brahmajala Sutta (I 10): Walshe 1987: 71–2.

[30] Sammaparibbajaniya Sutta: *Sutta Nipata* 360.

[31] Vasettha Sutta: *Sutta Nipata* 648/*Majjhima Nikaya* 98 (II 126) – Nyanamoli and Bodhi 1995: 806.

[32] Brahmanadhammika Sutta: *Sutta Nipata* 284–313.

[33] Dhammapada 394–5 – Sangharakshita 2001: 129 (adapted).

[34] Ibid. 393 – Sangharakshita 2001: 129.

[35] Assalayana Sutta: *Majjhima Nikaya* 93 (II 147) – Nyanamoli and Bodhi 1995: 763.

[36] Kutadanta Sutta: *Digha Nikaya* 5 (I 134) – Walshe 1987: 134–5.

[37] Canki Sutta: *Majjhima* Nikaya 95 (II 167) – Nyanamoli and Bodhi 1995: 777.

[38] Brahmayu Sutta: *Majjhima Nikaya* 91 (II 144) – Nyanamoli and Bodhi 1995: 753.

[39] Sundarikabharadhvaja Sutta Nipata 481.

[40] Assalayana Sutta (MN II 148).

[41] Kevaddha Sutta: *Digha Nikaya* 11 (I 221) – Walshe 1987: 178 (abridged).

[42] Tevijja Sutta: *Digha Nikaya* 13 (I 238) – Walshe 1987: 188.

[43] Pingya-manavapuccha Parayana Thuti Gatha: *Sutta Nipata* 1135.

[44] Apannaka Sutta: *Majjhima Nikaya* 60 (I 401).

[45] Aganna Sutta: *Digha Nikaya* 27 (III 81) – Gethin 2009: 118.

[46] Ambattha Sutta: *Digha Nikaya* 4 (I 90) – Walshe 1987: 113.

[47] Kutananta Sutta: *Digha Nikaya* 5 (I 144–7).

[48] Cullavagga 6. 4. 2.

49 Sudatta Sutta: *Samyutta Nikaya* 10: 8 (I 211) – Bodhi 2000: 312 (abridged).

50 *Dhammapadathakatha* (III 440) 21: 1 – Burlingame 1990, 3: 171.

51 Ratana Sutta: *Sutta Nipata* 222–4.

52 *Samyutta Nikaya* 19: 10 (II 258) – Bodhi 2000: 703.

53 *Si-Yu-Ki* – Beal 1906, 2: 156.

54 Sonadanda Sutta: *Digha Nikaya* 4 (I 116) – Walshe 1987: 117–18.

55 Tirokudda Kanda Sutta: *Petavatthu* (*Khuddhaka Nikaya*) 1: 5.

56 Saleyyaka Sutta: *Majjhima Nikaya* 41 (I 285).

57 *Anguttara Nikaya* 8: 36 (IV 241).

58 Mahanama Sutta: *Samyutta Nikaya* 55: 21 (V 370–71) – Bodhi 2000 (adapted).

59 Susima Sutta: *Samyutta Nikaya* 2: 29 (I 64–5) – Bodhi 2000: 160 (adapted).

60 Dhammapada 195–6.

61 Sigalovada Sutta: *Digha Nikaya* 31 (III 188–9) – Gethin 2009: 135.

62 *Anguttara Nikaya* 4: 61 (II 66) – Nyanaponika and Bodhi 2000: 99.

63 Mahaparinibbana Sutta: *Digha Nikaya* 16 (II 86) – Gethin 2009: 48 (abridged). Vinaya I 226 has a usefully expanded version of this teaching.

64 Mahavacchagotta Sutta: *Majjhima Nikaya* 73 (I 491) – Nyanamoli and Bodhi 1995: 597.

65 Anathapindikovada Sutta: *Majjhima Nikaya* 143 (III 261) – Nyanamoli and Bodhi 1995: 1111.

66 Pancaraja Sutta: *Samyutta Nikaya* 3: 12 (I 79) – Bodhi 2000: 175.

67 Dhammacetiya Sutta: *Majjhima Nikaya* 89 (II 121) – Nyanamoli and Bodhi 1995: 730 (abridged).

68 Piyajatika Sutta: *Majjhima Nikaya* 87 (II 107).

69 Dahara Sutta: *Samyutta Nikaya* 3: 1 (I 68).

70 Ibid. (I 69).

71 Kandaraka Sutta: *Majjhima Nikaya* 51 (I 346).

72 Atthakarana Sutta: *Samyutta Nikaya* 3: 7 (I 74) – Bodhi 2000: 170.

73 Tuvataka Sutta: *Sutta Nipata* 927.

74 Ibid. (922, 928–32, abridged).

75 Dhammannu Sutta: *Anguttara Nikaya* 7: 64 (IV 113).

[76] Dhammacetiya Sutta (II 122) – Nyanamoli and Bodhi 1995: 731 (abridged).

[77] Appaka Sutta: *Samyutta Nikaya* 3: 6 (I 168–9).

[78] Appamada Sutta (II): *Samyutta Nikaya* 3: 18 (I 87).

[79] Kannakatthala Sutta: *Majjhima Nikaya* 90 (II 128) – Nyanamoli and Bodhi 1995: 736.

[80] Donapaka Sutta: *Samyutta Nikaya* 3: 13 (I 185–6) – Olendzki: ATI.

[81] Appamada Sutta (I): *Samyutta Nikaya* 3: 17 (I 86).

[82] Attarakkhita Sutta: *Samyutta Nikaya* 3: 5 (I 72) – Bodhi 2000: 169 (abridged).

[83] Pabbatopama Sutta: *Samyutta Nikaya* 3: 25 (I 102) – Bodhi 2000: 192–3.

[84] Kosala Sutta: *Anguttara Nikaya* 5: 49 (III 57).

[85] Kannakatthala Sutta (MN II 126) – Nyanamoli and Bodhi 1995: 734.

[86] Bandhala Sutta: *Samyutta Nikaya* 3:10 (I 76–7) – Bodhi 2000: 172.

[87] Mahadukkhakkhanda Sutta: *Majjhima Nikaya* 13 (I 87) – Nyanamoli and Bodhi 1995: 182 (abridged).

[88] *Arthashastra* 6: 3 – trans. R. Shamasastry.

[89] Jatila Sutta: *Udana* 6: 2 (Ud 64) – Ireland 1997: 84.

[90] Kutadanta Sutta (DN I 135). Trans. Richard Gombrich in *Theravada Buddhism*, pp.82–3.

[91] Agganna Sutta (DN III 92).

[92] This rendition (and the accompanying interpretation) is taken from Penner 2009: 177ff.

[93] *Anguttara Nikaya* 3: 14 (I 109).

[94] Lakkhana Sutta: *Digha Nikaya* 30 (III 147) – Walshe 1987: 443.

[95] *Samyutkta-agama* 1077. Translations and references are from Analayo: 'The Conversion of Angulimala in the Samyutkta-agama', *Buddhist Studies Review*, 25. 2 (2008) 135–48.

[96] *Theragatha commentary* II 157.

[97] Adhimutta Thera: *Theragatha* 715.

[98] Angulimala Sutta: *Majjhima Nikaya* 86 (II 100) – Nyanamoli and Bodhi 1995: 711.

[99] Ibid. (II 104) – Nyanamoli and Bodhi 1995: 715.

[100] Dhammapada 5 – Sangharakshita 2001: 14.

[101] Angulimala Sutta (II 103).

8: CRISIS

1 Mahavagga 5. 1. 1 – Horner 1993, 4: 236.
2 Janavasabha Sutta: *Digha Nikaya* 18 (I 219) – Walshe 1987: 300.
3 Baddha Theri, *Therigatha* (110).
4 Punnovada Sutta: *Majjhima Nikaya* 145 (III 270).
5 Parayanavagga (Introduction): *Sutta Nipata* (978).
6 Jara Sutta: *Samyutta Nikaya* 48: 41 (V 216–17).
7 Gelana Sutta: *Samyutta Nikaya* 36: 7 (IV 211) – Bodhi 2000: 1266.
8 Parapariya Thera: *Theragatha* 920–48.
9 *Samyutta Nikaya* 16: 8 (II 208–9) – Bodhi 2000: 670.
10 Cf. *Samyutta Nikaya* ch. 17: Labhasakkarasamyutta – Bodhi 2000: 700ff.
11 *Samyutta Nikaya* 17: 8 (II 230) – Bodhi 2000: 685.
12 Bhaddali Sutta: *Majjhima Nikaya* 65 (I 445).
13 Samagama Sutta: *Majjhima Nikaya* 104 (II 243–4) – Nyanamoli and Bodhi 1995: 853.
14 Pasadika Sutta: *Digha Nikaya* 29 (III 117) – Walshe 1987: 427.
15 Samagama Sutta (II 246).
16 Ibid. (II 247).
17 Pasadika Sutta: *Digha Nikaya* 29 (III 125).
18 *Anguttara Nikaya* 1. 14. 1 – Woodward 1932, Vol. I.
19 Kokaliko Sutta: *Samyutta Nikaya* 6: 10 (I 150) – Bodhi 2000: 245.
20 Sariputta-sihanada Sutta: *Anguttara Nikaya* 9: 11 (IV 373) – Nyanaponika and Bodhi 2000: 232.
21 Cullavagga 7. 3. 1.
22 Ibid. 3. 11. 10
23 Thera Sutta: *Udana* 1: 5 (Ud 3) – Ireland 1997: 16.
24 Cullavagga 3. 2. 2.
25 Devadatta Sutta: *Itivuttaka* 3: 89 (It 83) – Ireland 1997: 213.
26 Cullavagga 7. 3. 14.
27 *Si-Yu-Ki* – Beal 1906, 2: 201.
28 Cullavagga 7. 3. 14.
29 Janavasabha Sutta (DN II 206) – Walshe 1987: 293.
30 Samagana Sutta: *Samyutta Nikaya* 3: 15 (I 84).
31 Dhammapada 201 – Sangharakshita 2001: 73.

[32] Sangama Sutta: *Sutta Nikaya* 3: 15 (I 85) – Bodhi 2000: 178.

[33] Samannaphala Sutta: *Digha Nikaya* 2 (I 47ff.) – Gethin 2009: 7ff.

[34] Ibid. (DN I 51) – Gethin 2009: 10.

[35] Ibid. (DN I 85). This and the following translations are by Michael Atwood in his essay: 'Did King Ajatasattu Confess to the Buddha, and Did the Buddha Forgive Him?' *Journal of Buddhist Ethics*, 15 (2008): 298.

[36] *Anguttara Nikaya* 10: 206 (V 294) – Nyanaponika and Bodhi 2000: 269.

[37] Samannaphala Sutta (DN I 86) – Walshe 1987: 109.

[38] Especially *Dhammapadatthakatha*, the commentary to Dhammapada 47.

[39] Atthakarana Sutta: *Samyutta Nikaya* 3: 7 (I 74).

[40] Dhammacetiya Sutta: *Majjhima Nikaya* 89 (II 118ff.) – Nyanamoli and Bodhi 1995: 89.

[41] Nyanamoli 1992: 285.

[42] Bhaddha-sala Jataka: *Jataka* 465 – Cowell 1895: 4: 96.

[43] *Ta-T'ang hsi-yu-chi* : fascicle 6, quoted in Nakamura 2005: 383.

[44] *Si-Yu-Ki: Fo-Kwo-Ki* XXII – Beal 1906, 1: xlix.

[45] Nyanaponika and Hecker 2003: 52.

[46] Cunda Sutta: *Samyutta Nikaya* 47: 13 (V 162) – Bodhi 2000: 1643.

[47] Sarabhanga Jataka: *Jataka* 522 – Cowell 1895: 5: 65.

[48] Ukkacela Sutta: *Samyutta Nikaya* 47: 14 (V 164).

9: THE FINAL JOURNEY

[1] Most references to the Sutta are to the Pali Mahaparinibbana Sutta, but some are from the Sanskrit versions of the text where this includes valuable additions. This is known as the Mahaparinirvana Sutra, and it should be distinguished from the Mahayana Nirvana Sutra, which was composed much later.

[2] *Si-Yu-Ki* – Beal 2: 152.

[3] Mahakassapa Thera: *Theragatha* 1162–70 – Olendzki: ATI (selected stanzas).

[4] *Si-Yu-Ki* – Beal 2: 153.

5 *Samyutta Nikaya* 16: 11 (2 217) – Bodhi 2000: 677.
6 Ananda Thera: *Theragatha* 1041–4 – adapted from Norman 1997, 1: 100.
7 Mahaparinibbana Sutta: *Digha Nikaya* 16 (II 72) – Gethin 2009: 39.
8 *Pan-ni – yuan-ching* (a Chinese translation of the Mahaparinirvana Sutta:) quoted in Nakamura 2005, 2: 35.
9 Mahaparinibbana Sutta (DN I 73) – Gethin 2009: 39.
10 Ibid. (DN II 74) – Gethin 2009: 39.
11 *Samyutta Nikaya* 20: 8 (II 267–8) – Bodhi 2000: 709.
12 Mahaparinibbana Sutta (DN II 76) – Gethin 2009: 41.
13 Ibid. (DN II 76) – Gethin 2009: 42.
14 Ibid. (DN II 77) – Gethin 2009: 42.
15 Ibid. (DN II 81) – Gethin 2009: 44–5.
16 Ibid. (DN II 84) – Gethin 2009: 47.
17 Ibid. (DN II 86) – Gethin 2009: 49.
18 Nagara Sutta: *Anguttara Nikaya* 7: 63 – Hare 1999: 69–71 (abridged).
19 Mahaparinibbana Sutta (DN II 88) – Gethin 2009: 49.
20 Ibid. (DN II 93) – Gethin 2009: 53.
21 Entry on Ambapali in *The Pali Dictionary of Proper Names*.
22 Vimala Theri: *Therigatha* 73 – trans. Susan Murcott in *The First Buddhist Women*, p.126.
23 Mahaparinibbana Sutta (DN II 96) – Gethin 2009: 55.
24 Ambapali Theri: *Therigatha* 252–70 (abridged).
25 Mahaparinibbana Sutta (DN II 99) – Gethin 2009: 57.
26 Ibid. (DN II 101) – Gethin 2009: 58.
27 Ibid. – Gethin 2009: 58 (abridged).
28 Ibid. (DN II 103) – Gethin 2009: 59.
29 *Samyutta Nikaya* 51:11 (V 264).
30 Cakkavati-Sihanada Sutta: *Digha Nikaya* 29 (III 77) – Walshe 1987: 404.
31 Mahaparinibbana Sutta (DN II 108) – Gethin 2009: 61.
32 Ibid.
33 Ibid. (DN II 115) – Gethin 2009: 65.
34 Ibid. (DN II 118) – Gethin 2009: 67.
35 Ibid. (DN II 120) – Gethin 2009: 68.

[36] Ibid. (DN II 122).

[37] Ibid. (DN II 124) – Gethin 2009: 70.

[38] Ibid. (DN II 127) – Gethin 2009: 72; his note explains that the literal translation is 'boar-softness'.

[39] Ibid. (DN II 127–8) – Gethin 2009: 73.

[40] Ibid. (DN II 132) – Gethin 2009: 75.

[41] Ibid. (DN II 134) – Gethin 2009: 77.

[42] Ibid. (DN II 137) – Gethin 2009: 78.

[43] Ibid. (DN II 138) – Gethin 2009: 79.

[44] Ibid. (DN II 140) – Gethin 2008: 80.

[45] Ibid. (DN II 141) – Gethin 2009: 81.

[46] Ibid. (DN II 143–4)

[47] Janussoni Sutta: Anguttara Nikaya 4:184 (II 175) – Gethin 2009: 258.

[48] Mahaparinibbana Sutta (DN II 147) – Gethin 2009: 84.

[49] Mahasudassana Sutta: Digha Nikaya (II 199) – Gethin 2008: 115.

[50] Mahaparinibbana Sutta (DN II 148) – Gethin 2009: 84.

[51] Ibid. (DN II 150–51) – Gethin 2009: 86.

[52] Ibid. (DN II 151) – Gethin 2009: 87.

[53] Ibid. (DN II 154) – Gethin 2009: 88.

[54] Ibid. (DN II 155–6) – Gethin 2009: 89.

[55] Gombrich, What the Buddha Thought, p.108.

[56] Mahaparinibbana Sutta (DN II 156) – Gethin 2009: 89.

[57] Parinibbana Sutta: Samyutta Nikaya 6: 15 (I 159) – Bodhi 2000: 253.

10: GAUTAMA'S LEGACY

[1] Mahaparinibbana Sutta: Digha Nikaya 16 (II 156).

[2] Ananda Thera: Theragatha 1046 – Norman 1997, 1: 101.

[3] Ananda Thera: Theragatha 1034 – Olendzki: ATI.

[4] Anando Sutta: Samyutta Nikaya 9: 5 (I 200) – Bodhi 2000: 297.

[5] Gopakamoggallana Sutta: Majjhima Nikaya 108 (III 8) – Nyanamoli and Bodhi 1995: 880–81 (abridged).

[6] Ananda Thera: Theragatha, 1035 – Olendzki: ATI.

[7] Brahmajala Sutta: Digha Nikaya 1 (I 46) – Walshe 1987: 90.

[8] Aggivacchagotta Sutta: *Majjhima Nikaya* 72 (I 486–7) – Nyanamoli and Bodhi 1995: 593.

[9] Brahmajala Sutta (DN (I 46) – Walshe 1987: 90.

[10] Mahaparinibbana Sutta (DN II 160) – Gethin 2009: 92.

[11] Schopen 1997: 126. The words are inscribed on a casket dating from the second century BCE found in Shinkot.

[12] Mahaparinibbana Sutta (DN II 167) – Gethin 2009: 96.

[13] This is the text of the Sanskrit Mahaparinirvana Sutra (41. 9), trans. in Schopen 1997: 117.

[14] Mahaparinibbana Sutta (DN II 141) – Gethin 2009: 81.

[15] Ibid. (DN I 154) – Gethin 2009: 88.

[16] Cullavagga 11. 1. 1.

[17] Ibid.

[18] Gombrich, *What the Buddha Thought*, p.100.

[19] Cullavagga 11. 1. 11.

[20] *Mahasanghika Sariputrapariprccha*, quoted in Bhikkhu Sujato, *Sects and Sectarianism*, epigraph (slightly adapted).

[21] Gotami Sutta: *Anguttara Nikaya* 8: 53 (IV 280).

[22] Parayana Thuti Gatha – Pingyamanavapuccha: *Sutta Nipata* 1142.

[23] *Ashokavadana* 26–7.

[24] Agganna Sutta: *Digha Nikaya* 27 (III 84) – trans. Richard Gombrich in *What the Buddha Thought*, p.189.

[25] Ray 1994: 47.

[26] *Vimalakirti Nirdesa Sutra* 3 – Luk 1990: 34.

[27] *Tathagatagarbha Sutra*, trans. Takasaki, quoted in Williams, 1989: 97.

[28] Major Rock Edict 13 – Dhammika: 15.

[29] Pillar Edict 2 – Dhammika: 23.

[30] Pillar Edict 7 – Dhammika,: 128.

[31] Pillar Edict 7 – Dhammika: 27.

[32] Major Rock Edict 12 – Dhammika: 16.

[33] Thurman 1998, pp.100–1.

[34] Joseph Goldstein, *One Dharma: The Emerging Western Buddhism* (London, 2002), pp.1–2.

[35] Mahasaccaka Sutta: Majjhima Nikaya 36 (I 246) – Gethin 2009: 183

APPENDIX: AN OUTLINE OF BUDDHIST HISTORY

[1] Major Rock Edict 13 – Dhammika: 29.
[2] Taranatha: *Taranatha's History of Buddhism in India*, trans. Lama Chimpa and Alaka Chatopadhyaya; quoted in Omvedt 2003: 170.
[3] Trans. Wendy O'Flaherty, quoted in Omvedt 2003: 169.
[4] Swami Vivekananda, quoted in Richard King, *Orientalism and Religion: Post Colonial Theory, India and the 'Mystic East'* (London and New York, 1999), p.138.
[5] *Dipavamsa* 4, 90–91; quoted in Sujato 2006: epigraph.
[6] Verse ascribed to the Indian monk Bodhidharma.
[7] Samuel 1993.

Index

The following publishers and/or authors have generously given permission to reproduce their original work:

Andrew Olendzski for translations of various Pali Sutta and Theragatha verses, many of which originally appeared in *Insight* journal.
Wisdom Publications (1 Elm St Somerville, MA 02144, USA.) for translations of Pali Suttas from the following volumes:

> *Connected Discourses of the Buddha: A Translation of the Samyutta Nikaya*, Bhikkhu Bodhi, Wisdom Publications, Boston, 2000.
>
> *In the Buddha's Words: An Anthology of Discourses from the Pali canon*, Bhikkhu Bodhi, 2001.
>
> *The Middle Length Discourses of the Buddha: A New Translation of the Majjhima Nikaya*, Bhikkhu Nanamoli and Bhikkhu Bodhi, Wisdom Publications, Boston, 1995.
>
> *Thus Have I Heard: The Long Discourse of the Buddha*, Maurice Walshe, Wisdom Publications, London, 1987.

Windhorse Publications for quotations from *Dhammapada: The Way of Truth* by Sangharakshita (Birmingham, 2001).
Oxford University Press for quotations from *Sayings of the Buddha: New Translations from the Pali Nikayas*, by Rupert Gethin (Oxford, 2008).
Equinox for quotations from *What the Buddha Thought* by Richard Gombrich (Oxford, 2009).
Taylor and Francis for quotations from the *Sutta Nipata*, by Ven. Saddhatissa (London, 1985).
Vistaar for quotations from *Numerical Discourses of the Buddha: An Anthology of Suttas from the Anguttara Nikaya* by Nyanaponika Thera and Bhikkhu Bodhi (New Delhi, 2001).
The Pali Text Society for quotations from

> *The Rhinoceros Horn and Other Early Buddhist Poems* by K. R. Norman (Oxford, 1986).
>
> *Poems of the Early Buddhist Monks* by K. R. Norman (Oxford, 1997).
>
> *Poems of the Early Buddhist Nuns* by C. A. F. Rhys Davids and K.R. Norman (Oxford, 1997).

Every effort has been made to identify and acknowledge the copyright holders. Any errors or omissions will be rectified in future editions provided that written notification is made to the publishers.